DATE DUE

MAR − − 2006		Annual	Date

DEMCO 38-296

The Career Mystique

The Career Mystique

Cracks in the American Dream

Phyllis Moen and Patricia Roehling

ROWMAN & LITTLEFIELD PUBLISHERS, INC.
Lanham • Boulder • New York • Toronto • Oxford

ROWMAN & LITTLEFIELD PUBLISHERS, INC.

Published in the United States of America
by Rowman & Littlefield Publishers, Inc.
A wholly owned subsidiary of The Rowman & Littlefield Publishing Group, Inc.
4501 Forbes Boulevard, Suite 200, Lanham, Maryland 20706
www.rowmanlittlefield.com

PO Box 317, Oxford OX2 9RU, UK

British Library Cataloguing in Publication Information Available

Library of Congress Cataloging-in-Publication Data
Moen, Phyllis.
   The career mystique : cracks in the American dream / Phyllis
Moen and Patricia Roehling.
      p. cm.
   Includes bibliographical references and index.
   ISBN 0-7425-2861-8 (cloth : alk. paper) — ISBN 0-7425-2862-6
(pbk. : alk. paper)
   1. Work and family—United States 2. Dual-career families—
United States 3. Women—Employment—United States. 4. Sex
discrimination in employment—United States. 5. Age
discrimination in employment—United States. 6. Career
develpment—United States. I. Roehling, Patricia. II. Title.
   HD4904.25.M638 2005
   306.3'6'0973—dc22

                                                        2004011009

Printed in the United States of America

⊖™ The paper used in this publication meets the minimum requirements of
American National Standard for Information Sciences—Permanence of Paper
for Printed Library Materials, ANSI/NISO Z39.48–1992.

We would like to thank Dick and Mark, our husbands, for their support and encouragement while we researched, wrote, and lived the career mystique.

Contents

Acknowledgments

Professor Urie Bronfenbrenner has said that "we are the people in our lives." *The Career Mystique* is no exception, representing as it does a synthesis of research evidence conducted by scholars from many disciplines: sociology, psychology, human resources, economics, demography, organizational behavior, policy analysis, history, and social work. We especially draw on findings from the *Ecology of Careers Study*, the culmination of years of interviews, focus groups, surveys, literature reviews, and analyses funded by the Alfred P. Sloan Foundation (#2002-6-8 2003-04; #96-6-9, #99-6-23, and #2002-6-8 1996-2003; #B1998-26) and the National Institute on Aging (#P50 AG11711-01, 2P50 AG11711-06, 1993-2003), with additional support provided by the McKnight Foundation, the University of Minnesota, Cornell University, and Hope College. We would like to thank Ralph Gomory and Kathleen Christensen of the Sloan Foundation for recognizing the import of the transformations in the U.S. workforce and economy for the life quality of employees and their families. The Cornell Careers Institute, funded by the Alfred P. Sloan Foundation, became the first of a series of multidisciplinary centers supported by the Foundation devoted to the study of this topic. We thank as well Sid Stahl and others at the National Institute on Aging for supporting our research on older workers as they move toward retirement. Phyllis Moen was also supported as a Fellow at the Radcliffe Institute for Advanced Study at Harvard University during the 2000–2001 academic year, a time made especially productive because of the efforts of Drew Faust, Paula Rayman, and Mette Sorensen. Prior to that, Nancy Tuma made it possible for Phyllis to develop early ideas while a visiting scholar at the Sociology Department at Stanford University.

Most of all, we thank the people of all ages and stages participating in the *Ecology of Careers Study*, conducted from 1998 through 2002. We deeply appreciate the thousands (4,637) of men, women, singles, single parents, couples, retirees, and employees who took the time to share with us their strategies, strains, and successes by participating in this study. Their experiences have provided us with a window into the real-life implications of people trying to cope with the mismatches produced by American policies and cultural myths out of step with twenty-first-century realities. We appreciate as well the assistance of the ten large employers who generously agreed to participate in this study. Human resources professionals and others at these workplaces provided important organizational information, as well as valuable insights. We have respected participating employers' requests for anonymity by using pseudonyms for these establishments, as well as for employees and spouses. (For details regarding this study, see *It's About Time* [2003], edited by Phyllis Moen, and *The New "Middle" Work Force* [2004] by Phyllis Moen with Donna Dempster-McClain, Joyce Altobelli, Wipas Wimonsate, Lisa Dahl, Patricia Roehling, and Stephen Sweet.)

The Career Mystique reflects the efforts of the many faculty colleagues, post-docs, graduate and undergraduate students, and staff we have worked with over the years. We are indebted to those who helped design the *Ecology of Careers Study* or were actively involved in conducting interviews and focus groups as well as data analysis: Kristine Altucher, Rosemary Batt, Ronald Breiger, Paul Callister, Noelle Chesley, Marin Clarkberg, Steven Cornelius, Stephan Desrochers, Emma Dentinger, Yasamin DiCiccio-Miller, Caroline Ebanks, Penny Edgell, Mary Ann Erickson, Francile Firebaugh, Judith Galtry, Shin-Kap Han, Heather Hofmeister, Andrew Hostetler, Robert Hutchens, Kathryn Hynes, Jungmeen Kim, Kimberly Kopko, Hyojin Kang, Yun-Suk Lee, Janet Marler, Stacey Merola, Fran McCormack, Hyunjoo Min, Steven Mock, Robert Orrange, Joy Pixley, Heather Quick, Mark Roehling, Rosern Rwampororo, Richard Shore, Susan Singley, Haya Stier, Mary Still, David Strang, Stephen Sweet, Raymond Swisher, Cate Taylor, Linda Tolan, Pamela Tolbert, Bickley Townsend, P. Monique Valcour, Ronit Waismel-Manor, Elaine Wethington, Lindy Williams, Sonya Williams, and Yan Yu.

We would also like to thank the staff of the Cornell Careers Institute who did the foundation work of collecting, organizing, preparing, and analyzing data, along with the faculty and staff of the Cornell Gerontology Research Institute, the Bronfenbrenner Life Course Center, and others at Cornell University who provided a larger view, managed the many details of the research enterprise, or offered key observations: Madhurima

Agarwal, Veronica Vargas Banks, Stuart Basefsky, Lisa Bloukahn, Fran Bensen, Fran Blau, Patsy Brannon, David Brown, Rich Burkhauser, Kristi Campbell, Carrie Chalmers, Larry Clarkberg, Lisa Dahl, Sarah Demo, Donna Dempster-McClain, Rachel Dunifon, Deborah Edwards, Bill Erickson, Kim Fenner, Jenny Gerner, Nina Glasgow, Krista Ham, Steve Hamilton, Doug Heckathorn, Tom Hirschl, Musarrat Islam, Joanne Jordan, Kara Joyner, Susan Lang, Shinok Lee, David McDermitt, Tammie Martin, Lauren Meritt, Sue Meyer, Liane O'Brien, Liz Peters, Rachel Poludniak, Karl Pillemer, Vandana Plassmann, Julie Robison, Mindi Rogers, Helen Rosenblatt, Leslie Schultz, Paul Streeter, Melissa Toner, Wipas Wimonsate, and Jerry Ziegler. Yasamin DiCiccio-Miller and her staff at the Computer Assisted Survey Team (CAST) collected excellent survey data for us, and participated actively in every phase of the research endeavor.

Thanks also to the people at the University of Minnesota who helped us put this manuscript together: Kelly Chermack and Jane Peterson. And the people at Hope College who also helped with research and manuscript preparation: Kathy Adamski, Anna Eriks, Travis Goldwire, Meredith Mick, Heather Swope, Pamela Van Dort, and Elizabeth Wilson.

We thank as well Rafe Sagalyn, our agent; Alan McClare, our editor; and Alden Perkins, production editor; as well as Jen Kelland, the copy editor. Joan Jacobs Blumberg kindly reviewed an earlier draft, providing helpful advice, as did a number of anonymous reviewers. We also appreciate the insights of Connie Ahrons, Roz Barnett, Hans-Peter Blossfeld, Bob Drago, Sonja Drobnic, Walter Heinz, Carla B. Howery, Erin Kelly, Deb Koen, Helga Krüger, Miles Maguire, Deb Moen, Jeylan Mortimer, Irene Padavic, Henry Walker, and Ansgar Weymann. Finally, we are grateful to our families who willingly lived with the day-to-day exigencies involved in the research and writing of *The Career Mystique*.

1

The Career Mystique

PROFILE: LISA AND DAVID

When Lisa was a teenager, she wanted to "have it all": a husband, children, and a stimulating career. This was the goal of most of the women of her generation (now in their late thirties), and American culture touted having it all as the path to gender equality.

David also wanted it all. He envisioned a future with a wife and children, where he was able to provide comfortably for them financially, as well as to be actively involved in raising his children.

Both did all the things necessary to attain their goals. Each graduated from high school and then from college. Lisa earned an undergraduate degree in business; David's was in engineering. Lisa's first job was working in the human resources department of a medium-sized corporation, Bright Manufacturing.[1] During her first month she met David, who was an engineer at the same corporation. Lisa was attracted to David's maturity and compassion. He was attracted to her outgoing personality and energy. Lisa and David fell in love, and they married two years later when Lisa was twenty-seven and David was thirty. Lisa enjoyed her work and was soon promoted to director of human resources. David was respected by his colleagues and supervised a large division within the corporation. Lisa and David felt like they were living the American Dream. They had successful careers, owned a nice home, had an active social life, and were in love.

When Lisa was thirty she became pregnant. Unfortunately, her pregnancy coincided with a time of corporate restructuring within Bright

1

Manufacturing, the company for which Lisa and David worked. The firm instituted large-scale layoffs. Feeling insecure about her job, Lisa took only a five-week maternity leave following their daughter Emily's birth, then went back to work full time.

Then things started to unravel. Finding full-time day care was difficult. The couple went through a series of day care providers. The first quit, and the second was a bad fit with their daughter. On the third attempt they put Emily in a day care center. Lisa's hours were very rigid. Because she was a director, she needed to be available and in the office from 8:30 A.M. to 5:00 P.M. David's job was even more demanding, and being concerned about the ongoing layoffs, he was afraid to signal to his boss anything but absolute commitment. He typically left for work at 7:00 A.M., not returning home until around 6:30 P.M. Lisa became exhausted with her daily routine of getting Emily up and out to day care before 8:30 A.M. At the end of her long workday she picked Emily up at 5:30 P.M., ran errands (e.g., groceries, dry cleaning, ATM), and then cooked dinner. Their evenings were filled with doing laundry, picking up the house, and getting ready for the next day. Lisa and David were both exhausted. Their social life dropped off the map. Something had to give.

Lisa decided to quit her full-time job, taking a job working ten hours a week in a physician's (her brother's) office. Two years later, in order to maintain their lifestyle (an expensive home and two cars), David left his job at Bright Manufacturing to move to a larger company. His hours increased dramatically, but so did his salary.

After eight years of marriage, Lisa and David divorced. They were still good friends and devoted parents, but their marriage had not worked out. When we interviewed them, they were sharing custody of their daughter.

After the divorce, Lisa found a full-time job in the human resources field. Full-time work was necessary to provide herself with medical benefits and to support her separate household. Emily went to day care after school and all day during the summer. For the next five years things went relatively well. Lisa and David both felt stretched by their daily routines, but were getting by. Each wanted to spend as much time as possible with their daughter, but both also wanted to excel in their careers. David's company allowed him flexibility, so he could take time off or work at home when necessary. Lisa's company was less flexible.

Things got much worse for Lisa, however, when her corporation merged with another. She kept her job, but others were let go in the consolidation. Those who remained had to take on the responsibilities of laid-off coworkers. Everyone in Lisa's department had to work at minimum a forty-eight-hour week. This wreaked havoc with Lisa's personal life. She saw far less of her daughter and had no time to develop other relationships. Lisa approached management several times, offering to take a different, less-demanding job or even a cut in pay so she could work fewer hours. Each time her request was denied. One evening, as she picked Emily up from David's house at 9:00 P.M., she decided to quit. At the time we interviewed Lisa, she had been out of work for two months. She was depleting her savings and considering dissolving her 401(k) retirement fund. Lisa was determined, however, to find a job that would give her more flexibility.

* * *

THE FEMININE MYSTIQUE

In the 1950s, things seemed simpler, at least for middle-class Americans. In the ideal world, men were the breadwinners, working full time in careers that promised security and a comfortable living for those willing to make work their top priority. Women were the caretakers of the home and family, supporting their husbands emotionally and socially so that they could focus single-mindedly on climbing career ladders or at least hanging on. Lisa and David, born in the 1950s, both had parents exemplifying this lifestyle. Lisa's father was an accountant; David's father worked in an office. Both of their mothers stayed at home throughout their childhood.

Although this lifestyle worked for some, it was never a reality for poor women or men, those on the fringes of the labor market. Still, the breadwinner/homemaker family became the icon of the American Dream. "Success" for men entailed a career that enabled their wives to stay home. "Success" for women meant being married to a "successful" man. Although not all families in the 1950s could afford this version of the good life, even those on the outside looking in—poor families, immigrant families, divorced or single parents—aspired to this breadwinner/homemaker lifestyle, replete with a house in the suburbs and a car in the carport, if not the garage. Books, movies, advertisements in magazines, and television shows depicted American women and men as homemakers and breadwinners, reinforcing and sustaining this gender divide.

But all was not well on the home front. Despite cultural consensus that marriage and motherhood are women's "master" roles, many emulating this archetype in the 1950s and 1960s felt a deep lack of fulfillment and a sense of unease. One of them, Betty Friedan, frustrated and depressed by the absence of opportunity to use her education and talents, actually began to write about this "problem with no name."[2]

In the 1950s Betty Friedan struggled to be a good homemaker, wife, and mother. Tucked into a residential suburb, she felt cut off from the mainstream, embroiled in her small world of full-time domesticity, of women and children isolated from the "real world" of business and industry. Frustrated by the absence of opportunity, she began to write about this "problem with no name," eventually calling it the *feminine mystique* (which became the title of her groundbreaking book). In that one phrase, Friedan captured the myth of middle-class womanhood in the middle of the twentieth century. Marriage and motherhood were touted as totally fulfilling, as a rewarding life peopled by children and other mothers in the new residential suburbs sprouting up in postwar America. Women were the family consumers, chauffeurs, cooks, and caregivers. They were also deft at handling contradictions, at being both sex symbols and the keepers of the nation's morals.

Leading to the feminine mystique were, first, jobs that paid a *family wage* (that is, enough to support a family on one income). A burgeoning post–World War II economy fit well with beliefs and values honed on the American experience, the American Dream of individual achievement and self-sufficiency.[3] The dream captures the frontier spirit of enterprise, energy, and optimistic expectations so emblematic of the United States. Success can be earned, people can pull themselves up by their bootstraps, anyone can move up the occupational ladder. For many in the middle of the twentieth century, this dream seemed within reach. Even blue-collar jobs with no such ladders offered a clear path to seniority and with it higher salaries, the wherewithal to own a home, and economic security. A measure of men's success became the fact that they could afford to support their wives as full-time homemakers.

In her book Betty Friedan showed the underside of this myth of domestic fulfillment. Many middle-class homemakers felt isolated, inadequate, alone, and unhappy. Sometimes living up to this ideal caused hardship for the rest of the family. Many girls saw their mothers grapple with being "just a housewife." Many families struggled to maintain a middle-class lifestyle on one salary.

The feminine mystique was only part of the story, half of the gender divide. It was, paradoxically, embedded in the American Dream that anyone could make it through hard work. Only, that "anyone" was assumed to be a man. What emerged for American men following World War II was a *lockstep* template—a one-way pathway from schooling through full-time, continuous occupational careers to retirement. This lockstep career path both *enabled the feminine mystique* and *was sustained by it*. Men could lead work-centered lives precisely because their wives took care of the daily details of family and home. Wives even supported their husbands' careers by entertaining bosses and relocating from state to state as their husbands followed jobs or moved up company ladders. Although men expected to fall in love, marry, and have children, their jobs were their main act, who they really were—doctors, salesmen, plumbers, and members of the growing white-collar bureaucracy that worked in offices, not on factory floors. For most middle-class households, there was one job—the paid one. Men's careers, thus, offered the only path to security, success, and status—for their families as well as themselves.

Women's lives in the middle of the twentieth century, by contrast, offered no such starring role. They were the stagehands, set designers, walk-ons, caterers, and coaches of others' lives: their husbands, their children, their neighbors, their friends. Still, most worked for pay before marriage or motherhood, as well as during World War II. Growing numbers of women attended college and developed occupational aspirations of their own. This mismatch created the cultural contradictions of the feminine mystique, a mythical vision of womanhood that limited options and idealized the breadwinner/homemaker family, even as many young American women were entering colleges or the workforce as a matter of course.

Whether people achieved it or not, the breadwinner/homemaker template provided cultural guidelines about careers, families, and gender that effectively *decoupled* paid work from unpaid family-care work, creating a fictional divide between them, a divide that became embedded in occupational ladders and prospects, assuming someone else—a wife—would attend to the details of daily living. In this way, an *imaginary divide* between paid work and unpaid work became a very real *gender divide*. Today the borders are both fraying and more permeable than ever before, but the roles, rules, and regulations about a lifetime of paid work remain in place, while care for the nation's families remains mostly women's unpaid work.

In *The Feminine Mystique*, Betty Friedan pointed out the cultural contradictions of assigning full-time homemaking to half the adult population. But she paid scant attention to its mirror image, *the career mystique*, the expectation that employees will invest all their time, energy, and commitment throughout their "prime" adult years in their jobs, with the promise of moving up in seniority or ascending job ladders. Some captured the reality of this mystification of occupational careers—C. Wright Mills wrote *White Collar*, William H. Whyte described *The Organization Man*, and Sloan Wilson painted a vivid fictional account in *The Man in the Grey Flannel Suit*. But none of these recognized that the *career mystique* rested on the premise of a gender divide, with men occupying the jobs offering seniority and ladders and women making men's homes, nurturing their children, and providing them with support and encouragement.

The Feminine Mystique was a bombshell. With it, Betty Friedan helped usher in the Women's Movement of the 1960s, 1970s, and 1980s, which, along with an expanding service economy, has literally transformed the lives of American women. But in rejecting the norms and values of the feminine mystique, much liberal feminism came to embrace men's lives as the yardstick of equality. The senior author recently overheard a young girl in a toy store saying she wanted boys' toys. This was, in essence, what feminism of the latter half of the twentieth century wanted as well: Many thought that the way women could be equal to men was through affirmative action, enabling them to have men's jobs and men's career investments and to reap men's economic rewards, advancement, and prestige.[4]

By the 1990s, most American women, like Lisa, took it for granted that they could—and should—have it all: career, marriage, and family. The world of paid work became increasingly important to middle-class women's lives—throughout all stages of their lives. Lisa, for example, explains how she felt after she reentered full-time employment following her divorce.

> Incredible, I was so stimulated and fulfilled. It's like this part of me totally woke up again, my intelligence and using my brain, incredible. I thought, "Thank you God, I am blessed. I love this job." It was so challenging and rewarding, and I gained so much self-confidence. When I got back to work full time we [Lisa and her daughter] almost immediately appreciated every bit of time that we spent together because we didn't have as much time together. I wanted to just be with her so much when I wasn't with her. I gave her better attention and our relationship improved.

In the last thirty-five years the workplace and family life have been transformed as record numbers of women have entered, reentered, and remained in the workforce. Women today are closer to approaching equality—using men's experience as the yardstick—than ever. But the domestic details and crises of daily life have not disappeared.

What *has* disappeared is the full-time homemaker, or else the role has become a short-term project for some when children are young. Three out of four employees in the U.S. workforce have no full-time homemaker to back them up on the domestic front.[5] When all adults in the family work for pay, no one is left to do the care work of families, homes, and communities, except as an overload, part of a hidden second shift.

Lost in women's push to equality was recognition that the *career mystique* (that Americans give their all to paid labor in order to "make it") rested upon the feminine mystique. The American Dream required hard work by *two* people—one at a job, one at home. Today, couples, much less singles or single parents like Lisa and David, cannot afford to hire a wife, to pay someone to be there for their children, their ailing relatives, the repairman, the FedEx delivery, and the myriad other minutiae of their domestic lives.

The career mystique remains a taken-for-granted attribute of the American experience. Almost all aspects of life in twenty-first-century America embrace a cultural regime of roles, rules, and regulations fashioned from this myth. Consider how Americans work the hardest, put in the most hours, and take the fewest vacation days of any advanced nation. Consider how various policies—health insurance, Social Security, unemployment insurance, pensions, vacations—all are tied to the presupposition of full-time, continuous employment. Consider the ways Americans structure time: week days, weekends, retirement, rush hours, lunch hours, blue Mondays, TGIF Fridays. All are embedded in the mythology of lockstep career tracks consisting of five-day, forty-hour (or more) workweeks—over a lifetime of employment.[6]

But reality is at odds with the myth, and there are growing cracks in the American Dream. Many men and women are trying to follow the career mystique, working long hours at demanding jobs only to climb ladders that lead nowhere or else to find the promised ladders no longer exist. Women and minorities often find that such career ladders as do exist have glass ceilings. In the past, sociologists and economists divided work and workers into two types: the *primary* workforce (mostly unionized or middle class with continuous full-time employment, full benefits, and opportunities for advancement) and the *secondary* labor market (mostly women, but also including men of color, immigrants, and those with few skills and little education). But today's global economy has an international workforce, new information technologies, and a never-ending story of mergers, buyouts, acquisitions, and bankruptcies. Ambiguities and uncertainties about the future abound in boardrooms and offices and on factory floors, coloring the sensibilities of employees and their families as many face the realities of corporate restructuring, in good times as well as bad. Restructuring, or downsizing, often means forced early retirements and layoffs for some, fewer benefits and greater workloads for others. This "risk" economy effectively places almost everyone in something akin to a secondary-labor market.

Americans in the 1950s also faced the specter of unemployment and financial insecurity. But the contract between employers and employees (official for unionized workers and unofficial for the nonunionized) was based on the seniority system, awarding advantages to those who would follow the lockstep mystique. Middle-class (mostly white) men with many years of employment were sheltered from economic dislocations. It was the last hired—typically women and minorities—who were the first fired. Today, the proportion of the workers under union contracts is at an unprecedented low. And the implicit contracts—trading mobility and job security for continuous full-time employment and unwavering loyalty—have disappeared, even for white middle-class men.

What has not changed is the *career mystique*, the myth that hard work, long hours, and continuous employment pay off. What has not changed is the *career regime*, the cultural bundle of roles, rules, and regulations built up around the mystification of this lockstep organization of paid work. Most employees—especially men—continue to make heavy investments of time and energy in their jobs—every day, every week, every month, every year— from the time they leave school to the time they retire. The regime of policies and practices built upon the career mystique means that occupational success is possible only for those engaged in continuous, full-time (or more) paid work. Not in the United States are there such European institutions as long summer and winter paid vacations, paid parental leaves of absence, and part-time employment with guaranteed benefits. Americans pride themselves on working hard, taking work home, staying late at the office, not even taking all of the few weeks of paid vacation they may accrue.

The purpose of this book is to show that most Americans—men and women—and most American institutions continue to presuppose the career mystique, even though it is out of date and out of place in twenty-first-century America. Although myths are important—providing a vision of what is possible—we see the career mystique as a *false myth*, standing in the way of creating new, alternative workplace and career flexibilities. It is "false" for five reasons. First, climbing the ladder of occupational success was never possible for all workers, even in the 1950s. Hard work paid off only for a select group of mostly white, mostly middle-class men. Second, the feminine mystique provided the platform undergirding the career mystique. It is no accident that those most successful in climbing career ladders in business and in government have been men with either homemaking wives or else wives who put their own careers on the back burner. Third, fewer and fewer jobs offer possibilities for security, stability, and advancement; the old contract trading continuous hard work for wage increases and seniority is long gone. Fourth, neither men nor women want to live with an old-fashioned and unequal gender divide. American women have not simply traded one mystique for another— moving from strictures about the "good" mother or the "good" wife to those embodied in the "good" worker; rather, many are trying to be it all—the good wife, the good mother, *and* the good employee. Growing numbers of American men are trying to be all as well—egalitarian husbands and caring fathers as well as productive and competitive on the job. They, too, find it almost impossible to do so. Fifth, very few men or women can live by the old rules. One job per family—the old breadwinner/ homemaker model—is often a ticket to economic privation given that wages have not kept pace with inflation or living costs, the minimum wage is a poverty wage, and "middle class" today means something very different in today's consumption economy.

Why do Americans cling to this patently false mystification of careers as the path to the good life? In part, because it epitomizes the American Dream. The career mystique incorporates both an endurance ethic and a work ethic, both crucial to American values of individualism and free enterprise. Sacrifice by working hard, the myth goes, and you'll reap wealth, security, status, health insurance, pensions, respect, love, admiration, and happiness. Like the sitcom reruns of the 1950s, the mystique remains. But the Faustian bargain of trading a lifetime of paid work for a lifetime of income security is probably gone forever. Still, children, young people, adults, retirees—along with CEOs, managers, union leaders, and government policy makers—buy into the career mystique. It is woven into the very fabric of the American way of life, making it hard to envision alternatives.

In the middle of the twentieth century, Betty Friedan captured the voices of suburban housewives asking (as did Peggy Lee), Is that all there is? Today, most American women feel liberated from the feminine mystique. The few who become, or remain, full-time homemakers tend to do so by choice, not because of the constraints of custom or cultural expectations. Many women of Friedan's generation aimed for an equality that would open to women the doors leading to men's occupational prospects and rewards. Many of these doors have opened. The feminist movement, the shift to white-collar service (rather than blue-collar manufacturing) jobs, changing technologies, and affirmative action legislation have made the possibility of equal opportunity in education and in occupations more attainable than ever before. But twentieth-century liberal feminism sought equality using the yardstick of occupational achievement. In other words, many women bought into the career mystique of climbing a ladder to success. The rungs of that ladder are increasingly available to women, and sometimes women's pay is even close to that of men's. However, the career mystique typically requires two conditions: (1) an expanding economy with upward or at least secure occupational paths, and (2) workers with someone else—a full-time homemaker—to provide backup on the domestic front. Today, these two conditions are seldom met for either men or women. Both are beginning to ask, of their jobs and their career prospects, Is that all there is?

Americans are living on a moving platform of change. The taken-for-granted social arrangements about work, retirement, schooling, and life no longer fit the realities of twenty-first-century America. The possibilities of fulfilling the career mystique may be dwindling, but its regime of rules, routines, and regulations remains deeply embedded in social policies, in occupational paths, in workplace regulations, and in the education-employment-retirement lockstep life course. Given the large-scale social upheavals characterizing the twenty-first century, the only thing clear to generations coming of age or moving toward retirement today is that their lives will not resemble those of their parents. How do Americans manage in a world where career ladders are precarious at best, where men and women alike live with incompatible and un-achievable goals?

We show in the pages that follow that most men and women typically go along to get along, adopting "work-friendly" strategies. They try to follow taken-for-granted blueprints for jobs, careers, and success that are ill fitting at best. Some draw on new information technologies to manage the multiple strands of their lives. (Picture a leading TV commercial; a mother at the beach with her two children frolicking in the waves while she is on a conference call.) Such technological advances permitting peo-ple to work anywhere, anytime, may be family-friendly, but they are also work-friendly, encouraging employees to work everywhere, all the time. Other key family-friendly business innovations, such as child care and flex time, are also work-friendly, making it possible for employees to pur-sue the elusive career mystique by devoting more time to their jobs. Even the watchword "balance" itself is work-friendly. Rarely do both spouses in a marriage balance their work and family goals and obligations. Rather, one spouse (usually the wife) typically scales back (balances) in order that the other spouse (the husband) can put in long hours, travel, be on call, and try to climb, or at least hang onto, an increasingly shaky career lad-der. We view the metaphor of balance as a cultural convention reinforcing gender inequalities at work and at home, while failing to challenge the ca-reer mystique.

We wrote this book to do three things: first, to describe how the career mystique remains part of the human experience of Americans at all ages and stages; second, to show the mismatch between the career mystique and contemporary reality, as well as to show how Americans accommo-date this mismatch; finally, and frankly, to lobby for change. Can Ameri-cans devise new, more realistic scripts—about success, about careers, about the roles of men and women? We believe that the nation is still caught up in the career myth precisely because it is so interwoven into the social fabric, such a taken-for-granted part of life—and work—today. We portray the career mystique for what it is, a social invention perpetu-ating a regime of roles, rules, and regulations reifying imaginary divides—between home and workplace, between men and women, be-tween paid work and unpaid care work. "All" that is required for Amer-ican society to move beyond the career mystique is imagination and the will to change.

We begin with a brief overview of how Americans came to the career mystique, along with describing the moving platform of change that characterizes life early in the twenty-first century.

HOW DID WE GET TO THE CAREER MYSTIQUE?

Families function as "role budget centers," allocating family members' time and energy to paid work, schooling, community engagement, and domestic activities.[7] Prior to the Industrial Revolution (occurring in the United States in the latter half of the nineteenth century), families operated as a cohesive unit; all family members, regardless of age or gender, typically engaged in productive labor—either on farms or in small family businesses. With this agrarian model, there was no concept of a career. Even during the shift to industrialization, the old strategy of all family members engaging in production persisted for a time, with wives as well as husbands, and children as well as older adults, expected to earn their keep through wage labor. This model still characterizes much of the developing world today. In Europe and the United States, as more men left agriculture for industry, they sought jobs that paid enough to support a family (a "living" wage). That, along with protective legislation, eventually produced a new blueprint, the breadwinner/homemaker model. Thus, industrialization sharpened distinctions, dividing activities into gender spheres of paid work and unpaid domestic work, of public and private life. Along with the living wage and the notion that women were only a secondary part of the workforce (leaving it when they married or had children if they could afford to), there developed identifiable career pathways in particular occupations.[8]

For most of the last century, those who could manage it financially "solved" potential paid-work–family-care work conflicts by having one spouse (typically the wife) serve as a full-time homemaker. This solution was truly work-friendly, freeing the other spouse (typically the husband) to concentrate exclusively on paid work and occupational development—to follow the career mystique. Advanced industrial societies were possible only because wives, daughters, and mothers did the unpaid care work of society, enabling husbands, sons, and fathers to invest their time, energy, and emotional commitment in being productive on the job. This created the three-phase, lockstep, career regime of middle-class men's lives: education, then continuous full-time employment, then the continuous full-time "leisure" of retirement, typically at age sixty-five. Occupational careers occupied most years of adulthood. Jobs were "greedy" institutions, assuming workers were able and willing to work long hours, to put in mandatory or "voluntary" overtime, to move for occupational advancement, to travel as needed, sometimes to work weekends, and, more recently, to work from home.

This lockstep blueprint, by and large, became the pattern of most blue-collar and white-collar men who grew up during the Great Depression and World War II, many of whom became the fathers of today's (aging) baby boom generation.[9] This meant completing schooling, getting married, and starting a family while simultaneously obtaining a job and launching a career. It meant having and raising typically two or more children while building seniority and establishing themselves at work, watching their children grow up and leave home, then retiring to the sidelines of society.

Compared to men, most women's life paths have been both more complicated and more family focused. Wives have often found their lives shaped by their husbands' careers (including geographical moves to advance their husbands' job prospects) and by their husbands' retirement. Most women in the years prior to and right after World War II, left paid work following marriage or motherhood (if they could afford it), with many returning part year, part time, or intermittently once their children were older.[10] Motherhood became women's absorptive, full-time (but not always completely fulfilling) occupation, despite the fact that growing numbers were getting a college education.[11]

What is key is that both the breadwinner/homemaker *gender divide* (of paid work and unpaid family-care work) and the life course as a three-part sequential *age divide* (education, employment, and retirement) are *social inventions*, products of industrialization, urbanization, suburbanization, and bureaucratization. They have become a taken-for-granted part of the landscape of American culture, shaping the institutions that sustain the American way of life. Thus, most colleges are geared to educate young people, even though growing numbers of "older" adults are returning to school to complete degrees, to retool or change careers, or simply to learn. Government legislation and corporate policies still reserve "good" jobs for prime-age adults, rewarding continuous, full-time employment by providing benefits in the form of health insurance, unemployment insurance, vacations, and pensions. Social Security provisions, as well as other pension regulations, along with declining training opportunities, encourage the retirement of older workers.[12] Those seeking success at work or even just job security believe both require continuous employment, long hours, and heavy occupational investment—in other words, following the lockstep model of the career mystique. Life in the suburbs began when middle-class families were breadwinner/homemaker families: One parent (the father) commuted to his job while the other (the wife) served as family chauffeur and full-time mother. The widening geographical distance between businesses and homes in post–World War II America became a spatial marker of the sharpening division between men's and women's life experiences, lending credence to the imaginary divide between work and family.

HOW DID WE GET TO THE MISMATCH?

A Changing Work Force

Consider these statistics: At the beginning of the twentieth century, only one in five American women worked for pay. Today, fully three out of five women are employed. As figure 1.1 illustrates, most dramatic has been the changing experiences of married women. Fewer than one in ten (6%) were employed in 1900; that number grew to one in five by 1950 and now has reached more than three in five. Having children no longer signals a retreat from the workforce. Today, unprecedented numbers of American mothers of young children, even mothers of infants, are employed (see figure 1.2). Growing numbers of women of all ages are working the way men have always worked: at year-round, full-time jobs (although still fewer women than men work full time or long hours). Today, knowing whether or not a woman is married or whether she has children tells us little about whether or not she is in the workforce. Lisa is typical of her generation. She has remained continuously employed through marriage, parenthood, and divorce. Unlike her mother, Lisa always assumed that she would have a job, regardless of whether she got married or had children.

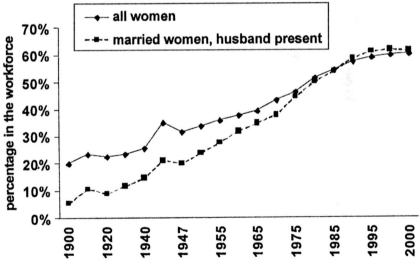

Figure 1.1. Unprecedented proportions of American women, married and unmarried, are employed. (Sources: U.S. Bureau of the Census, 1999 *Statistical Abstract of the United States*, Section 13, p. 11, and 2000 *Statistical Abstract of the United States*.)

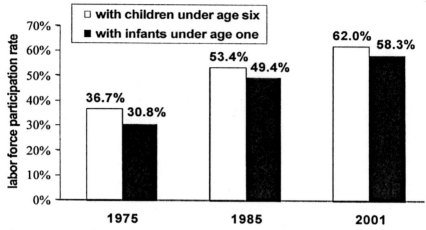

Figure 1.2.   Married mothers increasingly engage in paid work. (Source: U.S. Bureau of the Census, 2002 *Statistical Abstract of the United States*, p. 373.)

The fact that more women have jobs also means that there are more working families, that is, families in which all adults are wage earners. Half of all employees in the United States are now married to other employees. Husbands and wives are increasingly both working for pay. Neither they nor the rising numbers of singles and single parents have support on the home front, someone caring about the details of living while they are busy making a living.

More employees than ever before—whether single, single parent, or married—have child care, elder care, or other domestic responsibilities in addition to their job responsibilities, or will have them in the future. Few are prepared for the complications of combining work and family goals and responsibilities. Doing so typically falls to women, especially those who are mothers. As Lisa discovered,

> Beforehand, I didn't think there would be too much of a change when I had children. I'd go back to work and she would go to a babysitter. It was amazing. It surprised me how much everything changed. . . . I couldn't function in a full-time job. It was a lot harder than I thought. Hard to find balance and still keep your own identity as opposed to [being] just a mother. I didn't want to work full time. I couldn't balance it. I didn't have any time for her [Emily]. If I worked full time and spent time with her then I didn't have time for me.

David had less difficulty adjusting to parenthood. He felt less conflicted about pursuing the career mystique, handing off many of the caretaking responsibilities to Lisa. Although David was a very nurturing father who relished his time caring for his daughter, he saw his major role as being the breadwinner.

One key challenge of life in the twenty-first century is how to make incompatible roles compatible. Men are expected—and expect themselves—to pursue the career mystique, but most lack the backup of a wife at home. Women are increasingly expected—and expect themselves—to pursue the career mystique as well as to care for the people in their lives.

Increases in longevity, declines in fertility, and the aging of the baby boom generation are producing another challenge: a graying workforce and a growing "retired" force. The heyday of the breadwinner/homemaker lifestyle after World War II produced a large number of children—the baby boom of 1946 to 1964. Doing the math shows these seventy-six million baby boomers are now approaching their sixties. This means that the number of employees in their forties and fifties is reaching a historical high. Sixty-something boomers will not in any way resemble their sixty-something grandparents or parents. We believe baby boomers and the cohort just ahead of them are in the process of creating a new life stage, one that is *midcourse* between the career-building years and the infirmities of old age. Most Americans in their fifties and sixties are looking for new ways to phase into retirement, wanting jobs that are part time or part year. But the lockstep career regime of policies and practices offers but two options: full-time (often, in fact, long-hour) work or full-time retirement. Social Security and pension regulations reinforce this inflexibility around the paid work/retirement transition.

The new longevity is also changing the landscape of unpaid care work and family life. A large proportion of employees have at least one living parent who needs, or will need, care. Some will have to care for spouses as well. Growing numbers of contemporary employees have adult children (along with grandchildren), who may need support and may even return home for a time, between jobs or following a divorce or other personal crisis. The decline in the number of full-time homemakers means that few contemporary employees have someone else to take on the kin keeping or actual care of infirm or aging relatives, care work that typically has been the lot of adult daughters, daughters-in-law, wives, and sisters. Because neighbors, sisters, grandmothers, and aunts also have jobs, no one is at home, next door, or down the street to help out with children or infirm relatives or even to let the washing machine repair person into the house—in other words, to help make life work.

Five Societal Trends

The United States stands at something of a crossroads in the ways we think about, organize, and regulate careers and the life course. Five historical forces are creating a disjuncture between the mystique of an orderly, sequential, lockstep to success on the one hand, and the reality of (often disorderly) contemporary life-course experiences on the other. Long-hour, demanding, and insecure employment throughout adulthood can be at odds with employee health and well-being, as well as with the time parents need for their children, the time adult children need for their aging parents, the time neighbors need to build a sense of community, and the time individuals of all ages need for personal renewal. Particularly disconcerting is the experience of those who have followed the rules of the career game, putting in decades of hard work only to be downsized, laid off, or pushed into retirement. What happened?

First, recent shifts in marital and educational paths now challenge conventional notions of the transition to adulthood. Growing numbers of young people are delaying the school-to-work transition[13]—staying in and graduating high school, attending junior and four-year colleges, even going on to graduate or professional schools. This means that the demarcation between youth and adulthood has become blurred as many in their twenties, and even thirties, are still in school, remaining economically dependent on their parents, student aid, and government loans. Moreover, unprecedented numbers of adults in their thirties, forties, fifties, and beyond return to school to upgrade their skills, finish uncompleted degrees, or embark on new careers. Young people often delay—some even forgo—marriage or parenthood. Such traditional markers of adulthood no longer operate as such.

Second, there is a disconnect between the traditional (male) career mystique and the growing number of women in the workforce, a disconnect challenging conventional (gendered) work and family divides. Increasingly, the workforce consists of (1) men whose partners are in the labor force, (2) women whose partners are in the labor force, and (3) men and women without partners but with family obligations or other interests beyond their jobs. This is producing a crisis of care.[14] Despite this crisis, the career mystique remains the fulcrum around which American institutions are fashioned, meaning that Americans must organize (or aspire to organize) their lives according to its tenets. Care work, paid or unpaid, is relegated to the backwaters of public, governmental, and corporate concern. But the career mystique was made possible by the feminine mystique of women as providers of care. The "new" woman and the "new" man of the twenty-first century now expect (and are expected) to follow the career mystique *and* to be caring parents, spouses, and children. But career paths come prepackaged for those willing to give complete commitment; benefits, raises, and promotions are available only to those following the career mystique, giving all to their jobs. Responsibilities for family are off the business radar screen.

Third is globalization, and with it, the changing relationship between employees and employers. In the middle of the twentieth century, there was an implicit contract (a legal one in union settings) between those hired and those doing the hiring. It was this contract that set the stage for the career mystique. The rules of the game went like this: Employees traded their labor, work hours, and commitment for what frequently was a lifelong job or at least the steady income and job security that accompanied seniority. This contract has virtually disappeared. Today's global economy, with its emphasis on the bottom line, competition, and productivity, is a world of mergers and acquisitions, of restructuring and downsizing. Even middle-class managers and professionals at the apex of their careers may lose their jobs when firms seek to reduce labor costs. Employees, especially women, minorities, and immigrants, have always been vulnerable to a changing economy. But the downsizing trend means that midlevel managers and professionals are no longer immune from layoffs, even in good economic times.

Still, job ladders persist as cultural metaphors, yardsticks workers use in assessing their own work experiences. In fact, many employees put in far longer hours than did their parents' generation. The restructuring of work includes new technologies that "free" employees to work anywhere, anytime, hence, often everywhere, all the time.

Fourth are the revolutions in longevity and retirement, which are challenging conventional notions of old age. The aging of the baby boom generation, record low fertility rates, and increasing life expectancy mean a graying workforce and growing retired force. Since downsizing often takes the form of incentives offered to encourage early retirement, many employees in their fifties, and even in their late forties, find themselves suddenly encouraged to retire from their career jobs or else face the threat of unemployment. Those eligible for early-retirement incentive packages usually take advantage of this option, creating some very young retirees. In fact, retirement has become a very blurred transition. Many older workers leave their primary career jobs only to take on "second acts"; many retirees also seek second acts in paid work or unpaid community service.

Fifth, these enormous societal transformations characterizing life in the twenty-first century make existing cultural expectations and social policies out of date. Old customs and routines persist in the face of changing realities.

Today, a culture of occupational and educational equality among men and women coexists with the continuing gendered expectation that women should do the bulk of unpaid family-care work. But doing this second shift of family care[15] means moving in and out of the workforce, working part time or not at all.[16] This perpetuates gender discrimination in the types of jobs available to women, with employers presuming women lack long-term job commitment given that their checkered career patterns are at odds with the career mystique.

Increasing Work Hours

Still other changes suggest why some groups of workers today are putting in an unprecedented number of hours on the job. First, wages have not kept pace with living costs, requiring employees to work more hours to maintain their standard of living. Second, workers try to gain some measure of job security by signaling their commitment to their jobs and to their employers by putting in long hours, including working evenings or weekends. Third, the rising demand for consumer goods means that some workers work more to earn more to spend more. Fourth, women's increasing labor force participation means more total time spent on paid work by all adults in a household. Welfare reform legislation also presumes that poor women should support their families through paid work. More than nine in ten (95%) American workers reported (in a 1999 survey) being concerned about spending time with their immediate family. It is important to note that this is an issue for all employees—regardless of their age, income, race, ethnicity, or gender. Those with children under eighteen are especially concerned about having time to spend with their families.[17] Some researchers don't agree that working hours have really gone up,[18] but whether their actual hours are increasing or not, most American workers feel strapped for time.

THE END OF THE LOCKSTEP LIFESTYLE

In the 1950s most Americans finished school, found jobs, got married, and become parents before age thirty. The cultural template—on television, in middle-class suburbs, and in grade school readers—was the breadwinner/homemaker family, with gender dividing family and career even as commutes divided paid work from home life. Although some families could not afford a stay-at-home wife and mother, and others did not fit this two-parent, one-earner template, most Americans aspired to this vision of the good life, buying in to the career mystique for men and the feminine mystique for women. The conventional lockstep career shaped the life course not only of (typically male) breadwinners, but of their families as well.

Today, as we show in this book, there is no "normal" life path. Americans marry later or not at all, postpone parenthood, have fewer children (or none at all), move in and out of jobs, in and out of schooling, in and out of marriage or partnerships, and in and out of retirement. Most Americans hold values of gender equality; few now subscribe to the feminine mystique. But the career mystique of lockstep ladder climbing remains, even as the odds of achieving its promised success and security are smaller than ever. Most families still live in suburbs, only now all adults in the household are commuting to jobs, emptying neighborhoods for much of the day.

Career patterns in the United States remain one size fits all, with continuous, full-time employment a given for those serious about their jobs. The rhythm of paid work still shapes the (work-) day and the (work-) week. Career achievement and even popular notions of career paths continue to rest on the fragile edifice of hidden, unpaid family-care work.[19] As we show in the chapters that follow, somehow Americans manage to construct meaningful lives, in spite of outdated institutions designed for a different economy and a different workforce. Our years of research lead us to conclude that the costs of sustaining the myth of the career mystique —to individual and family life quality, to gender equality, to lifelong opportunity, and to a sense of community—are unacceptably high.

INTERNATIONAL TRENDS

These large-scale transformations in the United States mirror international trends. Sweden and China lead in their proportions of women in the workforce. Moreover, the revolution in family and lifestyle patterns characteristic in the United States is evident in the contemporary life course of individuals in most industrialized nations (see figure 1.3). In

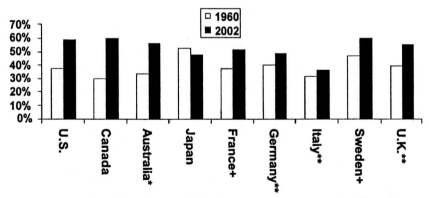

Figure 1.3. Civilian labor-force participation rates among women in selected countries, 1960 and 2002. (Source: U.S. Department of Labor, Bureau of Labor Statistics, 2004, "Comparative Civilian Labor Force Statistics for Ten Countries, 1959–2002.")
*1960 data was not available; 1964 data was substituted.
+1961 data was substituted for 1960 data.
**2000 data were not available; 1999 or 1998 data were substituted.

fact, in some European countries, marriage customarily occurs only in tandem with pregnancy—or not at all. Fertility rates are also at a historic low, with some countries, such as Italy, having children at less than replacement level (see figure 1.4).

Other countries both lead and lag in the development of policies and practices geared to the needs of the twenty-first-century workforce. Scandinavian countries have been on the cutting edge in adopting innovations that make it possible for both men and women to maintain their involvement in paid work and spend time with their families. Still, the Scandinavian workforce remains heavily segregated by gender, with men and women in Sweden, like those in many other countries, still reproducing many aspects of the gender divide. The age divide persists in Europe as in the United States, with older workers moving or encouraged into full-time retirement.

The lockstep pattern of lives—education, paid work, and retirement—remains the norm throughout Europe and Asia as well as the United States. This cultural blueprint both shapes and is shaped by social policies still geared to (1) full-time, continuous, paid work as the key to economic and occupational stability and success; and (2) the image of retirement as a one-way, one-time, irreversible exit from the workforce. The lockstep pattern of men's lives remains the yardstick against which all workers'—men's and women's—experiences are gauged.[20] However, contemporary American employees are more vulnerable to economic and other vicissitudes than are those in other countries. For example, while Canada, Sweden, Germany, and other countries in the European community experience high unemployment rates, they also maintain safety nets. Still, the trends toward early retirement, corporate restructuring, and the changing

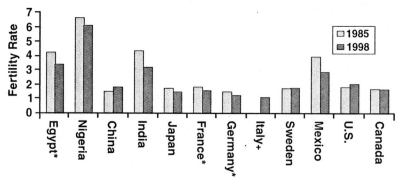

Figure 1.4.   Fertility rates in selected countries, 1985 and 1998. (Source: U.S. Bureau of the Census, 1998.)
*1990 data was used because 1985 data was unavailable.
+1985 and 1990 data was not available.

employer/employee contract are also evident in Europe, the Americas, and Asia. For example, state socialism in China used to mean secure state jobs (a situation known as the "iron rice bowl"); with the introduction of capital markets, however, state jobs are no longer as prevalent or as secure as they once were.[21]

REFRAMING THE PROBLEM

Sociologists, psychologists, economists, and anthropologists study paid work, unpaid work, retirement, families, education, and leisure—but typically not all together, not all at once. Understanding the pervasiveness of the career mystique requires putting the multiple strands of lives together, side by side with the institutions constraining them, that is, the outdated regime of rules, roles, and regulations shaping the contemporary life course. But social scientists are part of the very culture they study, frequently taking for granted the very lockstep of education, careers, and retirement that is at odds with contemporary lives. This is evident in the questions scholars investigate and the ways they define both issues and solutions.[22] For example, in the 1930s through 1950s, key work–family concerns were unemployment and stress, given the dislocations of the economic downturns of the Great Depression and World War II. Scholars focused on men's war absence and men's unemployment. Implicitly, if not explicitly, the breadwinner/homemaker cultural template defined their principal research questions.

In the 1960s and the 1970s, in light of discussions of the feminine mystique and the reinvigorated Women's Movement, many scholars turned their attention to the equality of opportunity for women in school and at work. Wage and occupational discrimination were prominent on researchers' agendas. But equality was defined in conventional male terms as equality on the job. Some feminists raised the issue of women's unpaid care work, but by and large that was not on the nation's research or policy agenda. Submerged in a culture embracing the conventional breadwinner/homemaker template, scholars investigated the possible harm to children of having a working mother. Having a working father was problematic only if men lost their jobs.

Note that poor women who combined paid work with family-care work were (and continue to be) part of welfare, not work–family, debates. Welfare legislation until the late 1990s made it possible for poor single mothers to continue as homemakers by depending on state support. Although growing numbers of middle-class working mothers could be seen as challenging old breadwinner/homemaker blueprints, by and large both the media and the scholarly community in the 1960s and 1970s defined this as simply women's problem. Researchers addressed how women could balance their paid work and unpaid family roles and continued to study the gender gap in earnings and status,[23] rarely questioning fundamental contradictions between the career regime and family responsibilities.

Feminist perspectives changed the work–family discourse in the 1980s and 1990s, bringing the division of domestic care work to the research agenda. Still, the balance metaphor persists in the framing of the work–family interface, with the burden of the balancing placed on women's shoulders. Proposed solutions to the problem of working mothers were "mommy tracks"—part-time jobs and/or less demanding occupations for women.[24] For men and women unwilling to lower their occupational aspirations, the career mystique of the lockstep career regime remained unchanged.

In the 1980s and 1990s, in response to the feminization of their workforces, large corporations began to move the *work–family* issue into the larger domain of *work life*, recognizing that not all their employees are parents or even married. In addition to information on subsidies for child care, many companies developed programs around elder care, flex time (changing start and stop times—either on a fixed basis or daily), personal days off, telecommuting, and parental leave. These changes accompanied the enactment of the Family and Medical Leave Act, signed by President Bill Clinton in 1993, mandating unpaid time off for new parents or those with sick children or other relatives (restricted to employees in organizations with fifty or more employees). Researchers began to follow suit, investigating work–life effectiveness along with the effects of the Family and Medical Leave Act and "family-friendly" initiatives in the private sector.[25] Gender issues related to equal pay for equal or comparable work remained on the research agenda. But few questioned the lockstep career regime: the roles, rules, and regulations that require committed employees to work long hours on a continuous basis, discouraging them from using family-friendly benefits for fear of seeming less committed to their jobs, and pit paid work against unpaid family work.[26]

Today many feminist scholars are shifting the terms of the debate from focusing on fitting women into the lockstep career regime to valuing unpaid (as well as paid) care work. Their studies show how family and community care work provides the scaffolding supporting not only men's career paths (as unencumbered workers), but the very infrastructure of communities, schools, and the market economy.[27] We argue that the issue is not how employees can balance their personal lives with the demands of their jobs, but how the career mystique and the regime of policies and practices built up around it constrain women's and men's options at every stage of their lives.

RETHINKING CAREERS

In the pages that follow, we focus on the career mystique as it permeates men's and women's life courses and document how individuals and families at different ages and stages think and strategize about their options and goals. We highlight (1) dynamic processes of development and change—from children envisioning their careers to those midcourse who are thinking about retirement; (2) the changing social, economic, and cultural environment that is the moving stage upon which contemporary Americans construct their lives; and (3) the significance of the career mystique and the career regime as outdated cultural metaphors, organizational arrangements, and social policies constraining life choices and life chances around paid work, unpaid family and community work, and retirement, as well as possibilities for gender equality.

In the 1950s, the career mystique matched the feminine mystique: Men in middle-class and unionized blue-collar jobs could focus on breadwinning because their wives did the homemaking. Just as they were in the middle of the twentieth century, today workers are expected to work long hours (including mandatory overtime and "choosing" to work evenings and weekends), to travel, and to relocate if their employers require it. The career mystique has persisted: Only now it is mismatched with the new risk economy and the needs of a new workforce that is more diverse, more female, and older than ever. This mismatch is a graphic example of *structural lag*,[28] in which old customs and routines persist in the face of changing realities. Although the feminine mystique, along with full-time homemaking, has become a relic of the mid-twentieth century, we show that many couples manage by prioritizing one person's job. They do so because the career regime relegates benefits, higher wages, and future prospects to those willing to follow the continuous, long-hour career mystique. Given the risks of the global economy, many adults feel that investing in at least one "good" job per family is the only way to achieve even a modicum of job and income security.

We also show that cultural expectations about the career mystique are changing at a glacial pace. Employers, men, women, and, frequently, even children take for granted that regular, paid work means spending five days, or forty or more hours, a week on the job (a standard enacted in 1938 by the Fair Labor Standards Act), that education is for children and young people, that retirement is a one-way, one-time, irreversible exit, and that family-care work is women's responsibility. This sense of the career mystique as "the way things are" creates, perpetuates, and exacerbates inequalities—financial and emotional—between men and women; strains working families; and fosters the rolelessness of retirement.[29] The myth of careers as long hours and lockstep only reinforces gender divides and gender differences in both salary and advancement prospects. When men earn more than women and have a greater chance of moving ahead in their jobs, it makes sense for couples to invest in husbands' occupational careers, even if it means shortchanging wives' own prospects. Thus, the weight of coordinating work and family responsibilities rests, for the most part, on the shoulders of wives, mothers, female single parents, and the daughters of ailing parents. The gendered nature of care work, in turn, reinforces and perpetuates inequalities between men and women in opportunities for on-the-job training and advancement. Both employees and employers buy into the notion that family-care work responsibilities are private troubles to be handled alone (and typically by women), rather than public issues requiring systemic changes in the career regime. Many also use gender stereotypes in the ways they hire and promote workers, presuming that women have (or will have) family responsibilities that will lower their productivity and tenure and increase their absenteeism. In this way, cultural myths about careers disadvantage women at all life stages, including retirement. But we also show that they disadvantage men as well, effectively reinforcing their provider economic role, meaning that men's time for their families, their communities, and themselves is curtailed.

BEYOND LOCKSTEP LIVES

Life in the twenty-first century is definitely not lockstep. Americans' transitions into and out of school, marriage, parenting, paid work, and care work are more varied than ever. People today are changing not only their jobs but also their occupations; returning to school at all ages or staying in school longer; marrying later, divorcing, or staying single; delaying childbearing or having no children; retiring early, late, not at all, or several times. The United States and, indeed, nations around the world stand in a whirlwind of demographic, economic, technological, and social change. But policies and practices remain caught in a time warp.

In this book we chart how the career mystique fosters a false divide between the two most fundamental life dimensions—job and family—as they play out over the life course. We show that most contemporary men and women want it all—including gender equality—but accommodate outdated and conflicting institutions through hybrid strategies—keeping one foot in the twentieth century and placing the other in the twenty-first—to deal with the risks and realities of contemporary lives. This means that women, wives, and single mothers still do most of society's care work without pay, even as they try simultaneously to maintain ties to the paid workforce. Men, husbands, and fathers put in long hours in paid work, even as many try to help out at home. Most Americans believe in equal opportunities for men and women but simply can't make it happen, even in their own families.

The lockstep regime of the career mystique also fosters an age divide. Most Americans in their fifties, sixties, and seventies want to remain engaged in some form of productive activity, but conventional employment and retirement patterns make it difficult to do so.

The career mystique developed during very different times, for a very different workforce, in a very different economy.[30] The chapters that follow examine the hybrid strategies Americans adopt at various ages and stages to manage the contingencies and contradictions of their lives. We begin with the ways even young children learn the career mystique.

2

Learning the Career Mystique: Where Do Values and Expectations Come From?

"When I grow up, I'm going to . . ." is a familiar refrain. Young people develop ideas about careers, gender, and their own futures very early, often by observing their parents and other adults and by absorbing the messages and myths of the society that envelops them. In rapidly changing times the lessons children learn about work, careers, and gender may well be out of date. Children's aspirations and goals change as they grow older to better match the changing realities in their lives. Still, what children begin to see as desirable or possible, for themselves or for others, can shape their subsequent life course. Such belief systems keep some doors open while effectively closing off other future possibilities. Nevertheless, children tend to hang on to certain cognitions as they move to adulthood, even as the world shifts beneath their feet. In this chapter we examine how children develop aspirations regarding their future careers and personal lives. These goals are influenced by their parents and peers, their educational experiences, and the messages received from the media and the broader culture. We show how many of the people and institutions in children's lives perpetuate the myth of the career mystique. Finally, we examine how children enter into the world of paid work and how those experiences shape their future.

CHILDREN'S OCCUPATIONAL ASPIRATIONS

Psychologists identify a series of stages that children pass through as they develop and refine their occupational aspirations. Studies show that even children between the ages of six and eight begin to develop career goals that fit with prevailing gender stereotypes.[1] Later, in elementary and middle school, when they reach ages nine to thirteen, children further refine these interests in light of their families' socioeconomic status. Typically, children in this age group begin to reject low-prestige jobs (relative to their own family's status), as well as those that they see as too difficult or beyond their reach.[2]

Parental Influences

According to social learning theory, children develop their values, attitudes, and expectations by observing and modeling the values, attitudes, and behaviors of the important people in their lives.[3] We expect, then, that young people whose parents have raised them in more traditional ways will tend to be more traditional themselves. Similarly, young people raised in more egalitarian families should develop less traditional values. In this way, outmoded but taken-for-granted templates like the career mystique are passed on from parent to child, with neither generation questioning whether there is a different way of structuring work, family, and the lockstep life course.

Research shows that, indeed, the behaviors and attitudes of parents do exert a strong influence on youths' and young adults' attitudes and expectations about work, family, age, and gender. For example, almost three quarters of high school students agree with their parents' values regarding women's roles.[4] Further, over the past twenty years teens' gender attitudes have increasingly converged with the attitudes of their parents, suggesting that, in these times of shifting values, young people increasingly look to their parents as guides. But, equally important, the last several decades have witnessed a culture-wide transformation in attitudes regarding gender. Both men and women have become more egalitarian in their thinking about the roles of men and women in the home and at work, with women's attitudes being consistently more egalitarian than men's. Consequently, young people, and particularly young women, are ever more apt to reject the gendered divisions between paid work and unpaid care work inherent in the assumptions of the feminine mystique.

However, changes in values and attitudes do not always translate into changes in behavior. Even though today's youth tend to believe that domestic chores should not be allocated by gender, sociologist Constance Gager and her colleagues find that ninth-grade girls spend, on average, two hours more a week doing domestic chores than do ninth-grade boys. This early gendered division of housework becomes even more pronounced with age. Three years later, by twelfth grade, these same girls perform nearly four hours a week more housework than the boys.[5] Despite believing that men and women should share housework equally, young people themselves often fall back into more conventional behavior when at home.

Mothers are especially important socializing agents for their sons and daughters, passing on cultural templates as to how family work and paid work should be managed and integrated. Studies find that young and adolescent girls' attitudes about children, marriage, and occupational careers are very similar to the attitudes of their mothers. Moreover, this similarity persists into young adulthood.[6] Fathers also play a role in the development of their children's gender values. Children whose fathers share more equitably in household tasks tend to have more egalitarian attitudes than children whose fathers do few household tasks.[7] Despite the importance of paternal modeling of gender behaviors, Grace Baruch and Rosalind Barnett show that mothers' gender values exert the strongest influence on children's development of attitudes and values about the roles of men and women at work and at home.[8] This can, in part, explain why many working women continue to cling to the vestiges of gender divisions, even as they reject the feminine mystique. Most women today were raised by mothers who were influenced by the myth of the feminine mystique, based on the notion that women were solely responsible for the care work of their families. Women generally adopt the values of their mothers. Hence, women today try to make their way in a world of work built on the career mystique (itself contingent on unpaid "women's" work) while they simultaneously embrace women's caregiving and domesticity.

As a case in point, consider twenty-two-year-old Constance (see profile), who emulates her mother's strategy for combining work and family.

PROFILE: CONSTANCE

The first thing that one notices about Constance is her warm and welcoming smile, which is frequently punctuated by a hearty, warm laugh. Constance, a twenty-two-year-old African American, recently graduated from college with a B.A. in biology. She is the youngest of three children, all of whom have graduated from college. Constance was born in Zambia, but when she was one, her family moved to the United States, where her father had received a scholarship to study chemistry at a prestigious university. When Constance was six her father received his Ph.D. in chemistry and began working for a large pharmaceutical corporation where he was still employed at the time of the interview. While in the United States, Constance's mother received a master's degree in social work but did not work outside of the home while her children were young. When Constance and her siblings were all in school, her mother worked part time in a human resources department. She did not want a full-time job because she wanted to be home when her children returned from school. Later, when Constance's father was transferred to another state, the only part-time job her mother could find was in a grocery store, stocking shelves. Constance's smile evaporates when she talks about her mother's career choices. Although her mother does not voice any regrets, Constance believes that her mother is not happy with her job. This is a plight Constance wants to avoid.

Although Constance was accepted into a graduate program in physical therapy, she decided to delay graduate school for two years so she could gain some work experience and save money. Constance does not plan on marrying but would like to have a child when she is in her mid-thirties, after her career in physical therapy is established. Once she has children, Constance believes her priorities will shift and that family will then take priority over work. Like her mother, Constance would like to work part time when she has children in order to spend more time with them. Unlike her mother, Constance does not want to find herself working in a job that does not challenge her or use her skills.

Constance plans to work only four days a week when she has small children. Her attitudes toward women's roles are more egalitarian than those of her mother, yet she still plans to make family care a priority when she has children. Constance is struggling with the question of how to satisfy the demands of the career mystique and still raise her future children.

Gender Values and Behavior

Do boys and girls have similar career goals and aspirations? As a result of the Women's Movement, equal-opportunity legislation, and greater cultural acceptance of gender equality, the answer appears to be yes. Teenage girls assign as much importance to their future careers as teenage boys.[9] Despite their ambitious goals, however, girls also place a higher value on marriage and family than do boys. Further, girls still expect to fashion their educational plans around the anticipated needs of their anticipated families, expecting either to truncate or interrupt their education as needed.[10] Even at young ages, both boys and girls subscribe to the myth

of the career mystique, believing that they can have it all by working hard
and excelling at their jobs. But most, like Constance, want more than simply to climb career ladders; they also want to have a successful family life.
They perceive only dimly, if at all, the incompatibilities between the career
mystique and the realities of family needs, even as both spouses or single
parents are caught up in jobs that expect employees to do more with less.
This incongruity is clear in a 1997 study, finding that while most high
school seniors agree that women should have the same opportunities as
men, over a third also subscribe to the belief that children will suffer if
their mother works.[11] This dissonance in cognitions and values is particularly acute for girls, whose lives will most likely play out in the seeking of
various resolutions to it.

Socioeconomic Influences

Family socioeconomic status influences children's expectations about
their own and others' occupational attainment, even at a young age. Susan Weinger found that children from low-income backgrounds believed
that economically disadvantaged children are unlikely to achieve the
same career goals as more economically advantaged children. As one
child stated about a hypothetical child living in a poor house, "She probably dreams of being something great, like a doctor, but in the back of her
mind she knows she's not gonna be a great person because of the family's
money or whatever. So she's probably like thinking about a bagger at the
store, like groceries."[12]

Vows and Values

Family values are also tied to the ways young people think about careers.
The latter half of the twentieth century witnessed a sea change in both values and behavior related to marriage and premarital sex (see chapters 3
and 4 for more information about changes in timing and rates of marriage). Divorce, childbearing out of wedlock, and cohabitation have all
risen dramatically.[13] These changes, in turn, influence the ways children
and youth think about commitment, marriage, and sexuality. Many teens
today consider cohabitation, premarital sex, and childrearing outside of a
marital relationship acceptable behaviors.[14] Still, most contemporary
teenagers view marriage as an important—if distant—goal. In a national
study, almost four out of five (78%) high school seniors reported that marriage and family life were extremely important to them, and about the
same proportion (80%) of high school seniors hoped to eventually
marry.[15] There is evidence that there may be a slight resurgence among
teens in traditional values associated with marriage. For example, teens

today have a more positive attitude toward monogamy than did teens in the 1970s.[16] Today, almost nine out of ten (88%) teens believe that the divorce rate is too high.[17]

Although most teenagers still value marriage, they are less optimistic about it in their own lives. In 1995, only three out of five (61%) high school students believed that it was very likely that they would remain married to the same person for life.[18] Girls are somewhat more optimistic that their marriages will last than are boys (64% and 59%, respectively).[19] Studies show that children and youth tend to have more detailed and optimistic plans for their occupational careers than for their family and romantic relationships.[20] Schools today place a great deal of emphasis on helping youth identify and work toward educational and occupational goals, but tend to neglect family and relationship planning. This is likely to leave young adults ill prepared to manage the complex responsibilities involved in integrating their work lives and personal lives, particularly when marriage and children are involved.

In sum, the research evidence shows that, generally, young people hold work, family, and gender values similar to those of their parents, but also that children tend to be less traditional than their parents. The move toward equality of opportunity has altered women's lives more than men's. It is not surprising, therefore, that—even in this time of uneven social change—girls and young women continue to be influenced by their mothers as they simultaneously move away from, and embrace the primacy of, family relationships in their lives. The stage is set in childhood and adolescence for both girls and boys to want to—and believe they can—have it all. They have little recognition of the difficulties of constructing lives in which both husbands and wives have high and equal occupational and family goals. An example of the belief that people can do whatever they set their minds to is Constance's conviction that she can be a single mother with a first-rate career. She may well manage to do so, but most single parents would describe very different scenarios.

LEARNING, LEISURE, AND OTHER WAYS TO SPEND TIME

Thus far we have examined children's values and beliefs about their lives as adults. In this section we consider their lives as children. Often they are children of dual-earner couples or single-earner, single parents. Having all adults in the household in the workforce affects children's lives along many dimensions. With a larger number of mothers working for pay, children today are spending more time with other caregivers and in preschool settings compared with children in earlier generations. They also spend their time differently. Children today, in both dual-earner and single-earner households, are more likely to participate in organized activities such as sports or art and music lessons. Conversely, children spend less time eating with their families, doing homework, attending religious services, or in leisure.[21] Further, children in single-parent households tend to spend more time watching television than do those living with both parents, and less time involved in music, hobbies, group activities, reading, religious attendance, eating with family, and household conversations.[22]

There are also gender differences in the way children use their time. Boys spend more time playing sports, using computers, and in free play than girls do. Girls spend more time than boys in household work, in arts and music activities, and in personal care.

TEENS AT WORK

Young people often develop knowledge and expectations about employment and career paths while on the job. In fact, it is the norm for American teenagers to work. Most older teens hold part-time jobs during the school year and many move to full-time work during the summer when school is not in session. In 1998 more than half (58%) of sixteen-year-olds in the United States worked during the school year, which was slightly higher than the proportion of Canadian teens doing so.[23] Although the percentage of teenage boys who work for pay has remained relatively constant in the United States over the past twenty years, increasing proportions of teenage girls have also entered the workforce (see figure 2.1).

Boys' and girls' early work experiences tend to differ. Boys are likely to take on jobs at an earlier age than are girls.[24] After the age of fourteen, employment rates for boys and girls are similar, although the types of jobs they engage in differ, reflecting the gendered nature of paid work in Western society. Teenage girls are more likely to babysit for young children and to work for family, friends, or people they know, and they are more intrinsically motivated to work than are boys.[25] Constance (see profile above), for example, spent the four summers while she was in college working as a nanny for a family that she had known for years. Even after graduating from college, Constance planned to spend one last summer working for this family. Teenage boys, on the other hand, are more likely to perform manual labor, which often pays more than the types of work girls do. As teens get older, this gender segregation continues; girls are more likely to continue to work for family and friends, while boys are more likely to be employed in a wider range of jobs.[26] Michael (see pro-

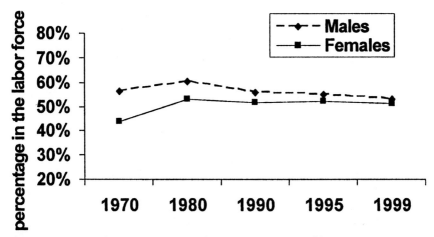

Figure 2.1. Labor force participation of teens 16 to 19 years old. (Source: U.S. Census Bureau, 2000 *Statistical Abstract of the United States.*)

file) is a good example of this progression. He began working very early in a restaurant as a dishwasher. By the time he was a senior in high school, he was doing highly skilled manual labor at relatively high pay. This type of occupational progression is rare among teenage girls. Michael's sister, for example, cleaned houses for friends of her family when she was a teenager.

PROFILE: MICHAEL

Michael is an unusually serious and introspective twenty-four-year-old with a piercing gaze and direct manner. At 6'1", Michael is a tall and muscular young man who takes pride in his work ethic and discipline. His parents are very hardworking people, and they impressed upon him the importance of being responsible and independent. Michael's father worked as a welder and his mother worked as a teacher's aid.

When Michael was eight his parents divorced. Following the divorce, Michael and his younger sister lived with their mother during the week, spending alternate weekends with their mother or their father. Michael's mother went back to school after the divorce to get a college degree. During that time Michael was often left at home to care for his younger sister, which may have fostered his strong sense of duty and responsibility. His parents appreciated Michael's maturity

and willingness to help out around the house and with child care. Today, he remains close to both of his parents and still looks out for the
welfare of his sister.

In high school Michael was an able student. However, his greatest love was sports. He played on the varsity basketball and football
teams. As a junior he worked approximately twenty-five hours a
week at various jobs, ranging from cooking in a fast food restaurant
to construction. During the last semester of his senior year in high
school, Michael worked full time for a builder. He used the money
he made to buy a car and spent what was left on recreation. Michael
found this work highly rewarding and was less and less interested
in his classes. After graduation Michael enrolled in college. However, he was bored at school, and after less than one year, he left and
took a full-time job with a builder. A year later, at the age of nineteen, Michael and a friend started their own construction company.
After two years, financial problems forced them to dissolve the
business, and Michael then took a job in a factory, working as a
welder.

Throughout high school Michael dated Sarah, a classmate. They
planned to marry once they were both financially secure. However,
when Sarah went away to college, they drifted apart and eventually
broke up. This occurred just as Michael's business folded. This was a
very difficult time for Michael. Two years later, at the time of the interview, Michael was still reeling from the double loss of his relationship with Sarah and of his business.

Since the breakup Michael has been reluctant to become involved
in another relationship. Marriage and a family are no longer among
his long-term goals. At the time of the interview, Michael was
twenty-three and working full time as a laborer in a factory. Feeling
directionless, he enlisted in the army and was leaving for basic
training the week after our interview. Michael was anxious about
the big changes that were about to take place in his life, but he was
also excited about the physical and personal challenges he would
encounter in the military.

Due to the early pay differential, as exemplified by Michael's story,
young men and women have differing expectations about how their
work is valued. Serge Desmarais and James Curtis found that teenage
girls, in addition to being paid less for their work, tend also to believe that
their work is worth less than do teenage boys. Desmarais and Curtis believe that young women develop lower expectations about what their la-

bor is worth because even as teenagers they and their same-sex peers are often paid less than teenage boys. This gender difference in the perceived value of their work persists into adulthood.

Children in the United States embrace the values associated with the career mystique. Even in their earliest work experiences, American youth place a high value on paid work and consider the mystique of employment the path to success and adulthood. As figure 2.2 illustrates, American youth spend vastly greater amounts of time in paid work than their counterparts in other industrialized nations. On average, American youth work about two-thirds of an hour per day. This is three times greater than the amount of time spent working by youth in Norway, the industrialized country with the second highest rate of teen employment hours. What activities do these teens forgo while they are working? According to a study by August Flammer and his colleagues, teens in the United States spend significantly less time reading for leisure than do teens in other nations (see figure 2.2). In every other country studied, Flammer found that youth spend at least twice as much time reading than working for pay. In the United States this relationship is reversed, with American youth spending approximately three times as much time at work than with a book. Young people in the United States are also less likely to spend time studying and playing music.

Why do teens in the United States work more than those in Europe? Typically, it is not because of economic need (as is often the case in third world countries, where teens work more hours than even American youth). In fact, teens from wealthier families in the United States are more likely to work for pay than youth from low-income families. For many

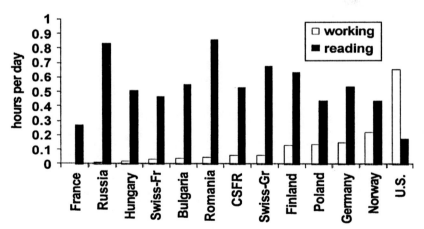

Figure 2.2. Average number of hours spent working and reading leisure material on a school day for children 13 to 17 years old in European countries and the United States. (Source: Flammer, Alsaker, and Noack 1999.)

teens, the desire to work is motivated by the desire for self-sufficiency, independence, and material goods, values inherent in the career mystique. As Michael reflects on his twenty- to twenty-five-hour-a-week job washing dishes while in high school, "I liked it a lot. I had lots of money and that was cool."

Another reason for the high rate of teen employment is America's low rate of unemployment compared to other industrialized countries. In 1999 the average jobless rate in the fifteen-nation European Union was 9.1 percent, twice that of the United States. A low unemployment rate translates to more jobs available for youth as well as others in the U.S. labor force. In France, the country with the lowest teen employment, unemployment among adults became so acute (12.5%) that in 1999 the French government officially reduced the workweek from thirty-nine to thirty-five hours.

The final reason so many American teens work is the much greater value American youth place on work and success than do their European counterparts, a reflection of the prevalence and lure of the career mystique as part of the American Dream. Jari-Erik Nurmi and colleagues compared U.S. and European teens' assessments of the importance they place on career, success, family, and leisure. Consistently, teens in the United States place a greater emphasis on their future career and occupational success than do teens in other countries. By contrast, American teens place less emphasis on the importance of social pleasure than do teens from Western Europe, and American girls place less importance on family than do girls from Eastern Europe.

The picture that emerges is that teens in the United States are among the most career- and success-oriented teens in the industrialized world, valuing economic success, often at the cost of family, education, and recreation. As we will see, this is another trend that persists into adulthood. These ambitious and hard-working American teens are not unlike their parents, who are among the hardest working in the industrialized world. The career mystique is a pervasive and deep-rooted cultural doctrine subscribed to by Americans of all ages, even adolescents.

The Effects of Teen Employment

Is teen employment beneficial or harmful? The evidence is mixed. Most of the jobs that teens in the United States hold are the least attractive and lowest-paid jobs in lower-level service industries.[27] Therefore, many of the skills that teens learn do not directly enhance their future employability. However, there are benefits associated with teenage employment.[28] Studies have found that students who work more hours while in high school have higher rates of employability two to four years after they graduate and are more likely to have prestigious jobs and make more money later in life. Teens who work for pay are also more autonomous and confident than those who do not have jobs and have better time-management skills, all of which are qualities highly valued in our individualistic and work-oriented society. Michael illustrates this point as he talks about working in high school:

> It made me be a more responsible person and realize that I have responsibilities and things to do, that people are depending on me to do them in order to make something work. So just being part of that, that made me realize what responsibilities are and how it works and what it is all about.

Employment is also related to higher levels of self-esteem, but only among teens who produce high-quality work, like Michael did in his construction job. For the most part, however, the majority of high school jobs do not have much of an impact on youths' work-related attitudes or values.

Teen work also has a down side.[29] A heavy work schedule predicts poor school attendance and can lead to a drop in high school grades. This occurred when Michael worked full time during his senior year. "I liked working a lot. It had an effect on my schoolwork, though. I felt like I owed my boss my responsibility. People were depending on me. It was easier to blow off a teacher. School seemed less important."

Teens who work twenty hours a week or more are also more likely to smoke cigarettes, to use drugs and alcohol, and to be involved in sexual behavior. The larger disposable income associated with a heavier work schedule can lead to increased spending on habit-forming substances and to activities which serve as an entryway to sexual involvement (e.g., dating, going to clubs).

Michael Frone hypothesizes that two processes are associated with teen work. For some teens, paid employment serves as a positive socializing agent, encouraging youth and adolescents to be more independent and to invest more in their education and career. These teens work hard because they believe that work will help them in the future. Other teens, however, may work relatively more hours because they have little attachment to formal schooling and, instead, invest in their after-school work. For the former group, the number of hours worked may be related to positive educational outcomes. For the latter, high work hours may reflect their already marginal investment in education. For Michael, his job was directly related to a declining interest in formal education.

CHILDREN WHO WORK

Most wealthy countries have laws to protect children from economic exploitation. In the United States the 1938 Fair Labor Standards Act (FLSA) restricts the ages, hours, and work settings of employed children. In industries the FLSA has set the minimum working age at sixteen. However, fourteen- and fifteen-year-olds can be employed for limited hours in occupations such as delivering newspapers, bagging groceries, washing cars, and stocking supermarket shelves. In the United States, children are restricted to working only three hours a day after school for a maximum of eighteen hours a week when school is in session. But agricultural work is largely exempt from the child-labor standards to which other industries are held. On commercial farms, a child as young as twelve is allowed to work if a parent also works on the farm, and work on family farms is exempt from all child-labor regulations.

Despite these laws, the illegal employment of young people is a significant problem in the United States. It is estimated that 156,000 children and youth worked illegally in America in 1996.[30] Illegal work is likely to take the form of either hazardous work or working hours that are longer than mandated. Michael, for example, who worked twenty-five hours a week as a junior and forty hours a week as a senior, was doing so in violation of the FLSA. Children who work illegally are not more likely to come from economically disadvantaged backgrounds. Rather than being driven by economic need, illegal employment is more likely to be driven by employer greed.[31] Indeed, Michael's employer, an independent businessman, paid Michael a lower wage than he did his adult workers and did not provide Michael benefits, which saved him a great deal of money. Michael, embracing the career mystique, believed that by working extra hours for his boss, he was earning himself both job security and the promise of future higher wages.

Migrant Farmworkers

A significant number of working children and teens are migrant workers, working alongside their family members as they make their way north in the spring, harvesting and planting crops. Their work experiences are very different from the experiences of most other employed teens working in the United States. Moreover, their work is often critical to their own and their families' survival.

Of farmworkers in the United States, 81 percent are foreign born, and 80 percent are male migrant workers who travel away from their homes to find work. U.S. child-labor laws are more permissive for migrant workers than for nonmigrant workers. With parental consent, migrant workers' children as young as ten may work in the fields with their parents. Ten- and eleven-year-olds can even work without parental consent if the farm obtains a waiver from the Department of Labor. Migrant children also have fewer legal protections than those working in other jobs. Children of migrant workers can be employed in agriculture for more than forty hours a week, even during the school year, unlike other children in the United States, whose hours are restricted when school is in session. A fourteen-year-old migrant farmworker in the United States can use knives and machetes, operate machinery, and be exposed to dangerous pesticides, whereas youth working in nonagricultural settings are not allowed to work with hazardous materials or dangerous machinery.

Farmwork poses a significant health risk to children. Agriculture is one of the most dangerous occupations.[32] Aside from their exposure to dangerous machinery and tools, almost half (48%) of migrant farmworker children have been sprayed with pesticides linked to childhood brain tumors and leukemia. The living conditions of migrant workers are often unsanitary. The rate of parasitic infection among migrant workers is estimated to be eleven to fifty-nine times higher than that of the general U.S. population. One in six farmworkers, who often work in the hot summer sun with pesticides and fertilizer, has no toilet and no access to clean water, which are essential to good health. Children working in the fields are even more vulnerable than adults to heat exhaustion and thirst. It is not surprising to learn, then, that the life expectancy for a migrant worker is forty-nine years, compared to seventy-three years for the general population.

Migrant farmwork has devastating consequences for the future of the children who travel across the country harvesting food. The rate of school enrollment for farmworking children is lower than for any other group in the nation. Many factors are responsible for this. First, because of economic need, many children work in the fields rather than going to school. Second, when children of migrant workers do go to school, they are often exhausted from getting up early in the morning and putting in several hours of work before school, only to work several more hours after school. This leaves little time for completing homework assignments or for sleep. As a result, migrant farmworking children have very high absentee rates.[33] And migrant-farmworker families are constantly moving, following the crops as they ripen. A migrant child will typically only be in a particular school for several weeks before the family needs to move to a new area. It is difficult for families to enroll their children in several different school districts throughout the year. It is also difficult for children to fit in socially and excel educationally when they move from school to school. As an eighteen-year-old migrant worker said, "It's hard. I'm always crying on the first day of school. . . . I just sit in a corner and after two weeks in one place, we move again."[34] Frequent moving and chronic absences result in migrant children losing motivation to attend school and eventually falling behind academically. It is no surprise, then, to find that only 45 percent of migrant farmworker children graduate from high school.[35] In fact, given the circumstances, one wonders how a migrant child could manage to attain a high school degree. By not completing a formal education, migrant farmworking children seriously curtail their chances to escape the cycle of poverty of which they are already a part.

BEYOND LOCKSTEP LIVES

Socialization—through parents, schools, and media, as well as their own observations and experiences—establishes children's expectations early about the nature of occupational paths and their importance in shaping life patterns and life quality. Research shows that even young children grasp the meaning of socioeconomic status and who is most apt to be a winner or loser—in terms of having an interesting job, good housing, and a high income—in American society.

We also see early internalization of taken-for-granted gender scripts and schema reflective of the broader culture. These play out in the allocation of unpaid (as well as paid) care work—with time diary studies showing girls (under twelve) already doing more housework than boys. Studies of teens who work for pay suggest some are in danger of buying into the career mystique early, endangering their future options by curtailing their educations in order to move into full-time jobs right after high school or even before they graduate.

The evidence points to how their parents' circumstances—maternal employment, single parenthood, educational attainment—affect the lifestyles and life quality of children. American children are busier today, as are their parents. The challenge of redesigning work and career paths in ways that make reasonable accommodations to working parents and other care providers has tremendous implications for the lives of their children and for the quality of childhood in contemporary society. The experiences of children in migrant families point to the futility of the career mystique for certain disadvantaged segments of the population. Still, the American Dream prevails. The myth of career success through hard work is learned early in life even if actual chances are slim.

3

Do Young Adults Still Believe in the Career Mystique?

The story of the transition to adulthood in twenty-first-century America (as in most of the developed world) is really hundreds of thousands of stories. When one of the authors (Phyllis) got married in the early 1960s, it seemed that all of the teenage girls in Atlanta and south Georgia were getting married right after high school, if not before. In the South in the 1960s, there were two options: marriage and motherhood or the career of the single woman. And Phyllis had met only one of the latter group, a thirty-five-ish professional who flossed her teeth all the time. Not surprisingly, Phyllis decided to take the marriage route at eighteen.

But times changed. In 1976, when Pat, the second author, was eighteen and living in the metropolitan Detroit area, the Women's Movement was in full swing and young women were determined to have it all. Pat and her female contemporaries delayed marriage until their mid-twenties, dreaming of having a family and a career, never realizing that these two goals would eventually come to loggerheads. Today there is even more variability in all the markers of growing up: whether and when to marry, to parent, to work, to go to school, to move out of the family home, and sometimes to move back in. The transition to adulthood now has no single script.

In this chapter we focus on young people mostly in their twenties—those who are moving into colleges or from schooling into jobs, who are beginning to form long-term relationships, sometimes cohabiting or marrying, sometimes having children. These people are on the borders of what, in the United States, is the main act: their occupational careers. How do they anticipate their future lives as they move into adulthood? The lockstep life course relegates education to childhood and adolescence. But for many, the twenties are almost a second adolescence, still a time of learning spent in and out of school and in and out of more casual paid work. Although some twenty-somethings have had jobs for years, some are already married, and some are parents, many others are still in college. Historical changes in the economy and in the educational system have transformed the transition to adulthood in contemporary society, with progressively more Americans not only graduating from high school, but also entering and remaining in college.[1] This is an early—and major—fork in the life-course path. Those without a high school diploma and those who go from high school graduation directly into full-time employment are often disadvantaged in an economy requiring skills and credentials. The earnings gap is widening between those with and without a college education. Gone are the days in which an industrious, hardworking man like Michael's father (see Michael's profile in chapter 2) could count on earning enough money to support his family without a college degree.

As young people in their twenties consider future occupations, as well as the possibilities of marriage and children, many begin to see the faintest outlines of the mismatch they will face, the mismatch built into a career mystique of continuous, long-hour, and long-term commitment to paid work. Young women especially begin to wonder how they can successfully have it all—an occupational career and a life that includes a husband and children. Their options are not as stark as those Phyllis faced in the 1960s, but many constraints remain; they are just subtler. Even in 2002, writers like Sylvia Ann Hewlett were advising women to choose between a professional career and a family.[2] Nor are women today as naive as young women, like Pat in the mid-1970s, who thought they could do and be it all with no costs to themselves or their families. Young men also face constraints as increasingly they, too, would like to be engaged in their families as well as their careers. As young men realize that the mothers of their children are likely to have occupational aspirations of their own, the dilemmas of integrating two careers with family goals often appear daunting. Moreover, the vagaries of a global information economy mean that twenty-something men and women can count on nothing—not on secure careers, guaranteed pensions, or even on the next paycheck with which to pay off their enormous student loans.

Research by sociologist Robert Orrange on professional school students (soon to graduate with law or M.B.A. degrees) shows that even these career-oriented young people (having invested their time, energy, and money to obtain the credentials to become lawyers and managers) rank family as a central focus of their lives.[3] But the uncertainties of their future life courses are a pervasive theme. For example, one law student sees family as more secure than career, although neither is certain:

Life in general is such a roller coaster. It's kind of like riding one forever. And the one thing that's always there is family. I mean, no matter if you lose your job . . . I guess none of them are guaranteed. I mean, family is not guaranteed, but neither is work . . . right now work is first, but hopefully someday, I think ultimately family is going to win out.[4]

Note that this student accepts the notion that occupational careers are top priority and that eventually family and career concerns will conflict before one eventually "wins out."

Where do young adults' expectations and plans come from? In part, they are generated by the socialization processes and experiences in childhood described in chapter 2. But socialization is ongoing. Young adults' beliefs and aspirations change as they confront shifting social and economic landscapes. In this chapter we show how the large-scale trends we discussed in chapter 1—the moving platform of multilayered change —shape the ways contemporary young adults experience and plan their lives.

AFTER HIGH SCHOOL: COLLEGE VERSUS WORK

College and postgraduate schooling are transforming both the timing and meaning of early adulthood. Despite the rising costs of education, the number of students attending and graduating from college in the United States has been increasing steadily since 1970. A little more than three out of five (63%) high school graduates enroll in college in the fall following their graduation. However, only about one-third of high school graduates actually receive their college degree within six years, with rates of completion approximately twice as high for whites as for African Americans or Hispanic Americans.[5] There is another change as well: Today, women are slightly more likely than men to attend college.

Factors Influencing College Attendance

Many factors influence whether young people go to college. A major determinant is whether they can afford the costs of higher education. As figure 3.1 illustrates, a higher proportion of young adults from high-income families attend college than those from low- or middle-income families. The disparity is even greater when we examine the socioeconomic status of those who actually receive a bachelor's degree.[6] In a longitudinal study of children in eighth grade in 1988, Steven Ingels and his colleagues found that by 2000 only 7 percent of children from the lowest economic quartile had attained a bachelor's degree, while 22 percent and

51 percent of those from the middle and upper quartiles, respectively, had done so.[7] This is important because a college diploma is the gateway to employability in today's competitive, global economy. Thus, opportunities for the success promised by the career mystique are not evenly distributed, effectively barring those without financial resources from gaining the credentials and skills so critical to a sustainable career[8] and perpetuating inequality between various subgroups of the population. Underprivileged minority groups are especially vulnerable to the low pay and layoffs that characterize jobs requiring little education. Increased financial aid to needy families has helped close the gap in college attendance between children from low- and middle-income families and those from high-income families, but children from high-income families still attend college—and graduate—at much higher rates (see figure 3.1).

Men and women tend to cite different reasons for not attending—or remaining in—college right after high school. Women most commonly report the need for child care and the lack of money as their reasons for not attending.[9] Additionally, approximately 60 percent of women who have a child while in college subsequently drop out.[10] For most teenage mothers, college is a financial and logistical impossibility. This quote from a research article by Helen Farmer illustrates the quandary faced by young mothers:

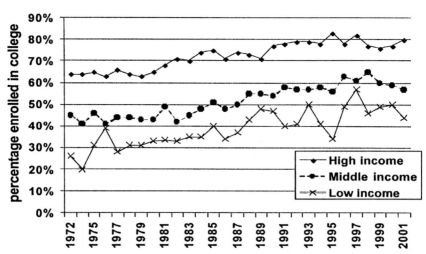

Figure 3.1.   Percentage of high school graduates ages 16 to 24 enrolled in college, by family income, 1972–2001. High income (top 20%), medium income (middle 60%), and low income (bottom 20%). (Source: National Center for Education Statistics, "The Condition of Education," 2003.)

In high school my plans were to go to college and get a career. Which those plans didn't work out. I only went to college like half a year and I dropped out. The reason was I had a child. First I had to worry about her. And then I was working while I did go to college so it was tough for me so I decided college is not for me.[11]

Men, on the other hand, are more likely to forgo college either because of a lack of interest or the belief that they can get reasonable paying jobs without a college degree.[12] Men who attend but eventually drop out of college often say they felt pushed into higher education and had not made the decision of their own accord. Michael (profiled in chapter 2) exemplifies this type of thinking:

I went to college because pretty much most everyone else was. After a month or two of going to college I realized it definitely wasn't a good enough reason to go to college. . . . I wasn't serious about my work. I wasn't keeping on track with it and getting it in on time. . . . I lost whatever desire I had to go.

A parent's attitude toward education can have a strong influence on a child's decision to pursue a college degree. Among students of color, parental encouragement and support are particularly important influences in children's educational and career decisions. In fact, research suggests that parental expectations have more of an impact on the career choices and development of African American, Mexican American, and Native American students than they do on those of European American students.[13] According to one student of color, "My parents made school a top priority. They placed a huge emphasis on education because they wanted me to have achievements for myself and my race."[14]

Similarly, Constance (see profile in chapter 2), an African American, credits her father with instilling in her the value of achievement and education. She spoke with admiration as she recalled his influence:

My drive and determination comes from him. He pushes us to succeed, to do well in everything that we do and I appreciate that. . . . I was talking to a guy who is nineteen and he works the night shift at Denny's. He said how when he was in high school he never thought about college. I was thinking how that was really never a question in my family. It was foreign to me to think that he went through high school not thinking that he was going to go to college. It was just expected that we were going to go to college and that was definitely from my dad.

Consequences of Educational Choices

Education, as the first part of the lockstep career regime, makes a difference in opening or closing occupational doors. Young men and women who go directly to jobs from high school are more likely to end up in lower-paying occupations that are traditional for their gender. Young women are more likely to work in "pink-collar" clerical or service-oriented jobs, such as food preparation or housekeeping, while young men, like Michael, are more likely to become blue-collar workers, such as laborers or machine operators. Thus, young men without a college degree tend to earn more than young women at the same educational level because they go into core-sector jobs that require expensive technology and contribute heavily to the gross national product. By contrast, the jobs typically held by young women with only a high school education (or less) are more often in the peripheral sector, in industries that operate in local and regional markets, have smaller assets, and hire fewer employees than core jobs.[15] Although core jobs tend to pay more than peripheral jobs, they are also more dependent on the vagaries of the economy, growing when the economy is good and drying up when it is bad; this makes young men without any higher education especially vulnerable to unemployment in economic downturns.

Michael, like many hardworking, ambitious young men, was initially seduced by the high salaries of core-sector jobs. Michael preferred work over school, in part because, as he said, he "had a lot of money and that was cool." However, these jobs seldom provide either opportunities for advancement or the job security common in the 1950s and 1960s.[16] Michael had operated under the assumption that if he worked hard and was loyal to his employer, then he would advance financially and professionally. But the promise of the career mystique did not materialize for him, no matter how hard he worked. Michael speaks of his disillusionment in terms of advancement opportunities at his job in the factory:

> They were always hiring [for management positions] from the outside. That was something that frustrated me. I worked with people that had worked there fifteen years and knew everything about the place and there would be this job opening for a supervisor with a salary, higher benefits and they would just hire one of the other supervisor's siblings out of the blue.

Although he was making a decent living, Michael saw that he did not have any options for moving up in his trade, and during economic down times, he was not assured of a job. So, he decided to join the army in order to have the opportunities and challenges that were missing from his workplace. When speaking about his reasons for joining the army, Michael reflects,

> Well I want to, I guess, be all that I can be. I mean that is their motto. But, that's what it comes down to. I think the way they challenge their soldiers or

their newcomers puts you in a position. You either do it or you don't. You see what you are made of. That is very appealing to me. I know I did my jobs well at the factory, working hard and everything. But I want to know if I'm capable of more than that.

In the long run, as Michael discovered, a lack of higher education constrains earning potential.[17] In 1999, men over twenty-five with only a high school education had a median income of $33,000; women with just a high school degree earned a median income of $23,000. By contrast, men and women with a four-year college degree had median incomes of $53,000 and $38,000 respectively.[18] Moreover, job prospects for those without a college degree have deteriorated over the past twenty years. Although in earlier times Michael's father, and others like him, were able to support their young families on the income paid to semiskilled laborers, there are now fewer manufacturing jobs in the United States than there were a generation ago, and the jobs that do exist no longer pay a wage high enough to support a family. The career mystique implies that employees willing to work hard on a continual basis, devoting vast amounts of their time and energy to the workplace, can achieve security and a comfortable life. However, even those in core-sector jobs can no longer count on lifelong employment, much less opportunities for advancement, as their fathers did. This leaves young employees like Michael vulnerable to an unpredictable economy and unable to support a family on their salaries alone.

Although there can be negative financial consequences associated with foregoing a college education, there seem to be few negative emotional consequences. Susan Gore and colleagues tracked the mental health of students in a Boston high school for four years, capturing information both before and after graduation.[19] They found that the students who went to work full time after graduation were initially more depressed than those who went on to college. However, three years later, those who had been working showed a substantial decrease in depression scores and became emotionally indistinguishable from those who went directly to college. The authors conclude that for some students, the transition from high school to full-time work is a healthy experience resulting in a significant improvement in their emotional well-being. This is particularly true for those unhappy in high school. Michael, for example, feels good about the psychological growth he has experienced since graduating from high school:

I am better off now because of the things I have gone through and what life has shown me. . . . Now I pretty much don't care about any of the things that I cared about in high school. I don't think anything is as important as I thought it was then, as far as being well off with money and

having the right clothes and the right friends, things like that don't matter
to me anymore.

For many young adults like Michael the transition from high school to
full-time work builds esteem, maturity, and responsibility. Unfortunately,
Susan Gore and colleagues also show that those who find themselves unemployed or underemployed (most often those with less education) three
years after graduation tend to have high scores for depression and distress.

Changes in Lifestyle Choices

Becoming an adult today is more complicated and less lockstep than it
was even thirty-five years ago. As figure 3.2 illustrates, compared to 1970,
households today are less likely to consist of married couples with children, the most common type of household in the 1970s. Rather, men and
women today are more likely to live alone and be childless than they were
in previous generations. In addition, more people are living in other
household arrangements, including living with friends and partners or as
single parents. Michael and Constance are examples of this growing
trend. Constance will be living with an unrelated family during the summer following college graduation and then plans to live alone. Michael
lives with his single father and will soon be in group quarters on a military base. Neither Constance nor Michael assumes that he or she will opt
for a "traditional" lifestyle in the future.

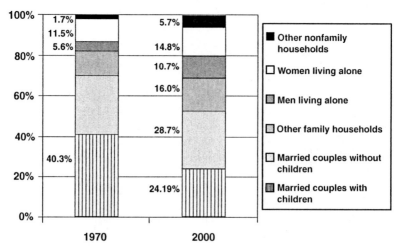

Figure 3.2.   Distribution of households by type, 1970 and 2000. (Source: Fields and
Casper, 2001.)

CHANGING MARRIAGE TRENDS AND VALUES

Marriage is inextricably bound to the career mystique, which assumes that those pursuing it have someone else, a wife, to care for their families and homes. On the other hand, precisely because of this assumption, young women may see marriage as an impediment to their own career goals. Three trends in marriage rates characterize the dramatic changes in lifestyle choices that young Americans confront today. First, there has been a significant decline in the number of people who get married. In 1970 only 9 percent of men and 6 percent of women in the United States had never married by their early thirties. In 2000, 30 percent of men and 22 percent of women in their early thirties had never married.[20] This is a remarkable change, with the proportion of unmarried men and women in their early thirties more than tripling since 1970.

In part, the decline in marriage is fueled by the rapidly rising number of men and women who cohabit outside of marriage.[21] Between 1990 and 2000 there was a 71 percent increase in the number of unmarried partners living together.[22] According to 1995 statistics, two fifths of all children have spent some time in a cohabiting family, and almost half of women between the ages of twenty-five and twenty-nine have cohabited with a partner.[23] Rob and Jennifer (see profile) are an example of a couple who have cohabited for eight years and have only vague plans to marry.

PROFILE: ROB AND JENNIFER

Rob and Jennifer have been together for eight years. They met in high school as juniors when they were both in a school play. Jennifer, who has a beautiful singing voice, had the lead role in the spring musical, "The Sound of Music." Rob worked on the stage crew. It took Rob an entire semester to work up the courage to ask Jennifer out on a date. They dated casually for the remainder of high school, occasionally seeing other people. Both Rob and Jennifer entered the workforce immediately after graduating from high school and soon began living together. For the first four years after graduation Rob worked in a series of jobs. He frequently moved from one job to another, often becoming dissatisfied with his employer or with the working conditions. During this period, Rob never worked for the same employer for more than six months. Jennifer also cycled through a series of jobs for the four years following high school. She worked as a waitress, as a clerk at a convenience store, and on an assembly line.

(continued)

Approximately three and half years after graduation, Jennifer discovered that she was pregnant. Although this was unplanned, Rob and Jennifer were thrilled when their child, Jacob, was born. Rob and Jennifer were both twenty-two years old when they had their first child. Because of their unstable work histories, they had saved little money and could not afford to buy a home or even make the down payment for a larger apartment. So, after Jacob was born, they moved in with Jennifer's mother both to save money and to get help with day care so that Jennifer could continue to work. Rob took a job with a roofer, and Jennifer, after taking several months off, got a part-time job at a restaurant. Eventually they saved enough money to buy a house, and when Jacob was two, they moved into their own home. Since Jacob's birth Rob has worked continuously for the same employer, as a roofer, which is the longest that he has ever held a single job (at the time of publication, two years after the interview, Rob was still working for this employer).

At the time of the interview, Jacob was three years old, and Rob and Jennifer, although unmarried, remained committed to each other. They originally planned to be married soon after Jacob's birth, but the date keeps getting delayed, and they still have no firm plans for marriage. They both believe that they will probably marry, but their experiences growing up (both had divorced parents) have made them pessimistic about marriage. Rob and Jennifer are part of the millennium generation that has grown up taking as given new information technologies and a global economy. But they find themselves on the wrong side of the digital divide, lacking the skills to benefit from high-tech job opportunities. Except that they are living together and have not married, Rob and Jennifer's lives and goals are more similar to than they are different from the high school educated couples of ten, twenty, or thirty years ago.

Rob and Jennifer are part of a trend among young people today. They have lived through the high divorce rate of their parents' generation. Consequently, single young men and women say divorce is one of their biggest concerns when considering marriage.[24] Couples like Rob and Jennifer view cohabiting as an opportunity to test how compatible they are and to avoid the pain and difficulty involved in a divorce.[25] In fact, 42 percent of a national sample of single adults report that they would only marry someone they had lived with first.[26] Indeed, in the early 1990s more than half (54%) of marriages followed a period of cohabitation.[27] Unfortunately for Rob and Jennifer, research shows that cohabitation does not mitigate the chances of divorce. Rather, marriages preceded by cohabitation are more likely to end in divorce than those that had not been preceded by cohabitation.[28]

The second major trend in marriage is its postponement: Those who do marry wait longer to tie the knot. In the United States in 1970 the median age at first marriage was 20.8 for women and 23.2 for men. By 2000, the age had risen to 25.1 for women and 26.8 for men.[29] This represents on average almost a four-year delay in the age of marriage over a thirty-year period. Rob and Jennifer, at ages twenty-six and twenty-seven, will be fairly representative of their generation (if they marry within the next two years).

The trends toward the rejection of and delay in marriage in the United States are evident across all ethnic groups. However, the delay and outright rejection of marriage is much higher among African Americans than it is among other groups.[30] Constance's attitude toward marriage is typical of many African American women. Demographers project that more than a fourth of African American women born in the late 1950s will never marry, while only one in ten European American women born at the same time will never marry. Consider Constance's viewpoint:

> I don't see myself getting married. . . . If something came up I would be very open to it, but I am not looking for anybody. In my head I am living in a comfortable apartment by myself and I am okay with that because I have lots of friends.

The young, unmarried population is also behaving differently than it did in past generations. In the early part of the twentieth century, most unmarried adults continued to live with their parents, often working in a family business or helping care for other family members. Unmarried women, especially, were expected to care for their aging parents. Now, in the twenty-first century single men and women tend to establish their own independent households if they can afford to do so. The number of young, single adults living on their own in the United States is remarkable, a phenomenon not witnessed at any other time in history. This trend is not peculiar to the United States; declines in marriage rates and increases in single households are occurring as well in most industrialized countries.[31]

The Independence Theory of Marriage Delay and Singleness

There are several potential reasons for these declines and delays in marriage.[32] Many theorists propose that the decreasing popularity of marriage is linked to women's increased independence and economic freedom, given that the decline in marriage rates has closely paralleled the
rapid increase in the participation of women of all ages in the workforce.[33]
Prior to the 1970s, women's economic opportunities were limited; hence,
many women looked to marriage for economic security. Now there is a
broadening acceptance of women in the workforce, be they married or
not, mothers or not (see chapter 1). Moreover, women's earning power
has slowly been gaining relative to that of men's and is getting closer to
parity in pay with men's.[34] Increasingly, women in good jobs (those paying a living wage) are able to support themselves and their families. At
the same time, men's wages have not kept pace with inflation. Thus,
women today see marriage more as a choice and less as an economic necessity. Indeed, women with higher levels of education and higher paying
jobs are less likely to marry or to marry early than other women.[35] Further,
the better the female labor market, the lower the marriage rates tend to
be.[36] Constance, for example, plans to be economically self-sufficient as a
physical therapist. In a previous generation, this would have been much
more difficult. Constance does not realize, however, that most occupations are based on the career mystique of unencumbered workers who do
not have to grapple with family or home needs while at work. The existing regime of long hours and heavy job demands throughout the childrearing years makes it difficult for single parents to realize their dual
goals of career and family.

Economic instability may be a key factor in the lower marriage rate of
African American men and women.[37] African American men are more
vulnerable to economic insecurity and earn on average less than white
men, white women, and African American women. This undermines both
African American men's attractiveness as potential spouses and their decisions about whether to marry. Many African American men and
women, like Constance, do not see marriage as conferring as many advantages as white Americans do.[38]

Marriage may enhance a man's economic potential. Longitudinal studies show that men who are married or cohabiting earn more, on average,
than those who have never married.[39] In part, this reflects the fact that
men who marry are more economically secure.[40] But marriage provides
an added advantage even when we take into account a man's premarital
income.[41] Despite societal changes, marriage for men is congruent with
the breadwinner/homemaker undercurrent in the career mystique. Married men typically work more hours than their wives, investing more

heavily in their careers, while their wives are more likely to work shorter workweeks and take on the bulk of the responsibilities at home. This arrangement provides advantages to men's careers by allowing them to live more consistently with the ideals of the career mystique, especially when their wives are either homemakers or at least not pursuing a career mystique of their own.

The Economic Security Theory of Marriage Delay and Singleness

Economic uncertainties may also contribute to marriage postponement. Many men and women, like Rob and Jennifer, do not want to marry until they are economically secure, but a globalizing economy has widened the gulf between those at the top and those at the bottom of the income hierarchy in the United States.[42] Although the expanding economy of the 1990s resulted in an increase in skilled jobs, it also meant a decline in highly paid, unskilled production jobs, many of which moved offshore as corporations sought low-wage workers in other countries. As a result, men in the United States with few skills and little education are now less able to earn a living wage and, therefore, may be delaying marriage until they are more secure and stable financially. Indeed, Sharon Sassler and Robert Shoen find that the most economically attractive men, that is, those who earn the most money, are more likely to marry in their early twenties. By contrast, those less economically stable are less likely to marry early, if they marry at all.

According to a study by Barbara Whitehead and David Popenoe, men and women still wish to be married, but the meaning of and reasons for marriage have changed over the past three decades. In the 1970s and earlier, marriage was the socially and institutionally approved context within which couples engaged in sexual relationships and became parents. Further, marriage provided economic security to women who, given the prevailing breadwinner/homemaker cultural template on which society was modeled, had relatively few viable options for supporting themselves. Today, premarital sex and parenthood outside of marriage are commonplace and accepted behaviors by most young Americans.[43] Rather than marry for religious, economic, or reproductive reasons, men and women today are looking to marriage for emotional fulfillment. And their expectations are high. In a survey of adults in their twenties, 94 percent of the men and women surveyed felt that finding a soul mate was the most important consideration when searching for a spouse.[44]

The relationship between education, economics, and marriage exemplifies the interlocking layers of the life course as well as the significance of the career mystique and its resulting regime of roles, rules, and regulations about work and occupational advancement. A college education increases the likelihood of at least a chance for income and job security, which, in turn, affects the likelihood and timing of marriage. Among women, a good income may lead to delaying marriage and possibly even to a decision to remain single. Among men, a good income promotes earlier marriage and possibly increased marriage rates. Thus, economic wherewithal buys women independence, decreasing their likelihood of marrying young; men's economic wherewithal, by contrast, increases their eligibility for marriage and attractiveness as a partner, thereby increasing men's chances of marrying early.

CHANGING ATTITUDES AND VALUES

Both young men and young women increasingly endorse women's participation in the paid workforce, with women consistently showing more egalitarian attitudes than men.[45] Data from the General Social Survey, an annual survey of a nationally representative sample of the U.S. population, illustrates this change (see figure 3.3). Between 1972 and 1991, the percentage of young men and women approving of a woman working outside the home, even if she has a husband who is capable of supporting her, increased markedly and has recently leveled off.

Attitudes toward women's roles in the home have also become increasingly egalitarian, with men and women today less likely than twenty

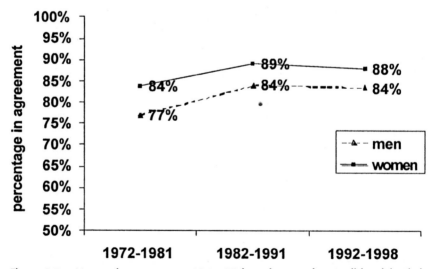

Figure 3.3.   Men and women ages 18 to 25 have become less traditional in their gender-role attitudes. (Source: Data from the General Social Survey.)

years ago to believe that women must be primarily responsible for the home.[46] Figures 3.3 and 3.4 illustrate both the decreases in traditional gender values and the fact that women consistently hold more egalitarian values than men. This is a robust finding. In Europe and across ethnic groups in the United States, women generally report more egalitarian gender-related values than men.[47]

A recent study of young, unmarried, college-student couples finds that these young men and women are actively thinking about and planning how they will eventually manage career and family. This is particularly true for couples engaged to be married and for women pursuing nontraditional career choices.[48] Many young men expect to have children but do not think it will impact their occupational careers. Rather, they expect their work life to follow the career mystique—a linear, upward, lockstep trajectory—punctuated by steadily increasing responsibilities and pay. When developing future plans during college, young men struggle with their occupational choices, viewing their occupational careers as central to who they are and where they want to be.[49]

When Robert Orrange interviewed graduate students in business and law, he found that these young men report egalitarian beliefs but that their dominant orientation is toward their own occupational careers.[50] The men in his study often expressed a desire to find a partner who would take responsibility for raising the children or take responsibility for ensuring that the children were well cared for. They tended to be open to

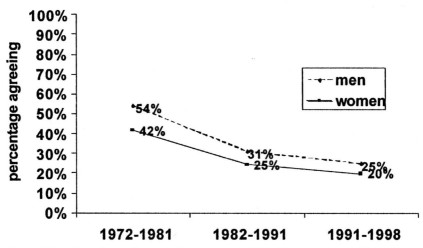

Figure 3.4.   Percentage of men and women ages 18 to 25 who agree with the statement, It is best if men achieve outside the home while women take care of the home and family. (Source: Data from the General Social Survey.)

the possibility of their wives working as long as they could also manage the home:

> I'll probably always be the so-called breadwinner. What I would like is for her to have a lot of options. That we can both agree upon, because I'll work, and I'll enjoy my job. . . . But I would like her to have the option, you know, if she wants to stay home and take care of the kids, more power to her. But, if she wants to work and get some help until they're old enough to take care of themselves, we can do that too. Whatever she wants to do I would support her, but at the same time realizing that the family would be the most important consideration.[51]

This quote reflects other research findings showing that many young men feel that it is fine for a woman to work for pay as long as it does not interfere with her duties in the home or impinge upon her husband's career.[52] When conflicts between work and family occur, men are much more likely to believe that wives should change their work schedules or else leave work to meet the needs of their families.[53]

Women, on the other hand, have more diverse, often ambivalent, orientations about managing work and family goals and obligations. Some women, a minority in Orrange's study of graduate students in business and law schools, express a neotraditional orientation, expecting their own careers to take a secondary role to those of their husbands and to their own family obligations. However, there are also many women seeking a more symmetrical way of synchronizing the work and family dimensions of their lives.[54] These women expect their future spouses to share equally in the unpaid care work related to home and family. As one law student described her feelings,

> Ideally I'd like [for us to have] shared roles. Just because I plan to be working too. And, if I wasn't working, then I could see a justification for me having to be the one taking on the family role and raising children, if any, or keeping up the house. You know, but if I'm going to be working too, then I think of it as a sort of a shared responsibility that we have.[55]

Although most women feel that housework should be shared equally between men and women, many also believe that it is their responsibility to make work adjustments, when necessary, to meet the needs of the family. This reflects the finding that female college students tend to place a greater importance on their future parental identity than do male students.[56] Even today, many young women both believe in gender equality and expect to take a hiatus from work or to reduce their hours when they have children.[57] Constance, who does not plan to get married, would still like to interrupt her career as a physical therapist temporarily when she has children:

Ideally, I'd love to take off a year or more to be at home and be a mom. That's a big job and I'd like to dedicate a full amount of time to that. But if that is not possible then at the very least, the very, very, very least, six months.

Constance also believes that becoming a mother will change her priorities and her orientation to work:

Obviously, once you have a child you have decreased flexibility as to when you can work. When you have a baby you can't just up and go to work at two in the morning if you feel like working. Or, if you have something pressing that you need to get done the next morning that is not always a reality. Having a child will be a major reorganization of priorities. Because then being a mom would come first over a job.

These are the priorities that today's young adults observed in their mothers and that remain built into the prevailing career mystique that undergirds much of American culture and its institutional arrangements and that was clearly based on the backup of a wife managing family concerns. Both Constance's and Michael's mothers took jobs that underutilized their skills and abilities in order to meet the needs of their families and to prioritize their husbands' careers.

We can see that these gender templates set the stage for future conflicts when young men and women eventually try to combine paid work and unpaid family-care work in fashions other than neotraditional, that is, with the husband still the main breadwinner and the wife still the main homemaker, even when she is also in the workforce. Within the broader culture, most Americans now believe women should work for pay. However, men and women continue to hold different expectations regarding housework and other unpaid family-care work. Most women have higher expectations than men for the sharing of household duties, and these different expectations may result in future marital conflict. Additionally, most young women and men expect that when they become parents, the wife/mother will take on the majority of the child-care responsibilities. Moreover, women tend to underestimate the difficulties that they will encounter when trying to do it all, successfully combining paid work and unpaid family-care work.[58] Constance displays this optimism as she imagines her future as a single mother:

If everything works out the way I want it to work, which won't happen of course . . . if everything will work out perfectly, then I will be putting in a lot of time, but I can handle it. Things will be a lot easier if I can find really good child care and things will be easier if I find a job with a lot of flexibility. . . . How hard is it to find good child care?

HOURS SPENT AT WORK

Work-family concerns usually focus on the overloads and strains of mothers with young children. But the career mystique also places considerable overload and strain on those in their career-building years, regardless of whether they are parents. For example, young working men and women in their twenties and thirties who do not have children tend to work far more than the standard forty-hour week. Using data from the 1997 National Study of the Changing Workforce, we find that men under the age of thirty put in an average of 44.7 hours a week on the job. Childless women under age thirty also put in close to that amount, on average 42.3 hours per week. As we see in chapter 4, this drops precipitously when women become mothers. In fact, twenty-something men and women without children are the most equal in terms of hours put in on the job, compared to those at other life stages. But even among this early-adult group, men tend to spend more hours at work than do women, a trend that will be observed across the life course. Still, single and married men and childless women in the early years of employment act as if the career mystique might turn out to be true. They work long hours and report experiencing high levels of overload and stress.[59] If hard work and long hours do pay off, these young employees are ready to reap the rewards. Most would like job security at least for all their efforts.

BEYOND LOCKSTEP LIVES

Young workers are at the beginning of their work lives; they are also part of a new generation coming of age in the twenty-first century. Almost half (45%) of young workers (18–25) have been employed in their current jobs less than two years; contrast this to only one in five (20%) of workers in their thirties and forties and less than one in ten (8%) of workers in their fifties and sixties. These differences in job duration reflect the nature of career development over the life course, but may also signal historical changes in the implicit contract between employers and employees for different generations. For example, Michael's career options as a young man differ from those his father had at the same age. Most young adults no longer truly believe in the lockstep life course of the career mystique, even though many hedge their bets by working hard and putting in long hours. From their vantage point, young people can see the traditional sequence of education, then job, then retirement unraveling. Many are thinking about ways to cope, how to customize their own biographies. For example, almost three-fourths (72%) of young workers plan to get additional education and training. Others, like Michael, look to the military for a career.

For those coming of age in the twenty-first century, marriage and parenthood are no longer markers of adulthood, but rather optional roles typically taken on later than ever. Nor are full-time employment and economic independence key indexes of having grown up given the extended period of higher education for many young people, along with periodic bouts of joblessness that cause some to return to their parents' homes for a while.[60] The twenties and even the thirties are now a period of uncertainty, ambiguity, and ambivalence, with the boundaries between youth and adulthood increasingly blurred.

4

If Real Work Is Paid Work, Can New Parents Follow the Career Mystique?

The previous chapter shows that traditional markers of adulthood now occur at a wide range of ages: Some teens have children, many in their twenties remain in school, and growing numbers delay having children to their forties or else choose not to become parents. Still, contemporary occupational career building and family building most commonly take place among Americans in their thirties. We define the *launching stage* as including all men and women with preschool-age children as well as the growing numbers of childfree men and women in their thirties who are also launching their occupational careers while creating their own single- or dual-earner households.

Parents of all ages with preschoolers, as well as thirty-something childfree men and women, face tough choices and often make compromises, either at work or at home, in order to negotiate and synchronize the multiple dimensions of their own lives and the complex interlocks linking their lives with those of coworkers, children, spouses, and parents. This is the period when adults begin to assess whether their earlier career aspirations are truly viable. Research shows that most young people do, in fact, set unrealistically high goals, and this is a stage of life where men and women adjust their expectations for their occupational futures.[1]

The launching stage, then, is the period in the life course when people confront the built-in contradictions between the career mystique and contemporary reality. It is a pragmatic time; earlier aspirations and expectations give way to real-world constraints—a world of work with little job security, one that pays lip service to gender equality and family friendliness but still operates on a foundation of imaginary gender divides. Boys and girls in grade school, like young men and women in high school and college, tend to be more similar than different—wearing the same kinds of jeans, eating the same foods, taking many of the same classes. But marriage and, especially, parenthood change all that. Not surprisingly, given the still prevailing (male) breadwinner/(female) homemaker career mystique, men and women moving through their thirties, especially those who become parents, have very different experiences. Although race, ethnicity, and socioeconomic status also shape the developing life course, people from all circumstances face similar challenges managing families and demanding jobs in a world designed for a career regime based on but one "real" career per two-parent family. Americans across class and ethnic divides experience similar difficulties in fashioning meaningful lives, given that the years of career building (as mandated by the lockstep regime) are also the years of family building (with social as well as biological mandates). What makes this quandary especially real for new parents are egalitarian norms suggesting that any avenues or ladders of opportunity should be available to both men and women and that both mothers and fathers should be equally involved in caring for their children. One possibility for achieving this equality would be to have someone else care for the children and the home. But few working parents have—or can afford to hire—a full-time homemaker at a period in the life course when both job demands and family demands are especially high and earnings are especially low. And many would not want to outsource their family life even if they could afford to do so. New mothers—married or single—who have bought into the promise of the career mystique find themselves falling short of their own career and maternal expectations and goals for work, for motherhood, and for life. New fathers who really believe they are different from their own dads suddenly find themselves falling back into the breadwinning role, putting in long hours to be good providers, especially given the uncertainties surrounding most jobs.

In this chapter, we examine how men and women navigate this period of life, trying to launch occupational careers in a world of mergers, downsizing, and layoffs, while often starting to raise children. The answers we find, for many, are to reduce either the "family" or the "work" sides of the work–family equation, or both. We aim to capture the complex interplay between family, employment, and gender in a twenty-first-century economy and workforce still saddled with a twentieth-century career myth. We begin by looking at the family side of life, documenting trends in fertility.

HAVING CHILDREN OR NOT? AND WHEN?

Decisions about whether and when to have children and how to manage it are interwoven with the career mystique and, moreover, can set the future trajectory of people's life courses. Over the last thirty years, most industrialized countries have experienced three major changes in childbearing patterns: (1) an increase in women bearing children out of wedlock, (2) a delay in the timing of the birth of the first child, and (3) an increase in the number of men and women who choose to remain childless. Each of these trends is affected by the career mystique and, in turn, affects the way gender divisions continue to be constructed for each new generation.

Increase in Childbearing among Unmarried Women

Although birth rates among unmarried American women jumped dramatically during the 1970s and 1980s, recent data indicate that they may have leveled off, or at least slowed, since the mid-1990s (see figure 4.1). In the 1940s, fewer than one in twenty births were to unmarried mothers; this number rose to one in six in 1960, and has leveled off now at around one in three.[2] Among low-income households, this trend may even be reversing. Between 1995 and 2000 the proportion of children living with low-income single mothers declined by almost 4 percent.[3]

Still, one in every three children born in the United States now has an unmarried mother, a remarkable statistic. Several factors contribute to the increased rate and acceptance of premarital childbirth, including the postponement and rejection of marriage (see chapter 3) and the increased cultural acceptance of bearing children outside of marriage. With fewer women marrying during their prime childbearing years and with the decreasing stigma attached to single parenthood, some deliberately choose

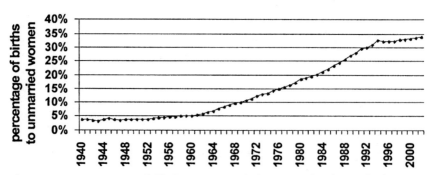

Figure 4.1. Percentage of births to unmarried women in the United States, 1940–2002. (Sources: Ventura and Bachrach 2000; Martin et al. 2002.)

to have a child out of wedlock. Figure 4.2 uses data from the U.S. Census Bureau to document the percentage of first births among unmarried women by race and ethnicity. Note that although different subgroups have different birth rates among unmarried women, all ethnic groups in the United States have seen an increase in these rates. Recall (from chapter 3) that African American women are less likely to marry than are women in other ethnic groups; it is not surprising, therefore, that African American women experience the highest out-of-wedlock birth rate. Many African American women, like Constance (see profile in chapter 2), want to have children and do not see their marital choices or chances as an obstacle to that desire. Constance says,

> I have confidence in myself and my ability to be a mother and a "father." It is something that I have known for awhile. The same way that I know that I don't want to get married, I've also known that I want to have a child.

Contrary to popular myth, most births occurring outside of marriage, like Rob and Jennifer's (see profile in chapter 3), are not the result of teenage pregnancy (although 86 percent of births to teenage mothers do occur out of wedlock).[4] Births outside of marriage are actually most likely to occur among women in their twenties, and almost half of unwed mothers were cohabiting with the fathers of their babies when they gave birth. In fact, the proportion of nonmarital births that occur among teens has actually declined over the past thirty years, from 50 percent in 1970 to 34 percent in 2002.[5] The above statistics represent a remarkable shift in the

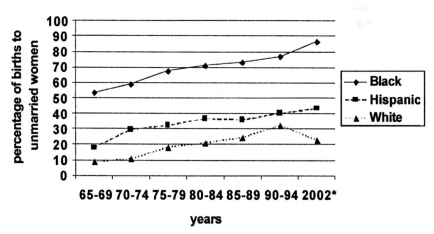

Figure 4.2. Percentage of first births to unmarried women ages 15 to 29, by race, 1930–1934 to 1990–1994, and of all births for women at all ages, 2002. (Sources: U.S. Census Bureau, *Current Population Reports*; Bachu 1999; *National Vital Statistics Report*,* Hamilton, Martin, and Sutton 2003 [for 2002 data].)

timing of births out of wedlock, reflecting the conscious decision that many individuals and couples make to have children before or without marriage.

Another remarkable demographic change is the growing number of single-father households, suggesting a trend toward increased parental responsibility among men. The 2000 census reveals that households headed by single fathers increased by almost 62 percent between 1990 and 2000, which was greater than the 25 percent increase in single-mother-headed households during the same period.[6] Despite this increase, most single-parent households are headed by women. In 2002, approximately 23 percent of all households with children were headed by women; only about 5 percent were headed by men.[7]

Single parents have a unique set of needs and challenges precisely because of the career mystique. The regime of paid work and career paths is not designed for people with family-care responsibilities. Schools, workplaces, medical clinics—all sorts of social arrangements—presume that at least one parent is available at varied hours to transport and care for children, a remnant of the days of the feminine mystique. Even workplaces have neglected the needs of single parents when designing their "family-friendly" workplace policies.[8] Single parents report feeling squeezed for time in all domains: work, family, and personal.[9] To examine the experiences of single mothers, sociologists Rosanna Hertz and Faith Ferguson interviewed a sample of women who intentionally embarked on single motherhood.[10] The researchers found that one strategy that single mothers use to cope with the mismatch between conventional organizational arrangements and the needs of their families is to develop an extensive network of family members and fictive kin (close friends who are "like family") to help them manage the care of their children.

Many of the mothers that Hertz and Ferguson studied planned for and structured their finances in order to be prepared for their new families. But, as the following quote illustrates, unexpected expenses, such as medical problems, can be devastating for single parents who have no one else to fall back on, either financially or physically:

> The last six weeks of my pregnancy I had toxemia and I was supposed to have complete bed rest, but I couldn't do it. I couldn't afford to do it. If I did that, the money I'd saved for my maternity leave would have been used up and then I wouldn't have had a maternity leave. Plus, my boss would have fired me.[11]

Single parents risk being both time poor and income poor. Approximately six out of ten children in single-parent homes are at or near the poverty line.[12] Children of never-married mothers are especially vulnerable to poverty, more so than children of divorced mothers.[13] Because men earn higher wages than women, children living with their fathers tend to be better off financially than children living with their mothers.[14]

As a result of 1996 legislation reforming welfare, single parents are now expected to pursue the American Dream embodied in the career mystique, pulling themselves out of poverty through hard work, not government assistance. Unfortunately, unwed parents are twice as likely to have dropped out of high school and less than half as likely to have attended college as their married counterparts. Thus, their earning power is seriously restricted.[15] Several barriers, aside from a lack of education, make it difficult for former welfare recipients to find a job or to work themselves out of poverty.[16] Even when they are able to find work, most of these women are employed in low-paying jobs, with wages near or below the poverty line. Thus, they are unable to afford consistent, quality day care; nor are they likely to have reliable transportation. Both of these are essential for maintaining a job, much less advancing to higher pay. Moreover, single parents with few employment skills frequently have jobs lacking the flexibility and benefits (such as sick leave and paid vacation time) needed to mesh their obligations at work and at home.[17] Finally, many poor single mothers have medical problems that make it difficult for them to find work.[18] Chapter 7 discusses more fully the Welfare Reform Act and its aftermath. For the present, note that the uphill battles faced by the growing number of adults and children in single-parent-headed homes only underscore the outdatedness of the career regime, the policies and practices predicated upon the myth of success for all those willing to invest the preponderance of their time and energy in their jobs.

Delays in Childbirth

One way Americans adjust to the "greedy" demands of the career regime is by reducing family demands—postponing parenthood, having fewer children, or having none at all. Thus, in tandem with women's increased labor-force participation, we have witnessed another trend, a delay in childbearing. The peak age for childbearing among women has shifted from the early twenties to the late twenties and the early thirties. By 2001 the median mother's age at first birth in the United States was 24.8, up from 22.1 in 1970.[19] (Postponement is occurring in other countries as well. For example, in Canada in 1971 only 7 percent of first births were to mothers over the age of thirty. By 1997 that number had grown to 31 percent.[20]) The delay in childbearing is more prevalent among whites than among other American ethnic groups.[21] This postponement by some but not others produces wide variability in yet another marker of adulthood, the transition to parenthood. America has moved from a lockstep of almost universal marriage and parenthood before age thirty (characteristic of the

1950s and 1960s) to a panoply of life-course paths. Women become mothers from adolescence through their early forties.[22] Men become fathers from early adolescence through their eighties (especially as men tend to marry much younger women in their second, third, or fourth marriages). Scholars cite both higher levels of education and reliable birth control as major reasons why women are delaying childbirth.[23] Women in the United States (and other industrialized countries) who have attained a higher level of education often wait longer to have their first child.[24] This makes sense for two reasons. First, women pursuing an advanced degree typically wait to have children until they have completed their schooling. Second, women more highly invested in their education are more likely to want to establish themselves in their occupational careers before becoming pregnant.[25] Constance explains why she wants to wait before having children:

> My mother got married at twenty-six and immediately started a family. I think she kind of regrets that because she got her masters degree while she was pregnant with my sister. She never did anything with her degree because she had a baby again right away and she had two other small children. She was kind of limited in what she could do. . . . Right now she works part time in a grocery store. I think she regrets that a lot. . . . The timing was not good for her. She got a degree and never used it.

Parents, particularly mothers, also have a strong influence on daughters' timing of childbearing. Jennifer Barber, using a sample of 835 mother–child pairs, found that mothers' preferences (for their children) are an even stronger indicator of the timing of first birth than the adult child's own preferences.[26] This was true for both men and women. We can see how her mother's attitudes are related to Constance's plans for a family (Constance would prefer to have her first child around age thirty-five):

> I'd love to stop doing everything and have a baby right now. I don't want to regret that decision later the way that my mom has. I am working really hard for this degree, I don't want to never use it.

A key theme of this book is that the outdated regime of policies and practices based on the career mystique still permeates every aspect of the life course including choices about parenthood. As career paths are currently organized, parenthood, especially motherhood, has long-term career repercussions, especially for women. Young women like Constance are increasingly aware of both the immediate stresses and long-term costs of trying to combine paid work with the care work of parenthood, care work that continues to be disproportionately borne by mothers. Unlike motherhood, fatherhood is closely linked to being the family breadwinner and thus is not at odds with the regime of roles, rules, and regulations formulated for the career mystique. In our college classrooms, young women commonly ask us when is the "right" time to have children so as not to jeopardize their careers (rarely do the men in our classes pose this question to us). Given the ways career paths come prepackaged, we both say that there is no single, right answer to that question. The solution, we believe, is more complicated but also more radical; it involves designing a new range of career paths with no long-term costs tied to one path versus another and easy (re)entries and exits along the way. Right now, employees are often able to scale back by temporarily leaving the workforce or else taking a part-time job, but they are seldom able to go on to "good" jobs further down the road. We discuss this and other possibilities in chapter 8.

Declining Fertility, Increasing Childlessness

For almost twenty years, American women have tended to give birth to two children, on average, during their lifetimes.[27] However, recent census data indicate that this birth rate is on the decline. Compared to the early 1900s, women clearly are having fewer children. One reason for the declining birth rate is that many dual-earner couples limit their family size because of the difficulty of combining work and family, given the way career paths come prepackaged.[28] A thirty-nine-year-old mother of two discusses her decision not to have a third child:

> Thinking about having a third child. It was something we decided against. . . . If I didn't have a career, I think I would have had another baby. . . . But to be the kind of parent I wanted to be, and that I was, and wanting to work and needing to work, I just couldn't do justice. . . . It was me deciding that I didn't have enough left over, I didn't have the time to be with my kids if I was going to have more.

An even more startling statistic, however, is the dramatic increase over the last twenty-five years in the proportion of women remaining childless (see figure 4.3). In 1976, only 10 percent of women in the United States between the ages of forty and forty-four had not had children. By 2002, that number had almost doubled; today 18 percent of women in their early forties are childless.[29] Most of this increase in childlessness is among women who are (or were) married. From 1970 to 2002, the number of ever-married women between the ages of forty and forty-four who were childless nearly doubled (from 8% to 12%) while the number of never-married women who were childless declined (from 89% to 63%).[30] This declining birth rate is not only an American phenomenon; the same drop

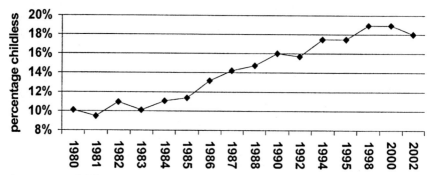

Figure 4.3. Childlessness per 1,000 U.S. women ages 40 to 44, 1976–2002. (Source: U.S. Bureau of the Census, 2002a.)

in fertility and rise in childlessness is occurring across most Western European countries, with the birth rate often below replacement levels.[31] (Italy, for example, has the lowest fertility rate in the world.)

The increase in childlessness has occurred in tandem with the increase in women's employment. Scholars suggest these two trends are related through two mechanisms.[32] First, as more women enter the workforce and as barriers to women's employment are removed, more career-oriented women may choose to pursue an occupational career in lieu of motherhood. Indeed, Susan Bram finds that many women who plan to remain childless do so because they feel children will have a negative impact on their achievement, lifestyle, and marriage.[33] Theresa, a thirty-five-year-old, echoes this sentiment:

> I was fairly sure I didn't want kids early on. There were a lot of reasons. I was afraid it would hold me back from attaining the goals I was pursuing in my career. I wanted to be able to move around, relocate if necessary, and it wouldn't be good for kids. In a lot of ways, it seemed like it wouldn't be fair to them.[34]

A journalist echoes this feeling:

> I love my life and feel completely fulfilled. My husband is a litigator and I, a journalist. We both work incredibly long hours (60- to 80-hour weeks). We are steeped, emotionally as well as horologically, in what we do. We feel we are making important contributions through our work . . . as well as keeping bill collectors at bay.
>
> We play as hard as we work. We love to travel and spend at least one month overseas each year. . . . Could I have children and do everything that I do now? Absolutely not. First, it would be a financial impossibility. I could not pay two mortgages, monthly stall board [for her horse] and international travel bills if I were buying extra food, clothes and day care while trying to save simultaneously for college. Second, each of my commitments would

suffer. I could not work as hard, spend as much time with the child, or have enough time for myself as necessary.[35]

Childlessness is also related to education.[36] The more education a woman has, the less likely she is to have children. Renbao Chen and Philip Morgan believe that many professional women do not make a conscious early decision to remain childless; rather, a series of decisions to postpone childbirth lead to the eventual conclusion.[37] Diane, age thirty-five, explains how this occurs:

> You can keep postponing it up until a certain point, and a lot of my friends talk about a biological clock, presumably after thirty-five something magical happens. . . . It's more difficult to have a child. . . . It's a higher risk for the mother. It's a higher risk for the child. The cutoff for me would be sometime in my forties. I think as you get older your career makes it more difficult to have a child. I know five years ago when I was in a comparatively low place in the organization, it would have been a much easier time for me than now, because I have greater responsibilities. There's much more demand where my time's concerned, much more stress . . . and I travel approximately once a month.[38]

Diane finds herself at a point in her career where it may well be difficult to have children. She is approaching the end of her childbearing years and is faced with a dilemma that confronts many women who choose to delay childbirth. Because of the career mystique and the whole edifice that has been built up around it—a regime of expectations and timetables, of many exit portals, but no reentry ones—Diane can see no options for having both a meaningful, successful career and a family life.

A second explanation for the growing incidence of childlessness is easy contraception. Economists Claudia Goldin and Lawrence Katz propose that the availability of the contraceptive pill to young single women has transformed women's role in society.[39] They suggest that the pill has had a domino effect, allowing women in the 1960s (and since) to delay motherhood, thereby clearing the way for their subsequent greater investment in education and paid work. That investment then leads to a decline in fertility, given the cost of earnings forgone if women do not pursue the elusive career mystique. This process is being duplicated on a global stage. With the broader dissemination of reliable birth control, even women in developing countries are beginning to participate more in paid work and having fewer children.[40]

In terms of life satisfaction, there seem to be few differences between those with children and those who remain childfree. Some studies have found higher life satisfaction among childless couples; however, this

difference tends to disappear when researchers take into account the income and age differences of those who have children and those who do
not.[41] There is, however, consistent evidence that childless couples have
higher marital satisfaction than couples with children.[42] According to
Ione DeOllos and Carolyn Kapinus, childless couples place marriage at
the center of the relationship, whereas couples with children often
place the children at the center of the relationship. As a result, marital
satisfaction can suffer.[43] There is some evidence that in their later years
and during major life transitions, childless women question their decisions about remaining childfree.[44] However, this is an area that has
been little researched.

PARENTHOOD

The transition to parenthood is one of the most, if not the most, conse-
quential life-course transitions, upending men's and women's lives in
often unexpected ways. Rosalind King estimates that, on average,
Americans spend 65 percent of their adult lives as parents to at least
one child under the age of eighteen.[45] At certain ages, parenthood is
clearly the norm; in 2000, 81 percent of adults between the ages of
thirty-five and forty-four had children (see figure 4.4). At all ages,
African Americans are more likely to be parents than are European
Americans; they also tend to have more children and to begin having
them earlier.

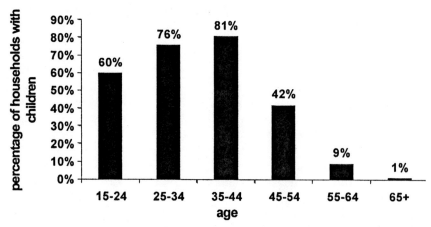

Figure 4.4.   Percentage of U.S. households with children under 18 by age of house-
holder, 2000. (Source: U.S. Census Bureau, 2002, *Statistical Abstract of the United
States*, p. 53.)

The Impacts of Parenthood on Occupational Careers

Parenthood is a taken-for-granted aspect of the career mystique: Family breadwinners are seen as hardworking, conscientious, ambitious employees. The problem is, the career mystique was developed in tandem with the feminine mystique: Someone else would be tending—and attending to—the children. So, while both motherhood and fatherhood have profound impacts on career development, the magnitude and the nature of these impacts vary significantly by gender. Throughout most of the twentieth century the cultural norm was for working women making the transition to motherhood to leave the workforce if they could afford to do so.[46] This has also been characteristic of women's life course in Eastern and Western Europe, Japan, and Latin America, where the presence of small children in the home is a deterrent to women's workforce participation.[47] However, over the last thirty years, as attitudes about women's roles have become less traditional, government policies have protected the rights of working mothers and mothers-to-be.[48] And, as their incomes have become more essential to the family economy, women have become less likely to drop out of the workforce once they give birth (see figure 4.5). Even in the midst of the Women's Movement in the 1970s, only three in ten women with infants (children under the age of one) were in the workforce. Today, nearly two-thirds of mothers of infants are in the workforce, a major cultural shift. The contemporary cultural norm is to return to paid work after a brief period of leave (paid or unpaid). Still, a sizeable number of women in the United States, approximately 25 percent, do leave the workforce for a protracted period of time

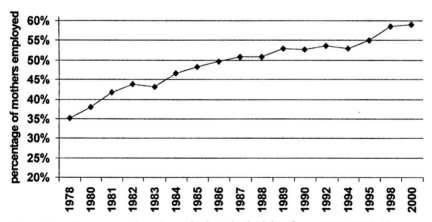

Figure 4.5. Percentage of mothers of infants in the labor force, 1976–2000. (Sources: Current Population Surveys, June 1976 to 1995; U.S. Census Bureau, June Current Population Survey, 1998; U.S. Census Bureau, 2003b.)

when they have children.[49] Numerous studies have documented the costs of motherhood in terms of wages, pensions, and advancement. Women in the second half of the twentieth century fought for equality at school and at work with remarkable success. But following the career mystique requires an occupational focus with no distractions. And life is about distractions, sometimes very positive ones. The path of the career mystique does not fit the plans of many contemporary parents.

Women, like men, feel they have to fit into existing arrangements, the ways work hours and career paths are prepackaged. To do so, some have fewer children, later in life, or no children. Others give up on the career mystique, taking up a series of part-time or flexible jobs with little coherent connection between them and no future prospects. Still others leave the workforce for a time altogether. Still, women today have more options than ever in the past.

There has been little broadening in men's options. Cultural norms about men's life paths remain relatively intransigent, and few men have become full-time caregivers. In 2002, among married couples, only 4 percent of fathers in families with preschoolers were out of the workforce while their wives "brought home the bacon," compared to almost two out of five (39%) families of preschoolers where fathers provided for their families, while mothers focused full time on family-care work.[50]

Brad is one of the rare 4 percent. He has traded in the traditional breadwinner role for that of unpaid caretaker. In most respects, Brad and his wife, Joan, an accountant, are like all the other thirty-something couples that populate their middle-class suburban neighborhood. But the couple decided it would be best if Brad stayed home with their son (now four years old) while Joan remained in the workforce. Brad, who has a degree in philosophy, did not have a clear career path when their son was born. Although they are both very happy with their decision, Brad constantly feels the stigma associated with bucking tradition:

> It's a big problem when we go into a social situation and there are men around and they say, "What do you do?" There is still a big stigma about that [a man being a full-time homemaker]. They'll have a funny, uncomfortable reaction and usually someone in the group will say, "Oh that's admirable for you to stay home and let your wife work," but there are a few of them you can just see are saying, "You're letting your wife work and you're staying at home!" But they don't say it to your face usually. I have run into some older gentlemen who would say, "You are letting your wife do that, well that is just ridiculous!" . . . I never see it from the women, just from the men generally.

Although women are usually supportive of Brad's choice to stay home with his son, he still feels like an outsider among the few parents in the neighborhood who also stay home with their children (all of whom are women). Regarding his relationships with other full-time homemakers, Brad says,

> I feel most comfortable in the conversations with women talking about rais- ing their kids. But there still is a little standoffishness, a man–woman gender separation. I'm not really sure how to explain it. They aren't really comfort- able allowing a man into their little group. I don't see myself being able to fit into a woman's group.

As Brad has found, even in this society paying lip service to gender equality, there is still a great deal of intolerance for men who break with the male tradition of following the career mystique.

Influences on Women's Employment Decisions Following Childbirth

What has driven the trend for mothers to remain in the workforce? Soci- ologists, as well as economists, propose three theories to explain this phe- nomenon. The first explanation draws on the human-capital theory,[51] based on the idea that women who have invested a great deal in the de- velopment of their careers (obtaining a high level of human capital, that is, education, skills, and experience) will want to protect that investment by remaining in the workforce. Consider how the Women's Movement, the shift to a service economy, and the declining growth in men's wages all fostered a dramatic rise in women's educational and employment op- portunities and incentives over the second half of the twentieth century. Women flowed into colleges and professional schools, developing strong occupational aspirations and attachments. Women who have made such investments of time and energy are aware that any gap in the lockstep regime of continuous, full-time employment can decrease future earnings and attainments and render skills out of date.[52]

There is evidence to support the hypothesis that women with higher human capital are in fact less willing to leave the workforce for an ex- tended period following childbirth. Educational level, a key ingredient of human capital, is positively related to the employment of mothers across the board. Women in the United States, Europe, and Latin America with higher levels of education return more quickly to the workforce following the birth of their children than those with lower levels of education, par- ticularly those without a high school education.[53] Wage rates, one out- come of human capital, are also related to maternal employment. Women with the greatest prebirth incomes tend to return to their jobs more quickly than those with lower prebirth incomes.[54] Finally, older women, who presumably have accumulated higher levels of human capital be- cause of their greater investment in work experiences, are more likely to return to the workforce following childbirth than younger women.[55]

PROFILE: RICK AND DONNA

Rick, age forty-six, and Donna, age thirty-nine, are both professionals with high-powered careers and are examples of people following the career mystique. Rick and Donna both grew up in the outskirts of New York City. Donna's father was an executive and instilled in each of his children the belief that they would work hard and achieve successful careers. Rick's father was also a professional, and Rick always envisioned himself becoming a successful businessman. Both Donna and Rick earned master's degrees in business. Rick moved around for the first several years of his professional life, but for the five years prior to the interview, he has worked in the telecommunications industry. Donna, on the other hand, is a high-level executive at a multinational corporation where she has been continuously employed for fifteen years.

Rick and Donna met at a professional conference when they were in their thirties. Career was a top priority for each, and neither had been married, although each had active social and dating lives. When they met, they quickly fell in love and began adjusting their priorities so that they could spend time together. This was particularly difficult for Donna, who worked extremely long hours and spent a great deal of time traveling for her employer. However, both Rick and Donna were ready to settle down into a serious relationship. Rick and Donna lived together for four years before they got married. Two years after their marriage they had their first child, Madison, who was ten months old at the time of the interview.

Donna's job is very demanding, and she has continued to work at the breakneck pace she maintained before Madison was born. However, since Madison's birth, Donna has become very conflicted about her work. Her job requires her to travel, which means being away from Madison for several days, even weeks, at a time. When she isn't on the road, she only sees Madison for a few hours a day. Rick, whose career is less demanding, spends more time with Madison. Nonetheless, Madison is in day care for ten hours each weekday. Both Rick and Donna are frustrated and unhappy with their current lifestyle. Although it would mean a significant drop in their income, Donna is seriously contemplating leaving her job to spend time at home with Madison.

Donna (see profile) has a high degree of human capital. She has invested a great deal of time, energy, education, and experience in the pursuit of the career mystique and earns a six-figure salary. With the birth of her daughter, however, Donna realizes that her pursuit of the career mystique is incompatible with the type of family life she would like to have. Donna recognizes that if she scales back at work she is at risk of relinquishing her rung on the career ladder:

> I'm not sure what that does for me [reducing her hours] in the long run, does that put me back a couple of steps? You can say, "I can deal with that, what does it matter if I go back a couple of steps?" And that's true. However, there is something to be said about stepping back after spending all this time to get where you're at.

A second explanation for the increased number of women and mothers in the workforce is financial need.[56] In the last thirty years we have witnessed a substantial decline in the real wages of many unskilled workers, and the income gap between the high-income and low- and middle-income families has increased.[57] In general, wages have not kept up with inflation or with rising demands for consumer goods. Contemporary workers holding full-time jobs are more likely to fall below the poverty line than workers holding full-time jobs in the 1970s. This drop in earning power, in tandem with a rising standard of living, means that one person's income is frequently insufficient to support a family adequately or to meet family lifestyle goals. The decline in men's relative earnings, especially for those with marginal educational and employment experience, constrains women's options to become full-time homemakers.

Indeed, economic necessity does appear to play a role in new mothers' decisions to work. According to the 2000 census figures, women who are divorced, separated, or widowed, and therefore have limited financial support, are the most likely to be in the workforce following the birth of their children.[58] Among married women, those whose husbands have lower incomes are more likely to return to work following childbirth.[59] Before their first child is born, women generally do not take finances into consideration when thinking about their future lives. However, after the baby arrives, finances play a role in their ultimate decisions. Consider the case of Jennifer (see profile in chapter 3). She initially did not want to return to work when her son, Jacob, was born, but both she and Rob felt it was necessary in order to save money for a home.

A third reason for the increase in the number of working mothers has to do with shifting values.[60] Surveys of employed expectant mothers show that their intentions to return to work are strongly influenced by their gender values.[61] Expectant mothers with more egalitarian values about men's and women's roles are more likely to plan to remain in the workforce and to return to the workforce earlier than are those with more conventional values. The shift in maternal employment, in part, reflects this shift in societal values. The difficulty, as we see with Donna, occurs when women (and men) want it all—to spend time with their newborns and to succeed in their careers. The lockstep career regime makes it almost impossible for dual-earner couples and single parents to juggle all the balls tossed into the air during the career- and family-building years.

The Impact of Parenthood on Work Hours

Becoming a parent not only changes the amount of time people spend in leisure and family care, it also has a profound effect on the number of hours they work for pay. For men, the transition to parenthood typically means more, rather than less, involvement in paid work. In line with the breadwinner aspects of the career mystique, men are more likely to become stable members of the workforce after the birth of their first child, often increasing their work hours, particularly if their wives reduce their hours or leave the workforce.[62] For example, prior to the birth of their son, Rob (see profile in chapter 3) was constantly moving in and out of the workforce, rarely working more than six months at one job and working variable hours. After Jacob's birth, Rob's orientation toward work changed and he has since remained continuously employed with the same employer for more than three years. Rob explains his changed outlook:

> I've just gotten a lot more serious about my work and I realize that everything is going to be more expensive now, so I don't have the luxury of taking time off, I need to be working consistently all the time.

There are some exceptions to the above finding. First, men whose wives continue to work following childbirth are not under as much pressure to earn money and, in fact, have been shown to put in slightly fewer hours in paid work following childbirth.[63]

Second, older fathers are less likely than young fathers to increase their work hours following parenthood.[64] Men and women who have children later in life are typically better established in their occupational careers, already owning the homes, furniture, cars, and other goods that younger couples also want but are only beginning to acquire. Younger fathers generally have not established themselves financially and occupationally and may feel more pressure to provide for their new families and therefore work longer hours. The values of older and younger fathers may also differ, resulting in different approaches to employment following childbirth. Men who have children relatively early in their adult life course may take fatherhood as a given. But couples moving into parenthood later in life may have postponed starting a family or considered remaining childless; thus, the new child reflects a conscious lifestyle choice to embrace parenthood.

We see the above processes at work with Rick and Donna, older, professional, first-time parents. Donna's job is higher paying, more time intensive, and requires more travel than Rick's. Since the birth of their daughter, Madison, Donna has remained continuously employed and has not reduced the number of hours that she puts in. Rick, on the other hand, responded to Madison's entry into their lives by decreasing the amount of time he devotes to work. Because Donna has remained continuously employed in a high-paying job, Rick does not feel the same pressure to provide for the family that Rob has felt. Rick explains the changes he has made to his schedule following fatherhood:

> She [Madison] is the highest priority, so there are a lot of conflicts and Madison wins almost every one of them. I go into work later than I had ever gone to work. . . . I get there by nine, ten o'clock [the nanny arrives at 8:00 A.M.]. I leave work earlier than I ever used to.

Rick recognizes that this orientation would change if Donna were to leave her job as she has been contemplating. If this does happen Rick expects to increase his own job commitment, at least in terms of the hours he devotes to it:

> [If Donna leaves work] I'll be able to go to work earlier and I could spend more time . . . she could take on all the activities that take me away from working, so I would be able to rewrite my goals. I don't know if I would be more invested in work mentally, but I would spend more time.

Workplace and community policies and practices developed around the career mystique with its breadwinner/homemaker template, with no provision for workers with heavy child-care responsibilities. Consequently, most couples adapt to parenthood by adopting a strategy of having someone, typically the wife, scale back.[65] Jennifer scaled back her work hours when she returned to work. Rick has scaled his back, but will increase his hours if Donna works less. Although it has become the norm for women with young children to work for pay, it is not the norm for them to work full time. In fact, the number of hours worked by new mothers declines by almost half (45%) following childbirth (see figure 4.6).[66] Phyllis Moen and Steve Sweet refer to this scaling-back strategy of working mothers as a *neotraditional* arrangement: Both parents may be employed, but husbands put in long hours on the job while wives put in long hours on care work, still remaining in the workforce, but with reduced

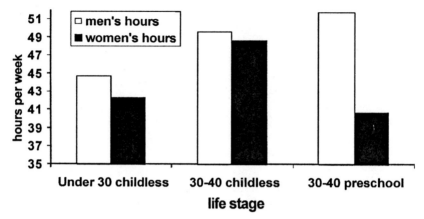

Figure 4.6. Total number of hours worked by married U.S. employees at selected life stages. (Source: Data from the 1997 National Study of the Changing Workforce, *n* = 3,035.)

hours. This is the modern version of the traditional breadwinner/homemaker division of labor, a strategic response to the dearth of options for new mothers and fathers.[67]

Shelley MacDermid, Mary Lee, and their colleagues have examined the experiences of professional women who have reduced their work hours in order to better manage their work and family lives.[68] For the most part, these women felt that the cutting-back strategy was successful. The majority of the women felt that their work continued to be interesting and challenging and that their career advancement was either not stalled or only temporarily affected. On the whole, most women felt that the benefits of the arrangement outweighed the financial and career-mobility costs. The minority of women who were unhappy with the cutting-back strategy typically lamented that they felt resentment from their supervisors and coworkers and that their careers had been seriously stalled. MacDermid and Lee caution that the reduced-load strategy is likely to be successful only if employees receive support from their supervisors and if the workplace culture is accepting of alternative career paths and work arrangements.

Note that the impacts of parenthood are not as dramatic for men's paid work as they are for women's. Although many new mothers drastically reduce the number of hours that they work (or even leave the workforce for a time), most men's occupational career paths remain pretty much the same, with the exception that some may devote more hours to their jobs. But this is due to couples' decisions to prioritize husbands' careers, a realistic choice when men's wages and prospects are typically better than their wives'. But this also reflects the taken-for-granted gender divide in family-care work as well as paid work.

Parenthood affects not only work hours, but also punctuality and absenteeism. Linda Boise and Margaret Neal report that women with children have higher rates of absenteeism and tardiness.[69] This reflects the neotraditional attitude that when there are conflicts or problems at home (such as sick children or child-care emergencies), it is generally the mother who must cope by altering her work schedule or by finding alternative strategies for managing the problem. These behaviors reinforce cultural stereotypes about working mothers and may have long-term negative impacts on performance evaluations and promotions. They also enable men, but not women, to pursue the career mystique best.

The Impact of Parenthood on Income

The transition to parenthood also impacts the family economy and the earning abilities of each parent. Women who leave the workforce for a year or more following childbirth show a significant decline in income when they do return to work.[70] Among women who remain continuously employed, there is no immediate decrease in their income associated with childbirth. Still, as we will see in later chapters, in the long run, women with children earn significantly less than women without children. This is especially the case for women who have children in their early twenties, before they have time to establish themselves in their careers.[71]

The relationship between fatherhood and income is a different story. In contrast to women, the birth of the first child is associated with an increase in men's earnings.[72] This is true for husbands regardless of whether their wives remain in or leave the workforce. Surprisingly, before having children, fathers-to-be typically earn less than nonfathers. However, by the time that the first child is born, this trend is reversed and, on average, fathers earn more than nonfathers. Again surprisingly, the wage increase tends to be greater when the child is a boy rather than a girl.[73] Part of this wage increase is certainly due to the longer hours some new fathers (especially those married to women who work only intermittently following childbirth) put in on the job. However, new fathers whose wives remain continuously employed (but often working fewer hours following the birth of their child) also tend to experience an increase in wages. This may reflect something deeper than simply their (typically) greater time on the job, possibly their new and deeper commitment to the breadwinner role. New fathers, taking their provider role more seriously, may gravitate toward higher-paying and more secure jobs in their efforts to pursue the career mystique. When Rob (see profile in chapter 3) became a father he moved out of the restaurant industry to begin a career in roofing. Although Rob enjoyed the lifestyle involved with the restaurant industry, the money and culture associated with construction work were more conducive to providing for a family:

> When Jacob was born I wanted to get out of cooking because there's not enough money in it, and you work late at night. It's just not a very conducive job to have if you're a family man. . . . I know people do cook for a living and have families, but there's generally a lot of partiers in that business and I wanted to remove myself from that atmosphere a bit, and at the same time get better hours. . . . Get this roofing thing down good, because I know I can take care of a family on the wages that roofers make, and it's also a trade that I can sell anywhere in the country.

In sum, parenthood has profound impacts—but in opposite directions—on the career paths of both men and women. New mothers typically scale back, either cutting their work hours or leaving the workforce. But because they thereby move outside the conventional career regime, their wages are adversely impacted and their career prospects stalled. Fathers, on the other hand, tend to become more invested in their jobs, often earning more money and putting in longer hours than nonfathers. The next chapter examines the long-term consequences associated with these gendered strategies in response to the fundamental mismatch between caring for an infant and the expectations associated with the career mystique.

Division of Labor—At Work, at Home

We have shown that motherhood means more dramatic life-course changes than fatherhood because the career mystique is congruent with men's family breadwinner role that encourages men's continued—or even increased—investment in the lockstep career regime. But that same regime relies on women to do the unpaid care work of families, meaning that new motherhood puts employed women in a double bind. Our point is that the overloads and conflicts many employed mothers experience are not inevitable; rather, they are the consequence of the current social organization of work hours and occupational paths in line with the career mystique, making no accommodations for the family or personal lives of employees. Despite the sea change that has occurred in women's labor-force participation, the gender divide in both paid work and unpaid family domestic work has been relatively resistant to change. Women in the workforce experience one job for which they get paid and a second shift of domestic and care work waiting for them at home, leaving very little time for leisure or relaxation.[74] We return to this issue in chapter 5.

CARING FOR CHILDREN

The prevailing career mystique means that women generally bear the primary responsibility for the care work associated with raising children (thereby freeing husbands and fathers to compete for income and advancement). This is true, not only in the United States, but in most countries.[75]

In the market-based labor society of the United States, where long hours on the job are rewarded, valued, and expected, paid work has primacy over unpaid family-care work. Although caring for children represents a tremendous investment in the future of the country (and the future workforce), parents who reduce their work hours or leave their jobs to care for their children pay a price for doing so. As one example, they will face reduced or nonexistent Social Security benefits in their later years in return for their care work. In contrast, other countries recognize care work as important and valuable. For example, many European countries recognize unpaid labor when calculating their gross domestic product.[76] This recognition acknowledges that those who perform this work are providing important services valuable to the economy and society. By making this work invisible and unacknowledged, the United States sends a very different message about the value attached to parenting and household management.

Father Care

The role of fathers in American society has been slowly changing, with father care becoming an increasingly common phenomenon in the United States, particularly among low-income couples.[77] Even as late as the 1970s, care work was not viewed as part of a father's role. Employed mothers typically arranged for a paid caregiver or for a female family member to care for their preschool-age children while they were at work, even if the husband was available. However, by the mid-1990s most men who were available to care for their young children while their wife worked did so.

Often, father care is a matter of both changing gender-role expectations and economics. Men are more likely to take a greater share of responsibility for the care for their children when their wives earn substantially more than they do. Economically, this makes sense. When the wife's time on the job has substantially more value associated with it than the husband's, it is more cost-effective for the husband to take care of the children so the wife can spend more time at work. This is the arrangement that Rick and Donna have adopted. Because Donna earns

more than Rick, he is the one who gets Madison ready for the nanny in
the morning and is the first one home at night. A side benefit of father
care is that children whose fathers are more actively involved in caring
for them tend to have higher self-esteem and less stereotyped gender-
role attitudes.[78]

A second situation which lends itself to father care is shift work. Couples in which one member works a nonstandard shift (evenings, nights,
weekends) are more likely to have fathers regularly involved in the care
work of the children.[79] Many couples adopt this strategy in order to avoid
the use of day care (see below).

It is interesting to note that men have been much more amenable to
sharing child care with their partners than they have been to sharing
household chores. We believe that this is part of the changing norms of
society. Sociologist Sharon Hays proposes that in the last 150 years the
value attached to children and to their care has changed dramatically.
Rather than relegating the care of infants and children to governesses,
wet nurses, and younger siblings, as in earlier centuries, families in the
United States have placed increasing value on mother care. Children today are viewed as more precious and in need of nurturance and protection than they were in previous generations (witness child-labor
protection laws and mandatory education). These societal changes
have given rise to what Hays terms the culture of "intensive mothering." Parents today work to provide their children with a sheltered and
rich educational and emotional environment, which is the new standard for which middle- and upper-class parents strive. The following
quote from a mother we interviewed illustrates how some parents today orient their lives around making sure that their children receive
this intensive experience:

> My family life is completely chaotic [laughing]. Most of the time, it's very
> busy. Three boys keep me very busy. Every one of them plays an instrument,
> takes music lessons, one is a member of Boy Scouts. Everyone plays sports,
> and they go to Sunday school. You have to keep track of who is supposed to
> be where and when. When I get home at three o'clock, I am often driving and
> organizing things. So, in fact, working is the easiest part of my day. The sec-
> ond shift is very demanding. Many times I have to do a lot of the homework
> supervision, oversee the music practice, and the driving before my husband
> gets home.

We propose that this shift in values is responsible, in part, for the increase in the number of men who spend time caring for their children.
Parenting has taken on increased value in our society.

COMMON STRATEGIES FOR MANAGING
COMPETING DEMANDS OF WORK AND FAMILY

Shift Work

Working a nonstandard shift (evenings, nights, rotating shifts, or week-ends) is a common practice among couples with young children. Accord-ing to Harriet Presser, almost one third of dual-earner couples with pre-school-age children are split-shift couples with one member of the couple working days and the other working evenings, nights, or rotating shifts, and more than half have one member working on the weekend.[80] In al-most all of those cases the father cares for the child while the wife is at work. This is a tremendous bonus for the family, and many families con-sciously pursue this strategy as a way of managing work and family. Stag-gered shift work allows fathers to be more actively involved in raising children, the family saves on child-care expenses, and parents do not have to trust others to care for their children. However, working staggered shifts can come at significant cost to the marriage. Divorce and separation are much more common among couples with children who work oppo-site shifts.[81] Nancy (see profile in chapter 6) worked a rotating shift when her children were young. She speaks about the difficulties of working nonstandard hours:

> Well we both agreed that we had to do it [dual-earner, nonstandard shift] if
> we wanted to be able to have a good life and security for ourselves and the
> kids. But there were times when it was difficult to make choices, to request
> time off for this but not for that. There were some things that I would miss
> because I was working weekends like little league games and those types of
> things. It was probably more stressful just for me because I thought I should
> be everywhere.

Single mothers, particularly never married mothers, are more likely than married mothers to work nonstandard shifts. In fact, nearly one third of never married mothers work a nonstandard shift.[82] Although married couples use nonstandard shifts as a strategy for managing work and fam-ily, single mothers often work nonstandard shifts because their jobs de-mand that they do so.[83] Many single mothers have limited job options and must therefore settle for the work that they can find, which often means working at odd or unpredictable hours. If these women do not have a family member available to assist them, finding day care is difficult and can be an impediment to work. Single mothers who work nonstandard shifts often find themselves locked into a continued cycle of poverty.[84] For them, the promise of the career mystique is always out of reach.

Self-employment

There are many reasons why people choose to pursue self-employment—potential financial rewards, job security, and the desire for autonomy are reasons frequently cited by men for starting their own business.[85] Women, on the other hand, are much more likely to pursue self-employment for family-related reasons, particularly when they have young children in the home.[86] There are three ways in which self-employment eases the burden associated with combining work and family. First, many self-employed women work out of their homes, allowing them to earn money while they care for their children. For women with few work-related skills or little education, this is the only way in which they can afford to work, for the cost of child care can be prohibitive.[87] This is the motivation behind many women who become home day care providers, one of the major forms of female self-employment.[88]

Second, self-employment gives parents the flexibility to structure their work schedules around their needs and the needs of their families. Karyn Loscocco studied self-employed men and women and found that women who were self-employed protected and valued the flexibility associated with self-employment.[89] This is illustrated by the following quote from one of her respondents, a beauty salon owner:

> One of the reasons I like what I do is because I can have flexibility to—if I need to take a day off to do something I have that flexibility and I don't have to ask anybody's permission, you know, I could just take that day and do it, and do what I want to do.

In contrast, the self-employed men in her study did not place as high a value on flexibility, and they were less likely than women to structure work around their family. A male restaurant owner in her study illustrates this point:

> I have always put business before family. That's the way I grew up. I'm very sorry if that's wrong, you prove it to me. . . . I've always felt that I'm willing to work and I'll do everything I can and if that means I'm away from my family—and my kids have paid the price a little bit there—if that means I'm away from them, so be it.

Third, self-employment gives people control over their workload. As this chapter has chronicled, most women work fewer hours following the birth of their first child. Unfortunately, many employers do not give their employees the option of reducing their hours, whereas people who are self-employed can dictate the amount of work that they will take on.

On average, full-time self-employed women earn approximately one third of what full-time self-employed men earn.[90] This reflects the different motivations that men and women have for being self-employed. Women are much more likely than men to use self-employment as a strategy to give them flexibility in managing both work and home. As a result, self-employed women spend more time than self-employed men on housework and child care, which, according to Greg Hundley, accounts for much of the earnings differential.[91]

Self-employment can also have its down side. Rather than facilitate the meshing of work and family, self-employment can result in work overtaking one's home and personal life. Self-employed individuals also report feeling isolated and lonely.[92]

Couples' Time-Based Strategies for Managing Competing Demands of Work and Family

We have shown that the most common responses to new parenthood are for women to reduce and for men to sustain or increase their work hours, but there are other, less common strategies for managing the dual demands of work and family. Moen and Sweet drew on a sample of over 850 middle-class dual-earner couples to identify five couple-level arrangements (see figure 4.7).[93] Most typical is the neotraditional strategy in which the husband puts in long hours and the wife works fewer (less than full time) hours. The second most common pattern is the high-commitment arrangement in which both members of the couple put in long hours (45+). In couples with an alternative commitment, both members work relatively few hours. In dual-moderate couples, the fourth most common strategy, both work full time, but neither puts in

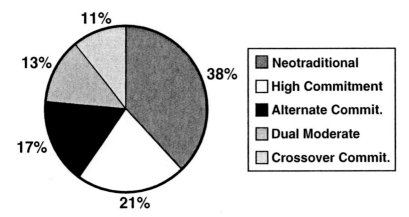

Figure 4.7. Work-hour typologies among middle-class dual-earner couples. (Source: Moen and Sweet 2003.)

more than forty-four hours, and in most cases each spouse puts in forty hours a week. Finally, in the least common typology, the crossover-commitment strategy, the wives work long hours, and their husbands work at most full time.

Moen and Sweet found that these work-hour strategies were responsive to the varying family-time needs and demands inherent in different life stages. Couples with children tend to adopt neotraditional, dual-moderate, or alternative-commitment strategies, which all include a scaling back of work hours for one or both spouses. The high-commitment strategy occurs frequently among childfree couples but rarely among parents of young children unless they rely heavily on paid day care and other household services.[94] Lynn Polasky and Carole Holahan found that women who try to maintain a high commitment to work while continuing to be the primary caregivers in the home pay a price.[95] They may maintain their upward career trajectory, but they also report higher levels of depression than women who cut back on their responsibilities either at home or at work.

WORK–FAMILY CONFLICT AND SPILLOVER

Work–Family Conflict

Is life more difficult for dual-earner couples and employed single parents who are raising young children than for other workers? We have seen thus far that parenthood transforms the lives of husbands and wives. Because jobs are designed for workers unencumbered by domestic concerns, employed parents of young children are especially hard-pressed in managing the multiple dimensions of their lives. They commonly experience conflict when the tasks and responsibilities of one role intrude upon the other.[96] For example, work–family conflict occurs when a parent leaves an important meeting at work to pick up a sick child from day care or when a parent receives a work-related telephone call while at a child's sporting event. Work–family conflict has important ramifications for individual well-being. High levels of work–family conflict and spillover have been related to depression, anxiety, lower levels of overall quality of life, poor physical health, job dissatisfaction, psychological distress, marital strife, and heavy alcohol consumption.[97]

Fortunately for employers, but unfortunately for families, paid work interferes more with family life than the reverse.[98] This again reflects the strategies employed parents make to accommodate the career-mystique template shaping employment norms, policies, practices, and occupational paths. This template is invariably at odds with the fact that most say family is more important than work. The fact is jobs are much more regimented and inflexible than family life. Even the most tolerant employer has limits as to how frequently an employee can take care of family or personal business on work time. On the other hand, home life tends to be much more flexible, particularly in two-parent households, which explains why employees are more apt to protect their work life from the intrusion of family concerns than they are to protect their home life from job-related intrusions. Because women are more likely to do the care work of families and society, it is not surprising that employed women, particularly mothers, report the highest levels of work–family conflict.[99]

Workplace policies that increase demands on employees exacerbate work–family conflicts. Studies in the United States and Canada show that stressful jobs, high workloads, and long work hours increase the chances that employees will experience work–family conflicts.[100] And studies in the United States and Finland reveal that those with low levels of job security also report higher levels of work–family conflict, presumably because workers feel they need to go the extra mile at work in order to retain their precarious jobs.[101]

The family side of the equation also leads to work–family conflicts. The more housework women do, the greater their work–family conflict. Similarly, the more (younger) children employees have, the more work–family conflicts they experience.[102] Employed women experience the most work–family conflicts while their children are in their preschool years; however, the age of their children doesn't predict whether or not fathers report work–family conflicts.[103]

The quality of family relationships also plays out in work–family conflicts. Marital distress and parent–child discord often result in higher levels of work–family conflict.[104] What matters as well is the match (or mismatch) between gender-role values and couples' work and family lifestyles. If couples' circumstances are not consistent with their values and beliefs, then work and family roles are likely to conflict. For example, Nancy Marshall and Rosalind Barnett found work–family conflict to be higher among dual-earner couples when husbands preferred that their wives not work outside of the home and wives believed that their husbands preferred they not work for pay.[105] People who are unhappy about the choices they have made as a couple may be less likely to share the burdens associated with those choices. For instance, husbands who do not support their wives' employment may abstain from participating in stereotypically feminine household tasks, leading to greater work–family conflict for their wives. Wives who wish that they could invest more time in their own careers may resent supporting their husbands' careers (by doing all the laundry and other chores, entertaining husbands' coworkers, etc.), leading to more work–family conflict for these wives.

But conflict is not the whole story. Given the isolation of homemakers and society's devaluation of care work, women in the workforce also experience the highest levels of work–family gains. In fact, there is overwhelming evidence that employment enhances the mental and physical health of both men and women.[106] Women who work full time, particularly those who are able to manage their multiple roles successfully, tend to experience less anxiety and depression and better physical health than full-time homemakers.[107] Work also provides a buffer for the stresses in the home, a network of social relationships, and opportunities for meaningful engagement and success that are not available to those who are not employed.[108] Studies show that paid work is especially beneficial to women who have a high degree of social support, good family relationships, and egalitarian gender-role values.[109]

Work–Family Spillover

Another important concept in understanding the well-being of employed men and women is the concept of work–family spillover. David Almeida, Elaine Wethington, and Amy Chandler describe work–family spillover as the transfer of mood, affect, and behavior from one setting to the other.[110] Spillover can be either positive or negative and is bidirectional, meaning spillover can happen from work to family and from family to work. For example, positive family spillover occurs when family life energizes and motivates an employee at work. Conversely, negative family spillover occurs when a person is in a foul mood at work because of marital or parental difficulties at home.

The concept of work–family *spillover* is clearly related to that of work–family *conflict*, with two important exceptions. First, theory and research about spillover tends to focus on how emotional reactions in one setting influence emotional reactions in another setting. By contrast, theory and research on work–family conflict focus on how the tasks and time demands of each realm conflict with the demands made by the other realm. Second, spillover can be either positive or negative, pointing to the costs and benefits of combining work and family roles, whereas scholars studying conflict focus exclusively on the strains and difficulties of meshing work and family roles.

Positive Work Spillover

We know relatively little about the factors associated with positive spillover because researchers have tended to focus on the negative side of the work–family equation. What studies there are tend to concentrate on relatively well-educated, dual-earner couples, most of whom are employed in professional occupations. The conclusions may, therefore, not apply to those with less education and in nonprofessional occupations. However, we do know that women in middle-class, dual-earner couples report higher levels of positive work spillover than do their husbands, meaning that work enhances women's home life more than it does men's. Again, we see that despite the difficulties associated with managing work and family, women's life quality is often enhanced by their employment.[111]

Negative Work Spillover

Using data from a representative sample of all workers in the United States, figure 4.8 shows that negative work spillover (events at work negatively impacting mood while at home) is highest for women with preschool-age children. Shifts in negative work spillover may well reflect the fact that the career-building years are also the child-bearing years, with the way jobs and career paths are structured producing overload and spillover of stresses from work into one's personal life.

But when we focus on the middle-class men and women in dual-earner couples whom we interviewed,[112] a different picture emerges. In this largely professional sample, those with a preschool-age child tend to have less negative work spillover.[113] It may be that middle-class couples have more resources to relieve some of the stresses associated with combining

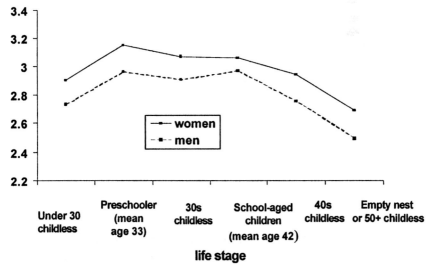

Figure 4.8. Negative work-to-family spillover among U.S. employees at selected life stages. (Source: Data from the 1997 National Study of the Changing Workforce, $n = 2,877$.)

work and family (such as hiring help with cleaning or consistent, quality day care). For these professional women, caring for young children may actually serve as a welcome change of pace and may act as a buffer from some of the stresses associated with work, thereby decreasing any negative impacts on their personal lives.

Positive Family Spillover

Positive family spillover, where family life enhances one's work life, is highest among women. The more highly involved employees are with their families, the greater the positive spillover tends to be. For highly involved parents, family life can serve as a respite, a haven to escape the pressures of work.[114] This is particularly true when children are older, no longer requiring the constant care that preschool-age children need.[115]

Negative Family Spillover

In the U.S. population at large, the presence of young children increases the spillover of negative feelings from the family into the workplace for both men and women, but especially for women.[116] A second factor affecting negative family spillover is housework. Not surprisingly, the more household chores a person does, the more likely negative emotions flow from home to work. Demanding family obligations tend to drain energy from employees when they are at work as well as at home. Additionally, the more hours that their spouses work, the higher employees' negative spillover from home to work.[117] Presumably, a spouse who works long hours is less available to help out with household tasks and is also less available emotionally, which can have a negative impact on employees' mood at work.

BEYOND LOCKSTEP LIVES

Studies of spillover demonstrate that, on the whole, most parents find that the rewards of combining employment and parenthood outweigh the strains.[118] In Nancy Marshall and Rosalind Barnett's 1993 study of working couples in Boston, 72 percent of fathers and 79 percent of mothers noted significant gains from combining work and parenthood. In fact, only 20 percent of the fathers and 27 percent of the mothers reported major strains in combining these two roles. Similarly, in our "Ecology of Careers Study," 71.7 percent of men and 78.8 percent of women with preschoolers report that family life enhances their experiences on the job (positive spillover) and only 7.4 percent of men and 13.3 percent of women with preschoolers see their family lives as detracting from their performance at work (negative spillover). Thus, despite the difficulties inherent in combining parenting and paid work roles, most parents who remain in the workforce find the task manageable and enriching. But these are the success stories. Those who can't cope are likely to have one spouse (the wife) leave the workforce or else change to a less demanding job. Single parents who can't manage are also more likely to drop out of paid work.

We find that Americans in the early years of launching both their careers and their families often make strategic selections in order to accommodate the outdated career regime. Thus, new fathers typically take their provider role more seriously than ever, while new mothers are apt to scale back on both their occupational aspirations and their work hours. This is not because couples suddenly become more traditional in their attitudes, but because they can see no other way to fit into the demands of jobs that expect employees to do more with less. Wives typically leave even good full-time jobs for less demanding, but also less challenging, jobs or else drop out for a time. In order to insure their earnings and job security, husbands focus on their jobs, leaving the family-care work largely to their wives. But for many Americans, this neotraditional strategy is far from satisfactory. The fact is, most husbands, wives, singles, and single parents in their early career years want to work fewer hours, but the costs to their economic security and future advancement are too high for most men and most single women. Women with young children continue to pay these costs precisely because they can manage no other way.

What would most help those in these early years of career and family development? Two key resources are time and money, with young adults in their twenties and thirties—especially those who are parents—typically short on both.

The 1993 Family and Medical Leave Act is the principal piece of federal legislation addressing the difficulties of working parents (see chapter 7). It provides up to twelve weeks leave, thereby addressing time needs, but is unpaid, making it too costly for most parents, particularly first-time single mothers.[119] Moreover, this act only covers workers in businesses with fifty or more employees.

Those in low-wage work typically lack even sick leave, much less any form of paid parental or personal leave. This is in marked contrast to the extended periods of paid leave provided by European employers. In her book *The Widening Gap: Why America's Working Families Are in Jeopardy and What Can Be Done about It*, Jody Heymann points to the importance of paid leaves for making families work.[120] Studies have shown that parental leave contributes to women's employment continuity[121] and men's involvement with children.[122] However, most men take little time off to care for a newborn after the first few days following the birth.[123]

The neotraditional solution (of wives working less) for most new parents in the United States is more work-friendly than family-friendly, providing (1) a workforce (of relatively unencumbered men) willing to put in long hours at demanding jobs as required by the career regime, along with (2) a contingent workforce (of encumbered women) willing to engage in low-paying, insecure contract, temp, and part-time work in order to have time for their families. Flexible paid leave policies are needed to be sure, but also essential are phased work and phased career paths that permit people to reduce hours or investment temporarily (for a period of months, for example), but that do not entail long-term costs in future opportunities or earnings.

Finally, we need to reassess the culture of 24–7 work in the United States that employees, as well as employers, take as given. The United States is one of the only industrialized countries that does not require, by law, that employees be given paid vacations, and Americans take fewer vacation days than people in other industrialized countries (see table 4.1). Burned out, overworked employees are not the most effective—on the job, at work, or at home. Rethinking the lockstep regime based on the

Table 4.1.   Cross-National Comparison of Vacation Days

Country	Days by Law	Average Days Taken
Sweden	25	25–35
Austria	25	30
Denmark	25	30
Germany	24	30
Italy	20	30
Norway	21	30
Spain	25	30
France	25	25–30
Switzerland	20	25–30
Ireland	20	28
Australia	20	25
Finland	24	25
Netherlands	20	25
Portugal	22	25
United Kingdom	20	25
Belgium	20	24
Greece	20	23
Japan	10	17.5
China	15	15
United States	0	10.2

Source: Valenti (2003).

career mystique is essential to make it possible for men and women to synchronize the work and family dimensions of their life courses and to construct more egalitarian gender relations. Rhona Rapoport, Lotte Bailyn, and their colleagues argue that to do this, organizations need to evaluate and challenge gender-based assumptions about competence and commitment in the workplace.[124] They work with organizations to identify outmoded workplace norms and replace them with practices that will create gender equity and work–personal life integration. These changes have not only increased the well-being of the workforce (of both men and women), but they have increased the effectiveness of the participating organizations. Such innovative programs and partnerships are essential for transforming the workplace.

5

Living the Career Mystique: Making It, Giving Up, or Slipping Behind?

In 1998, 773 CEOs were asked at what age they believed an employee's productivity peaks. Their average response was age forty-three.[1] The forties may be prime career-establishing years, but for many Americans life in this decade is a lot more complicated. Some forty-somethings are just starting their families. Others are seeing that the decision to postpone parenthood may well have turned into a decision not to have children. Still others have school-age children. The same variety exists in their occupational circumstances. Some have just begun serious jobs after years of schooling and casual employment. Others feel good about past occupational success and future possibilities. But many more are insecure about their futures. High-paid as well as low-paid employees in their forties are often laid off, their jobs shipped off-shore to be done more cheaply. Others are downsized to make room for contract workers or younger employees who will work more hours for less pay. In fact, 26 percent of age discrimination suits in 1996 were brought by plaintiffs in their forties, up from 18 percent between 1968 and 1986.[2] Increasingly, employees of all ages find they cannot rest on their past accomplishments. Those who do not continue to produce at the same level risk losing their jobs. Even highly productive employees may find themselves laid off.

Few Americans in their forties experience, or can count on, the typical lockstep progression through family and work promised by the career mystique. They may have expected, but not found, a linear path of focused and fulfilling employment, economic security and advancement. For the baby boom generation, being in their forties often entails less settling in to any prescribed pattern than rewriting the script as they go along. Many move in and out of jobs and sometimes even in and out of the workforce. Growing numbers return to school for additional training or to obtain a new set of credentials. People in this age group lead very diverse lives, marrying, divorcing, remarrying, developing cohabiting relationships, or constructing single lifestyles. Women and men moving into or through their forties acknowledge the biological realities of women's reproductive age by having (or trying to have or adopting) a second or third child or else by accepting the status quo—that their childbearing will be limited to children already born (including children from previous marriages). For childless individuals and couples, the forties represent a time of finalizing earlier choices about not becoming a parent, coming to terms with the fact that nondecisions around childbearing and adoption are in fact decisions to remain childless, or else moving rapidly toward parenthood by trying to have or adopt a child.

For many, the forties are a time when people reflect on their lives, either recommitting to the course they may have planned or stumbled into or else adjusting that course.[3] This chapter focuses on the experiences of men and women in these years of what has become early midlife: those who are parents of school-age children and those forty-something who are childfree.

WORK–FAMILY STRAINS AND CONFLICTS

In the last chapter we noted that Americans are often just launching their occupational careers at the same time that they are starting their families, a period where they are vulnerable to high levels of work–family conflict and negative spillover. The story for those in their forties depends in large part on the presence or absence of children. Among the middle-class dual-earner couples in our study, childfree women in their forties report minimal negative spillover from family. Such is not the case for women with school-age children, however, who experience higher rates of negative family spillover intruding into their life at work. We find that having school-age children requires a real juggling act for employed parents. School holidays, half days, snow days, or a child's high fever can send parents of elementary school children scrambling for a care provider, or else one parent (usually the mother) has to take time off from the job. Thus, even when their preschoolers enter kindergarten or first grade, parents (especially mothers) continue to experience relatively high levels of conflict and spillover at work because of their family responsibilities. These strains begin to decrease when the youngest child is around twelve, the age at which many parents see children as being old enough to care for themselves for at least short periods.[4] But, as we discuss later on, parenting teens and preteens brings its own set of difficulties for employees.

By contrast, the presence or absence of children has little effect on the degree of negative family spillover that *men* experience. This is consistent with the well-documented finding (discussed later in this chapter) that women continue to be primarily responsible for managing as well as performing household and child-care tasks.[5] In line with the career mystique of the unencumbered breadwinner, men whose wives are full-time homemakers experience even lower levels of negative spillover from home to work.[6]

By contrast, negative *work* spillover is actually lower for parents of school-age children than for those in their forties without children.[7] There are several possible explanations for this. First, women with children may have learned to compartmentalize the stresses and strains of their jobs in order to be more present and spend more quality time with their children. A thirty-nine-year-old single mother of two (ages 6 and 8) we interviewed, who is both employed and back in school, explains how she uses compartmentalization to cope with the demands of parenting, even though there is not enough time in her day:

> I compartmentalize everything. There are concerted times that I give to each thing, and it's never enough time for any of it. So what I do is at night, while the children are awake, I just say, "Forget it. I'm not going to get any work done." So if I'm there, I cook them dinner, I give them a bath, do bedtime stories. They're in bed by 9:00. Hopefully the coffee has kicked in, and I can stay up until 2:00. So, 9:00 to 2:00, I work on school.

A second reason for less negative job spillover for parents of school-age children (compared to nonparents) is that children's lives are invariably distracting. Parents often spend evenings and weekends driving children to extracurricular activities, watching sporting events, helping with homework, and volunteering at school, activities that may act as a diversion from, or place in larger perspective, any negative aspects of their jobs. By contrast, many of the childless couples we interviewed talked about working all the time. It is as if they lack the excuse of family demands to provide respite from their job demands.

A third, and related, explanation is that, for women, parenthood often means scaling back on occupational aspirations, work hours, or both. Because many mothers seek out or cobble together jobs with fewer hours, less stress, and lighter workloads, they may also experience less negative work spillover compared to women without children who typically invest heavily in their jobs.[8]

MONITORING SCHOOL-AGE CHILDREN

Finding appropriate child care can become even more complicated as children move into and through elementary and middle school. With preschool children, child-care needs are fairly consistent from one week to the next. However, once children are in school, child-care needs often vary from week to week and month to month. The school calendar is punctuated by holidays, teacher conference and training days, and the unpredictable inclement-weather days (in the Midwest and Northeast, at least four inclement-weather days per year are built-into the school system's calendar). Responsibility for finding child care on those days falls primarily to the mother.[9] During school holidays parents often either stay home with their children or impose on the goodwill of friends, neighbors, or relatives to watch them. Sometimes full-time homemakers resent always being asked to watch the children of employed friends and neighbors.

The child-care problem becomes even more acute during the preteen years. Although self-care, rather than formal day care or after-school care, is relatively rare in the early grades (first through third), with each passing year self-care becomes a more popular choice among children and parents. Research by Deborah Belle, Sara Norell, and Anthony Lewis shows that most children whose parents work for pay begin spending unsupervised time at home by the ages of ten or eleven.[10] By the fifth grade, students begin dropping out of after-school programs in droves.[11] One reason for this is that many after-school programs do not meet the needs of older children. Most after-school care settings combine all elementary school children into one center, and older elementary school children view these programs as being boring and babyish, according to Rivka Polatnick, who interviewed twenty-two preteens and their parents about their feelings regarding after-school care.[12] One sixth-grade girl describes her after-school program:

> Little kids [were] running around calling you "mommy." . . . [They] were always following us everywhere. . . . You could never get rid of them.

Another common complaint of children and parents is that these centers do not provide appropriate times or places for the older children to do their homework. Accordingly, many parents of older elementary school–age children end up constructing a patchwork of solutions. For example, Julia Roehling, the daughter of the second author of this book, at age ten (fifth grade), spent two hours after school on Mondays at home with an older sibling. She went to a structured day care center on

Tuesdays and Thursdays, and to the home of one of her friends (whose mother was paid for her care) on Wednesdays. On Fridays she attended Girl Scouts. A completely different arrangement was worked out for the summer when school was not in session. This potpourri was sometimes confusing, particularly for Julia's father, who occasionally picked his daughter up on his way home from work. On more than one occasion he found himself running from one place to another trying to find his daughter. However, this patchwork arrangement allowed Julia some independence from the structured after-school setting at the YMCA, which she felt she had outgrown. According to the U.S. Census, using multiple day care arrangements for children between the ages of five and fourteen is the norm. On average, these children are cared for in 3.4 different day care arrangements per week.[13]

After-school care becomes an acute problem once children reach middle school. In American society, many children view the transition from elementary school to middle or junior high school as a rite of passage from childhood into adolescence. Given this new-found and socially prescribed maturity, most preteens vehemently oppose any organized care setting and instead lobby for self-care.[14] Yet this is a time when children are at risk of engaging in risky and delinquent behavior if left unsupervised.

Societal institutions clearly lag behind the needs of working families by failing to provide viable supervision for preteens. In most communities there are virtually no options available for middle school or junior high school students.[15] Elementary schools in many communities provide much-needed after-school care for their students. But by middle school such resources dry up. Furthermore, after-school activities that are available often revolve around sports or tutoring programs, which are not appropriate for or interesting to many children. As a result, most working families end up leaving their preteens unsupervised during the after-school hours or else come up with creative solutions, as did another mother in our study:

> My daughter who was fourteen when she made the switch to middle school was ready to go home on the school bus alone but I wasn't ready for her to do that. . . . There wasn't any after-school program and she didn't like the idea of a baby-sitter, so we really kicked into this whole system of two or three kids going to one house together on a day that one parent would be there.[16]

This can be a serious problem for families and communities. Although the research is conflicting, there is some evidence that adolescents who are unsupervised after school are more likely to engage in risky behaviors such as drug or alcohol use, sexual experimentation, or other acts of delinquency.[17] A mother of a sixteen-year-old in our study remarks,

> I have a need to be around more, not just for the younger kids, but for the older one. Teenagers being teenagers, they feel they want to spread their

wings more. They have less of an opportunity and they are probably less tempted to do that when there is an adult around.

Older Child Care—An International Perspective

In many non-Western cultures children often receive more supervision from their older siblings than from their parents.[18] In these countries, children in elementary school, who in the United States would still be attending structured after-school programs, are responsible not only for themselves, but also for their younger siblings. Children in these cultures are expected to behave (and do behave) more maturely and responsibly than children in Western cultures. The fact that other cultures routinely expect younger children to be independent and act responsibly suggests that parents in the United States have relatively low expectations for their school-age children. However, others argue that American culture is fraught with temptations and dangers that children in non-Western cultures are typically not exposed to and from which our children need to be protected. As one mother describes her eleven-year-old daughter,

> She's a very striking-looking young lady. . . . I've had other mothers say to me, that guy over there is looking at your daughter. Men, grown men. . . . I need to protect her. And she knows that she's going to be in a protected atmosphere for the next couple of years.[19]

One of the challenges for working parents and communities is to identify which children are responsible enough to be independent in the preteen years and to develop safe, engaging alternatives for those who are not.

THE DIVISION OF LABOR AND LEISURE

Employed parents, especially mothers, have less leisure than employees without children.[20] Consider the case of Lynn (see profile), a college professor and mother of two, and her husband, Harold, a health care administrator, both of whom were part of our study. Lynn explains their division of family work, which results in her second shift:

> He can come home at night and he doesn't say this, but I've seen this in men. It's almost like they deserve to sit down and relax. Deserve to see the paper, watch a game, if something's on. Not run around like crazy like I do, folding the laundry, feeding the dog, helping the kids with homework, cleaning the dishes. [Harold] will come out and do the dishes if I ask him, remind him that it is just a ridiculous night and I can't do it all. He will dry the dishes. If I ask him, he will take out the trash. He literally doesn't see it unless I ask him.

PROFILE: LYNN AND HAROLD

Harold is part of the baby boom generation. He was born in 1951 in the aftermath of World War II when couples like his parents began their families in earnest, making up for lost time. He got a bachelor's degree and began teaching high school, which, along with coaching the football team and helping out with driver's education after school, came to about a sixty-hour workweek. While in his twenties he went back to graduate school, at first at night and then full time, where he met and fell in love with a college senior, Lynn.

Lynn, too, was a postwar baby born in 1953. She graduated from high school in 1968 as the second wave of the Women's Movement was under way. Both she and her parents took for granted that she would go to college, at least to a community college. She originally planned on a nursing career and actually got a two-year degree in nursing. She then enrolled in a university, lived in a dorm, and was completing her bachelor's degree when a friend introduced her to an "older" graduate student, Harold, who literally swept her off her feet. He liked dancing as much as she did; rock music of the early seventies became the background of their romance. They married when Lynn got her undergraduate degree. She was twenty-four; he was twenty-six.

The early years of marriage were also graduate school years. Harold went on to earn a master's degree and then an M.B.A., getting a full-time (sixty hours a week) job in a nonprofit organization. Lynn earned a master's degree and then a Ph.D. in nutrition, getting her first job teaching nutrition in a college in 1982, when she was twenty-nine. She left a few months later, trying her hand at a government job, which seemed less demanding (requiring only forty hours a week), but left this job as well at age thirty-one when their first child, Mark, was born. A year later they had a daughter, Heidi. When Mark was born and Lynn quit her job, Harold felt he had to earn more. So, he made the move to yet another small nonprofit, where he became the CEO, working at least eighty-five hours a week.

When Mark entered kindergarten and Heidi, age four, could go to preschool, Lynn took a full-time job doing college teaching. She had to leave that job two years later when the family moved so that Harold could get an even better job across the country as vice pres-

(continued)

ident of a much larger nonprofit where he could cut back to sixty hours a week. Since then, Lynn has held several jobs and is currently teaching at a local junior college. Harold became tired of his long work hours and switched jobs once again. He is currently putting in an average of fifty hours a week at a medical center. When we interviewed Harold and Lynn, Mark (18) was just graduating from high school, and Heidi (17) was a junior. Harold (49) and Lynn (47) both earn good salaries, although he earns about a third more than she does. Both agree that Harold's career has taken priority. They are still dancing, but only a few times a year.

Lynn says that with two (messy) teenagers requiring lots of food for friends and clean laundry almost daily, she does about five hours of family work each weekday. Harold says he puts in an hour a day. This inequity of responsibility for household labor is typical of most couples. Research finds that women in the United States perform on average between 70 and 80 percent of all household chores.[21] This gender stereotyping and unequal division of family-care work is not unique to the United States. Across nations, even across continents, women who work for pay outside the home are also primarily responsible for the unpaid family work within the home.[22] This second shift of family work, in part, accounts for women's inability or unwillingness to meet the demands—and reap the rewards—of the lockstep career mystique.

To be sure there have been some changes in the division of household labor now that wives as well as husbands are in the workforce. The previously large gap between the amounts of time men and women spend on housework has been narrowing. Suzanne Bianchi and her colleagues found that while in 1965 women did 6 times as much housework as men, this differential decreased such that they only did 1.8 times as much by 1995 (see figure 5.1).[23] In part, this narrowing is due to the fact that men are doing slightly more around the house. However, much of the change results from women themselves doing less housework, whether or not they are employed. The past thirty-five years has witnessed a decline in the importance that men and women place on housework. As Lynn states,

There was a time when I wanted everything perfect. Now I don't care quite as much about it. I clean every other weekend and there is never a health hazard.

This dramatic shift in values is occurring in other industrialized countries as well.[24] The steepest decline in the amount of housework, surprisingly,

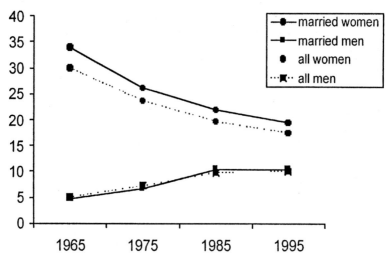

Figure 5.1.   Hours spent in housework by women and men ages 25 to 64. (Source: Bianchi et al. 2000.)

is among women who are full-time homemakers. One common corollary of the death of the feminine mystique has been diminished expectations about cleanliness, cooking from scratch, and other domestic standards commonly adhered to by these women's mothers.

In addition to different amounts of time spent on family work, there is also a gendered distribution of household chores. Research shows that tasks considered part of women's domain are rarely performed by men, and vice versa. For example, women are more apt to do the laundry and the general cleaning, while men are more likely to perform maintenance and outdoor tasks.[25] In general, "feminine" tasks tend to be the tedious jobs that need to be performed on a regular basis and are noticed only if they are not completed. "Masculine" tasks, on the other hand, are performed less frequently, are more varied, and overall, take less time than stereotypically feminine tasks. Harold illustrates this:

> We do a lot of sharing but we have more of what you may call traditional roles. I certainly help out with kids and help with the inside chores, but I am basically the outside guy and she is basically the inside person. I do all the traditionally male chores, I'm afraid—mow the lawn, shovel the driveway, wallpaper rooms and that stuff, and she does the meals and all that stuff. She does handle all the finances for the household.

Women also have primary responsibility for meeting the needs of children.[26] When fathers do watch their children, they often view it as "helping out" or as child care rather than parenting. When children are sick or when they have other needs during the day, the mother more often interrupts her work to care for the child. One frustrated insurance professional in our study lamented,

> He [her husband, a software programmer] says it is embarrassing when he takes a day off for a sick child. He always expects me to take the day off. He sees my job as less important than his.

A less visible, but equally important, aspect of caring for home and family is household management. This involves ensuring that the tasks necessary for keeping the household running are completed and includes knowing when (sports, music, play) practices and (doctors, dentists, tax, teachers, play date, car maintenance) appointments are scheduled and getting family members to and from them, arranging child care, making sure that there are clean clothes and food for lunches and dinner, deciding when children should go to bed, remembering and buying cards and gifts for birthdays and holidays, paying the monthly bills, calling repair people, and making sure someone is home when workers come to install or fix appliances or to perform home maintenance. Wives and mothers are not only primarily responsible for household tasks, they also take the lead in household management.[27] Lynn confirms this in her marriage:

> I do all of the phone calls, the bills, the doctor's appointments. When they were young, I took the kids to all their activities, signing them up for this and that. Just planning the family type activities, that kind of thing. It's just that there are a lot of things that he doesn't see.

Harold recognizes this: "[Lynn] does a lot of housework, and she does a lot of the organization of maintaining schedules. I am guilty of that. I don't take initiative, but I help out." He voices what research evidence consistently shows: Women see and are seen by their husbands as primarily responsible, while men view their role as helping out. As we shall see below, this same dynamic operates in caring for children.

FACTORS INFLUENCING THE DIVISION OF HOUSEHOLD CHORES

Marital Status

Marital status has a profound impact on the amount of housework people do.[28] Sanjiv Gupta, using a longitudinal, representative sample of American men and women age nineteen and over, estimates that when couples marry, the amount of time that a woman spends doing housework increases by approximately 17 percent, while a man's decreases by 33 percent (a third!).[29] When a man divorces or is widowed, he typically increases the amount of housework he performs by 61 percent and 71 percent, respectively. By contrast, divorced women spend less time on housework than they did when they were married. It appears that once a man has lived with a woman, he becomes less tolerant of housework left undone. As a result, should he become single once again, he will do more housework than he had prior to (or during) his marriage. Gupta suggests that the demographic trend of delaying or forgoing marriage may in part be due to the reluctance of working women to enter into an institution which, in terms of housework, is clearly to their disadvantage.

Time Spent on Paid Work, Housework, and Child Care

The amount of time men and women spend on housework is also influenced by the amount of time they spend on paid work.[30] Not surprisingly, women who do not work outside of the home tend to do the greatest share of housework, followed by those who work part time, with women who put in full-time hours on the job devoting the fewest hours to housework.[31] However, time spent at work is not related in the same way to time that women spend on child care.[32] Time caring for their children remains a priority for women and is typically unaffected by their hours of paid work. When time is at a premium and women have to decide what to let go, they tend to be less diligent about housework or give up on sleep rather than spend less time with their children. Sharon Hays refers to this as the ideology of intensive mothering; many women will sacrifice job, time, sleep, and energy to be there for their children.[33]

Like women, men's hours on the job affect the amount of housework they do. Men putting in long hours at work tend to do less housework.[34] Does this mean that nonemployed men with wives in the workforce do the majority of the housework? Not necessarily. Two studies—in Canada and in Norway—both show that nonemployed husbands do more housework than men who are employed.[35] However, even in this situation, their wives still do most (60%) of the housework.[36] We see this in the case of Joan and Brad (see chapter 4). Recall that Joan works full time while Brad stays home to care for their son. Still, Joan is responsible for approximately half the household tasks:

> Tuesday is laundry day and he'll do laundry and if I want laundry done any other time then I do it. . . . It's at least 50/50. He does the laundry and mows the lawn. The meals are 50/50. He might run and get burgers, but I am making the fries and salad. So I would say it is 50/50, if not Brad doing a little

more. But yet on the weekends I don't see him cleaning much at all. I am cleaning and doing the toilets and things like that. . . . He'll do other projects like putting the grill together. They are projects that he wants to do and never gets a chance to do it all week. That is his special time to do the projects on the weekend and then I'm cleaning.

Children

Parenthood is an enormous transition, a time when even modern dual-earner couples find themselves suddenly following neotraditional arrangements. As we have discussed earlier, the majority of couples with children adopt a neotraditional gender-based arrangement. Both parents may still remain in the workforce following the birth of their first child, but fathers become serious breadwinners while mothers do the bulk of the family work. Parenthood thus becomes another tipping point toward reinforcing the career mystique for men but not for women. Gender disparities in earnings, promotions, and pensions begin to widen as women specialize more in the house and care work of the family.[37] Sandy, a forty-eight-year-old mother of two in our study recalls that when their first child, Sarah, was born, the inequitable division of labor between her and her husband became more pronounced:

> His life didn't change any. He still got up, went to work, came home. Where I get up, get breakfast, get myself ready, get Sarah ready, get her to the day care which was just a block from the house. I'd pick her up at 2:15, come home, we'd play. I'd still do all the chores that needed to be done. Lots of times it would be 8:00 at night before I would take off my shoes and relax.

Prior to the birth of Sarah, Sandy and her husband had a fairly egalitarian arrangement.

Other societal institutions, such as schools, assume that mothers are responsible for the children, including arranging for alternative care when necessary. A thirty-two-year-old mother of two in our study illustrates this point:

> I had someone very good, but whenever [there was a problem], I'd mention it to Mario [her husband] and he'd say, "Oh, just hire somebody else"! Like you just go out on the street. [Laughs] Okay! Another thing I think is hilarious is that they have both phone numbers at school, you know, Mommy's and Daddy's. And they never call Daddy!

Despite the Women's Movement, there are still strong societal norms for what constitutes a good mother and a good father, and these norms often involve gender divides with tremendous consequences for men's and women's biographies. What we have shown throughout this volume is that the career mystique shaping the lockstep life course is fundamentally at odds with taking time for family care. Thus, deeply ingrained images of the good mother are incompatible with the career mystique while images of the good father are not.[38] Additionally, ample research demonstrates that with increasing numbers of children, the amount of time women spend on housework increases, while men's time doing housework remains the same or increases only slightly.[39] The younger the children, the more housework women do.[40]

Figure 5.2 illustrates that among the middle-class dual-earner couples in our *Ecology of Careers Study*, having preschool-age children means a much larger amount of time spent on housework for women than for men. Sanjiv Gupta, using a nationally representative sample of Americans, estimates that, on average, each child under the age of five increases the time mothers spend on housework by over three hours a week (more than what we find among the middle-class, dual-earner couples in our study).[41] In contrast, having young children in the home increases the father's amount of housework by only about one hour a week (also more

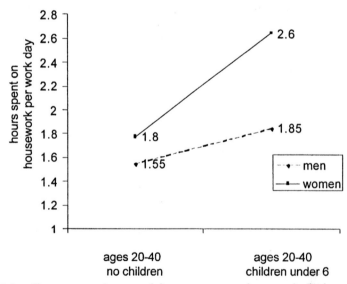

Figure 5.2.   Time spent on housework by young men and women in dual-earner couples with preschool children and without children. (Source: *Ecology of Careers Study*, 1998, *n* = 382.)

than we find), but only when children are under the age of five. For mothers, however, the presence of a son of any age in the home continues to result in more housework. Daughters, on the other hand, stop adding work to their mother's workday when they become teenagers.

Attitudes about Housework and Gender Values

Myra Ferree has found that most men and women view housework as unpleasant.[42] Men's feelings about housework relate to the amount of time that they spend doing it, with those who dislike it the most doing less. But for women, feelings about the unpleasantness of housework are unrelated to the amount of housework they actually perform. Rather, the amount of time a woman spends on housework is related to how much either she or her husband cares about the cleanliness of their home. The more either cares about having a clean house, the more time the wife spends doing housework. Although the feminine mystique of the full-time homemaker may have been cast aside, homemaking work remains a fact of life, and women continue to feel, and to be, responsible for it. Many women believe they should be it all—a good mother, a good wife, a good housekeeper, and a good worker. A clean and orderly house becomes an outward manifestation of their being successful as mothers and wives.

Gender-role values also predict the amount of housework men and women do. In the United States and in other countries, men with the strongest beliefs about gender equity are more likely to do a greater share of the housework, while those with more traditional attitudes tend to spend less time on household chores.[43]

Occupational Status

For women, the job prestige/housework relationship is relatively straightforward: The higher their job status, the less housework women do. For example, the more money that a woman makes, the higher status her position, and the more education that she has (all measures of prestige), the less time she typically spends on household chores.[44]

Also important is a woman's relative status, her job prestige compared to her husband's. This conforms to both exchange and feminist theories of power within the household, with relatively more earnings and job prestige translating into power. The greater one's relative power, the less housework one performs. April Brayfield's study of Canadian dual-earner couples shows that for every level higher a wife's job is than her husband's, her share of the housework is reduced by 4 percent.[45] The same effect, albeit more modest, occurs for relative income. For every $10,000 more that a woman earns compared to her husband, her share of the housework is reduced by 1 percent. Other studies in the United States and in China also find evidence of this relationship.[46]

Any reduction in the relative share of housework among women in high-prestige jobs does not reflect an increase in their husband's housework. In fact, wives' earnings are unrelated to the amount of housework husband's do.[47] Women with high-prestige occupations simply do less housework than other women, thereby decreasing their relative share. High-status women manage by hiring others—often less advantaged women—to do their families' housework. Only by outsourcing home-making can women ever follow the lockstep career mystique. For example, Donna (the mother of one-year-old Madison; see profile in chapter 4), who has a high-prestige job, does relatively little housework. She and her husband, Rick, have three employees: a full-time nanny, a housecleaner, and a third person to do laundry, grocery shopping, and dry cleaning. When at home, Donna and her husband share equally in the care of their daughter and in the remaining household duties, but neither of them spends a great deal of time on tasks that are not related to Madison. But this solution means that other women, typically poor immigrants, are doing the family-care work for low pay and few, if any, benefits.[48] Even though it appears that Donna may be succeeding in her pursuit of the career mystique, it still has left her conflicted and unhappy with the way her travel impacts her family: "I don't like being away from Rick, but that I could manage. I hate being away from Madison that long. It's just torture to me."

The relationship between occupational prestige and housework is less straightforward for men than it is for women. Consistent with what is true for women, the greater the economic power a man holds in a relationship, the less housework he does relative to his wife. This reflects both a decrease in the amount of time he spends in housework and an increase in the amount of time spent by his wife. It is as if men who earn more than their wives "buy themselves out" of the housework. Sandy, discussed earlier in this chapter, recalls how the unequal division of labor at home is linked to unequal earning power: "One thing I have never forgiven him [her husband] for is when one time we talked about him doing more housework, and he said 'let's compare salaries.'" Two years later Sandy stopped working and became a full-time mother/homemaker.

Men at the low end of the job hierarchy, those struggling to fulfill their role as breadwinners, are, surprisingly, even less likely to perform housework than those with greater earning potential. Some scholars propose that men who experience difficulty as breadwinners see doing housework as a threat to their masculinity.[49] Performing stereotypically feminine tasks, such as housework, may further undermine their already fragile sense of self, so they opt out of them. This hypothesis has been supported by research showing that men who hold positions of low autonomy do less housework than those with more autonomy.[50] Men in subordinate positions whose wives also earn more than they do are even less likely to spend time in housework. Presumably these men feel a double threat to their masculinity—at home and at work—and are therefore even less inclined to engage in the stereotypically feminine behavior of housework. Not surprisingly, then, men with at most a high school education typically do less housework than those with more education.[51] It appears that among men housework is linked to the idea of "doing gender."[52] Men who feel insecure about their abilities as family providers are reluctant to engage in "women's" care work associated with maintaining the household.

In summary, economic power and prestige (as measured by income, education, and authority on the job) are related to doing less housework for women and men as well. This is consistent with an economic model. The more value assigned to a person's time, the less likely he or she is to use it performing unskilled, undervalued tasks. However, men with relatively low earning potential, along with those in subordinate positions at work, may avoid housework as well so as not to further undermine an already shaky sense of masculinity.

Ethnicity and Housework

African American families appear to be more egalitarian about housework than white families. Yoshinori Kamo and Ellen Cohen,[53] as well as Daphne John and Beth Anne Shelton,[54] using a sample representative of the U.S. population collected in the late 1980s, found that African American men spend more time on household chores than do white men, even when factors such as income and number of hours spent in the work place are accounted for. Data from the 1997 National Study of the Changing Workforce (see figure 5.3) shows that this difference has persisted into the 1990s. Furthermore, in the 1980s, African American men and women in the workforce typically spend more time on household chores than do European American men and women in the workforce.

DIVISION OF LABOR, PERCEIVED FAIRNESS, AND MARITAL SATISFACTION

What is the effect of the unequal division of labor between spouses on the quality of their relationship? Surprisingly, many men and women tend to not perceive the gender disparity in housework as unfair. In fact, women will perform up to 66 percent of the housework before they begin to feel

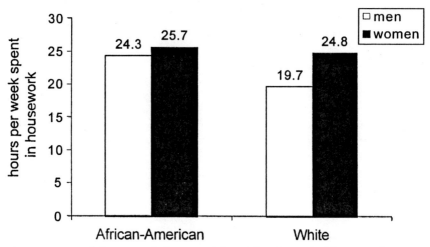

Figure 5.3.   Total time spent in housework by adult white and African American men and women in the workforce. (Source: Data from the 1997 National Study of the Changing Workforce, *n* = 3,003.)

that it is unfair.[55] Also, the more a woman enjoys doing housework and feels that she is good at it, the less likely she is to view the disparity as unfair.[56] Dynamics within the marital relationship also have an impact on a spouse's feelings regarding how fair the household division of labor is. A spouse's acknowledgment of and appreciation for the housework that the other partner does can go a long way in mitigating any sense of inequity.[57] Finally, the division of household labor will more likely be perceived as unfair if husbands and wives have unequal access to leisure.[58] Because men tend to spend more time in the workplace than women, many couples feel that the unequal divisions of household and paid labor even out. However, when women have less leisure time than their husbands, feelings of unfairness are more likely to arise. Not surprisingly, people are more satisfied in their marriages when they feel that the division of labor is equitable.[59]

PARENT–CHILD RELATIONSHIPS

There has been an ongoing debate since the 1950s about the effects of maternal employment on the relationship between a mother and her children, with the consensus being that the effect of maternal employment *depends* on whether mothers are employed by choice, on job conditions, on fathers' attitudes and behaviors, and on the supports available to the family.[60] Ellen Galinsky, in a survey of over one thousand children in grades three through twelve, compared the evaluations of school-age children with employed mothers with those of children with nonemployed mothers. Her findings are reassuring: "In not a single analysis was mother's employment status related to the way a child sees his or her mother or father. Neither is working part time or full time"[61] Despite the time their mothers' jobs entail and the stresses at work, children with employed mothers grade their mothers as highly as children with nonemployed mothers in terms of the quality of their parenting and the quality of the parent–child relationship. The cost of working often falls on the women themselves in less sleep and in effort. Lisa (profiled in chapter 1), the single parent of a nine-year-old child states,

> I want to be there for her as much as I can, but I tell you it is very taxing on me to keep a household going, going to work and being there for her, I'm trying to be as much a part of her life as possible . . . so she ends up on the right road.

Mothers who work outside of the home do spend less time in the presence of their children than mothers who do not work outside of the home. However, the difference between the two groups in terms of the amount of time that they spend interacting with, helping, and teaching (often regarded as quality time) their children is not as large as one would expect, with one study finding that working mothers spend only 4.75 hours fewer per week on these activities than mothers who do not work outside of the home.[62] As if to make up for this difference, fathers of children whose mothers work spend more time interacting with their infants than fathers of children whose mothers do not work.[63] Further, researchers have found no difference in the quality of parenting between employed and nonemployed mothers. Lisa, for example, feels that her relationship with her daughter improved when she began working full time following her divorce:

> When I got back to work full time we almost immediately appreciated every bit of time that we spent together, because we didn't have as much time together. And I wanted to just be with her so much when I was with her. I gave her better attention and our relationship improved. Our relationship improved after I went to work.

Note the dearth of research on the impact of *fathers'* employment on their relationships with their children. In fact, scholars tend to reinforce conventional stereotypes by focusing on the impact of maternal *employment* and paternal *unemployment*.[64]

Family members' lives are linked with one another in a complex web of undercurrents. What happens at work influences family relationships. Ellen Galinsky found that children are acutely aware of spillover from their parents' jobs and highly attuned to the moods of their parents at the end of the day.[65] As one nine-year-old girl explains,

> My mom—she's very expressional. If she comes and picks me up from the babysitters and says "Come on, just hurry up, I really want to get home," I know that she's had a really bad day. My dad keeps everything inside. He's not very talkative. But I can tell by the expression on his face.[66]

Children monitor their parents' moods with good reason. A series of studies demonstrate that both mothers and fathers are less accepting of, more withdrawn from, and experience more tense and conflictual interactions with their children when they are stressed on the job.[67] But children tend to be understanding of the stresses their parents bring home from work. Nancy Galambos and Jennifer Maggs found no relationship between the level of a mother's work-related stress and either her overall relationship with her children or her children's psychosocial adjustment.[68] That is not to say that children don't recognize that their parents sometimes have difficulty controlling their emotions. When Ellen Galinsky asked children to grade their parents on a variety of dimensions reflecting the quality of parenting and the quality of the parent–child relationship, overall, the children gave parents very high marks. However, they gave their parents the lowest grades on their ability to control their tempers. Only 28 percent of mothers and 31 percent of fathers received an "A," while 22 percent of mothers and 23 percent of fathers received a "D" or "F" from their children. A thirteen-year-old girl illustrates the ways negative moods spill over from parents' jobs:

> If my brother and I are fighting or if I don't do something the minute she tells me, she yells at me. It's usually because she's had a bad day at work. Because some days she doesn't care, and sometimes she does. She'll say, "I've had a bad day. Just leave me alone."[69]

Galinsky also discovered that many children develop strategies for managing their parents' negative moods when they come home from work. Some have learned to avoid their parents, as one teenage girl explains:

> When you are in a bad mood, you don't want to do anything but sulk. So, if [my parents] have had a bad day, I just leave them alone. When I am in a bad mood, I don't want to be bothered. So I give them time to cool down. Usually their moods will change after a while.[70]

Other children are more proactive in their approach to managing their parents' moods, like this twelve-year-old girl:

> I try to make her feel better. My friend can make people laugh so easy. And so usually I'm like, "Chris, my mom feels kind of bad right now—you wanna come over and cheer her up?" and in just five minutes my mom is laughing so hard.[71]

When children were asked about the worst thing involved with having an employed parent, the most common response (30%) was that the parent was stressed out by work.

PARTNER RELATIONSHIPS

Stress on the job not only creates distress for individual workers and their children, but it also affects their spouses and spousal relationships.[72] A key study by Niall Bolger, Anita DeLongis, Ronald Kessler, and Elaine Wethington asked people to monitor their experiences in the workplace during the day and also at home in the evening.[73] They found that people who argue with coworkers during the day are more likely to also have arguments with their spouses that same evening. Bolger and his colleagues refer to this transmission of stress from work to home as stress contagion. High stress on the job can also have long-term consequences for individuals and their spouses. In another important study, Rosalind Barnett and Robert Brennan interviewed employed men and women twice, about a year apart.[74] They found that employees whose jobs became more stressful during the intervening year were more distressed at the second interview, as were their spouses, another example of stress contagion.

Wives may be more vulnerable to stress contagion than their husbands. A study of dual-earner couples in England shows higher levels of distress among wives' whose husbands report both high levels of conflict and low levels of support at work.[75] However, the reverse is not the case; husbands' well-being is unrelated to characteristics of their wives' jobs.

A heavy workload on the job creates pressure on the domestic front as well. But this has different ramifications for husbands and wives. On days when men report being overloaded at work, their wives report being overloaded at home later that evening.[76] It appears that husbands, when feeling they have too much to do at work, neglect their household responsibilities. Their wives compensate by picking up those tasks, which results in an overload for them at home. Thus, it appears that wives adjust their own domestic workloads to absorb the tasks of their (work) overloaded husbands. Men, however, do not seem to make the same adjustments when their wives are overloaded at work. Rather, when women are overloaded at work, they report an increase overload the next evening at home. It appears that wives, like their husbands, neglect some household tasks when they feel they have too much to do on the job. As a result, neglected household tasks are often left undone until the following evening when wives complete them, resulting in a feeling of overload at home the next evening.

There are also gender differences in the extent to which paid work and unpaid family-care work influence people's moods. Among men, evening mood is more heavily influenced by events occurring on the job. For women, the relationship is reversed, with stressors on the home front accounting much more for wives' evening moods than job-related stressors.[77] These differences mirror traditional gender expectations, the primacy of men's paid work and women's unpaid care work. This helps explain why women with preschool- and school-age children are more immune to spillover from their jobs than are women without children and men. Managing life at home tends to overshadow life on the job for women when there are children at home.

SHIFTING CAREER PATHS

Although young men and women start out with similar occupational aspirations, parenthood, as we saw in chapter 4, often entails reverting back to some modified version of traditional gender schema. This is not only a matter of socialization; neotraditional patterns are also the pragmatic adaptations of men and women playing out the gender expectations of motherhood and fatherhood in a society fashioned for one-career, two-adult families. Government and corporate policies that are more job-friendly than family-friendly make it difficult to pursue two lockstep careers in dual-earner households or a single lockstep career pattern in single-parent households. In the neotraditional household, all adults work for pay, but women disproportionately accommodate their paid work to their family-care work, scaling back on work hours and goals, moving into more feminized occupations or temporary jobs, turning down promotions that require travel or relocation, declining the after-work social engagements that are often crucial for developing networks, and even leaving the workforce altogether for a period of time.[78] For many women scaling back is a way of achieving a sense of balance; they forgo ladder climbing to spend more time with their children. However, these scaling-back strategies entail unanticipated costs that become increasingly evident in midlife. Although often temporary, occurring when childrearing demands are heaviest, scaling back has a permanent impact upon women's career trajectories as they fall behind their male coworkers in salary, security, seniority, and advancement. For example, in 2002, among full-time, year-round employees, the median income for women was 77 percent of that for men.[79] With few exceptions, women across all job categories earned less than men. The strategies women use to cobble together jobs, community service, marriages, and children take them off track. Many find themselves still on the "mommy track" at work long after their children are grown and gone. These gendered pathways, which widen gender divide in resources and recognition, are the rule for women and men in Europe as well as in the United States.[80]

The Glass Ceiling

Not only do women make less money than men across job categories, they also advance more slowly up career ladders, particularly among high-earning professionals.[81] The term *glass ceiling* was coined in a 1986 *Wall Street Journal* article describing the barriers women encounter as they approach the top of the corporate hierarchy.[82] Despite the fact that women have entered and remained in the workforce in record numbers, they are still rarely in positions of power or influence within organizations. According to a study by Catalyst in 2002, only 8 percent of individuals holding the top positions in Fortune 500 companies were women.[83] In fact, in 2002 there were only six women CEOs in the Fortune 500 group of corporations, up from only two women CEOs in 2000. The situation is even worse for women of color.[84]

Scholars offer a range of explanations for the failure of women to advance professionally at the same rate as men. One frequent explanation is cultural: Gender scripts and schema dictate that unpaid family-care work is "women's" work. As we have chronicled, women commonly scale back at work to accommodate these demands. Doing so both removes women from the pipeline to the top and distances them from the informal networks that are crucial to ascending corporate ladders.

Despite a plethora of success-story anecdotes, studies show that women who are successful occupationally are more likely never to be married or to have a spouse who does not work, to be childless, or to have delayed childbirth until their forties.[85] For some, prioritizing their occupational careers is a conscious choice as they recognize that the only way to succeed along the lockstep template is to be, in fact, what it demands: an unencumbered worker. Sarjol Parasuraman and Jeffrey Greenhaus found that 63 percent of the women executives they interviewed gave up marriage, family plans, and social relationships in order to be successful.[86] Generally, women who have made the decision to forgo children in order to pursue their careers feel positively about the decision.[87] As one executive in the our study remarked,

Oh, I think a lot of people, a lot of women have horrible problems [balancing work and family]. And I've been lucky, I've not had children, so I've been relatively free to make a commitment to work. This is the big thing, when you have children.

Some women find that the cost of occupational success is too high. Take, for example, Brenda Barnes, formerly the North American CEO of Pepsi-Cola. She was one of the first women to crack the glass ceiling in a Fortune 500 company. However, in 1997, feeling the cost of success was exacting too high a price on her family, she resigned from Pepsi-Cola to spend more time with her husband and children, ages seven, eight, and ten.

Donna, the executive we profiled in chapter 4, did resign from her position soon after our interview. She plans to take two to three years off before returning to work. These women are not alone. In one study of married women who had changed jobs, almost two out of five (39.5%) reported wanting to spend more time with their children as a major reason for the change.[88] In this same study, about the same proportion of mothers (39%) reported being overwhelmed by the competing demands of work and family.

For men, having a family is often an asset rather than a liability to their career success. Married men, regardless of whether their wives work outside of the home, tend to make more money than unmarried men.[89] This is because the career mystique behind the way jobs are structured assumes someone else, a wife, will serve as backup and support on the home front. Not surprisingly, then, men whose wives are full-time homemakers are the most successful.[90] Men with children tend to be more successful and make more money than men without children, again, a product of the fact that the career mystique is congruent with family breadwinning.[91] For men, family success means success as the family provider, which means success in the world of paid work. This is true in other countries as well. For example, a study in Australia shows that, as in the United States, having a family has a negative impact upon women's careers but a positive impact on men's.[92]

Married women who manage to be successful in their occupational careers are also more likely to have a spouse who does not work.[93] Carly Fiorina, the first woman CEO of a Fortune 100 company (Hewlett Packard), is an example. Her husband retired at forty-eight from his job as vice president at AT&T to stay at home and support her in her career. Such support can be critical to succeed in a demanding career.[94]

The difficulty that women encounter as they try to advance up career ladders is indicative of the lag between their needs and the career mystique, which provides many paths to opt out of careers but few portals of reentry. One option is to start fresh at a new organization. Jill Barad (formerly of Mattel) used such a strategy, leaving a job with an advertising agency after the birth of her first child. When she reentered the workforce, she started at a different company, Mattel, where she rose to become CEO.

The glass ceiling is not only a result of women failing to follow the traditional (male) lockstep career mystique; it also reflects the culture of (female) care. Managers making decisions about hiring, raises, promotions, and training view women as a status group, a group with heavy family-care responsibilities. Sociologists term this *statistical discrimination*; even unmarried, childless women are viewed as workers who will marry or will have children and, therefore, who will be less committed to their jobs than their male coworkers. Statistical discrimination is more subtle, but also more difficult to erase, than more overt, blatant, gender discrimination.

The glass ceiling is not just an American phenomenon. Women throughout the world are denied access to high paying jobs. For example, while the European Community has equal pay laws, they are seldom enforced due to the lack of affirmative action policies regarding hiring.[95] Even in Sweden, which has some of the most progressive laws promoting gender equality, there is evidence of a glass ceiling for women.[96]

JOB-RELATED RELOCATION

Relocating for a job is commonplace in the United States. According to 2000 Census data, almost one third of nonlocal moves are made for work-related reasons.[97] Many employees change jobs, either within an organization or by joining a new organization, in order to advance professionally, and many firms expect their top employees to relocate as they ascend the corporate hierarchy.[98] This explains why highly educated and well-paid employees are the most likely to relocate.[99] Typically, a spouse and children are uprooted to move with them.[100]

Relocation and Gender

Historically, women are much less likely to move for work than are men, although there is evidence that this trend is slowly changing.[101] In 1978, women made up only 4 percent of those who moved for their jobs. By 1993, the number had risen to 17 percent (see figure 5.4), still a vast underrepresentation of women.

Two processes appear to be involved in the gender disparity in relocation. First, women are less likely than men to be given the opportunity to relocate.[102] Consider, for example, the mostly professional employees we

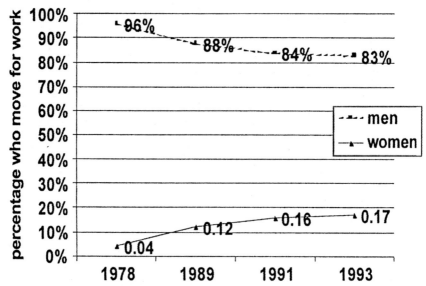

Figure 5.4. Employees who move for work broken down by gender, 1978–1993. (Source: Hendershott 1995.)

surveyed; 42 percent of the men, but only 20 percent of the women, in that sample had been offered a career opportunity that required relocation. Positions requiring relocation are usually offered to employees pursuing the career mystique—on the fast track to upper management. Women are more apt to be sidelined than fast tracked. The same gender biases responsible for the overrepresentation of men in upper management may be responsible for the dearth of opportunities for relocation among women.

Second, when offered one, women are less likely to accept a relocation assignment than men.[103] Again, among couples in our study, more than half (55%) of the women who had been offered jobs involving relocation had declined, while only 42 percent of the men refused such an offer. Traditionally, women have been less likely than men to place the needs of their careers ahead of the needs of the entire family, making them less likely to want to relocate for their jobs.[104] Men tend to be less concerned about the impact of a move on their wives' careers than women are about the impact of the move on their husband's career.[105] Lynn illustrates the reluctance of women to move unless moving benefits the entire family:

[Following a move for Harold's career] I do remember him saying to me, "Next time, it'll be your turn." Meaning that he knew that he was taking me away from my job and next time if we have to move, it'll be because of what

I might want to do. But I have to be honest with you. I highly doubt that will ever happen. It's not that he wouldn't do it for me. But he makes more money than I do. I guess you can say he is the primary breadwinner, although both of us work hard. . . . It's a little nontraditional for the wife to say, "Okay, let's go here because of me." It is certainly something that we would discuss. I wouldn't be given a "no." I just think that I would hesitate uprooting him if he were well established in what he were doing.

The Trailing-Spouse Syndrome

Moving from a community where one has developed social and occupational networks is stressful, especially for the spouse of an employee who has been relocated. This trailing spouse, often the wife, when placed in a new community, is bereft of the support networks and human capital she built up in her previous community and previous employment. She often moves without having a job lined up at her new residence and is in the unenviable position of having to establish herself anew in an unfamiliar community. If the couple has children, then the trailing spouse is often the one who bears the burden of ensuring their smooth transition into the new neighborhood and school system. The situation can be even more difficult for trailing husbands. Consider the observations of a childless architect in her mid-forties:

> So we moved about a year ago. That was really hard, because he had to give up his friends. He was a member of a biking team in Colorado and that was more of a career to him than his job was; it was a lot more than a hobby. He had to give up his job there and move here and just be "Jane's husband." I was the only female that was transferred, and that was really hard. All the wives of the guys that moved up here did stuff, and he was the only husband. I felt really weird too because the people who came up from Colorado would go out, and I would be the only female.

Moving for a spouse's job can be detrimental to the trailing spouse's professional life. Some trailing wives, particularly those with conventional orientations, leave the workforce following the move to a new community.[106] Many trailing spouses who stay in the workforce often accept jobs beneath the positions they held previously and find it hard to reestablish their credentials in the new setting. For example, Pat, the second author of this book, left a tenured position at a small liberal arts college in the Midwest when her husband accepted a tenure-track position at a university in the East. When she first arrived in the new town, she accepted temporary, adjunct teaching positions which, when combined, paid 20 percent of what she had been paid previously and offered no benefits or job security.

Trailing husbands are more likely to get assistance finding employment from a spouse's employer than are trailing wives.[107] Trailing husbands are also less likely than trailing wives to settle for a position that is significantly inferior to their previous position.[108] This may reflect the fact that women are less likely to move unless it is in the economic interest of the entire family, which means that there would also be a professional opportunity for the husband in the new community. If it means that their husbands will incur a serious loss in professional status, most women are reluctant to accept a move. Finally, there is evidence that employers are more inclined to assist in finding a job for the husband of a relocated employee than they are to find the wife a job.

Men and women make sacrifices emotionally and socially when they relocate for work. Most people who relocate do so because they believe that the financial and professional gains will offset the losses incurred by leaving their communities. Is the trade-off worth it? Several researchers have demonstrated that relocation does not benefit men and women equally. Among men, changing jobs and relocating for work are strategies associated with attaining a higher salary.[109] However, neither of these strategies appears to make a significant positive impact on the amount of money that women earn.[110] Relocation, then, is a strategy that literally pays off more for men than for women.

Commuter Marriages

When faced with the decision to relocate, many couples decide to embark upon a commuter marriage rather than uproot the entire family and disrupt one spouse's career. In a commuter marriage, a couple maintains two separate households, and one member of the couple resides at a separate residence for at least three days a week. A recent study estimated that 7 percent of corporate relocations end up spawning commuter marriages.[111] Most couples who maintain two households do so because of the potential trailing spouse's job or because they do not want to move the children. Commuter marriages come at a cost. They often have negative impacts on the marital relationship and can lead to social isolation, particularly for the spouse who sets up the new household. The upside of the commuter marriage is that both members of the couple have more freedom to tailor their schedules to meet their needs, and the worker who commutes can be more productive when away from the distractions and responsibilities of home.[112] This, of course, is not the case for the spouse who does not commute, particularly when there are children in the home. These employees (usually wives) have sole responsibility for the home and children while their spouse commutes, making them less available for their own jobs, giving them less control of their time, and removing them even further from the good-worker template fashioned around the career mystique.

Travel

Many employees are required to travel overnight for their jobs. Again, we find that men are more likely to engage in time-intensive work-related activity, such as overnight travel, than are women.[113] This relationship is even more polarized when children are in the home. Women with dependent children are less likely to travel than those without children, whereas men's travel is not affected by parenthood (see figure 5.5). Length of time spent traveling is also affected by gender and parental status. In the *Ecology of Careers Study* sample, we find men who travel spend an average of 5.5 nights away from home over a three-month period, whereas women spend only about 3.8 nights away. Women with children spend even less time away from home (2.9 days), but the presence of children does not impact time spent away from home for men in our study.

Not surprisingly, work-related travel has an impact on people's personal lives. Christy Fisher interviewed five hundred frequent business travelers, finding that travel is hardest on those with young families.[114] Most parents who travel fear that their children are stressed and disappointed by their frequent absences. On the other hand, Fisher found that the majority (80%) of business travelers felt their trips have no

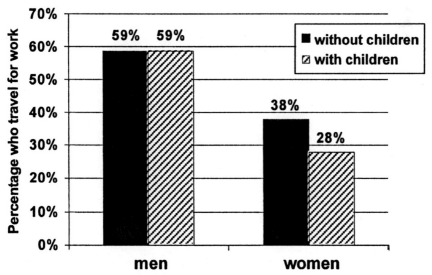

Figure 5.5. Percentage of men and women who travel for work, by parental status. (Source: *Ecology of Careers Study*, 1998.)

impact on their marriages, and 12 percent believe that travel helps their marriages, compared to only 9 percent who report that their marriages are hurt by their travel. Patricia Roehling and Marta Bultman, using data from the *Ecology of Careers Study*, found that the impact of travel on marriage is complex. Work-related travel is related to lower marital satisfaction only when it is inconsistent with couples' gender-role values, particularly when children are present in the home. Specifically, egalitarian couples with children are generally less happy when either member of the couple travels for work. Take, for example, Rick and Donna, very much an egalitarian couple (see profile in chapter 4). Both are unhappy about the amount of time that Donna travels. Rick states, "That [Donna's travel] is very difficult because then you feel like a widower. It's constant, you have no relief . . . you have no partner to regenerate with."

Among parents with traditional gender values, husbands' travel (which is more consistent with traditional gender expectations) is associated with higher or stable marital satisfaction, while wives' travel (inconsistent with traditional gender roles) is associated with lower marital satisfaction.

Lifelong Learning: Going Back to School

Women (and many men) are returning to school in record numbers, further evidence of the growing obsolescence of the lockstep life course (see figure 5.6).[115] In 2000, 20 percent of full-time students in degree-seeking institutions were over twenty-five years old; even more—two thirds (67%) of part-time students were over twenty-five.[116] According to a 1999 survey, 46 percent of American adults have participated in adult education activities at some point in their life course, up from 32 percent in 1991.[117] A similar trend is occurring internationally. The number of mature (nontraditional age) students in the United Kingdom doubled between 1982 and 1992, and in Australia the majority of students entering higher education are now mature students.[118] According to Maggie Ford, the president of the American Association of University Women, the notion of an educational and career ladder is outdated; rather, she believes the appropriate metaphor for the twenty-first century is a spiral: "The spiral captures the likelihood that women will move in and out of formal education throughout their lives, by choice or necessity, to fulfill a variety of economic and personal enrichment goals."[119]

People go back to school in their thirties, forties, and fifties (or even later) for two major reasons. The first is very similar to the reason that people often seek a job change—personal enrichment. According to a

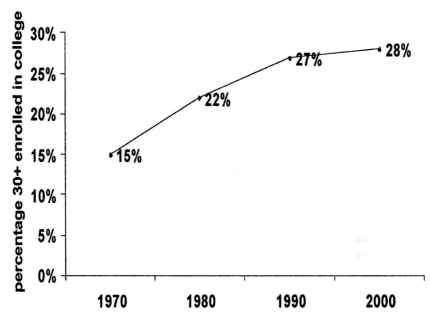

Figure 5.6.   Percentage of total fall enrollees in degree-granting institutions that are 30 years old and older, 1970–2000. (Sources: U.S. Department of Education, 2000; Gerald and Hussar, 2002.)

study by the American Association of University Women, 85 percent of women and 78 percent of men who return to college from full-time work cite personal enrichment as a very important motivating factor.[120] Many of these men and women are questioning the lockstep life course dictated by the career mystique. They have not found that their commitment to the workplace has yielded sufficient growth and enrichment. For those experiencing the threat or reality of downsizing, additional schooling can update their skills and credentials.

Second, family issues can play a large role in people's decisions to (re)-enter college. For example, as we saw in the last chapter, many women interrupt their careers when their children are born. As their children grow older, these women seek to reenter the workforce but frequently discover that their skills are out of date or that their prior career is now a poor fit and does not offer the flexibility they require, or that they can't reenter the rigid career track. Often these women reenter school to learn new skills so that they can be competitive in the job market.

A significant number of women postpone higher education because of the financial demands of living or parenting and instead move directly into paid work after high school. As their children grow older such women find themselves in a more financially secure position and with fewer child-care demands. They are finally in a position to pursue, often on a part-time basis, the college education they put off when they were younger.

There are other paths to school as well. Many women unexpectedly find themselves in the role of sole provider (either through divorce or through the disability or death of their spouse) for which they are ill-prepared. Restructuring due to mergers and "right" sizing of corporations means that growing numbers of men and women in their forties find themselves once again on the job market. In these instances, many attend college to develop or upgrade their skills and credentials.

The vast majority of older students are managing both paid work and unpaid family-care work obligations as well as school. Recognizing this changing demographic, institutions of higher education are beginning to develop programs that make it easier for nontraditional students to mesh these roles. A good example of such a structural lead—of institutions changing to meet new needs—is the recent and dramatic growth of distance-learning classes and programs. Distance-learning courses take place primarily or exclusively online so that students can view lectures and take tests at their convenience. In 2001 most public two-year (90%) and four-year (86%) institutions of higher education offered some form of distance education.[121] Even the most prestigious schools are embracing distance learning. Britain's Oxford University and the Harvard School of Public Health are two examples of schools that are developing online degree programs. Students of all ages find that the flexible class times associated with distance learning make it easier for them to combine school with family responsibilities.[122] Additionally, distance learning makes higher education available to people who are tied to geographic areas where educational opportunities are not otherwise available. Take, for example, Ruth, a recent divorcee with fifth-grade twins. Prior to her divorce, Ruth, a respondent in our study, did not work outside of the home. She is now struggling to support herself and her two children with a part-time job while she is enrolled in a distance-learning master's program in library science. A job in this field, she believes, will provide her with a living wage and a flexible schedule. Ruth only needs to be physically present in the classroom for one week each semester. For the rest of the semester, she corresponds with her professors and classmates by e-mail. She completes assignments and views lectures at her convenience. According to Ruth, without this distance-learning opportunity she would not have been able to manage work, home, and school.

Another popular option for men and women who return to school is attendance at community colleges, which are often geared toward working adults. Many classes are held in the evening and are designed to work around the busy schedules of those with multiple commitments. Additionally, community colleges are typically less expensive than four-year institutions.

Although on-the-job training has long been part of the organizational landscape, most employers have been slow to adapt to the rapidly expanding group of adult learners. Some of the more progressive corporations provide financial incentives for their employees to attend classes. A survey of women who received such financial support from their employers finds that 75 percent see these incentives as an important factor in their return to school. Other workplace supports that older students find beneficial are access to the workplace during evenings and weekends to study, flexible work hours during exam times, and support for study groups within the workplace.[123] Schooling is not only a means of obtaining job skills; it also contributes to people's reassessment of their established values and attitudes and moving their lives in new directions.[124]

Involuntary Job Change

Job insecurity is a stark reality in today's global information economy. Gone are the days when slavish devotion to the career mystique—hard work and commitment—were rewarded with job security and steady advancement. Once laid off, employees in their forties (or older) can find it difficult to get another job. According to David Opton, executive director of Exec-U-Net, a network of five thousand executives looking for leads on new jobs, "I often tell people who are between 40 and 45 and thinking of getting a new job to hurry, because the door closes at 45." Indeed, a 2002 study by the Economic Policy Institute finds that the long-term unemployed are most likely to be over forty-five, professional, and college educated.[125] Such employees who do find another job are often forced to take a substantial cut in pay. Mike B., age forty-six, was earning $130,000 as head of sales and marketing at a small firm. He was replaced by a twenty-eight-year-old. He was able to find another job, but it only paid him 40 percent of what his previous job did. Mike summarizes his dilemma: "Should I go out and retrain myself? Perhaps. But how can I? I am supporting two kids in school. I support my wife. You get caught between a rock and a hard place."[126]

The effects of losing one's job can be devastating. Richard Price and his colleagues report that job loss is associated with increased levels of depression, anxiety, feelings of incompetence, alcohol abuse, violent behavior, and even suicide attempts.[127] The longer one remains unemployed, the more severe the negative psychological effects.[128] In many cases the severity of the above symptoms depends on the degree of economic hardship that results from the job loss. For this reason, the effects of layoffs are often more severe among those who do not have a spouse who works for pay. Men and women in dual-earner couples have second incomes to fall back on when coping with job loss, dampening its negative effects.

The anger and alcohol abuse associated with job loss may translate into higher rates of spousal abuse, marital strife, and depression among wives of men who have lost their jobs.[129] Children also suffer when parents lose their jobs. Aside from the higher rates of depression, alcoholism, and aggression noted above, fathers who have lost their jobs are more punitive toward their children and focus more on their children's negative traits. Although men who are out of work report that they spend more time with their children after losing their jobs, the increased contact may have a negative effect. Children themselves are more likely to display higher levels of depression, more physical illness, and lower self-esteem when their fathers become unemployed. In addition, children of the unemployed are subject to the social stigma associated with a decrease in socioeconomic status, which may affect their relationships with their peers. Clearly, the effects of job loss can be far-reaching, touching the individuals who lose their jobs, as well as their spouses and children and even their children's social interactions.[130]

Families facing job loss in the United States have at best a meager safety net. Unemployment benefits are limited in terms of the amount and duration of benefits, and welfare supports are now predicated on paid work. Men and women who lose their jobs in their forties often have heavy financial burdens. Those who obtain new jobs often do so at a fraction of their previous pay. This is yet another way in which societal institutions have been slow to adjust to the changing needs of society.

BEYOND THE LOCKSTEP CAREER MYSTIQUE

The changing demography of the American workforce and the competitive global economy affects the needs, resources, and risks of contemporary workers in their forties, be they parents of school-age children or childless. There is considerable pressure on people in their forties to invest their time, energy, and commitment in their jobs, but the ladders they seek to climb are shaky indeed. Moreover, schools and medical services, as well as workplaces, continue to operate as if most households have someone to take care of the unpaid domestic work of life, including management of the household. As a result, many (especially women) suffer role overload as they try to work at demanding jobs with long hours and also manage a household with school-age children. Those in their forties who are childfree often put in even longer hours on the job and experience even greater demands, not having the excuse of children. Many forty-something men and women begin to question their lifestyles. Some embark upon a career change, seeking alternative ways to make life work. Others are forced into a career change due to downsizing and the changing economy of outsourcing, layoffs, buyouts, and early-retirement incentives. This is very different from the career trajectories of previous cohorts of white, middle-class men who typically remained in the same occupational career or with the same company for their entire work lives.

Schooling is another option. Adults are returning to school in record numbers. Institutions of higher education, in stiff competition for top students, have been one of the most responsive institutions to the changing workforce. Evening courses, distance-learning programs, and community colleges all cater to the needs of adults juggling paid work, unpaid family work, and school, helping many Americans in their thirties, forties, and beyond acquire new skills or even change occupational directions.

Workplaces have been less responsive than higher education to the historical shifts away from the lockstep life course. Employees juggling multiple goals and responsibilities in prime adulthood have little latitude in the hours they work in "regular" jobs (those offering benefits, for example). Actual ways to reduce hours, like job sharing, temp work, contract jobs, and part-time jobs, typically take workers (women) off the career paths that at least hold the promise of security and success. Most businesses still operate under the old assumption that loyalty and commitment can be measured by the amount of face time that employees put in on the job. In our study, many employees reported fearing that even asking to work less would signal low commitment. When women who are mothers do reduce their work hours, they often find themselves out of the mainstream, on something of a mommy track. As a result, women are underrepresented in high-level positions and earn less than their male counterparts. The advantages that accumulate for workers (typically men) who follow the lockstep template of continuous, long-hour work are mirrored in the disadvantages experienced by those who customize their career paths to make their lives, and the lives of their spouses and children, less frantic, as well as by those who find themselves unexpectedly downsized.[131]

Primary and secondary educational systems have also failed to adapt to the changing realities of working families, still assuming that someone is home to care for the family. Although many school systems provide important after-school programs for elementary school children, the options for middle school and junior high school students are almost nonexistent. As a result, millions of preteens and young teenagers are spending long afternoons in unsupervised settings. This situation is partially responsible for increased rates of juvenile crime and precocious sexual behavior. The problem is not that the mothers (or fathers) of these children are employed.

The problem is that contemporary societal institutions in the United States provide no viable options for these children.

The foregoing provides just a sampling of the ways in which policies, practices, and services lag behind the needs of contemporary Americans, reproducing gender divides at work and at home, rewarding for some the lockstep life course of the career mystique, but creating for many men and women a sense of overload and stress, along with insecurity, uncertainty, and ambiguity. Unpaid family-care work shapes women's, but not men's, lives, often accumulating disadvantages for women in terms of wages, job security, occupational attainment, pensions, and other benefits (such as health insurance). Gender scripts and schema around paid work and care work may be out of date, but they affect the career progression of almost all women, even those seeking to play by the rules of the (male) lockstep template of the career mystique and causes most men to invest their lives in their jobs. This is creating a situation where most workers—men and women—are exhausted and want to work less. We have come to the conclusion that what is necessary are flexible career paths—beyond the continuous, long-hour employment of the career mystique. Such flexible career paths could be *reasonable accommodations* to the needs of most working families at certain stages. They could permit renewal through schooling and sabbaticals and time for caring for children or other relations. Instituting more flexibility in work hours and in occupational careers could eliminate the artificial divides between jobs and family, paid and unpaid work, men and women—divides that continue to characterize adulthood in the United States.

6

Life Midcourse:
Are Retirement or Second
Acts Inevitable, Desirable,
or Even Possible?

According to the myth of lockstep careers, employees in their fifties and early sixties should not have to worry about their seniority and security. However, many people in our study face unexpected layoffs or forced early retirements just when they should be the most secure. Corporate mergers, downsizing, and outsourcing mean that many older employees work harder but feel less secure.

One fifty-something woman in our study makes this clear:

> At this time we are running a big project, and it's very demanding. However, there is a lot of uncertainty and strain at our company, and I can't be sure whether I'll even be there after a while.

Some reflect back on earlier paths taken and not taken, as is clear from another women's view:

> I had a family a lot later in life than I had anticipated. Work is definitely not turning out the way I had expected, but that is probably due to the fact that I did not know much about corporate America until I got into corporate America. Neither one [work or family] has turned out the way I expected.

Nancy (profiled below) says,

> I never thought I would be working full time because when we got married wives didn't. They worked part time or not at all.

Most older workers would probably agree that neither their work nor their personal lives have turned out the way they expected. And few can envision the shape the next phase of their lives will take. This is part of the growing disarray around the mystique of the lockstep life course. For example, it is not adulthood alone, at least in terms of financial independence, that is now delayed as young people stay in school longer, marry later, and remain economically dependent on their parents (often well beyond age eighteen). Just as the line separating youth from adulthood has blurred, so too has the line delineating old age. What do we mean by old? Aging baby boomers in their fifties can't envision being old at sixty, sixty-five, or seventy. People in their fifties, sixties, and seventies see themselves as (and are) younger than their parents and grandparents were at those ages. The fact is, growing numbers of older workers find themselves in a new life stage bridging the time between the early-career and family-building years, on the one hand, and the frailties we associate with old age, on the other. Just as adolescence became a way of extending childhood, this new *midcourse stage* extends prime adulthood. Social transformations are delaying middle adulthood, postponing poor health and creating a cadre of adults who imagine possibilities for "second acts," either in or along the way to retirement. Some baby boomers are not willing to go quietly into the ranks of seniors or the elderly. In this chapter we focus on this new stage, where Americans are in the process of shifting gears as their children leave home and job pressures or uncertainties escalate. Many are thinking about or actually retiring from their primary occupations; many are thinking about or actually moving into their second acts—second or third careers, possibly in the form of civic engagement.[1] They are part of the demographic, biological, and social transformations that are increasing the health, longevity, and number of older workers, who may have another thirty or more years of vital adulthood after they retire from their career jobs.

RETIREMENT IN FLUX

How did we get here? The whole notion of retirement from work is a relatively recent phenomenon. In earlier times and in other places, older people, as well as children, have been expected to work, to be productive members of society. Retirement became institutionalized in the United States with the Social Security Act of 1935 and with the pensions employers began to provide following World War II. Retirement has typically meant later-life withdrawal from the workforce, typically at sixty-five or sixty-two, often in conjunction with public and/or employer-provided pension benefits.[2] In fact, trends in government financial support in the later years of adulthood (Social Security and Medicare) and employer-provided pensions have been key in shaping the later adult life course, such that retirement has been institutionalized as an almost universal status passage for workers in the United States.[3] Retirement may be a relatively recent social invention, but it has become a key dimension of the lockstep life course. Today, Americans view childhood as a time of preparation and learning; many see later adulthood as a time of leisure, a second endless "childhood" of sorts, with no real responsibilities.

The fact that growing numbers of older Americans are or will soon be seeking second acts is creating a real challenge to individuals and institutions alike. In the 1950s, men worked full time until they could no longer do so—poor health or mandatory retirement meant a sharp exit from continuous employment to continuous leisure and old age. But policies and practices governing retirement are no longer so clear-cut. Even though the 1967 Age Discrimination in Employment Act eliminated mandatory retirement, most employees today retire from their career jobs well before age sixty-five, while others never retire.

Taken-for-granted expectations, Social Security benefits, and private pensions set retirement apart from unemployment as a job exit that can be planned for and anticipated.[4] By the 1950s, Americans came to see retirement, effectively, as the passage to old age. This American experience of retirement was a reality for generations of white-collar and unionized blue-collar men: a single, one-way exit, commonly at age sixty-five as a consequence of mandatory retirement policies, Social Security policies, and social norms. By the middle of the twentieth century, retirement had become a scripted and distinct stage in the clockwork of the lockstep life course. Retirement remains part of the lockstep career mystique, a clockwork regime of social and organizational policies and practices affecting the timing and expectations of later-life employment exits.

For older workers today, both their jobs and retirement have been upended. A global economy means that seniority no longer guarantees job security.[5] Mergers, downsizing, and offshore outsourcing make career prospects and retirement possibilities increasingly uncertain.[6] Shifting policies (such as prohibiting mandatory retirement, outlawing age discrimination, and delaying Social Security eligibility) add to workers' sense of ambiguity and ambivalence about retirement.[7] Concerns about financial security and health care complicate retirement plans even further. Many corporations are trimming or eliminating retiree health insurance and pensions. There is a common perception (whether or not it is a real possibility) that Social Security no longer provides a reliable safety net.

Today retirement from one's career job no longer means a final exit from the workforce, as many people take on postretirement jobs. In fact, we see two twin trends: Many employees retire from their career jobs early, while the age at which employees actually make a final exit from the workforce seems to be increasing.[8]

The result is tremendous variation in the age at which people retire and growing uncertainty and insecurity regarding retirement, jobs, income, and health care.[9] At such times of social change, when old patterns don't fit and new patterns aren't on the horizon, people strategize[10] on their own—customizing, where possible, their own retirements and second acts.

Economists and sociologists are documenting the fuzziness of contemporary retirement.[11] Many older workers want, and some find, "bridge" jobs, either scaled-back versions of their career jobs or else some new line of work. Jim (profiled below) retired early but took on two bridge jobs.

PROFILE: JIM AND NANCY

Jim and Nancy are both fifty-eight, born in 1946, and were raised under conditions of poverty. Following the Great Depression, their parents struggled to meet their family's economic needs. Jim and Nancy met in high school, marrying after graduation. Neither had money for college, so they both found jobs right away. Jim worked in a manufacturing warehouse. Nancy worked in a hospital as a nurse's assistant.

Like so many couples they knew, in their mid-twenties they had the first of three children. Given their relatively impoverished childhoods, they placed a high priority on economic security. Unlike many women in this time before the rebirth of feminism, Nancy continued to work part time after her children were born. They wanted enough money to support their family comfortably and to save for college and retirement. Nancy worked a rotating shift in the evenings and on weekends. Jim took care of the children while Nancy worked, and Nancy cared for the children during the day when Jim was at work. This arrangement was difficult, but fit with their economic and family values. Nancy felt guilty about missing baseball games and other family events, but both felt her employment was necessary for their economic well-being.

When their youngest child entered high school, Nancy took a full-time, regular-hour job, which also offered her a promotion. Jim, in the meantime, had also moved up the career ladder, having been promoted to foreman. Jim's job became more and more stressful as the company grew and business got more competitive. He frequently worked sixty hours a week and was constantly feeling stressed.

All three of Jim and Nancy's children went to college. Like their parents, they were bright and hardworking. Each had earned an academic scholarship, so much of the money saved for college was converted into retirement savings.

When Jim was fifty-four his company introduced an early-retirement plan. Jim had never even considered early retirement, but the package was attractive. His financial advisor determined that they could *both* afford to retire. After much waffling, Jim accepted the early-retirement offer.

Nancy enjoyed her work and had no interest in retiring, but she wanted once again to work only twenty hours a week. She stayed full time, however, to keep building her retirement benefits.

After two months of retirement, Jim felt bored. Suddenly, he was home alone with nothing to do but household chores. He found a part-time job a few blocks from his house washing rental cars. The next month he took a second part-time job driving a delivery truck. He now works thirty hours a week and is happy with his jobs, saying they are low stress and fun. He swims at a gym two mornings a week and spends time with his grandchildren. Nancy would like to retire in her early sixties and then volunteer more at her church and take guitar lessons. Both hope that they can travel. Even though their financial advisor says to spend money, they continue to save money each month.

This new phase of life offers real opportunities for second acts. For many it can be a time of personal growth and renewal. For someone like Jim it can be a time of cutting back and reducing stress. But the existing clockwork of health insurance, pensions, Social Security, and early buyouts, along with the lockstep career myth, make second acts difficult to achieve. Older workers are on their own in trying to figure out their next steps. Jobs remain structured for those willing to work full time (or more) for the full year on a continuous basis, meaning that many employees, like Nancy, do not have the option of scaling back without incurring penalties.

Birthdays at age sixty, sixty-two, or sixty-five still come with the labels of "senior," "elder," "old," or "over the hill." But baby boomers will not, we predict, accept conventional notions about retirement, much less the stereotypes of age. In 2004 Tina Turner turned sixty-five. Will Mick Jagger or Cher ever be "senior" citizens?

THE CHANGING BIOGRAPHICAL LANDSCAPE

For most adults, paid work is a major, if not their principal, source of purposive activity, social relations, independence, identity, and self-respect. Being employed is the way Americans become connected and acknowledged as adult members of the larger community. Employment is virtually isomorphic with contemporary notions of productivity and achievement. But as their children leave home and their options at work narrow or dry up altogether, we find many older employees beginning to reassess their lives. One man we interviewed captures this shift:

> I think that, in terms of time, but maybe even more importantly than time, in terms of energy, and what I thought about, and what drove me on a week-to-week, year-to-year basis, was all workplace issues. And now I tend to think a lot less about that.

However, short of retirement, older workers find that the lockstep career mystique offers them few next-step options. This man goes on to say, "I don't feel that my job offers me a lot of choice, in that there are things that need to be done, there's no choice whatsoever about them."

Without doubt, Americans will spend an increasing proportion of their lives in retirement. Most older workers still go from full-time, continuous employment to full-time, continuous leisure, with few alternative pathways (such as phased retirement in the form of part-time or part-year jobs) and little assistance in developing life plans for the next several decades of their lives. And yet retirement as perpetual leisure can be what scholars call a roleless role, with some rights but little responsibility, recognition, or relevance. With increasing longevity, many people will be retired from their primary career jobs for a longer period than they spend in those jobs.

A whole industry has developed around vocational counseling and career development; but with retirement, the focus has been on financial, not lifestyle planning. Jim, while financially able to retire, was completely unprepared for this major transition:

> It came too quick. I mean I was fifty-four when I retired. I never paid attention to retirement. I just mean all of a sudden they offered this package. I figured it wasn't going to get any better so I might as well grab it and get out. I figured I was going to work at least another five years, if not seven. But then they came out with this package so I had less than a month to think about it. Right up to the last minute at 5 o'clock, to the last day, she [Nancy] called me about 4:30 and wanted to know what I decided because we still could have called personnel and canceled it. She called me at 4:30 because I still wasn't really definitely sure because I hadn't prepared myself for it. . . . I always look

at retirement as the last big decision to make or second to the last big decision of your life, the other one is death. That is it.

Life midcourse is limited by the myths about and policies shaping the clockwork of both careers and retirement. Neither the career regime nor the retirement regime has kept pace with demographic realities. This life stage also reflects personal biographies, the culmination of earlier choices, constraints, and chance encounters in schooling, work, and personal relationships. Some in their fifties, sixties, and seventies who have followed the career mystique are now reaping the advantages promised by the American Dream, rewarded for a lifetime of hard work or good luck with high earnings, health care, status, and challenging opportunities. Many men (with the support of homemaking wives) have been especially advantaged, reaping the rewards of the conventional lockstep clockwork in the expansive economy of the 1950s and 1960s. Others are reaping accumulated *disadvantages*; careers of intermittent, part-time, or temporary jobs produce little by way of pensions, savings, health insurance, or security.

PROFILE: DEB AND STEVE

Deb and Steve are just beginning their midcourse years. At fifty and fifty-one they have lived a fairly conventional lifestyle. They were high school sweethearts who managed to remain together even though they went to separate colleges. Deb earned a degree in business and Steve earned one in political science. After graduation, Deb began work as an accountant in a small business, and Steve went on to law school. During his last year of law school, Deb and Steve were married.

After marriage they settled into "good" jobs. Steve got a job in a prestigious law firm, and Deb worked for a small mortgage company. Five years later, their first child was born. Deb, strongly influenced by the Women's Movement and the promise of gender equality, was committed to staying in the workforce after childbirth. So, after a two-month maternity leave she returned to her full-time job. Steve's hours at the law firm were long; he was rarely home before 6:30 P.M. Deb, who was responsible for most of the household management and housework, received little help at home. She found it difficult to manage her work and home life and wanted to spend

(continued)

more time with her daughter. She asked her employer if she could reduce her hours and leave work each day at 3:00 P.M. rather than at 5:00 P.M. When her manager turned down her request, Deb left her job and became a full-time homemaker. Soon afterward, she became pregnant with their second child.

Steve excelled at his job and was eventually lured away from his law firm to serve as counsel for a major corporation. He continued to work long hours and traveled frequently. Deb became active in the community, volunteering at her children's schools and also in local clubs and organizations. They were a close family and whenever possible the entire family would travel with Steve on his business trips.

When their children reached middle school, Deb decided that she wanted some outside stimulation, so she took a minimum-wage job working for an upscale department store near her home. She wanted a job that could work with Steve's and her children's schedules. The department store gave her this type of flexibility. She only remained in this position for three years, however. Once the children were in their teens, Steve dug in harder at work. He shifted his hours from forty-five to fifty-five hours a week. He felt there was less need for him at home and his job was greedy for his time.

Their youngest child, Scott, was very active in high school athletics and played on the football, basketball, and soccer teams. Deb and Steve were both avid sports fans and found their weekends and many of their evenings filled with high school sporting events. Deb became the president of the high school booster club and Steve volunteered when he could. They also socialized extensively with the other parents on Scott's sports teams.

When their youngest child graduated from high school, Deb found that she had an enormous amount of time on her hands. She had been out of the professional workforce for twenty years, and her skills were sorely out of date. After four months of unsuccessful job hunting, Deb decided to go back to school and start a new career. At the time of our interview, Deb was in her second year of a master's program in social work.

Steve met with great success in his career. He eventually worked his way up to president of his corporation. After his children graduated, he decided to put in fewer hours, going from seventy to fifty hours a week. Since his children left home Steve has taken up cycling. Recently, he convinced Deb to begin cycling also. Now, on weekends Deb and Steve often pack up their bikes and travel to remote regions for relaxation and exercise.

For parents such as Steve and Deb (see profile), midcourse represents a time of shifting gears, especially from active parenting as their children grow up and leave home. Popular stereotypes of this empty-nest transition define it as stressful, but research shows little negative and, in fact, many positive outcomes for parents as their children move into adulthood.[12] Indeed, although both Steve and Deb were concerned about how they would adapt when their children left home, they have each developed new interests and friends in this new stage of their lives and are renewing their relationship. Steve has become a competitive bicycler, and Deb is embarking on her second act by developing a new career.

For many of the people we interviewed in their early fifties, the cost of their children's college education is a source of stress. Prior family decisions can have long-term implications for the midcourse years. For instance, those who postpone having children until their forties worry about the costs of college tuition at a time when their same-age coworkers are thinking about retirement.

We find that for many, the midcourse years can be a time of changing values and reordering priorities about work, family, and personal relationships. A study of British and French male executives finds that during the thirties and forties the primary focus of their lives shifts from their jobs to their children.[13] By their fifties they may also experience another shift away from children to their partners. Steve (profile above) reports that since his children have left home, he and Deb do more together and are closer. Joy Pixley and Elaine Wethington also find in their research a tendency for employees at midlife to cut back on their career commitments.[14] Figure 6.1, presenting nationally representative data on working Americans, shows that, indeed, older workers tend to reduce their hours.

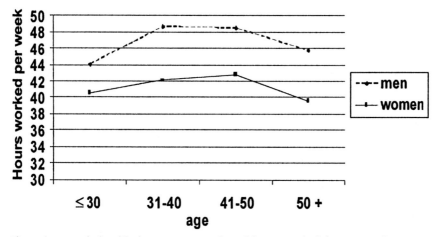

Figure 6.1. Relationship between age and total hours worked for men and women. (Source: Data from the National Study of the Changing Workforce, 1997.)

Rather than formally going part time, however, many scale back closer to a forty-hour workweek, which is Steve's goal. Among dual-earner professional couples we see a slightly different picture. Using data from the *Ecology of Careers Study*, we find that women are more likely to increase their hours when they are in their fifties. Such women include people like Deb, who either drastically reduced their work hours or left the workforce when their children were at home and recommit themselves to their work in their fifties as part of their second acts.

Older workers without children or whose children are grown often consider next steps, deciding to remain in their current jobs or thinking about retirement and possible second acts either in paid jobs or unpaid community service. Women who put their occupational goals on hold while raising children often invest more fully in their jobs.[15] Nancy waited until her children were in high school before taking a full-time regular job. Now that Deb's children have left home, she is starting a whole new career, energized by the prospects: "I want to be able to support myself; I want a career. I have at least fifteen years to work." By contrast, Jim moved from what he saw as a career as a foreman to what he describes as a job, doing part-time work.

Sociologists often explain social change by using the concept of cohort replacement: As new groups of individuals move through life, they challenge obsolete, taken-for-granted roles, rules, and relationships. Today, the baby boom cohort is growing older as conventional conceptions of jobs, career paths, retirement, and gender are in flux. As a result, they are constructing their own second acts, making their midcourse years up as they go along.

THE CHANGING SOCIAL LANDSCAPE

According to the career mystique, retirement should be a time for enjoying the fulfillment of the American Dream, the golden years. In real life, the years before and after retirement are increasingly times of variability. Some in their fifties and sixties have children in college and are putting in long hours on the job to manage tuition costs. Some are back in college themselves, taking courses for fun or to learn a new occupation. Others are watching as their adult children begin the bumpy launching of their own careers, marriages, and families. Still others are helping to raise their grandchildren. Some have young children of their own, having started parenthood late or a second family later in life. Some are already into their second acts of new paid or unpaid work; others are counting the days to a long-anticipated retirement from a stressful job. Being fifty, sixty, or even seventy is far different in the twenty-first century than in the 1930s, the 1950s, or even the 1970s. Then sixty-something was considered old. Today retirement is no longer the gateway to old age.

Americans in their fifties, sixties, and seventies come in all shapes and sizes and from all kinds of ethnic, racial, religious, occupational, and educational backgrounds. Some must shift gears because their jobs disappear; others want to scale back work hours and job commitments. Still others, often women, feel they are just getting started. But all Americans in this new life stage have one thing in common; they have no blueprint for the future. The career mystique and the retirement mystique are clearly at odds with the real lives, capabilities, and desires of this growing segment of the population in twenty-first-century America. Baby boomers moving toward their sixties, along with members of the pre–baby boom generation just before them, are typically healthy, educated, energetic, and young in every sense of that word. Most want to do meaningful work, paid or unpaid, but do not want to put in the long hours or put up with the inflexible demands of their present jobs. The growing numbers of Americans fitting into neither the lockstep career box nor the lockstep retirement box present a real challenge to existing policies and practices fashioned for a bygone era.[16]

The graying of the U.S. workforce reflects advances in longevity (life expectancy has increased), reductions in fertility (women are having fewer children), and the aging of the post–World War II baby boom generation (born 1946–1964). The median age today in the United States is 35.3.[17] This means that half of the population is now over thirty-five. Demographers project that the median age will peak at 39.1 in 2035 and then remain fairly constant. Seventy-five million Americans are now in their fifties or older, a number that will only increase over the coming decades.[18] But America is still a comparatively young country. The aging trend is even more striking in other countries (due to remarkably low fertility rates). The median age in Japan is 41.2 and is projected to rise to 49.0 by 2050. It is almost that high in Italy, which projects a median age of 53.2 by 2050. Globally, the number of people over sixty is expected to triple by 2050, and the number of those over eighty is expected to rise fivefold.[19]

This changing age distribution calls into question the meaning of aging and the period defined as old. The leading edge of the baby boomers (born 1946–1957) begins turning sixty in 2006. Conventional arrangements—continuous long-hour employment in prime adulthood followed by the continuous permanent leisure of retirement and old age —is simply out of step with contemporary reality.

Gendered and Diverse Retirements

This is the first American generation in which large numbers of women are experiencing retirement. It is also the first in which many American couples are facing two retirements, his and hers. Women may make up almost half the workforce, but they typically come to retirement with checkered work histories. As we have seen throughout this volume, most American women follow Yogi Berra's advice; they take two forks in the road—trying to pursue both the career mystique and, if not the feminine mystique, at least the "good mother" mystique.[20] Many find doing both is difficult, if not impossible. Many manage by scaling back, having fewer (or no) children, having them later in life, or postponing occupational goals.[21] Thus, women are unlikely to have followed the expected lockstep path; few worked continuously on a full-time basis throughout most of their adulthood (take, for example, Nancy and Deb).

This matters, because continuous, full-time employment is the backbone of private and public pension programs, as well as health insurance systems. Common scaling-back work strategies—part-time jobs, contract and temporary work, moving in and out of the workforce—mean that many women are off track as far as Social Security and pensions are concerned, making them especially vulnerable financially as they age. (Deb, who was out of the workforce for twenty years, is completely dependent on her husband's retirement income.) Because divorced women are less likely to remarry than divorced men and because statistically women live longer than men, older women are more apt to be or become single, further increasing their financial vulnerability. At age thirty-nine, Lisa (see profile in chapter 1), for example, has little retirement savings and has accrued only six years of full-time work toward earning Social Security benefits.

Men with few skills, immigrants, and minorities who have been discriminated against often find themselves in the same predicament as most women: They are unable to follow the full-time, continuous, lockstep career regime to retirement. Consequently, those whose lives fall outside the career mystique come to retirement with little or no private pension coverage, low Social Security benefits, and uncertain or even no health insurance.[22] Some find they are not eligible (not having put in the requisite years of continuous full-time employment) for lucrative buyout packages available to other coworkers. With little savings and few benefits, many feel they can't afford to retire. The financial costs of putting family first are especially pronounced for divorced and single women who lack the cushion of a spouse's pension. Additional long-term costs kick in for married women when they become widowed. Much to many new widows' surprise, pension and Social Security checks (based on couples' income needs) can shrink dramatically once their husbands pass away. In this way, gendered and unequal (by race, class, and education level) life scripts and options produce distinctive life-course patterns for older men and women, often reproducing earlier inequalities once more in later adulthood.

Families in Flux

People in the United States are and will be spending an increasing proportion of their lives unmarried. Increases in longevity, divorce, widowhood, the postponement of marriage and remarriage, and choices to remain single all mean that a growing portion of older Americans live alone. Locate this demographic trend within another reality—the fact that scholars find marriage a source of both social support and economic security,[23] conducive to health and well-being. This raises a number of questions yet to be answered by research. What kinds of relationships can provide those on their own in later adulthood with the same kinds of supports that marriage has typically provided? What are the effects on occupational careers and life quality of spending a significant portion of one's life course in, or out of, marriage? How does the timing of becoming single (whether from divorce or widowhood) or remarriage affect life midcourse?[24]

Older Americans can also expect to overlap more years with their children as adults. Older workers are often adult children themselves, having to care for their aging parents. Some are also older parents, starting their own families later in life. In this way, most Americans are spending increasing proportions of their lives in three-, four-, and even five-generation families. There is a concept in sociology called "the strength of weak ties." Some relationships with adult children, siblings, and even distant or fictive kin (such as cousins, great aunts, family-like friends, former sons- or daughters-in-law) will be activated and reactivated as family circumstances and needs change or as individuals make geographical moves. Matilda White Riley and John Riley call this form of kinship structure a "latent web of continually shifting linkages."[25] Older workers and young retirees often find themselves enmeshed within a rich network of kin, both near and far, including adult children and grandchildren, with all the stresses, joys, responsibilities, and resources such ties entail. Neither the career mystique nor the retirement mystique prepares people for the care they will provide to aging and infirm relatives, much less for the possibility that they themselves may someday need such support.

SHIFTING CARE WORK

The same medical advances promoting more years of health and vitality also increase the likelihood that midcourse Americans have older relatives who currently (or will eventually) require their care. The reality of aging parents, aunts, uncles, brothers, sisters, and even spouses means that many people in their fifties, sixties, and seventies suddenly find themselves responsible for ailing loved ones. It is estimated that 80 to 90 percent of medical care is provided informally by family members, especially wives, daughters, and daughters-in-law.[26] Roughly 7 to 12 percent of the American workforce has current adult caregiving responsibilities.[27] Many must argue with infirm kin about their driving abilities, negotiate with them about housing options and realities, and deal with health care providers, often from long distances.

Still others want to be there for their loved ones when they are ill. The following quote from a fifty-two-year-old female executive in the *Ecology of Careers Study* illustrates the difficult choices that employees today must make and the consequences of those decisions:

> I'm thinking of one thing that's really depressing, so I hope I won't depress you too much, but you asked me if there was anything I regretted in terms of work–family balances or decisions I made. I have one decision that I made that was a really bad one. . . . But it is certainly something that comes into the regret category. And that is that I made the decision that I needed to be here in [a city in upstate New York] doing work while my mother was having open-heart surgery, under the premise that I would be able to pick her up after her surgery and bring her back to [city in upstate New York] and help her get better. And she died after the surgery, and I did not make it to see her alive.

The grim reality is that most older workers are either caring for an aging or infirm family member or expect to do so at some point in the future. Women are the most apt to provide this care.[28]

Nancy's father, for example, has Alzheimer's disease. Nancy's mother, age eighty-one, still cares for him, but Nancy takes him for one day a week to give her mother some respite. She also helps her mother with household tasks and decisions.

Caregiving takes a toll on older workers, producing heightened levels of work–family conflict, lower work performance, and absenteeism, particularly among women.[29] Caring for relatives with dementia often means health problems for workers themselves, higher levels of stress hormones in their bloodstream (which can lead to hypertension and diabetes), and lower levels of antibody production (which can lead to decreased immune functioning).[30]

Growing numbers of older Americans also care for their grandchildren. Between 1970 and 1998, the percent of children living in the homes of their grandparents almost doubled.[31] In 2002, 8 percent of all children in the United States were living in a household with a grandparent present. In most cases the child lives with the grandparents, and in almost half of these cases no parent is present.[32] How to facilitate employees' ability to care for grandchildren as well as aging family members is an important policy consideration, broadening the need for flexibility and reduced hours beyond simply the challenges of working parents, and further erasing the imaginary divide between work lives and personal lives.

Older women workers with caregiving responsibilities often resort to the same strategies they used when their children were young, such as using flex time, taking longer lunch hours or scaling back their work hours.[33] Women in blue-collar and service professions often can't adjust their work schedules and may be forced to take unpaid time off from work for elder care.[34] These strategies are not unique to American women; in both Japan and Australia women who engage in elder care are also apt to reduce their hours at work.[35]

SHIFTING OCCUPATIONAL GEARS

Social researchers are coming to see retirement as a *process*, possibly involving a number of transitions into and out of paid and unpaid work.[36] It is now a longer and fuzzier transition as retirees from primary career jobs, like Jim, increasingly take up second or third careers, often part year or part time. One seventy-year-old retiree, rehired by his former employer as a contract worker, told us he has difficulty filling out company forms, not knowing whether to put down "retiree" or "electrician." Steve plans to follow a similar course; when he retires he wants to be a part-time consultant with his company. The boundary separating retirement from employment is now less clear-cut, and retirement from a primary career job is no longer fixed at any set age. Older Americans find themselves in a quandary: The social regulation of retirement has weakened at the very same time that unprecedented numbers of women as well as men are retiring. Just as baby boomers approach retirement, previously taken-for-granted pensions and health insurance are now both less certain and less secure.[37]

The mystique of a lockstep life course—full-time schooling followed by full-time paid work, culminating in full-time leisure—is at odds with the shifting realities of a graying workforce and a growing "retired" force. For example, medical advancements have extended the average length of life to an impressive degree, but public- and private-sector retirement policies encourage workers to leave the labor force at progressively earlier ages. Most American employees in their fifties and sixties want to work less, not to stop working altogether. But we find those wishing to scale back typically have but two options: to keep working full time across the full year at their jobs or to retire altogether. This reflects a regime of outdated policies and practices built on the obsolete lockstep mystique. Very few businesses offer the possibility of phasing down to fewer hours a week or fewer weeks a year. Jim is an example of the two-option scenario: to retire or to continue in his full-time job. He was not ready for retirement, but he *was* ready to reduce his time commitment to work. Nancy also wanted to reduce her hours after Jim retired, but she faced serious financial consequences associated with moving into part-time work as a way of phasing into retirement:

> As I understand it, if you retire from Vantech, your retirement is based on the last five years that you worked. So, if you cut down to part time in the last two years, it could diminish the amount of retirement income that you would make, which makes me kind of angry.

For Nancy, working part time before retirement would substantially reduce her retirement income.

Moving to a different part-time job is often not an option either, given that such jobs remain on the edge of the labor market, lacking health insurance and other benefits at a time when health insurance is especially valued (given that midcourse workers under sixty-five are not eligible for Medicare and have to rely on their employers for health coverage). If Nancy went to part-time work, she and Jim would be without health insurance coverage; thus, it does not pay for Nancy to reduce her hours. Still, American workers are increasingly exiting their full-time career jobs at progressively earlier ages, wanting, but not always finding, a second career that is part time or part year.[38]

One reason for the decreasing age of retirement is that pension incentives have promoted progressively earlier retirements (see figure 6.2).[39] In

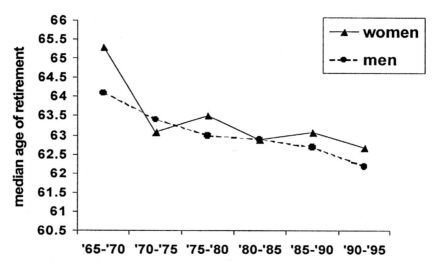

Figure 6.2.   Median age of retirement for men and women in the United States, 1965–1970 to 1990–1995. (Source: Gendell 1998.)

1950 almost half (45.8%) of men aged sixty-five and over were in the workforce; by 2000 this number had dropped to 17.5 percent. In 1950 almost all (86.9%) men aged fifty-five to sixty-four were in the workforce; by 2000, only about two thirds (67.3%) of men in this age group were in the workforce, a decrease of almost 20 percent (see figure 6.3).[40] Corporate policies increasingly phase out people like Jim and Steve in their fifties by encouraging early retirement. Steve says he plans to retire in his early sixties because

> When I retire the company has ten years to pay out my stock. I want to be alive and enjoying my health when they pay me. I would never retire when I am seventy because I wouldn't see the stock come to me and get a chance to use it.

But Social Security is now phasing in incentives for workers to retire at progressively later ages.[41] Economists Joseph Quinn and Richard Burkhauser predict that these changes may reverse the trend of a decreasing age of retirement.[42] Moreover, even workers who bought into the career mystique, working hard, often more than full time throughout their adult years, now find they can no longer rely on the promise of future

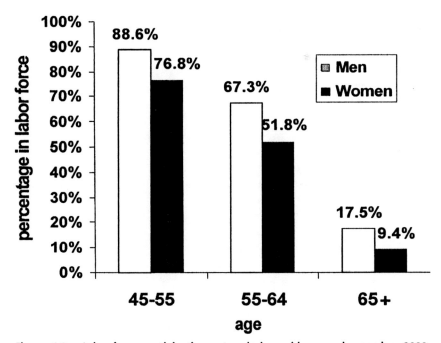

Figure 6.3. Labor-force participation rates during midcourse, by gender, 2000. (Source: U.S. Census Bureau, *2001 Statistical Abstract of the United States*, no. 568.)

financial and health care security. With the fall of the stock market and the corporate scandals of the early 2000s, even workers with "good" jobs worry about the viability of their employers' retirement plans and are increasingly distrustful that their employers are looking out for their retirement interests.[43] These concerns are grounded in reality; employers have been slowly restructuring the nature of retirement benefits in ways that can lead to economic or health care insecurity for retirees. In 1975, 68 percent of all workers eligible for retirement benefits were enrolled in defined-benefit retirement plans, guaranteeing retirees a fixed pension, depending on their length of service and salary (again rewarding the lockstep path). Only 13 percent of eligible employees in 1975 were enrolled in a contribution plan such as a 401(k).[44] By 2000, this had reversed. Only 22 percent of employees in private industry with retirement benefits were enrolled in a defined-benefit plan, while fully 44 percent were covered by a contribution plan.[45] Such plans depend heavily upon the vagaries of the economy and on the size of employee contributions, meaning that in times of economic downturn, retirees are vulnerable. Nancy and Jim are among the lucky ones: Both have defined-benefit plans and both invested in 401(k)'s. Future generations will not be so lucky.

Because Social Security benefits are based on average earnings during most of a worker's adult years, being out of the workforce is costly. For example, economists predict that the Social Security retirement incomes of single-parent women who relied moderately or heavily on welfare will put them at 30 to 74 percent below the poverty level.[46] These low-income women are unlikely to have saved for retirement or to have worked for employers providing pensions, leaving them in an extremely precarious position.

Leading life-course scholar Glen Elder maintains that understanding any transition (such as retirement) requires placing it in the larger contexts of both current circumstances and other life pathways.[47] Renowned developmental psychologist Urie Bronfenbrenner also points out that the way people view themselves and their circumstances depends both on the characteristics of the person and features of the environment, as well as the processes that shape and bind the two over time.[48] Research, including our own *Ecology of Careers Study*, shows how earlier experiences shape subsequent retirement transitions. For example, following the career mystique by remaining in the workforce full time throughout adulthood affects whether employees can even afford to retire. Whether jobs are demanding, boring, physically taxing, or challenging also affects employees' desire to do so.[49]

Individuals located in different social ecologies experience the midcourse years in disparate ways and view retirement from different vantage points. For example, Steve is at the top of his career and his profession. He wants to continue working into his sixties, but he also wants to slowly decrease his hours. Because he is president of the company, he believes that he will have that kind of flexibility. Deb, at fifty, is just beginning to think about starting her new career and is far from preparing for retirement. Jim, who is fifty-five, has already retired from his main job, but expects to keep working at his two part-time jobs for several years. Nancy, also fifty-five, expects to retire at around sixty, but she too wants either to work part time or to volunteer for her church.

We find that people of different ages view retirement in different ways. Michael (see profile in chapter 1) is still in his twenties and has just joined the army. Although he has thought very little about and has saved no money toward retirement, he recognizes the value of the army's retirement benefits. When asked whether the army's retirement benefits influenced his decision to join the military, Michael responds,

> No, I don't think about it so much as everyone keeps bringing it up to me [army retirement benefits]. "Yeah, you got to retire from the military. It's a good thing to do." And I just say, "Yeah, I know it's a good thing to do." I've kind of made a habit of not thinking too far into the future about that kind of stuff. I do now and again. But, I don't plan my life around it right now because it's just so far away.

Lisa, a single mother (see profile in chapter 1), has done virtually no planning for retirement. Lynn and Harold (see profile in chapter 5), both working full time with teenaged children, are both highly committed to their jobs, working long hours. They agree that Harold's job has priority. Lynn, at forty-seven, is 90 percent certain she'll keep her job until she retires (although she doesn't know when that will be). By contrast, Harold, at forty-nine, is less certain of keeping his job and is pretty sure he will not be in this job until retirement (for him, expected to be at age sixty). Even though Lynn likes her job a lot, feels very successful at it, and isn't sure when exactly she'll retire, she has already done considerable planning for retirement. Harold is planning for retirement as well, but less than Lynn.

HIS AND HER RETIREMENTS

Americans typically think of retirement in terms of men's lives, although its effects clearly ripple across family relationships.[50] But almost half the contemporary workforce is now female. Most older workers today are married to other workers. For the first time in history, most people are making plans around *two* retirements: his and hers. Retirement is increasingly a *couple's* transition; contemporary husbands and wives must strategize about and synchronize two career paths, two retirements, and

two lives after retirement.[51] Women in particular are likely to tie their retirements to their husbands', whereas men rarely base their retirement
plans on their wives' plans.[52] Deb, for example, believes that she and her
husband will retire together, although she has not put any thought as to
when that will be. Steve, on the other hand, did not mention Deb's work
status when he discussed his reasons for wanting to retire at sixty-two. Although some couples are making conscious choices about retirement timing and whether or not to retire together, few think much about the ten,
twenty, or even thirty, years of life—and marriage—once they leave their
career jobs.[53]

Retirement for one or both spouses can be a major family transition.[54] It
can crystallize latent discrepancies in couples' views and expectations of
their work, their marriage, their division of housework, and their future.
For example, both husbands and wives typically expect husbands to
spend more time on domestic chores following his retirement, which may
or may not come to pass.[55] Husbands' increasing presence at home can
impinge on wives' routines. Nancy describes her ideal retirement in terms
of her *husband's* employment:

> Part of my ideal retirement situation is for him to keep working a couple of
> days a week. Just because I do enjoy having just some quiet time to read or
> meditate or whatever. Go along to lunch with a friend without thinking, oh,
> that he would have me do something different. So, I would hope I would
> have time for my own choice of things.

For herself she says,

> Mostly the ideal is to have the flexibility to kind of go with what today feels
> like. Not to have to always be someplace. I wouldn't sit and do nothing. I
> want to have options, and not be tied to a schedule all the time.

There are often discrepancies in couples' actual or desired retirement
timing. For example, we find that some wives in their fifties are enjoying
their jobs, just starting new lives once their children have left home. Simultaneously, many of their husbands are counting the months until retirement. This is true for both Deb and Nancy. Deb will be starting her second act just as Steve thinks about winding down his career. Nancy is
enjoying her professional identity while her (retired) husband sees his
part-time jobs as diversions. Both Deb and Nancy started their career jobs
later in life and are not yet ready to give them up.

A large body of research documents the importance of homophily (similarity between two individuals) for marital quality. Spouses with similar
religions, values, ages, and education levels report higher satisfaction in
their marriages than those who differ in these areas.[56] We find that simi-

lar timing in retirement also affects marital quality. Couples who retire at about the same time report less marital conflict than when one spouse retires and the other continues in the career job.[57] Some spouses may not technically have retired, but may be out of the labor force for other reasons, as is the case of homemaking wives who have never worked for pay or others who leave employment because of disability or a layoff.

Our research shows that the actual transition to retirement increases the amount of marital conflict reported by both husbands and wives, with the most conflict and the lowest marital satisfaction reported by retired men and women married to someone who is not yet retired.[58] This is the situation that Jim found himself in. He did not like being home alone with little to do while his wife worked. He solved this dilemma by returning to the workforce.

We also find that, in the long run, retirement can be good for couples. Those who have been retired for more than two years report better marital quality compared to couples still in their career jobs.[59] There is also evidence that following retirement there can be more equality between men and women in the sharing of household tasks and in decision making.[60] Consistent with this, Nancy reports that Jim now does most of the cooking and more of the household chores than he did prior to retirement.

SUCCESSFUL AGING

Scholars have proposed several theories for promoting health and a sense of well-being in the later adult years. One is the notion that aging successfully is a consequence of continuity[61] in behavior and relationships.[62] This theory emphasizes the importance of ongoing activity. People need to maintain relationships that are important to them as they ease out of one role and into another. Successful aging means remaining active, replacing the time spent in former roles with other similarly purposeful activities. Jim maintained his activity level and his sense of accomplishment by engaging in new jobs. Deb and Steve replaced the time they spent with their children with cycling and they have formed new relationships with people in a cycling club. Such activities have been shown to promote a successful life after retirement.

The obverse of continuity theory points to the importance of disengagement, of shifting down from the demands of prime adulthood by scaling back from demanding social relationships and role obligations.[63] Jim scaled back from his high-stress job to low-stress retirement work:

> My part-time jobs are "no-brainers." At the rental car agency, I wash the cars. No responsibility. At the florist, I'm driving a van. You meet a lot of nice people.

I like that. Again, it's a "no-brainer." It doesn't take any intelligence at all to do it. No responsibility. I figure if I am going to be retired, I don't need that or I would have stayed at Utilco where I had people working for me as a foreman. I had up to twenty people working for me at one time. I don't have their problems now. If I don't like what I am doing or I don't want to do it, I can walk out at the end of the shift or whenever I want.

A variant of both continuity and disengagement approaches to successful aging is *social selectivity theory*,[64] whereby individuals selectively retain some relationships while forgoing others. Once Steve and Deb's children graduated from high school, they lost contact with most of the other parents that they socialized with at high school sporting events. However, they have held onto a few of these key relationships and have even gotten one of the couples involved in cycling. Both Steve and Deb and Jim and Nancy remain engaged with their adult children.

Still another theory of successful aging suggests the significance not of activity alone but of social integration and productive engagement, that is, doing meaningful work (whether paid or unpaid) that sustains a sense of contribution and connectedness.[65] This may be achieved through volunteer work, paid work, or helping family members and friends. Steve talks about the need for continued productive engagement:

When you get older what becomes more important is helping younger people and passing along what you know and less of "where do I want to get?" I'm doing much more volunteer work than I have ever done. It's more rewarding for me to help them because I am helping the community in some way.

All of these theories emphasize the significance of maintaining roles and relationships for health and well-being in later adulthood. Roles and relationships may well matter because of the lifestyle routines they foster, for example, not smoking, maintaining a reasonable weight, eating healthy foods, and exercising. Our research, as well as research by others, shows that both employment and civic engagement may be key in themselves, providing routine, social networks, and a sense of accomplishment, all of which are important for life quality. But the retirement mystique works against the social integration and productive engagement of older Americans by limiting employment possibilities for older adults. Similarly, most nonprofit organizations recruit younger people, not retirees, as volunteers.

The evidence for the health and well-being effects of social participation in paid and unpaid work is especially compelling, so long as such engagement is made by choice and offers older Americans flexibility and a sense of meaning. The issue is how to foster and promote such second acts. This points to the importance of yet another, more structural theory of successful aging, focusing on how institutional arrangements, policies, and practices constrain possibilities for the meaningful engagement for older workers and retirees.[66] From this perspective, few social institutions include people across age divides, given the primacy of lockstep ways of thinking. Moreover, there are few arrangements that can assist Americans of all ages and stages to think about, plan, and investigate possibilities for second acts.[67] Midcourse Americans often view this life stage as a time of shifting gears occupationally: changing jobs or careers, returning to school, scaling back on work hours or aspirations, retiring from their primary career jobs. But there are few community, employment, or government policies and practices that facilitate such gear shifting.

SECOND ACTS

Most Americans retire from their primary career jobs earlier than age sixty-five or even age sixty-two. Many do so because they have little or no choice as companies downsize, close plants, merge with other companies, lay off workers, or offer retirement-incentive packages that are too good to refuse (or can't be refused). This is the case for a fifty-nine-year-old machine operator we interviewed who left his emergency-maintenance job (where he had worked for the same company since age twenty-two) to pursue a lifelong interest in building machine replacement parts. Retired at age fifty-four (early because of a downsizing retirement package), this father of eight children views his second act as a craft, one that is critical for sustaining older tool-and-die machines in local businesses in his community. He also helps out friends and neighbors, using his construction, electrical, and mechanical skills. Doing so, he says, "provides a sense of contribution to the overall welfare of my community."

Some people retire early to take control of their lives. We interviewed a sixty-three-year-old retired occupational health nurse who left nursing at age fifty-eight when she reached a certain 401(k) financial goal. Prior to that, she was forced to move to another location when her plant closed and hated working with a new set of people at a new plant. After retiring from Bright Manufacturing, she was invited to work as a nurse in the local hospital, but said, "No way." Instead, she decided her second act would be community service. Rather than getting a paid job, she works as a volunteer coordinator for the surgical waiting room at that same hospital. She also organizes and delivers for a local meals-on-wheels program. Her husband says, "I think she volunteers out of a need to keep busy." He retired earlier from Vantech, where he had worked as a machine repairman since 1959. His second act involves becoming a self-employed handyman.

Growing numbers of Americans find themselves suddenly retired with little preparation.[68] Jim had less than a month to decide whether to retire at fifty-four. He did not finally make this major life decision until the last hour of the last day on which early retirement was offered. In retrospect, he feels that retirement came too quickly. He had not looked at other options or thought about what he would do following retirement. He now feels that he wasn't adequately prepared.

Most who retire from their primary careers enjoy their lives, but many miss the routines and social relationships of their old jobs. Some feel socially isolated, out of the mainstream of an America that revolves around paid work.[69] This may explain why more than one in four retired men age sixty-five and older works in some type of alternative arrangement, as does one in seven older women (see figure 6.4). A sixty-two-year-old commercial-art specialist who now works as a consultant told us he feels at loose ends, even though he is relieved to be away from the stress of his career job in graphics and display. He volunteers some for his synagogue but feels he is not qualified for many of the volunteer possibilities open to him.

Employment after retirement typically has salutary effects. Jungmeen Kim and Phyllis Moen found that retired-then-reemployed men report higher morale and fewer depressive symptoms compared to those still in their career jobs and those who are retired completely. Working after retirement also appears to reduce women's experience of marital conflict.[70]

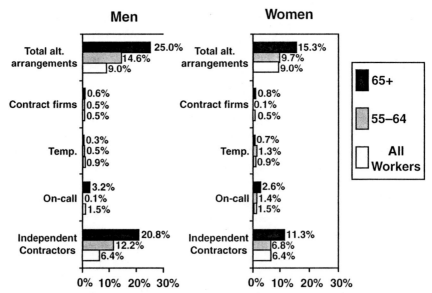

Figure 6.4. Alternative work arrangements during midcourse, by gender, 2001. (Source: U.S. Department of Labor, 2001.)

The growing "retired" force is an important, untapped social resource for American families, communities, and, indeed, society at large. Trends in longevity, good health, and early retirement (from primary careers) and the aging baby boom generation are coalescing to rewrite the midcourse life script. The challenge is to open up possibilities for second acts.[71] What many in this "age wave" want are options for productive activity, civic engagement, and some form of identity-defining status within society. Many want their second acts to make a difference, to make their communities and American society a better place. They *don't* want to give up the freedoms and flexibilities that come with retirement. This means providing new, more flexible jobs and new, more flexible opportunities for civic engagement—part time, part year, or as contract work. But the career and retirement regimes—the policies and practices built up around the career mystique—make such options difficult to find.

Unretirement: Paid Work after Retirement

The traditional definition of retirement as a final exit from the labor force is obsolete as Americans in their fifties, sixties, and seventies move in and out of paid (and unpaid community) work. Americans may come to define retirement in several ways: as the first exit from a primary career job following eligibility for pension, Social Security, or early-retirement benefits, and as the final exit from all paid work.[72]

Many older workers and young retirees want a second career, an entirely different type of job, and others want to stay in their first act but at a reduced level. Still others find employment following retirement (or not retiring at all) less of an option and more a necessity. Edward Wolff, an economist at New York University, reports that between 1989 and 1998, the majority of the population saw a decrease in expected retirement income.[73] Only households with holdings above $1 million saw a consistent increase in retirement earnings after inflation. Black and Hispanic households experienced a 19.9 percent drop in expected retirement income, and those headed by people without a high school education had a 39 percent drop in expected income. Wolff attributes this disparity in retirement income to the decline of traditional defined-benefit pension plans and the rise of contribution retirement plans, benefiting wealthy, older Americans but hurting middle- and lower-income Americans. With the vagaries of the stock market, older employees who are dependent on contribution plans often feel at financial risk. Second acts for those on the lower rungs of the employment ladder may be a necessity given their economic circumstances.

How can America bridge the gap between this vital and growing coterie of seasoned citizens and the stereotypes, policies, and practices defining old age? One way is to disconnect retirement from age. Military personnel often retire early only to begin other, second careers. Many athletes retire in their twenties and thirties, only to go on to do other things. By contrast, politicians and judges often "age in place," with only severe illness or death moving them out of their jobs. Competency-based employment is also a way of separating age from retirement, with ability, not age, determining continued employment.

Another possibility is for American businesses and governments (federal, state, and local) to remove the disincentives and increase the options for flexible workweeks, flexible work years, flexible careers, and flexible retirements. Flexible jobs after retirement are often qualitatively different from those people hold before retirement. Take, for example, the disparity between the work that Jim did as a foreman, supervising twenty employees, and the work that he now does washing cars and delivering flowers. Jim is happy to have reduced stress and greater flexibility.

Community Service

Another type of second act is unpaid work, be it informally helping out one's neighbors or actively volunteering in a community program. Individuals who retire, however, do not necessarily replace their career jobs with unpaid civic engagement.[74] Susan Chambré found that employees actually volunteered at higher rates than retirees, but that retirees who are active volunteers tend to have a significantly higher level of commitment than volunteers who are still in the labor force.[75] Similarly, in a recent study of 762 retirees and not-yet-retired workers between the ages of fifty to seventy-four, Phyllis Moen and Vivian Fields found little difference in community participation by retirement status.[76] Those who volunteer before retirement, however, tend to increase their volunteer hours once they retire. Deb and Steve, already active volunteers, are likely to become even more involved once they retire. Deb affirms this prediction:

> I will always want to do something. I wouldn't mind helping out in the schools or as a real old senior citizen being a greeter at Wal-Mart. Something that would keep me up and out, still being productive.

Research shows that community service is positively related to well-being.[77] Socially active retirees report the most positive attitudes about retirement.[78] Although there are few statistics on volunteer work, some suggest that 40 percent of those aged sixty-five to seventy-five volunteer for community organizations; this number drops to 26 percent after age seventy-five. Phyllis Moen and Vivian Fields found that volunteer community service predicts the well-being of retirees, but not that of those older workers not yet retired from their career jobs.[79] Moreover, the salutary effects of such community participation appear only for those retirees who are not also in postretirement employment. This suggests that unpaid community participation may help to replace the social relationships that occur naturally in the world of paid work, with regular volunteer activities becoming their work. There is also some evidence that retired men may benefit more psychologically from both paid work and volunteering than do retired women.[80]

Changes in Self-concept

According to Robert Atchley, a proponent of continuity theory, people's self-concepts remain stable between pre- and postretirement.[81] Ongoing family and friendship relations continue to serve as sources of self-esteem, with self-esteem remaining fairly stable as people move from employment into retirement.[82] Elizabeth Mutran and colleagues found that people who see themselves as being more competent workers (i.e., who have a positive worker identity) and those who have higher self-esteem are more likely to have positive attitudes about retirement.[83] But workers on the brink of retirement may feel real ambivalence. American society places a high value on paid work. Who we are in contemporary American society equates, for most American adults, to what we do, how we earn a living. Many of those who retire from their career jobs and do not take new jobs enjoy the leisure of retirement, but don't want to be completely cut off from the mainstream of society.

BEYOND LOCKSTEP LIVES

Retirement is not only a personal transition; it is also a social transition in flux.[84] Americans in their fifties, sixties, or seventies at the beginning of the twenty-first century are vastly different in their resources, expectations, and experiences from those in their fifties, and sixties, seventies in the mid-twentieth century. Most people continue to view retirement as part of the taken-for-granted career mystique, even though the "gold watch" type of lockstep retirement (where employees of a certain age are given a gold watch as they are ceremoniously retired) is increasingly rare.

Most older workers want to phase gradually into retirement, but face two options: work full time (and often at long hours) or else quit their jobs (retire) completely. Moreover, given the structural shifts of a global economy (as jobs are moved overseas or replaced by new technologies), a growing number of midcourse workers confront the choice of either retiring (with an early-retirement incentive) or being laid off. Risk and uncertainty have replaced the security that used to accompany seniority. In light of these dislocations, many Americans are forging new paths around retirement, second acts involving changing occupations, starting their own businesses, engaging in volunteer service, going back to school, or learning a new craft.

The career and retirement regime of policies and practices designed for the lockstep life course of the 1950s is clearly out of step with the growing proportion of the older American population refusing to equate retirement from a primary career job with old age. Public policies to date appear to encourage two opposing scenarios for older Americans: a continuous second childhood of unending play, travel, and rest, or no retirement and extended adulthood with unending pursuit of the career mystique through long hours and continuous employment. Most recent policy proposals involve the second solution, extending the lockstep pattern of employment by simply delaying the timing of retirement. This is evident in the 1983 amendments to the Social Security Act, phasing in a gradual change in Social Security eligibility from age sixty-five to age sixty-seven. Many policy makers believe that eligibility should be pushed back even further, in effect forcing older workers financially dependent on Social Security to delay retiring from their career jobs until closer to their seventies or even later.[85]

But this does not enable older workers to do what our research suggests most want to do: to work less, switching to something more flexible, less demanding, and, often, more meaningful. In other words, most want *second acts*. Policies forcing older workers to delay retirement from what are often physically demanding or high-stress jobs in effect reduce rather than expand midcourse Americans' options for productive engagement. (The trend toward restructuring by encouraging older workers, often earning high salaries, to retire and ongoing age discrimination in the hiring process, in tandem with policies promoting later retirement, could create real problems for older Americans.)

The United States is beginning to recognize and respond to the fact that many men and women want to continue some form of work after their official retirement. In 2000, President Clinton signed into law the Senior Citizen's Freedom to Work Act. Prior to the passage of this law, those between the ages of sixty-five and sixty-nine who continued to work and earned more than a specified amount were penalized by a reduction in their Social Security benefits. The passage of this legislation allows those over sixty-five to work for pay without being penalized for doing so. But most retirees who want to work are under sixty-five, and need health insurance, especially to bridge the years between retirement and Medicare eligibility.

Government, community, and corporate policies offering a cafeteria selection of paid (and unpaid) work with a range of hours, durations, and benefits would better fit with the demographic realities and aspirations of this new stage of the life course. Business, educational, and governmental institutions have opportunities to expand the possibilities for midcoursers, using their time and talents to strengthen communities as well as to provide a reliable, productive workforce.

Psychologist Erik Erikson describes mature adulthood as vital involvement in generative activities, in other words, active participation in meaningful roles.[86] America's policy regime promulgating the lockstep life course is at cross-purposes with the growing number of vital, talented people in their fifties, sixties, and seventies either experiencing or contemplating retirement. Envisioning flexible retirement exits—phased exits—could offer new possibilities for personal growth, for service, and for sustaining a skilled, motivated workforce. Even more radical options for second acts could create a third force of Americans dedicated to civic renewal.

Clearly, existing myths about retirement and age need themselves to be retired. Doing so could open up a panoply of possibilities providing flexibilities to employees, employers, and communities. Especially promising would be the fostering of second acts of civic engagement—part-time, part-year opportunities for community service, possibly offering minimum pay, possibly providing health insurance.

7

Policies and Practices: Maintaining the Status Quo or Challenging the Career Mystique?

In the United States in the 1950s and 1960s, neither government nor business was concerned about family-friendly policies; rather, the focus was on a booming postwar economy. "Good" jobs were those that provided sufficient income to support a family. Families subscribed to the career mystique of one breadwinner and one homemaker if they could afford to do so. Welfare aimed to fill the economic gap for single-parent families, assuming that mothers would (and should) stay home.[1] But a confluence of forces propelled wives and mothers into the workforce, and with these changes came grudging recognition of the need for family-friendly initiatives. "Work–family" and later, "work–life" became the dyads that described the difficulties of combining paid work with unpaid family-care work.

PUBLIC POLICY DEVELOPMENTS

As the nation ended the twentieth century, work–family issues (but not the career mystique) began to appear on the policy agenda. The federal government considered (if it did not always pass) legislation related to working families, and employers saw family-friendly policies as tools for recruiting and retaining a skilled, competitive workforce.[2]

Federal legislation can have a profound impact on the types of family-friendly benefits companies provide.[3] But the impact of legislation in the United States has been modest, largely because of its limited scope. Although federal and state governments have produced little in the way of work–family legislation, public discussion (often prompted by legislative initiatives) has been an impetus for employer–provided benefits and protections. For example, discussion about the employment rights of pregnant women encouraged many corporations to discontinue their policy of firing pregnant employees long before protective legislation was enacted.[4]

Businesses have historically opposed the involvement of the federal government in work–family issues, arguing that changes in employment conditions and benefits should remain voluntary and not be mandated by federal and state governments. This has been a major impediment to the drafting and enactment of legislation. For example, both the Chamber of Commerce and the National Association of Manufacturers vigorously attacked parental leave bills introduced in Congress (see below for a discussion of the Family and Medical Leave Act [FMLA]) on grounds that, if enacted, such legislation would be excessively costly, particularly to small businesses. Their opposition remained strident despite the fact that none of the bills introduced applied to employers with fewer than fifteen workers (the eventual bill passed was relevant only to those with more than fifty workers) and the General Accounting Office estimated that the bills would entail only modest costs to companies. This has, in fact, proved to be the case.[5]

Pregnancy Discrimination Act of 1978

Prior to the 1970s, it was common for women to be fired from their jobs when they became pregnant. Take, for example, a recollection of Cynthia's from 1953, when she was in her early twenties. Cynthia and her friend Judy were friends who taught at the same elementary school. They both supported their husbands, who were third-year law students. In the late fall, Judy became pregnant. It was the policy of their school system that a woman resign when she became pregnant. Judy's salary was essential; she could not afford to leave her job. So, when school administrators noticed Judy's growing size and asked her about her condition, Judy denied being pregnant. Cynthia laughed as she recalled Judy finishing the school year, obviously eight months pregnant, still assuring her principal that she was, indeed, not expecting.

The Pregnancy Discrimination Act was adopted in 1978 to protect the rights of women like Judy. This act made it illegal to discriminate against (e.g., fire or refuse to hire) a woman due to pregnancy or childbirth. Women like Judy no longer needed to hide or lie about their pregnancies in order to remain employed or get a job. Nor could they be fired if they missed work for childbirth or pregnancy-related complications. The Pregnancy Discrimination Act had a large impact on the work behavior of pregnant women. In the four years following the passage of the act, the number of women who worked during pregnancy increased by 30 percent.[6] Today, more than 80 percent of pregnant women work full time.

The Family and Medical Leave Act of 1993

The FMLA, signed into law by President Clinton in 1993, was major legislation to address the lag between outdated breadwinner/homemaker assumptions and the new demography of the American workforce. Family leave was not on the policy agenda in the United States during the first half of the twentieth century when the majority of middle-class, married women did not work outside of the home, and those who did—principally single, poor, and minority women—had sisters, mothers, aunts, and neighbors who could help out. As the majority of American women came to enter, reenter, and remain in the workforce, policy makers at both state and federal levels began to see the need for providing some kind of time off. Prior to the FMLA, there were no national standards for the granting or duration of family leaves for the care of a newborn infant. Nor were there protections for men and women who missed work to care for a sick child, an ailing spouse, or an infirm parent. Although some states adopted protections for the care of newborns and family members, in other states leaves were left to the discretion of employers. For example, Sandra, a college professor and friend of one of the authors, had her first child in 1972, before the enactment of the FMLA. The university where Sandra worked did not provide maternity leave for their employees. When Sandra's daughter was born in the middle of a semester, she was responsible for making sure her classes were taught. During the week following childbirth, Sandra paid a colleague to teach her classes. After that first week, Sandra went right back into the classroom. She recalls crying late at night while she graded papers between nighttime feedings. Sandra was in an all-male department and received very little support from her colleagues or the administration.

The FMLA requires employers with fifty or more employees who work within a seventy-five mile radius of their worksite to provide up to twelve weeks of unpaid, job-protected leave per year to eligible employees to care for a newborn, newly adopted, or foster child, or a child, spouse, or parent with a serious medical condition. It also can be used for a serious health condition of the employee, including maternity-related disability. Eligible employees are those working for the same employer for at least 1,250 hours in the previous twelve months.[7] (Key employees—those paid the top 10 percent in an organization—may be exempted from FMLA benefits.)

Hailed as landmark legislation, the FMLA provides valuable protections but falls short of meeting the needs of contemporary working men and women.[8] For instance, it covers only slightly more than half of the nation's working population.[9] Part-time, temporary, and seasonal workers, new employees, and employees in small businesses are excluded. Neither Jennifer nor Rob (see profile in chapter 3) is eligible for a job-protected parental leave because each of their workplaces has fewer than fifty employees. Consequently, Jennifer lost her job when she took two months off following the birth of her child.

Moreover, almost half of eligible workers fail to take advantage of the FMLA.[10] The fact that the FMLA offers only *unpaid* leave is a serious deterrent to its use. The vast majority cannot afford to take unpaid time off (see figure 7.1). Others feel it would jeopardize their job security or career trajectory. In a 1999 study of U.S. households, Naomi Gerstel and Katherine McGonagle found that one quarter of those who did take a family or medical leave in the previous year had to borrow money, and over one in ten (11%) had to depend on public assistance for support while on leave. Women who do take leave around the birth of a child rarely take the full twelve weeks the FMLA allots. In fact, census data shows that only one fourth of new mothers take more than eight weeks leave. Had they been eligible for the FMLA, Jennifer and Rob are a prime example of a couple who could not have afforded to take advantage of it. Recall that when their son was born, they had to move in with Rob's mother to stay afloat financially.

Yet another criticism of the FMLA is that it does little to integrate the realities of both paid work and unpaid family-work obligations. At the time it was enacted, many large employers already voluntarily provided

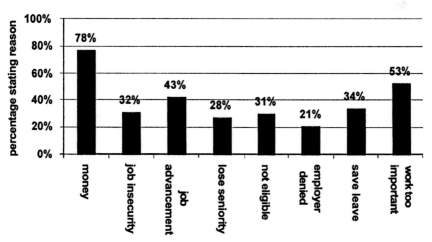

Figure 7.1. Reasons for not taking a leave covered by the FMLA. (Source: Cantor et al. 2001.)

leaves that were at least as, and often more, generous than those the FMLA mandated. Rather than forging innovative social policies for the new American workforce, the FMLA closely adhered to the minimal standards already adopted in the marketplace. It has had minimal impact on workplace policies: Gerstel and McGonagle found no differences in the number of leaves taken by employees in firms covered and not covered by the FMLA.[11] William Campion and Janice Dill found that most (74%) of the human resource professionals they surveyed saw the FMLA as having little impact on corporate policies.[12]

Despite these criticisms, the FMLA provides legitimacy for taking time off. The most dramatic impact of the FMLA has been the increase in the number of employers who offer leaves for new fathers and employees with ill family members.[13] According to the Department of Labor's Commission on Leave, after the FMLA was enacted, 69 percent of covered worksites changed their policies to provide leave for fathers to care for seriously ill or newborn children.[14] Note that the majority of employees using the FMLA typically do so for reasons other than parental leave (figure 7.2).

In September 2002, California enacted the first law in the United States mandating *paid* family leave for the care of a new child or an ailing relative.[15] This law requires up to six weeks of paid leave for employees with a family emergency (which includes care of a newborn child or an ill relative). The pay is derived from employee contributions to a state fund, and there is a cap on the amount to be paid out ($728 a week). Unlike the FMLA, all employees in California are eligible for this benefit, regardless of their length of tenure, work-hour status, or workplace size.

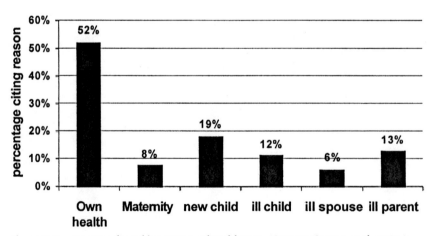

Figure 7.2.   Reasons for taking FMLA-related leaves. (Source: Cantor et al. 2001.)

International Perspective on Family Leaves

The FMLA represents a step forward in policies supporting working Americans, but falls woefully short of the policies adopted in other developed countries. Although the ideology of the career mystique has also permeated Europe, alternatives to the full-time, full-year, continuous, lockstep life course are available, particularly for women (or else used disproportionately by women). In 1992 the European Union (EU) issued a directive mandating a paid, fourteen-week maternity leave for employees in EU countries. Other international groups have adopted similar standards. In June 2000, the International Labor Organization (ILO) Convention on Maternity Protection adopted a new world standard for maternity leaves. The ILO recommended that women be afforded a fourteen-week maternity leave during which benefits should be provided "at a level which ensures that the woman can maintain herself and her child in proper conditions of health and a suitable standard of living."[16] This contrasts starkly with the shorter (twelve weeks versus fourteen weeks), *unpaid* leave afforded to some U.S. workers. In fact, the United States stands alone among industrialized countries in terms of the brevity of parental leaves, their nonuniversal coverage, and the lack of financial compensation. Of twenty-nine advanced industrialized countries in the Organization for Economic Cooperation and Development (OECD), only three, the United States, South Korea, and Australia, have no policy of mandatory paid maternity leave.[17] Table 7.1 illustrates how poorly the United States compares to other countries. In OECD countries, the average childbirth-related leave is forty-four weeks, and the average duration of pay is thirty-six weeks. In addition, eight countries mandate a paid paternity leave. These benefits are available to all employees, while only a little more than half of U.S. workers are legally entitled to the (unpaid) protections of the FMLA.[18] This highlights the mismatch between the reality of working parents in the United States and the career mystique assumptions that committed workers don't have family responsibilities.

U.S.-Scandinavian contrasts are even more marked.[19] Swedish parents are allowed an eighteen-month job-protected parental leave, consisting of fourteen weeks of maternity leave and two weeks of paternity leave following childbirth, along with six weeks of maternity leave before birth. The first year of leave garners 80 percent of one's full salary. Three more months are paid at a lower rate, with the final three months available without pay (but still with job protection). Mothers not in the workforce at the time of childbirth also receive a minimum paid benefit. Parents with children under age eight have the right to work 75 percent of a normal workweek. Either parents or grandparents have the right to take paid time off to care for an ill child under the age of twelve. Such innovative

Table 7.1   Maternity, Paternity, and Parental Leaves in the OECD Countries, 1997–1999

Country	Type and Duration of Leave	Wage Replaced	Paternity Leave
Australia	1 year parental	Unpaid	Shared parental
Austria	16 weeks maternity	100%	Shared parental
	30 months for 1 parent, 36 months if shared	Flat rate	
Belgium	15 weeks maternity	75%–80%	3 days and
	3 months parental	Low flat rate	shared parental
Canada	17 weeks maternity, 35 weeks parental	55%	Shared parental
Czech Republic	28 weeks maternity	69%	Shared parental
	3 years parental	Unpaid	
Denmark	28 weeks maternity	90%	2 weeks, 100%
	10 months parental, up to 52 weeks during child's first 8 years	60%	pay and shared parental
Finland	18 weeks maternity	65%	18 days flat
	26 weeks parental	Flat rate	rate and parental
France	16 weeks maternity	100%	3 days
Germany	14 weeks maternity	100%	Shared parental
	3 years parental up to eighth birthday	Flat rate	
Greece	17 weeks maternity	50%	Shared parental
	3.5 months parental	Unpaid	
Hungary	24 weeks maternity	70%	Shared parental
	3 years parental	Flat rate	
Iceland	3 months maternity, additional 3 months parental	80%	3 months at 80% and shared parental
Ireland	18 weeks maternity	70%	Shared parental
	14 weeks parental	Unpaid	
Italy	20 weeks maternity	80%	Shared parental
	Additional 10 months parental	30%	
Japan	14 weeks maternity	60%	Shared parental
	1 year parental	Unpaid	
Korea, South	8 weeks maternity	Unpaid	
Luxembourg	16 weeks maternity	100%	Shared parental
	6 months parental up to fifth birthday	Flat rate	
Mexico	12 weeks maternity	100%	

Country	Type and Duration of Leave	Wage Replaced	Paternity Leave
Netherlands	16 weeks maternity	100%	6 months
	Additional 6 months maternity	Unpaid	unpaid
New Zealand	12 weeks parental	100% of lowest wage earner's pay	Shared parental
Norway	52 weeks parental	80%	4 weeks at flat rate and shared parental
Poland	16 weeks maternity	100%	
	Additional 24 months	Flat rate	
Portugal	5 weeks maternity	100%	Shared parental
	Additional 2 years parental	Unpaid	
Spain	6 weeks maternity, 10 weeks parental	100%	Shared parental
	Parental until child is three	Unpaid	
Sweden	18 months parental until child is 8	80%	Shared parental
	3 months	Flat rate	
	3 months	Unpaid	
Switzerland	16 weeks maternity	Varies by canton	
Turkey	12 weeks maternity	66.67%	
United Kingdom	18 weeks maternity, 13 weeks parental	6 weeks at 90%; 12 weeks at flat rate	Shared parental
	Additional 11 weeks for employees with 1 year of tenure	Varies by employer	
	13 weeks parental up to fifth birthday	Unpaid	
United States	12 weeks family leave (includes maternity)	Unpaid	Shared parental

Source: Kamerman, Sheila B. 2000. "Parental Leave Policies: An Essential Ingredient in Early Childhood Education and Care Policies." *A Publication of the Society for Research in Child Development* 16:3–15, available from the Clearinghouse on International Developments in Child, Youth, and Family Policies at Columbia University at www.childpolicyintl.org/issuebrief/issuebrief5table1.pdf.

policies undoubtedly account for the high employment rate of women in Sweden and other Scandinavian countries.[20]

Still, family care remains gendered care, even in Scandinavia. In 1998 less than one third (32%) of new Swedish fathers used parental leave, and those who did, did so only for a brief period.[21] Moreover, job segregation by gender is extremely high. Swedish men are far more likely than Swedish women to be in fast-track, private-sector jobs. Men pursuing the career mystique in the private sector seldom take leaves for any significant period. Sweden has created a version of the "mommy"[22] or "parent" track for some employees. This provides them with both time and money during the early childhood years. But those who take it may find their career paths constricted.

New Mothers' Breastfeeding and Protection Act

Research consistently shows that breastfeeding has strong benefits for both infants and mothers. Breast milk reduces the incidence and severity of illnesses in infants—including diarrhea, respiratory infections, and ear infections. Mothers who breastfeed accrue protections against breast cancer, ovarian cancer, and osteoporosis.[23] Accordingly, the American Academy of Pediatrics recommends that infants be breastfed exclusively for the first six months of life. In order to ensure that working women are able to continue to breastfeed their children during the first crucial year, the New Mothers' Breastfeeding Promotion and Protection Act was introduced in Congress in 1998. The bill would have protected women from being fired or discriminated against for expressing milk or breastfeeding by requiring employers covered by the FMLA to provide an hour of unpaid break time for women to express milk during work. To date, the bill has not been passed. However, a handful of states (Minnesota, Tennessee, and Hawaii) have enacted legislation requiring employers to establish private space for new mothers either to breastfeed their infants or to express their milk.

International Perspective on Breastfeeding

The United States ranks far behind most other countries in promoting breastfeeding among working mothers. Currently eighty countries have provisions for women to take nursing breaks. In many countries these breaks are paid.[24]

Welfare and Welfare Reform

Welfare policies throughout much of the twentieth century implicitly endorsed the breadwinner/homemaker template by providing financial assistance, first through Aid to Dependent Children (ADC) and then through Aid to Families with Dependent Children (AFDC), to single mothers so they could stay home and care for their children.[25] However, with the rise in maternal employment, policy makers began to question the practice of providing poor women with money to stay home with their children when almost half of middle-class, married mothers were working outside of the home. This led to the passage in 1996 of the Personal Responsibility Work Opportunity Reconciliation Act (PRWORA), ending the federal guarantee of support for single mothers and replacing it with Temporary Assistance for Needy Families (TANF), a time-limited benefit tied to job training and employment.[26]

Through TANF the federal government turned the welfare system over to the states by providing block grants for states to use to cover benefits, administration, and services to poor families. Although states have a great deal of latitude in deciding how and to whom to administer their block grants, each state must meet administrative and federal guidelines. First, the length of time that people (women) can receive assistance is limited to five cumulative years. After this five-year time limit, a family is no longer eligible for cash benefits. By contrast AFDC placed no time limits on the receipt of welfare support. Also unlike AFDC, benefits under TANF are tied to work-related activity, which can include paid work, education, training, or community service. However, after an initial period of job search and training, to continue receiving benefits single parents must work at least thirty hours per week, and two-parent families must work at least thirty-five hours per week. There are some exceptions to these requirements. For example, states may exempt up to 20 percent of their caseload from the five-year time limit, and the work requirement can be exempted for single parents of infants and for those without adequate day care. But these exemptions are at the discretion of each state. States can also impose more stringent restrictions. For example, almost half of the states have implemented time limits of less than five years.[27]

Challenges for Welfare Reform

In the 1960s, policy makers saw the proper role of mothers as mothering; poor, single women without a male breadwinner were to be given (minimal) subsistence by the state. Today single mothers are to be both mothers and breadwinners. Legislators have unwittingly modeled welfare policy reform on the career mystique, the American Dream that hard work pays off.

States face real challenges moving low-income families into the workforce and off public assistance. First, most women on public assistance have few work skills and live in areas with little economic opportunity, which means they are likely to find, at best, low-wage work that won't enable them to support their families and pay for day care.[28] The Economic Policy Institute found that in 1999 almost half the families leaving welfare for full-time, full-year work encountered a financial crisis, such as being unable to pay for food, housing, or day care. Former welfare recipients in the workforce encountered more economic hardship than families remaining on welfare during the same time period.[29] To survive, low-income single mothers either need income subsidies or jobs that pay an adequate wage.

Second, TANF was signed into law during one of the country's most expansive period of economic growth and full employment, meaning that welfare recipients were facing a favorable job market. Economic downturns affect former welfare recipients more than other employees. Increases in the unemployment rate of low-income single mothers tend to outpace increases in unemployment among the general population.[30] There has been a dramatic decline in the number of retail jobs, one of the largest employment sectors for low-income single mothers.[31] For TANF to work, jobs must be available for low-skilled employees that pay wages sufficient to support a family. The welfare reforms may have sounded reasonable to some in the economic climate of the late 1990s, but they became a serious mismatch during the jobless recovery of the early 2000s. TANF families who cannot find work and bump up against their five-year benefit time limit face economic disaster, even homelessness.

Third, TANF requirements place a heavy burden on single, low-income mothers. Recall that most married mothers of very young children work part time (see chapter 4) and have both financial support and backup from their spouses. Under PRWORA, single mothers who have exhausted their benefits must take full responsibility for raising their families while also working full time, often with little or no other systems of support. If the intention of welfare reform was to update expectations of single mothers to be consistent with the experiences of married mothers, then PRWORA has swung the pendulum in the other direction. Whereas AFDC asked little of single mothers in terms of economic activity, PRWORA expects low-income single mothers to shoulder a heavy work–family burden.[32]

A fourth (and related) challenge is the absence of workplace benefits necessary to manage job and family responsibilities successfully. Jody Heyman and Alison Earle found that employed, former welfare recipients are less likely to have paid sick leave, paid vacations, or flexible work schedules, compared to women who have not been on welfare.[33] Low-income, single mothers already lack the option of trading off child-related responsibilities with a spouse, making them even more in need of such workplace flexibilities. The absence of paid leaves and flexible arrangements to accommodate family emergencies undermines the possibility of a successful transition from welfare to work.

A fifth, and perhaps the most obstinate, hurdle facing women as they move off welfare is their difficulty in finding affordable, quality day care.

It is nearly impossible to pay for full-time day care and adequately meet family financial needs while earning a minimum wage. Although TANF provides child-care funds to some women as they move into work, the adequacy of these funds varies by state and locality, and they are often underutilized.[34] Two recent studies of women making the transition from welfare to work show that finding affordable, quality day care is a major, if not the major, deterrent to employment[35] (other deterrents include lack of transportation, difficulty taking time off for sick children, heavy family responsibilities, and limited employment opportunities[36]). A recent case in Michigan is illustrative: Elizabeth McCallum, a single, employed mother working a third shift, fell asleep on the couch after coming home from work. While she was sleeping, her daughter climbed out a window and was found by a motorist wandering in the middle of a busy street during the lunch-time rush hour. Many people in the community criticized McCallum's decision not to hire a day care provider while she slept, ignoring the difficult, almost impossible, dilemma that low-income women face as they strive both to financially support and to raise their families.[37] New welfare laws require them to work for pay, but most states do not adequately assist low-income working mothers in finding and paying for adequate care for their children. Further, many former welfare recipients have such low incomes that they benefit little or not at all from the income tax credits many working families receive to help defray the costs of child care.

The rationale behind welfare reform is compelling; movement off of welfare and into the workplace generates positive outcomes. Single mothers in the workforce learn skills and develop an employment history, making them more employable in the future. In addition, they earn important future Social Security benefits.[38] Indeed, a landmark study shows that maternal employment appears to benefit the children of former welfare recipients. Lindsay Chase-Lansdale and colleagues found teenagers whose mothers had moved from welfare to work displayed improvements in mental health and cognitive skills as well as decreased drug and alcohol abuse.[39] Children whose parents have left welfare are also less likely to drop out of high school, presumably because of the positive role model the employed parent represents.[40] Clearly, leaving welfare for work can have positive effects on the families of those able to find and sustain viable employment.

International Perspective on Welfare

Only families in the most economically precarious positions receive welfare in the United States. By contrast, in Scandinavia, welfare is an integral part of society, used to equalize income and to ensure that everyone makes a living wage. More conservative European countries, such as Germany, depend less on welfare, using it as a form of social insurance to protect people when they are out of work.[41]

Although European countries do support single mothers, there is a movement in many of these countries, as there is in the United States, to compel single mothers to enter the workforce by placing limits on the length of time that they can receive assistance without working.[42] Jane Millar's 2001 paper found that welfare without a work requirement is available to single mothers with children under the age of three in Austria, Finland, France, and Germany. In the Netherlands mothers can receive welfare without being employed until their youngest child is five, in Luxembourg until the age of six, and in Norway until the age of eight. In the United Kingdom single mothers can be supported on welfare with no work requirement until their youngest child is sixteen. There is no fixed age limit in Denmark, Sweden, Italy, and Spain, but single women are generally expected to work for pay. Some European countries compel fathers to contribute to the financial well-being of children who are being raised solely by their mothers.[43] Note that in many European countries single mothers' earnings are supplemented so that a single woman can support herself and her family. This also enables single mothers to work part time, which places a more reasonable burden on her and her children. No such supplementation is provided to single mothers in the United States. As with parental leave, the United States, in comparison with other Western, industrialized countries, offers little assistance to single mothers in their efforts to mesh work and family.

Child Care

The U.S. government has taken a largely hands-off role in providing, subsidizing, and regulating child care.[44] Accordingly, the vast majority of child-care settings are privately run. Many do not require licensing and therefore have no federal or state oversight. Even when applicable, standards for obtaining a child-care license are usually minimal.

In the United States financial support for child care goes only to families who can demonstrate financial need.[45] The federal government has made money (in the form of block grants to states) available to women in TANF to pay for child care. However, having a small level of savings or even owning a car renders families in many states ineligible for child-care assistance.[46] The Child Development Fund also provides (often inadequate) money for child care to low-income parents, but very few of the families who are eligible for these subsidies actually receive them. Janet Gornick and Marcia Meyers report that only 16 percent of eligible low-income families receive this money.[47] There are several reasons for this underutilization.[48] First, day care providers are often reluctant to work with children receiving subsidies because of the paper work and delays in receiving payment. Parents also find that subsidy eligibility changes frequently and is affected by changes in employment. Thus, parents cannot rely on their subsidies being consistently available. Finally, the bureaucratic procedures involved in applying and reapplying for subsidies can be overwhelming.

Parents can also deduct some of their child-care expenses from their taxable income through either (1) the Dependent Care Assistance Plan (as part of a flexible spending or cafeteria benefit plan), which allows parents to exclude up to $5,000 in child-care costs from their taxable wages, or (2) the Child and Dependent Care Tax Credit, which allows parents to deduct a portion of their child-care expenses from their taxable earnings. But, deductions are limited to between $480 and $720 (depending on one's income) for one child, and between $960 and $1,440 for two or more children.[49] Because child-care expenses for one child typically range from $4,000 to $10,000 a year, these tax credit options, while providing some relief, still leave a heavy burden, particularly on those with more than two children.[50] And, tax credits give little to no relief to families with incomes near or below the threshold for paying taxes.

International Perspective on Child Care

Several European countries take a more active role in both providing and subsidizing child care for working parents.[51] In some Scandinavian countries, such as Sweden, Denmark, and Finland, all children are extended care services from the time that parental leave ends until the child is old enough to attend school, with the government paying for approximately 80 percent of the costs. France and Belgium provide full-day preschool for all children beginning around age two and a half.

Elder-Care Policies and Benefits

Caring for infirm parents is increasingly common for America's (aging) workforce. Two major pieces of legislation provide for such care. The FMLA provides full-time employees in medium and large firms with the option of twelve weeks of unpaid leave to care for a seriously ill parent or spouse. (Recall that these are the same leave benefits extended to new parents and to those with a serious illness). The National Family Caregiver Support Program, enacted in 2000, provides caregivers with information and services, including counseling, support groups, respite, and other home and community based services.[52]

CORPORATE POLICIES AND BENEFITS

The U.S. government has few mandates for employer-provided benefits. Unions focus primarily on wage and seniority issues, with few bargaining for family-friendly benefits. Employers thus have wide latitude in the number and types of benefits they choose to offer. Those that do tend to adopt new personnel policies and benefits for three major reasons: (1) to attract and retain workers in a tight labor market, (2) to enhance productivity and reduce absenteeism, and (3) to be socially responsible in the eyes of the public.[53] There is disparate evidence as to the number of companies providing supports to working families (such as child care, flexibility as to time and place of work, and reduced hours), but larger firms are more apt to do so.[54]

Figure 7.3 lists some of the most popular family-friendly benefits and the proportion of employees in private industry eligible for them.[55] For full-time employees, paid holidays and paid vacations are almost universal. Unpaid family leave is now almost universal among full-time employees at medium- and large-size organizations (93%), given the FMLA. For part-time workers (not protected by the FMLA), unpaid family leave is only available to about half of the employees in medium- and large-size organizations (54%). Family-friendly benefits that incur a direct cost to employers, such as paid personal leave and paid family leave, are rarely

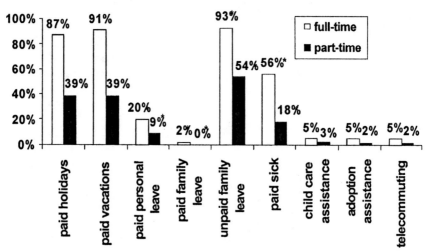

Figure 7.3.   Percentage of employees in private industry eligible for selected employee benifits.
*Medium and large businesses only; data from 1997.
(Sources: U.S. Department of Labor, Bureau of Labor Statistics, 2003 [2000 data]; U.S. Department of Labor, Bureau of Labor Statistics, 1999 [1997 data].)

available. In fact, the U.S. Department of Labor estimates that only 2 percent of organizations extend this benefit to full-time employees, and almost none provide paid family leave to part-time employees. Other family-friendly benefits that have a direct cost to employers, such as child-care assistance, are also rare. This suggests American employers are reluctant to go beyond federally mandated protections. Furthermore, part-time and temporary workers, usually women with children,[56] who could benefit most from family-friendly policies, are the least likely to be eligible for them.

Below we outline several of the most popular family-friendly benefits, identifying who uses them and their implications for employee behavior and morale. Although many family-friendly policies involve either an initial financial investment on the part of employers or a reorganization or change in long-standing practices, facilitating employees' integration of work and family has potential long-term benefits for employers as well as employees and their families.

Family Leaves

Businesses increasingly offer some time off for family concerns, be it in the form of family leave, personal leave, or maternity leave. Mostly women take such leaves, typically for maternity.[57] Leaves are more likely to be available to professional and managerial men and women than to low-income employees, who may be most in need of such support.[58] Family leave is also less likely to be available to men and women who work in highly sex-segregated occupations or companies. Thus, those who work in a predominantly male (e.g., engineering firm) or a predominantly female (e.g., child care) setting are less likely to have access to family leave than those in a setting with a mix of men and women.[59]

Leaves have important ramifications for employees and employers. First, longer maternity leaves appear to be better for women's mental health. One study found that mothers taking short maternity leaves (less than twenty-four weeks) tend to have poorer mental health than those who take leaves longer than twenty-four weeks (which is relatively rare in the United States, given the twelve-week provision of the FMLA).[60] This negative effect is exacerbated when women return to work quickly and face other stresses, such as marital- or work-related problems. These women are at heightened risk for depression.[61]

Employers may well benefit indirectly from generous family leave policies: longer maternity leaves mean not only employees with better mental health, but also greater commitment, who are less likely to quit their jobs.[62] Whether a leave is paid or unpaid may also influence employee commitment.

Most American men and women do not take advantage of the parental and family leaves available to them. Many cannot afford to take an extended unpaid leave. And those who can afford to often fear that an extended leave may signal less commitment to the career mystique of continuous, full-time (or longer) employment.[63] There may be some validity to these fears. Michael Judiesch and Karen Lyness examined the personnel files of almost thirteen thousand managers in a large multinational financial organization[64] and found that men and women taking leaves (including maternity, paternity, and sick leave) received fewer promotions and lower raises in subsequent years, compared with their colleagues who took fewer or no leaves.

Child-Care Assistance

Child-care assistance varies dramatically in form and financial costs to employers. The most commonly offered child-care benefits are the inexpensive ones: day care referral services (in 2000, available to 14 percent of all U.S. workers)[65] and flexible benefits plans (withholding pretax money used to pay for day care, available to 13 percent of full-time employees in 1997).[66] On-site day care is rare, is expensive to administer, and can incur financial liabilities (available to only 2 percent of the workforce).[67] Child-care subsidies are also costly and rare (only 5 percent of employees receive this benefit).[68] To date, researchers have failed to demonstrate a relationship between on-site day care and positive worker outcomes such as productivity and low employee turnover, less work–family conflict, or lower absenteeism.[69] Because on-site day care is costly and provides few tangible benefits for employers, it is not surprising that so few workplaces provide it. Research has shown that child-care assistance policies in general (including child-care referral and flexible benefit plans) have a positive effect on employee loyalty, especially among women with school-age children and among men of childbearing age, and are also associated with less work–family conflict.[70]

Despite the costs, some forward-thinking corporations do provide their employees with quality child-care options. For example, Amgen, a large biotechnology company, operates one of the nation's largest day care centers, offering day care for up to 430 children between the ages of six weeks and five years.[71] Amgen charges 10 to 15 percent below the cost of most private day cares, making it affordable for a broad cross section of their employees. Eastman Kodak has also been innovative in helping employees meet child-care needs, developing an on-site program for school-age children to attend during the summer and on school holidays (Camp Kodak).

Elder Care

Most employees who are eligible for unpaid family leave are able to use their leave to care for elderly relatives. Other benefits specifically designed for elder care are rare. A few larger, more innovative companies provide employees with information about elder care and a referral service for elder-care needs. However, researchers have found that, when available, elder-care benefits are vastly underutilized.[72] Again, this underutilization is likely due to a fear of retribution in the long term. Taking time off to care for an ailing relative is not consistent with the career mystique. Not surprisingly, because elder care is compatible with the general caregiving role of women in our society, female employees are more likely to use elder-care benefits than male employees.

Part-time Work

Recall that a popular strategy for working couples is for one member of a couple to pursue the career mystique, while the other (typically the wife) reduces her work hours, particularly when young children are in the home (see chapter 4). Granting an employee reduced hours is a policy that costs employers relatively little. In fact, because part-time employees generally do not receive the same insurance, retirement, vacation, and paid leave benefits as full-time employees, the employer may actually save money by allowing an employee to move from full-time to part-time status.

Providing part-time work, even with prorated benefits, makes business sense for employers. Women who are allowed to reduce their hours following childbirth are more likely to return to work and also to return to work more quickly than those who return to a full-time job.[73] Recall Donna (see profile in chapter 4), who had a high-commitment job that required frequent travel. After her daughter was born, she found her job to be too time-consuming: "Continuing with what I am doing is not an option for me. My options are quit entirely or ask for something on a part-time basis, or ask for a couple of years' leave of absence." During a follow-up interview with Donna, we learned that she had requested a decrease in hours. When her request was denied, she took a protracted leave from her job.

There is also some evidence that employees are more productive when they move from full-time to part-time status. In one study of Fortune 100 firms, more than half of the employees who moved from full-time to part-time status said their workload did not change (although their financial compensation did), and fully 10 percent reported that their workload actually increased.[74]

Employees also benefit when they move to part-time work by choice. According to a 1997 study, 92 percent of workers who moved from full-time to part-time work said that the reduced hours improved their morale; 37 percent (like Donna) said that part-time work was essential for staying with their employers; and half reported that being able to move to part-time work increased their commitment to their companies. Finally, Janet Hyde and her colleagues found that mothers who work part time are less anxious than their full-time counterparts. [75]

But there are long-term costs to part-time employment because it is inconsistent with the clockwork and values of the career mystique. In many cases, working part time effectively moves people off the established career (mystique) track. Part-time jobs pay less per hour than comparable full-time jobs, have less potential for advancement, are less secure, and grant fewer benefits (such as paid vacation and leaves, retirement, and health insurance).[76] As such, the movement of women from full-time to part-time work contributes to gender inequality both within couples and within society. Further, the time that people (most often wives) save by working part time is often spent on household tasks, contributing even further to gender inequality in the home (see chapter 5).

Some employers recognize the importance of part-time work options for their employees and have taken steps to reduce the financial penalties associated with part-time work. Sears Roebuck and Winn-Dixie, for example, have extended benefits usually reserved for full-time employees to their part-time employees.[77]

International Perspective on Work Hours

European governments protect employees from working long hours. In the United States, full-time work is typically defined as (at least) a forty-hour week, whereas in most European countries, full-time hours are set at lower levels, typically ranging from thirty-five to thirty-nine hours a week. Further, many countries in Europe place a limit on the maximum number of hours that an employee can work (48 hours). This is not the case in the United States, where limits are only placed on work hours when they present a hazard to the public (e.g., the number of hours that truck drivers may drive or that pilots may fly in one day are limited).[78] As a result, Americans work, on average, far more than do Europeans.

Many European countries have also taken steps to ensure that part-time jobs are more commensurate with full-time jobs in terms of benefits and responsibilities so that workers (typically women) will not make long-term sacrifices in their career progression should they reduce their hours to manage their dual role as care providers and workers.[79] For example, the Directive on Part-time Work, adopted by the EU in 1997, provides key protections for part-time workers. First, it prohibits part-time workers from being treated less favorably than full-time workers in terms of pay, benefits, training, and opportunities for advancement. Second, it strongly urges employers to provide part-time opportunities for employees who request them. In particularly progressive European countries, the government mandates that employers must provide part-time work to employees with young children.[80]

European countries have also taken the lead in providing older workers with options for phasing into retirement. More than half of the EU countries have instituted some form of progressive retirement, which allows older workers to reduce their hours and at the same time provides them with a financial supplement to compensate for the reduced earnings.[81] This system permits the aging worker to ease more slowly into retirement without facing a financial penalty. The goals of progressive retirement are manifold. First, it keeps skilled workers in the workforce longer. Second, it provides more opportunities for older workers. Third, it places less of a burden on pension systems by reducing expensive early retirements. Fourth, it alleviates labor shortages. Most importantly, from our perspective, it allows older workers to remain active and engaged in the workforce as they ease into retirement.

Flexible Time

Flexible-time benefits are popular family-friendly policies that give contemporary workers greater latitude in managing the multiple strands of their lives. Flexible time includes a variety of work arrangements. The most widespread flexible-time benefit is *flex time*, where employees choose the time they start and end their days, as long as they are present during a specified core period and they work the required number of hours. Another innovative form of the flexible-time benefit is the *flexible week*, which allows employees to redesign their workweek. For example, one can work six short days or four long days (known as a compressed workweek). There is evidence that working a flexible schedule can make employees more productive as well as make them available to assist customers over a longer workday.[82]

Flexible-time benefits are widely used. In the United States and in Canada, approximately one fourth of employees take advantage of flex-time benefits.[83] Although used by employees at all ages and life stages, there is some evidence that flex-time benefits are most frequently used by parents.[84] Women are more likely to use flex time to reduce work–family conflicts, whereas men are more likely to use them to increase productivity.[85] Ironically, the group of people most in need of workplace flexibility, low-income women with children and single mothers, are the least likely to have the option of a flexible work schedule.[86]

Providing flexible-time options for one's employees does appear to have benefits for the employer. Patricia Roehling, Mark Roehling, and Phyllis Moen, studying a nationally representative sample, found that employees, regardless of family makeup or life stage, are more loyal to an employer when they are able to use flex time.[87] Another study found that the use of flex time is associated with greater job satisfaction and commitment.[88] Other studies show that the use of flexible time is related to lower levels of absenteeism, tardiness, sick time, and overtime; reduced turnover following childbirth; lower work and family role strain and interference; and lower levels of general distress.[89]

The use of flex time also appears to benefit families. Those who use flex time spend more evening hours with their families, and they spend less time commuting.[90] For men and women who do not have heavy responsibilities in the home, flex time is associated with increased levels of family and marital satisfaction. When used in the service of family needs, there is also some evidence that flex time use can breed some resentment within a marriage.[91] These negative effects, however, are small, and overall flex time is a valuable benefit that employees at all life stages enjoy.

Given that providing flexible-time options to one's employees costs the employer very little and is associated with so many positive outcomes, it is not surprising that this has become a widespread innovation in many contemporary workplaces. As with other policies discussed in this chapter, flexible-time benefits may be underutilized because of the message employees fear that flex-time use might send to their employer. Employees don't want to signal to their employers that they are not committed 100 percent to their jobs. One study found that flexible-time policies are most widely used among employees whose supervisors are relatively powerful within the organization.[92] This suggests that unless employees feel their request for flexible time is firmly supported by a strong figure in the corporation, they are reluctant to risk using the benefit.

Finally, it is important to point out that to call flexible-time policies family-friendly is a bit of a misnomer; rather, they are worker-friendly, appreciated by those with and without families and by those at all ages and stages of life. This is one innovation that can benefit both businesses and their workers. Creative employers and supervisors look for ways to optimize the flexible use of time among their employees.

Telecommuting

Telecommuting is a relatively recent innovation made possible by the technological advances of the past twenty years. Telecommuters work out of their homes for all or a significant portion of the workweek, keeping in touch with their employers and coworkers through the use of e-mail, fax, and telephone. Women tend to find telecommuting more attractive than men, and parents (particularly mothers) are more likely to telecommute than nonparents.[93] Telecommuting allows employees with families to remain in the home while they work. This can bring peace of mind to parents who can monitor the activities of their children while they are working, or it can engender additional spillover between work and family. Telecommuting options may appeal especially to employed parents with preteen and teenage children who are too old for day care but still need supervision. Despite its potential advantages, telecommuting is relatively rare. Christopher Higgins and colleagues surveyed public employees in Canada in 1994 and found that less than 5 percent use telecommuting.[94] Those who do telecommute report that they work out of their homes only during a fraction of the workweek.[95]

Research into the effects of telecommuting is also sparse and presents mixed findings. Telecommuting does tend to help employees meet the often conflicting demands of their jobs and their families. And telecommuters report that they are more productive and perform better when working at home because of reduced distractions and interruptions.[96] However, there are significant drawbacks to telecommuting. First, it can lead to professional and social isolation, curtailing employees' chances of advancement and professional development.[97] In addition, telecommuting blurs the distinction between work and home, which can lead to work–family interference, role overload, and negative work–family spillover, particularly among women.[98] Finally, family distractions can result in workers being dissatisfied with telecommuting.[99] Telecommuting, then, can be a double-edged sword. It helps employees integrate work life with home life, but at a cost in terms of professional advancement and personal well-being.

Workplace Support

Supervisor and coworker support, although not technically a policy or benefit, is an important aspect of the workplace environment that influences whether and how family-friendly policies are implemented. Studies have consistently shown that supervisor and coworker support is one of the most important, if not the most important, determinants of how family-friendly a workplace is. It is not enough to simply have family-friendly benefits on the books. If employees are to make use of those benefits, they must first feel that the environment is supportive of their doing so. In general, the more supportive the workplace climate, the greater the use of family-friendly benefits.[100]

Supervisor support has several other positive outcomes for both employers and employees. A supportive, family-friendly environment is associated with higher levels of employee loyalty and commitment, less work–family conflict, less turnover following childbirth, a more rapid return to work after childbirth, lower levels of employee stress, lower levels of employee depression and anxiety, enhanced work performance, and greater job satisfaction.[101] It is relatively inexpensive for employers to develop and maintain an environment in which workers feel supported in their efforts to mesh the sometimes conflicting needs of family and work. According to Ellen Galinsky, a leading figure in the area of work–family research, organizations can only be truly supportive of working families if they have a strong champion of work–family issues in a major position of authority.[102] A powerful champion at a high level will set the tone for the organization and ensure that managers are trained in identifying and being sensitive to the work–family issues facing contemporary workers.

Several of our case studies have illustrated how important support for work–family issues is to men and women in the contemporary workforce. Lisa, a single mother (see profile in chapter 1), was willing to leave her job because her boss would not support her needs. David, Lisa's ex-husband, has stayed with his employer because of the flexibility offered to him and the understanding of his family needs. Donna, the executive (see profile in chapter 4), and Deb, who stopped working when her daughter was young (see profile in chapter 6), left their jobs because their supervisors were unsupportive of their family obligations. The organizations willing to look beyond the rigid structure of the career mystique have a more loyal workforce.

UNIONS

Unions have historically played a pivotal role in winning basic rights and benefits for workers, many of which are crucial to the well-being of families as well as employees. For example, unions were instrumental in the passage of the Fair Labor Standards Act of 1938, which established a minimum wage and restricted the workweek to forty hours.[103] Unions were also strong advocates of the Family and Medical Leave Act of 1992, which gave employees covered by the act the right to take protected, unpaid leave to care for a newborn child or an ill family member. Unions have also worked to gain workers overtime pay, family health care plans, and vacation time.[104]

In general, unions have been active in lobbying for family benefits through the enactment of federal legislation, but they have not been as active in procuring traditional work–family benefits for individual union members through collective bargaining.[105] In fact, recent studies have found that workers who are represented by unions generally do not have greater access to work–family benefits, such as child-care assistance, work-hour flexibility, and part-time work options, than do those not covered by unions, and in some cases union members may have fewer benefits.[106] There is some evidence, however, that men who are protected by unions may have access to more family-friendly benefits than men not covered by a union. For example, a few studies have found that men who are union members typically work fewer hours, take longer leaves, and have more work–family benefits than nonunion members. However, this union advantage generally does not hold for women or for union members who work in female-dominated fields.[107]

But the nature of unions and what they bargain for is changing in tandem with the changing workforce. The largest group of union members today holds public-sector jobs, and women are now a key constituency. As more women gain positions of power within unions and as men increasingly come to value traditional family-friendly benefits, unions are beginning to take a more active role in procuring these benefits for their members.

POLICY LEADS

We have seen throughout this book that contemporary employees and employers are traversing an uncharted terrain. In the past, the clockwork of careers needn't mesh with the clockwork of families because different people (breadwinners/homemakers) attended to them. Even when poor women were the family breadwinners, other women provided the care their families required. Today, few workers have backup at home, but jobs remain patterned on the breadwinner clockwork. Unfortunately, most U.S. solutions are short-term Band-Aids. Employees expect—and are expected—to work out the multiple strands of their lives on their own.[108] Some resolve the mismatch by staggering each spouses' work hours. Some reduce their hours. Others temporarily leave the workforce. Still others hire help, outsourcing housework or elder care, for example. Government employers may offer some family-friendly options, but the clockwork of the career mystique—workdays, workweeks, work lives— remains largely intact. The federal government has yet to address (1) how outmoded rules and regulations constrain work-hour flexibility, or (2) the dearth of alternative paths that could offer more career flexibility. Some businesses adopt best-practice work–family or work–life policies, placing them on the books but rarely encouraging their use. Others try to ignore the problem altogether. What solutions exist remain piecemeal and narrowly defined.

Employers rarely adopt expensive work–life initiatives (such as day care centers or paid family or parental leaves); rather, they offer low-cost options such as child-care tax credits or child-care referral services. Work–family advocates often feel they must make a profit rationale for family-friendly benefits, touting the advantages they bring to the organization, such as decreased absenteeism and turnover. However, business commitments to these benefits tend to be shallow. During the 1990s, when unemployment rates were low and employers had difficulty attracting and retaining employees, many companies adopted work–life programs and benefits because it helped with recruitment and retention. In the early 2000s when unemployment climbed and the U.S. economy slumped, work–life programs were some of the first perks to hit the chopping block. A 2003 survey found that the number of companies offering job sharing, compressed workweeks, telecommuting, and flex time had dropped significantly from the previous year, underscoring the tenuousness of these initiatives.[109]

If flexible policies are only predicated on making business sense, then commitment to those programs will shift largely with shifts in the economic climate. Erin Kelly proposes that state and federal governments must play a stronger role in promoting and even mandating policies.[110] Kelly also proposes that work–family advocates go beyond merely making a business case for family-friendly policies to acknowledging and promoting the broader social goals that these programs address. For example, maternity leaves grew out of concerns over discrimination against women in the workplace; telecommuting and flex time evolved out of environmental concerns related to traffic congestion and pollution; child-care programs were initiated to combat childhood poverty.

To move past the Band-Aid approach, employers, unions, government, and community organizations must question the basic assumptions implicit in the career mystique.[111] Is the continuous, lockstep, high-face-time, full-time, and frequently long-hour template really the most efficient and effective arrangement? American business is successful precisely because of its willingness to change, to embrace new technologies, new demands, and new ideas. Can business now embrace the realities of a workforce of women and men; of workers married to other workers; of workers who need or want time out to care for children, parents, or themselves; of older workers and young retirees who want not endless leisure but flexibility and opportunity; of employees who want training or more formal education to gain the skills necessary in a global economy?

Structural Leads

We use the term *structural lead* to capture the idea of innovation, of new policies and practices that can pave the way for resetting career clocks and rewriting work scripts. One small example: The San Jose National Bank allows workers to bring infants to work with them for their first six months of life or until they begin to crawl, whichever comes first.[112] The manager at the San Jose National Bank instituted the policy in an attempt to reduce the costs of hiring and training temporary workers during employees' maternity leaves. But note: This lead may be more work-friendly than people-friendly, possibly encouraging new mothers to hurry back to their jobs.

Another small example is the provision of private settings in which nursing mothers can either breastfeed or express milk for their children while they are at work. Pediatricians recommend that infants be exclusively breastfed for at least the first six months of life,[113] and yet few U.S. workplaces allow new mothers six months of maternity leave. Although forward-thinking organizations provide women with a place and time to express milk for their infants, the larger issue of an institutionalized time-out, or work-hour reduction, for new mothers or others with heavy family responsibilities, remains unaddressed.

Finally, if gender equality at home and in the workplace is a goal for our society, then workplaces and families need new scripts. Janet Gornick and Marcia Meyers, in their book *Families That Work*, advocate for a dual-earner–dual-career society.[114] This means that both men and women shift their work and caregiving time commitments. For true equality, couples must share more equally the care work (what Jessica DeGroot, the founder of the Third Path Institute calls shared care) of the home as well as the paid work.[115] Women need to invest slightly less time in the home, whereas men need to invest less time in work and more in the home. For this to work, however, a more family-friendly marketplace must allow for temporary breaks in employment, quality jobs must require less than a fifty-hour-a-week commitment, and government policies must support caregiving work.

If policy lags represent outdated, obsolete arrangements and regulations, policy *leads* capture innovations geared to the twenty-first-century workforce and the twenty-first-century economy. Social scientists don't have solid evidence pointing to a single, let alone simple, solution to the outdated regime of educational, workplace, and retirement policies developed around the career mystique. Given the diversity in women's and men's lives, in families, and in jobs, a rich smorgasbord of options and possibilities may well be necessary. What might work best is a range of career "lanes"—with infinite switching possibilities at all ages and stages. We propose three sets of innovations that can begin to move the nation beyond the career mystique: the revaluing of care work, flexible work hours, and flexible careers.

Revaluing Care Work

Many Americans persist in believing the principal remedy to the work–family quandary to be a reduction in workers' family obligations,

for example, by providing day care for children. The goal is to free employees (from poor single mothers to highly paid professionals) from
family-care work so that they can focus full time (or more) on their jobs.
But this may be more work-friendly than family- or people-friendly.
Defining the problem simply as the absence of quality, affordable child
care leaves the conventional lockstep career template very much in place.
Clearly, the need for community-based child care and elder care are crucial to make life work for families in which all adults are employed. However, it tends to invoke an essentially one-sided response, requiring no
alteration in the fundamental structure of the workday, the workweek, career paths, or retirement, all of which shape the way people organize their
lives. The reality is that children are not simply a distraction. Many parents would actually like to spend more time with their children. Many
adults would also like to spend time with ailing (or dying) parents. There
can never be equality of opportunity in the workforce for men and
women and for mothers and fathers given the career mystique and the
gendered distribution. Neither can families function effectively as caregiving and childrearing units and places of emotional respite so long as
employment policies and practices remain predicated on the outdated assumption that employees can focus totally on and continuously on work,
investing long hours in their jobs, day in and day out, week in week out,
year in year out. Although affordable and quality child care is, of course,
a necessary step toward reducing the unpaid family-care work of those
with children, outsourcing care work only papers over the fundamental
crisis of care perpetuated by the career mystique. Recognition that most
employees have, or will have, family-care responsibilities and crises is
needed. Innovative flexibilities that permit them to fulfill their commitments at work and at home are required.

Flexible Work and Reduced Hours

Most workers want to work less, but are unable to do so without either
shifting to a different, part-time, low-wage job (often without benefits) or
else by leaving the workforce altogether.[116] Competitiveness in the
twenty-first-century global economy, along with high-commitment work
places, encourage an overtime culture of heavy time and emotional investment in jobs.[117] New information technologies encourage that work
can be done anywhere, which often translates into all the time, everywhere. We need to develop flexibility, as well as a range of work-hour options in existing jobs that better fit with the contemporary realities of today's—and tomorrow's—workforce.[118] Can government policy makers
create modern-day counterparts to such successful social inventions of
the past as Social Security and the Fair Labor Standards Act? These two

initiatives served to institutionalize the forty-hour, five-day workweek and retirement at ages sixty-two and sixty-five. But while these innovative policy enactments were insightful in the 1930s, today they are in some ways obsolete, hampering the recasting of work-hour policies and practices. Can business leaders refashion workdays and workweeks to offer employees more options and flexibility? Can policy makers reappraise wage and hour laws, pension and Social Security regulations, and the design of work more generally? With the aging of the workforce, employers may increasingly have to confront a shortage of skilled workers. Flexibilities and reduced work hours could be ways of recruiting and retaining valuable workers, as might "unretiring" retirees. Current pension, payroll tax, benefit, and work-hour regulations are the lags that make it costly, or even impossible, to do so.

Flexible and Phased Career Paths

Equally critical are new arrangements in the sequencing of schooling, paid work, family care, and leisure over the life course. How can career paths be fashioned to permit men and women to lighten their paid-work obligations without harming their long-term chances for promotion or benefits or limiting their future occupational options? Such a refashioning of occupational career pathways and ladders (to offer routes that could be exited or entered) along with a recalibrating of the workweek, could offer a wide variety of ways to be a valued employee and, at the same time, to pursue a valued family and personal life.

Parental leaves of absence and sabbaticals (for an interval following the birth of a child, prior to retirement, or simply for renewal) are two such structural leads, as is a cutback in hours (with prorated benefits) for a reasonable period at various times during the life course. Some innovative law firms are supporting the idea of part-time careers, even awarding partnerships to part-time employees. Other possibilities include flexible work schedules, opportunities to work at home, and extended time off for the care of children or infirm parents. These options are essential for those periods of the life course when family demands are particularly acute or when workers seek additional education, phased retirement, or relief from burnout. All of these opportunities are feasible in the United States, and the largest, most progressive corporations are adopting many of them. But none of them is in widespread practice. Permitting American workers to tailor their working hours—and their work lives—to their family circumstances and personal values might well reinforce their work commitment, enhance their work performance, generally contribute to the development of a more productive as well as more satisfied workforce, and further the goals of gender equality. But reduced hours and alternative career paths will not work as long as there is a culture of commitment predicated on the career mystique. Neither will these options work if they do not provide safety nets, security, and other necessities in today's risk society. People will take advantage of flexible work-hour and career options only if they are not one-way exits from real jobs, but are viewed as legitimate time-outs or alternative pathways.

8

Beyond the Career Mystique: Recasting the Lockstep Life Course

In 1989, social commentators, as well as social scientists, lambasted Felice Schwartz[1] for her (misunderstood) suggestion of a separate career track for mothers. Schwartz, then head of Catalyst (an organization dedicated to promoting women in business), recognized the difficulty of women having it all, pursuing existing career paths (fashioned lockstep in line with the career mystique) while raising children. The media promptly labeled her suggested alternative the "mommy track." Regardless of the merits of Schwartz's argument, many social observers were aghast at the very notion of a mommy track, of women somehow having less opportunity in the labor market then men. As a metaphor, the mommy track served to sustain the career mystique by placing women's experiences outside the conventional lockstep path. Men's career paths could remain intact if women were offered something else, a second, and a second-class, track. Those adamantly opposed to the mommy track idea took for granted two key assumptions: (1) pursuing the lockstep career mystique is the only *real* path to success, and (2) having both men and women pursue the career mystique is the only *real* path to gender equality. We believe neither assumption is correct. Schwartz was right, but her solution was too narrow. Americans do need more flexible—and more—career paths, but that is true for men as well as women, singles as well as marrieds, thirty-somethings as well as fifty-somethings.

Most crucial are multiple exit and entry portals in order to move away from the traditional lockstep pattern. Alternative exit and entry possibilities would permit Americans to begin second acts or revert back to an original, first act career at different ages and stages. The path to gender equality is not a forked road—follow the yellow brick road of the career mystique or else move off track to part-time, contingent, or intermittent work. We believe that true gender equality is only possible when the clockwork of careers becomes flexible enough to be compatible with the clockwork of the rest of life for all employees, regardless of their gender, their age, or their family responsibilities.

CAREER METAPHORS

Metaphors matter. Language describing careers as ladders to climb, as plateaus to reach or get stuck on, or as tracks to follow or be derailed from, paints more than just colorful images. It shapes not only American culture, but also social policies and what Americans envision as possible. In the preceding chapters, we have shown that the career mystique remains the dominant view of the way employment should work over the life course. But we also describe Americans—men as well as women—as uncertain and ambivalent about their career paths, wanting both more and less than the career mystique has to offer. The metaphor of the single-minded, singularly focused, lockstep career is becoming increasingly obsolete. Women's lives are a case in point; it is often impossible to chart women's career paths without information about their husbands, their children, and their aging parents.

American culture is replete with other stereotypes and images about the lockstep life course. Consider how we characterize retirees as "senior," "elderly," and "over the hill." Retirement itself is called "the golden years." Whole communities have emerged—such as Leisure World[2]—targeted to this growing segment of society. So, too, have sprouted special senior rates for movies, museums, and public transportation, even as growing numbers of men and women eligible for them are far from senior in their lifestyles, expectations, and goals.

The American Dream is itself a metaphor for occupational success, a metaphor that works for the winners of the educational and occupational career game,[3] but that remains elusive for growing numbers of men and women across age, class, educational, racial, ethnic, and geographical divides.

Still, the metaphor and mystique of careers remain a durable part of the American cultural landscape. They undergird a plethora of policies and practices creating and sustaining the clockwork of the lockstep education, work, and retirement life course. The career mystique is the great American fable, the story young people learn at early ages, the legend Americans of all ages accept as the way things are. But the ingredients of the career mystique—working hard and putting in long hours—no longer guarantee success or even job security. And, regardless of their security or future prospects, employees at all life stages are hard-pressed to manage the multiple clockworks of their job, family, and community obligations. Clearly the meanings and the institutional arrangements embedded in the lockstep regime of continuous, full-time schooling followed by continuous, full-time (or more) employment, followed by the continuous, full-time leisure of retirement, are out of step with contemporary reality.

We have demonstrated the perpetuation in policy, practice, and public perceptions of this view of divided lives, of a neatly packaged, lockstep life course. The career mystique became a full-blown part of the culture following World War II, hand in hand with the feminine mystique. Then, middle-class life meant the pursuit of both: Men pursued the lockstep career path backed up by their full-time, homemaking wives. As women sought to escape the feminine mystique, they traded it for the equality of the career mystique. But most men and women retained conventional values concerning the good wife, the good mother, and the good breadwinner. Social as well as business policies were grounded in the breadwinner/homemaker vision of the workplace and the home. With the Women's Movement of the 1970s came the push to make men's career opportunities also available to women. Since then, men's lives as breadwinners have changed little, with two important exceptions: They now seldom have the backup of a full-time homemaker, and few now have salaries sufficient to achieve and sustain a middle-class (or even working-class) lifestyle on only one income. Women's lives have become a lot more complicated. A new metaphor of balance has emerged as the hybrid solution: Women (especially) can *have it all* by balancing their paid- and family-work obligations, abandoning the career clockwork and working less, aiming lower, and occasionally leaving work altogether. The very language of *balance* reinforces the artificial division between paid work and unpaid family work, as well as the gender divide between the two. Women typically do the family balancing, while their husbands invest time, energy, and commitment in their jobs. As a number of researchers have pointed out, most women who follow the lockstep career clockwork to the top jobs and the legendary corner offices do not marry, or else they get divorced, have fewer children later in life, if they have any, or, in effect, "hire a wife" (other women to serve as the paid homemakers and caregivers for their families).[4] These strategies only underscore the fundamental incompatibilities of families and careers as they are currently organized.[5]

POLICY LAGS

The mismatch between real-life experiences and the regime of policies based on the career mystique points out how Americans take for granted beliefs about education, paid work, family-care work, and retirement.

Structural lag[6] is a sociological concept describing how the policies and practices of governments, corporations, and other institutions typically change at a far slower pace than demographic, economic, technological, and other social transformations. The nation is now experiencing such a period of structural lag in the ways American policies and practices organize education, retirement, and especially paid work. Structural lag is also evident when labor-market and occupational-career policies conspicuously ignore unpaid (and low-paid) care work, which is relegated to the private sphere of life and, generally, to women. We focus here on three instances of policy lag.

The Work–Family Mismatch

The *mismatch* between the career regime—the roles, rules, and routines we take for granted—and the family and personal needs of today's workforce exists precisely because of the *match* between the career mystique and the feminine mystique; each was predicated on the other. In the words of Arlie Hochschild,[7] we have a stalled revolution, one that changed women's educational and employment options, but not the career path options of either men or women. So long as the clockwork of jobs and career paths is predicated on the myth of the unencumbered worker,[8] they will remain at odds with twenty-first-century work–family realities.

As we move from an industrial to a global economy, few employees, regardless of their gender, have a full-time homemaker available to take care of the domestic details of their personal lives. But jobs remain designed as if employees were able and willing to focus exclusively on them. Jobs, schools, medical services, and many other aspects of contemporary life continue to assume that someone (a wife) is available during the typical workday to care for children after school, during the summer, or on snow days; to take children to the doctor or the dog to the vet; to have the refrigerator fixed or the new stove delivered; to engage in the civic activities that build communities. But the wives who facilitated men's careers now have careers of their own, as do the sisters, mothers, grandmothers, friends, and neighbors that working women relied on as backup in the past.

The highly competitive global economy, with its focus on 24–7 availability, long work hours, and doing more with less, only exacerbates the problems employees face as they strive to synchronize the multiple dimensions of their lives. The result? American workers report being frustrated, exhausted, and close to burnout. Working parents feel deprived of sleep. Their children's lives are frequently rushed and heavily scheduled, with their weekday experiences at home, especially before family members leave for school, work, and day care, often resembling controlled chaos.

The Lockstep Mismatch

The lockstep life course of, first, full-time, continuous education, then full-time, continuous employment, and finally full-time, continuous retirement is clearly at odds with the need and desire of growing numbers of Americans for *second acts*, that is for new or different jobs, skill-sets, or civic engagements at different ages or stages. To achieve such second acts, many want to return to school. Even though adult education is now taken for granted, options for career switching, credentialing, and skill upgrading for people long past their twenties remain limited. Americans have experienced only one truly effective policy promoting second acts and second chances: the post–World War II GI Bill. It not only enabled, but even paid, veterans to go back to school to develop job skills and acquire the education to prepare them for entry into new career paths or for progression along existing ones.

Legitimated, accepted *time-outs*—for schooling, for leisure, for raising children—are simply not part of the lockstep career clockwork, except for the presumably permanent time-out of retirement. But the clockwork of traditional institutional arrangements (hiring only young people for entry-level jobs, for example) forecloses second acts for older workers or retirees, making the growing ranks of those in their fifties, sixties, and seventies part of yet another stalled revolution. Americans in this age group are better educated, more vigorous, healthier, and more skilled than ever in history. But the regime of rules and regulations undergirding the career mystique means that they are also more apt to find themselves retired to the sidelines of society.

The need to reassess and update the governmental and business policies and practices shaping the lockstep clockwork of education, employment, and leisure is clear. New cultural blueprints that better fit twenty-first-century realities must incorporate older Americans' desire to remain connected and create avenues for second acts of paid work or unpaid community service. The tide of time and events is rendering obsolete traditional beliefs and values related to careers and age, retirement and age, gender and age. Still, the United States has yet to come to terms with the inconsistencies and contradictions of policies that marginalize older employees and retirees, constrain educational options to those who are just starting out, and ignore those of all ages and stages with heavy caregiving responsibilities, not only for the nation's children, but also for the nation's ill and infirm.

The Risk–Safety Net Mismatch

The reality obscured by the career mystique is that employment in the twenty-first century is replete with risks and insecurities. Layoffs, low pay, and loss of health insurance are now realities for employees regardless of their age, gender, ethnicity, education, or status. Corporate restructuring, mergers, and bankruptcies are now commonplace, as is the outsourcing of all kinds of jobs offshore to countries like China or India that have much cheaper labor. Despite their hard work, long hours, or personal loyalty, many Americans find themselves at risk of layoffs or forced early retirement.

Risks of poverty associated with single parenthood are now exacerbated by welfare reforms that assume that (1) jobs are available to low-skilled people, and (2) such jobs pay enough for people to work their way out of poverty. The risks of a health catastrophe are aggravated by the fact that jobs are increasingly packaged as contractual or temporary work; contractors or temps typically have to purchase their own health insurance or else do without. Even the gold standard of the career mystique—the "good" full-time job—is no longer a guarantee of affordable and medically adequate health insurance.

The risks of forced or strongly encouraged retirement from primary career jobs seem to catch many older employees unawares. In our research we find that people almost always retire before they expect to do so—often due to downsizing packages, a spouse's retirement, poor health, or the poor health of a family member. Declining pension benefits and reduced coverage, in conjunction with increasing longevity, mean uncertain prospects for a growing number of Americans approaching or living their "golden" years.

Europeans tend to recognize the risks of contemporary careers and lives better and to provide the appropriate safety nets. But in the United States policy makers are lowering the nets or else doing away with them altogether, even as risks and uncertainties escalate.

CONSEQUENCES

The Time Squeeze

Time has become a scarce commodity in American life.[9] This is especially problematic given the equating of work time with work commitment and employers' expectations of high commitment.[10] As a fixed commodity, time allocated to employment is necessarily unavailable for other activities, including family relations. When all adults in families are paid employees, the family gains in income. Employees themselves may experience a sense of productive engagement and self-esteem. What is lost when everyone is earning a living is time for living. We were surprised at the number of women in the *Ecology of Careers Study* who say they have virtually no leisure time on workdays. Stacey Merola shows that working men and women in the United States in 1997 reported having less free time than did working men and women in 1977.[11] There is, to be sure, a leisure gap between men and women, with men having more leisure; but men, too, would like more free time. Most American workers work at least full time and often more; most doing so voice a strong desire to work less.[12]

Insecurity and Unease

The story of the American Dream is predicated on the career mystique, the myth that strong work commitment, dedication, hard work, and continuous employment will lead to occupational attainment, security, and economic success. This has never been a realistic scenario for low-wage workers with few skills; still, many subscribe to its promise. The American Dream of the career mystique did fall within the reach of the many World War II GIs returning home to middle-class office jobs and houses in the suburbs, replete with children and homemaking wives. They worked hard to climb reasonably secure occupational ladders that became more secure with each year of additional seniority. Their wives typically managed the details of daily living and suffered from what Betty Friedan called the "problem with no name."[13]

Today most husband-wife families are dual-earner households. Mortgages on homes in middle-class neighborhoods commonly require two incomes. Few jobs now guarantee security with seniority. Even health insurance is no longer a taken-for-granted benefit. American workers at the bottom of the income distribution have always felt insecure, uncertain about their futures. But not since the Great Depression have so many middle-class households also experienced this anxiety.[14]

Quality of Family Life and Well-Being

Studies show that long hours and job demands, the clockwork of the career mystique, contribute to work–family conflict, especially in the absence of supportive supervisors. In turn, work–family conflicts and stressful work circumstances produce lower levels of marital quality.[15] For example, Ann Crouter and her colleagues find that husbands' stresses on the job lead to subsequent negative interactions with their wives at home.[16] Similarly, research by Rena Repetti and her colleagues show that stresses and overload at work lead to withdrawal and negative communications with children.[17] Both job characteristics (such as the number of work hours) and inequalities in work distribution at home spill over into the quality of workers' relationships with their spouses and children.

Still, the solution is not to revert back to old gender roles. Studies show that employment promotes well-being among women as well as men, even though women bear the greater burden in managing both paid work and family-care work.[18] Women who work for pay are typically less depressed and anxious and have fewer illnesses than women who are full-time homemakers. However, role conflicts and overload remain a hazard of contemporary living so long as the demands of work and home remain fundamentally incompatible. Furthermore, spillover, conflict, and overload have profound implications for workers' well-being.[19] Researchers find that stressors on the job and at home affect the mental health of both men and women.[20]

Short- and Long-Term Costs

Jobs in the United States have been designed for two workforces—the primary workforce following the career mystique and the secondary workforce. This secondary workforce (presumed to be comprised of young people or women) presumably does not require the wages, benefits, and security associated with jobs in the primary sector. Pursuing the career mystique has never guaranteed security or success, but there have always been penalties for *not* doing so. The costs of deviating from what has historically been the typical path of continuous, full-time (or more) employment (that is, the costs of being part of the secondary workforce) have always been borne by minorities, women, and the unskilled. Today, even in educated households, taking time out of the labor force or working a reduced schedule to raise young children, to care for aging parents, or simply to have a saner lifestyle can wreak havoc on seniority, salary, security, retirement income, and possibilities for promotion. Many workers try to solve the dilemmas of managing job, family, and personal life by controlling what is in their control: by delaying childbearing, having fewer children, or having none at all. This is a key point: Advanced nations, including the United States, are experiencing record lows in fertility precisely because most women and men want or need to be productively engaged in the workforce, and neither men nor women can figure out how to synchronize family-care work and paid work. Women have typically been paid less as part of the secondary workforce because it was assumed that they were married to (primary workforce) breadwinners. Traditional family responsibilities, along with traditionally lower salaries and fewer advancement opportunities, mean that few women follow the regime of full-time (or more) continuous employment. Research shows that most women frequently move in and out of the workforce or into part-time or temporary jobs in tandem with changing parenting or caregiving circumstances and/or their husbands' geographical relocations. These intermittent, part-time, and delayed-entry strategies on the part of women make sense in a world where occupational paths presume that primary employees have no family responsibilities and where husbands have higher earning potential than their wives. Both parents simply can't work everywhere, all the time. But stepping off the lockstep path is costly in terms of women's own occupational advancement, job security, future earnings, benefits, and retirement income.[21] Because pursuing two careers in a one-career world is so difficult, many husband/wife families prioritize one person's occupational career, usually the husband's.[22] In this way, gender inequalities, both within households and within society, are continuously reproduced.[23]

Occupational and family career paths thus play out very differently for most American men and women, even though both typically expect to invest heavily in their jobs when first starting out. But when the need comes to move to a different city or a different state to pursue a better opportunity or to retain one's current position, women are more likely to become "tied movers" or "tied stayers," following their partners or else staying put for their partners' jobs. Even single-parent women may choose to remain in a particular geographical area so their children have the chance to see their fathers on a regular basis. In addition, becoming a parent often means that women will scale back on their occupational plans and aspirations in light of the incompatibilities of family building and career building. New fathers, by contrast, typically invest even more in the family breadwinning role, which is compatible with career building, meaning that new fathers often put in even longer hours on the job.

THE CHALLENGE

Employees, especially those who are also wives, mothers, or caregivers of others, are exhorted in magazines and on television to balance the paid- and home-work aspects of their lives. But how? How do Americans put together the diverse pieces of their lives? We hold that the balance metaphor is not a good one; people want to be effective at both making a living and living, without being penalized for doing so. Americans today are managing as best they can. They do so through various hybrid arrangements, often involving men doing more paid work and women doing more unpaid family work. But many feel overworked and exhausted as they do. In fact, Americans in 2002 were less satisfied with their jobs than they were as recently as 1995.[24] Workers between the ages of thirty-five and forty-four—the typical career-building years, but also the typical family-building years—are the least content, with less than half reporting satisfaction with their jobs. Jennifer and Rob (see profile in chapter 3), who are just starting out with their first child, have worked out just such a neotraditional arrangement with Jennifer working part time. By contrast, Rick and Donna (see profile in chapter 4) are both highly committed to their professions. Their strategy has been to lessen family demands, delaying parenting as long as possible and having but one child. Deb and Steve (see profile in chapter 6) started out with a traditional arrangement when their children were young. Deb later returned to school and has started a new career in her fifties. In each of these cases, having two adults in a family facilitates such adaptive strategies. Lisa, a single parent (see profile in chapter 1), had to resign from her job because her employer refused to take her personal needs seriously. African American professional women are perhaps the most hard-pressed to have it all, often finding their dreams of marriage fading as they follow the career mystique.

The stories and the research evidence we have chronicled show that the twin forces characterizing adulthood in twentieth-century America—the lockstep career mystique and the breadwinner/homemaker gender divide—are obsolete cultural relics of a bygone era. Nevertheless, the regime of policies and practices built upon and reinforcing them continues to dictate the rules of the career game. Only, following the rules today can mean little—no job security, few raises, and fewer prospects for advancement.

The United States and, indeed, most nations thus far have not responded to the dramatic alterations in the social fabric of society. Needed are flexible policies and practices more in keeping with the new realities of contemporary experience, namely that (1) all adults in a family are probably in the workforce (in other words, that there are now few full-time homemakers); (2) there are risks in even what were once secure, well-paying jobs; and (3) with the increasing likelihood of and desire for second acts, retirement and retooling may occur several times in a person's life.

BEYOND LOCKSTEP LIVES

Corporations, governments, and communities have been much more adept in responding to *technological* challenges than to the *social* challenges we have described in this book: a changing (paid) workforce, a declining (unpaid) care workforce, a growing retired force, and a world economy fraught with risk and uncertainty. Yet, questions involving the human condition are both more perplexing and more critical to the nation's future than ever before. The challenge today is for the important agents of change—government, unions, corporations, and communities—

to work together to question old assumptions and to develop new ways of organizing paid work, unpaid family work, and community service work. By doing so, Americans can unlock the lockstep of the life course.

Revising the clockwork of paid work may seem radical, but in many ways it is a conservative response to the challenges Americans face. Rearranging career patterns to permit some work-time reduction during the childrearing, elder caregiving, and pre- and postretirement years would actually serve to bolster the sanctity and stability of families. Children would see more of their parents, family life would be less hectic, and neither spouse would be forced to sacrifice career for family or vice versa. Recasting the conventional patterning of work, education, and leisure over the life course to be more flexible could serve to reinforce the traditional function of families as caretakers of children and the infirm, while encouraging a partnership—between mothers and fathers, sisters and brothers, husbands and wives—to share caregiving and domestic roles.

In fashioning these innovative arrangements, it should be kept in mind that periods of childrearing, caregiving for ailing family members, and mid-career transitions are not long lasting. Parenthood has come to occupy a relatively short span of contemporary adulthood in the United States as a result of both reduced fertility and increased longevity. Indeed, today's parents will typically have very young preschoolers in the home for only a few years once or twice in their lives, while their average (paid) working life may well exceed forty years. What is required are more flexible clockworks both for the days, weeks, and years of paid work and for education, career development, and retirement.

Will American society legitimate alternative structural and cultural models and tempos for the clockwork of careers? Will they base policies on the fact that all workers, men and women, have or will have families and experience family demands? Will they recognize that most workers are or will become parents and are or will be married to someone who is also in the work force? Will employers and policy makers, along with the public, recognize that there is a new life stage in the making that is postponing old age, that most in these *midcourse* years would rather have a gradual reduction in hours as they move to retirement, or if retired would prefer to work for pay but not full time? Can the United States institutionalize a range of flexible career pathways, including possibilities for second acts and time-outs?

Like many individuals and organizations, the world of paid work is resistant to change. Existing social arrangements provide a guide to action (the rules of the game) and shared expectations that, in turn, foster a sense of security about the taken-for-grantedness of the way things are. Attempts to change existing arrangements are often resisted because they threaten this sense of security, make decision making more difficult, and disrupt routines.

New, more appropriate policies and practices will come about only when the economic and social costs of doing nothing outweigh the costs of change. We believe that time has come or is close at hand. Outmoded conventions, metaphors, and stereotypes about paid work, unpaid care work, gender, retirement, and old age operate as real impediments to productivity on the job, life quality at home, and community revitalization. Traditional, but now outmoded, institutional arrangements that gave substance to the career mystique *are* alterable. What is difficult is coming to terms with the need to do so.

In this book we have shown that most people do not, or cannot, follow the career mystique, marching lockstep through life from education to employment to retirement in a fixed sequence or schedule. Unforeseen circumstances (downsizing, mergers), as well as family transitions (a new child, an ailing parent), make it impossible to do so. Innovative policies permitting occasional time-outs, as well as "good" (with benefits) part-time or part-year jobs, could transform work as we know it. These arrangements could not only help meet the needs of working parents and the growing numbers of aging baby boomers, but also contribute to the creation of the more flexible and adaptable workforce required in this global, competitive, information economy.

If change is going to occur, Americans need to rethink and redesign educational, occupational, and retirement paths to be more flexible and integrative than lockstep. Consider, for example, the forty-hour workweek, a historical invention of the 1938 Fair Labor Standards Act. The forty-hour, five-day workweek seems legitimate or "normal" because (1) it is deeply entrenched in the ways we think about work, (2) there is a broad consensus about it, (3) it seems fair, and (4) so much of life is shaped around it. Consider how health insurance, pensions, Social Security, and other benefits are tied to at least full-time employment. The primary workforce (unlike those working part time, at temporary jobs, or moving in and out of the workforce) consists of those following some semblance of the career mystique by remaining in full-time employment throughout most of their adulthood. Much more is tied to full-time hours: rush hour traffic, when coffee shops are open, assigning federal holidays to Mondays, even the idea of the weekend. There are conceivably other possible ways to organize time. For example, Robert Kahn suggests the concept of four-hour work modules, where employees could contract for one, two, or three module days or for four to twelve modules a week for, say, a six-week or six-month period.[25] Other options, such as part-time or temporary work contracting for particular jobs, are already commonplace, but these arrangements now place workers at the fringes of employment, typically without health insurance, unemployment insurance, or job security.

What may push the United States toward such a revamping of the current career regime is the fact that this is an era of social and economic crisis. The nation stands at a critical juncture. Not only the needs of today's workforce, but the workings of a global economy, are challenging traditional ways of thinking about paid work and career paths. This could lead to a reconfiguration of the career regime (the jobs, rules, and routines around paid work throughout one's work life) in ways that create more options for both men and women in youth, early and middle adulthood, and the midcourse years.

A fundamental challenge to the nation in the twenty-first century is to create integrative, flexible careers—occupational paths that acknowledge rather than ignore personal and family goals and obligations, (re)educational goals and needs throughout adulthood, and midcourse inclinations for second acts, including postretirement employment and civic engagement. Careers will be flexible when they are compatible with the exigencies of peoples' lives. But that means that the United States must provide some way for people at all ages and stages to deal with the uncertainties and risks of our global economy. To build such flexibility and integration requires recognition of the career mystique as a historical invention, a powerful but obsolete metaphor that can, and should be, reinvented. All that is required is the will and the imagination to do so.

Notes

CHAPTER 1: THE CAREER MYSTIQUE

1. The names of both the people we interviewed and their employers are pseudonyms. This book represents the synthesis of findings from the *Ecology of Careers Study*, involving in-person and telephone interviews with 4,637 employees (or spouses of employees), as well as focus groups, conducted from 1998 through 2002. Most (3,893) of the people we interviewed were reinterviewed two years later to capture continuity and change in their lives. Where possible we interviewed both spouses separately. Further information about the first wave of the survey can be found in *It's About Time: Couples and Careers* (2003a), edited by Phyllis Moen. More comprehensive data on the Ecology of Careers Project can be found in a 2004 report, *The New "Middle" Work Force,* by Phyllis Moen and colleagues, available from her office at the University of Minnesota. The "Ecology of Careers Study" was supported by the Alfred P. Sloan Foundation and the National Institute on Aging.

2. Friedan's 1963 book *The Feminine Mystique* became a best-seller, fomenting the second wave of the Women's Movement in the 1960s and 1970s. See also Chafe (1972) and Rose (2001).

3. See also Hertz (1991), pp. 247–263.

4. In other words, many women discarded the feminine mystique only to replace it with the career mystique.

5. Sociologists and historians term this process of allocation and income distribution the *family economy*. This information was obtained from the Bureau of Labor Statistics "Families by Presence and Relationship of Employed Members and Family Type, 2000–2001," at www.bls.gov/news.release/famee.t02.htm (accessed June 20, 2004).

6. See Tilly and Scott (1978); Zerubavel (1981); Powell and DiMaggio (1991).

7. See Smelser (1959); Moen and Sweet (2003).

8. As a sociologist (Moen) and a psychologist (Roehling), we find the career concept useful as a way of linking individual lives with large-scale changes in culture and society. The concept of career is most typically defined as an orderly progression up an occupational ladder. But this is a mystification, a possibility for only a subset of employees, a figment of the American bootstrap dream of frontiers, expansive opportunities, and the exceptionalism of individuals. We term this the *career mystique*, reserving the term *career* to refer more generally to the patterns of employment over the life course, patterns that, for most Americans, are typically neither linear nor upwardly mobile. The term *career regime* refers to the policies and practices based on and rewarding those willing and able to pursue the career mystique of continuous, lockstep devotion to one's job. See also Griele and Elder (1998).

9. Coser (1974) discusses the concept of "greedy" institutions.

10. See Kessler-Harris (2001); Spain and Bianchi (1996); Moen (2003a, b).

11. Full-time mothering in surburbia leads to many women's sense of isolation and marginality from society, which Betty Friedan in 1963 called the "problem with no name."

12. Legislation also excludes children from the workforce, which we discuss in chapter 2. For an excellent overview of related social policy development, see the work of Skocpol (1992, 2000), and Kanter (1977), as well as work on the changing social contract (Rubin 1996; Freeman 1994).

13. See Mortimer, Harley, and Aronson (1999); Mortimer (2003); Macmillan and Eliason (2003); Heinz (1999, 2001); Modell (1989); Booth et al (1999); Buchmann (1989).

14. Several books address care work, e.g., Harrington (1999). Williams (2000) describes the policies perpetuating the gender divide. See also Appelbaum et al. (2002).

15. See Hochschild (1989).

16. Evidence of the whole process of choice and constraint reproducing gender inequality is provided by Crittenden (2001), England and Farkas (1986), Felmlee (1982, 1984), Goldin (1991), Reskin and Roos (1990); Reskin and Padavic (1994). For recent statistics on the wage gap, see data from the Institute for Women's Policy Research (2001). See Clarkberg and Moen (2001); Han and Moen (1999a, b).

17. See the Work Trends Survey by the John J. Heldrich Center for Workforce Development of Rutgers University; Townsend (2002); Bookman (2004); Hernandez and Myers (1993); Daly (1996).

18. See statistical analyses by Clarkberg and Moen (2001); Jacobs and Gerson (1998b); Robinson and Godbey (1997); Schor (1992).

19. The importance—and neglect—of unpaid care work is discussed by Harrington (1999); Williams (2000).

20. See discussion by Krüger (1996); Moen (2003a, b).

21. See the work of Zhou and Moen (2001a, b). In 1998, following economic reforms, the unemployment rate in China was estimated to be between 21% and 23%. See Benson and Zhu (1999).

22. See, e.g., Parsons and Bales (1955); Hill (1970); Komarovsky (1962).

23. See Blau (1977); Chafe (1972); Cott and Pleck (1979); Kanter (1977).

24. The discussion of alternate tracks for women was raised in an article by Felice Schwartz, founder of Catalyst, in 1989.

25. See Clacs (2000); Cooper and Kurland (2002); Kelly and Dobbin (1999); Glass and Riley (1998); Gornick and Meyers (2003); Haley, Perry-Jenkins, and Armenia (2001); Sandberg and Cornfield (2000); Scandura and Lankau (1997); Seward, Yeatts, and Zottarelli (2002); Standen, Daniels, and Lamond (1999).

26. See Bergmann (1986); Blau and Ferber (1986); Tilly and Scott (1978); Cohn (1985); Fuchs (1988); Goldin (1991).

27. See Appelbaum, Bailey, Berg, and Kalleberg (2002); Bailyn, Drago, and Kochan (2001).

28. Matilda White Riley is the intellectual force behind the notion of structural lag. See Riley, Kahn, and Foner (1994); Riley and Riley (1994).

29. Recent statistics on the persisting wage gap between men's and women's earnings are provided by the Institute for Women's Policy Research (1999). See also Finch (1983); Marshall et al (2001); Kessler-Harris (2001).

30. There is a vast literature on the work–family conflict. For more information see Beutell and Witting-Berman (1999); Friedman and Greenhaus (2000); Garey (1999); Goode (1960); Greenhaus and Beutell (1985); Gutek, Searle, and Klepa (1991); Hochschild (1989); Maume and Bellas (1999); Nelson, Quick, Hitt, and Moesel (1990); Marshall and Barnett (1993); Moen (1989, 1992, 2000); Moen and Yu (2000); Nippert-Eng (1996); Pleck (1977, 1985); Spain and Bianchi (1996); Townsend (2002). A classic on this topic was written by Myrdal and Klein (1956).

CHAPTER 2: LEARNING THE CAREER MYSTIQUE: WHERE DO VALUES AND EXPECTATIONS COME FROM?

1. Baruch and Barnett (1986) found that kindergartners are strongly gender stereotyped in their career aspirations. Ten-year-olds still display the stereotypes, but they are less extreme than those of younger children.

2. See Gottfredson (1981).

3. For an overview of social learning theory, see Bandura (1977).

4. University of Michigan, Institute for Social Research, "Monitoring the Future."

5. See Gager, Cooney, and Call (1999).

6. See Rollins and White (1982).

7. Thorn and Gilbert (1998) examined the relationship between paternal behaviors and the gender orientation of young men who were juniors and seniors in college. It appears that boys observed their fathers' role-sharing behaviors in the home and developed attitudes consistent with those behaviors.

8. See Baruch and Barnett (1986).

9. Johnson and Mortimer (2000), in a survey of high school seniors, and Stevens, Puchtell, Ryu, and Mortimer (1992), in a survey of ninth graders, found that girls' career expectations were at least as high as boys.'

10. Mahaffy and Ward (2002) found that girls who planned to have children early expected to abbreviate or interrupt their college education; boys did not see childbearing as affecting their plans (p. 412).

11. See Correll and Bourg (1999).

12. See Weinger (2000), p. 20.

13. See Martin, Martin, and Martin (2001) for a summary of this research.

14. See Martin, Martin, and Martin (2001) for a summary of this research.

15. Data from the "Monitoring the Future" survey as cited in Whitehead and Popenoe (1999). The study also found that girls placed more importance on marriage than did boys.

16. Data from the "Monitoring the Future" survey as cited in Whitehead and Popenoe (1999).

17. See Whitehead and Popenoe (2001) concerning a study conducted for the National Marriage Project.

18. Data from the "Monitoring the Future" survey as cited in Whitehead and Popenoe (1999).

19. Almost one fourth of teens in 1995 reported that few marriages are good or happy. Data from the "Monitoring the Future" survey as cited in Whitehead and Popenoe (1999).

20. See McCabe and Barnett (2000).

21. See Hofferth and Sandberg (2001a, b); Kinney, Dunn, and Hofferth (2000).

22. See Hofferth and Sandberg (2001a, b).

23. See Federal Interagency Forum on Child and Family Statistics (2003): see page 113 for U.S. data and the Canadian Council on Social Development for Canadian data.

24. See Flammer, Alsaker, and Noack (1999).

25. Mortimer, Pimentel, Nash, and Chaimun (1996) examine the different motivations for work and the value development of teens as they work.

26. See Desmarais and Curtis (1999).

27. These might include such jobs as dishwasher, cashier, or food preparer in a fast food restaurant; see Loughlin and Barling (1999).

28. For summaries of the research on the effects of teen employment, see Stone and Mortimer (1998); Vondracek and Profeli (2003). See also Mortimer (2003); Frone (1999).

29. See Stone and Mortimer (1998); Vondracek and Profeli (2003).

30. See Kruse and Mahony (2000) for more information about illegal child labor in the United States.

31. See Kruse and Mahony (2000).

32. See Piotrkowski and Carrubba (1999).

33. See Martinez and Cranston-Gingras (1996).

34. See Forman (1999).

35. See Forman (1999).

CHAPTER 3: DO YOUNG ADULTS STILL BELIEVE IN THE CAREER MYSTIQUE?

1. See review by Shanahan, Miech, and Elder (1998).

2. See Hewlett (2002).

3. See Orrange (2002, 2003b).

4. See Orrange (2003a, p. 462; 2003b).

5. For more information, see Digest of Education Statistics, 2001, at http://nces.ed.gov//pubs2002/digest2001/tables/dt185.asp (accessed May 18, 2003). According to the 2000 Current Population Survey (U.S. Census Bureau), college completion rates are much lower. Newburger and Curry (2000) report that 30% of women and 28% of men between ages twenty-five and twenty-nine have completed a college degree. The Federal Interagency Forum on Child and Family Statistics (2003) reports that in 2002, 29% had earned their degree. Black and Hispanic youth are much less likely to complete their college degree than whites (18%, 11%, and 36%, respectively).

6. Ingels, Curtin, Kaufman, Alt, and Chen (2002) found that children whose parents had completed college and were in the upper quartile of economic status were more likely to complete a bachelor's degree.

7. See Ingels, Curtin, Kaufman, Alt, and Chen (2002).

8. Ingels, Curtin, Kaufman, Alt, and Chen (2002), using a sample of respondents who were in eighth grade in 1988, found that 16% of African American, 14% of Hispanic, 46% of Asian, and 30% of white, non-Hispanic respondents had graduated from a four-year college or university in 2000.

9. Statistics in this section come from the American Association of University Women (AAUW) (1999).

10. See the U.S. Department of Education report by Bradburn (2002).

11. See Farmer (1997), p. 75.

12. See statistics in AAUW (1999).

13. See Clayton, Garcia, Underwood, McEndree, and Sheppard (1993); Dillard and Campbell (1981); Fisher and Padmawidjaja (1999); Lee (1984).

14. See Fisher and Padmawidjaja (1999), p. 141.

15. See Rubin (1996), pp. 34–35.

16. See Loughlin and Barling (1999).

17. See Coverdill (1988); Zandvakili (2000).

18. Data from the National Center for Education Statistics, Digest of Education Statistics, 2001, at http://nces.ed.gov//pubs2002/digest2001/tables/dt382.asp (accessed May 18, 2003).

19. See Gore, Aseltine, Colten, and Lin (1997).

20. See data from the U.S. Census Bureau reported by Fields and Casper (2001).

21. According to Raley (2001), the percentage of fifteen- to twenty-nine-year-old women who cohabit with men has tripled between 1970 and 1995 from 3% to 9%.

22. See Armas (2001) for a report on 2000 U.S. Census Bureau data.

23. See Bumpass and Lu (2000). Of women between twenty-five and twenty-nine, 47% had cohabited with men at one point in their life. Those with less education were more likely to cohabit than those with more education.

24. Whitehead and Popenoe (2001) found that 52% of single men and women surveyed agreed that one of their biggest concerns about getting married was the potential for divorce. Ferguson (2000) also found this a concern among Asian American women.

25. See Whitehead and Popenoe (2002).

26. See Whitehead and Popenoe (2001).

27. See Bumpass and Lu (2000).

28. See Bumpass and Lu (2000).

29. For statistics on marriage trends, see Bianchi and Spain (1996); South (1993). Data for 1970 and 2000 was reported by the U.S. Census Bureau (Fields and Casper [2001]).

30. According to the U.S. Census Bureau's America's Family and Living Arrangements (March 2000), 46% of African American men and 44% of African American women between the ages of thirty and thirty-four are unmarried, whereas only 28% of white men and 18% of white women are unmarried.

31. See discussion by McLanahan and Casper (1995), especially p. 14.

32. A large body of theory and research investigates the declining marriage rate. For the purposes of this book, we focus on that most germane to intersecting occupational and family careers.

33. See, e.g., Moen (1992); Goldscheider and Waite (1986).

34. See discussion in Cherlin (1992).

35. For black women, they found the reverse. See Van der Klaauw (1996); McLanahan and Casper (1995).

36. See Blau, Kahn, and Waldfogel (2000).

37. See Wilson (1996); Sassler and Schoen (1999).

38. See South (1993).

39. See Hersch and Stratton (2000); Cappelli, Constantine, and Chadwick (2000). According to Cohen (2002) the effect is even stronger if cohabiting men are excluded from the never married category (p. 346).

40. See Cappelli, Constantine, and Chadwick (2000); Clarkberg (1999, 2000); Graefe and Lichter (1999).

41. Graefe and Lichter (1999) controlled for economic advantage prior to marriage and still found the marriage-premium effect for men.

42. See the report by the Economic Policy Institute by Bernstein, Boushey, McNichol, and Zahradnik (2002).

43. Whitehead and Popenoe (2001) surveyed a nationally representative sample of 1,003 young adults as part of the National Marriage Project and found that 625 of these young adults believed that it is okay for women to have children on her own if she has not found the right man to marry.

44. Whitehead and Popenoe (2001) found that 88% believe that they have a special soul mate, and 87% believe that they will find the soul mate when they are ready to marry.

45. See Bryant (2003), p. 136.

46. See Bank and Spencer (1998); Correll and Bourg (1999); Jackson and Tein (1998); Zuo and Tang (2000).

47. For findings on Mexican Americans, see Gowan and Trevino (1998); for findings on European countries, see Crompton and Harris (1997).

48. See Peake and Harris's (2001) study of sixty-six nonmarried couples.

49. See Machung (1989).

50. See Orrange (1999).

51. See Orrange (1999), p. 10.

52. See Williger (1993).

53. See studies by Becker and Moen (1999); Covin and Brush (1991); Machung (1989).

54. See Orrange (1999).
55. See Orrange (1999), p. 23.
56. See the study by Kerpelman and Schvaneveldt (1999).
57. See Maines and Hardesty (1987); O'Connell, Betz, and Kurth (1989).
58. See Hallett and Gilbert (1997).
59. See Moen and Yu (2000).
60. In investigating the school-to-work transition in Germany, Heinz (2001) defines four behavioral configurations: strategic stock taking, step-by-step progression, taking chances, and wait and see. These may also characterize the experiences of young Americans.

CHAPTER 4: IF REAL WORK IS PAID WORK, CAN NEW PARENTS FOLLOW THE CAREER MYSTIQUE?

1. See Rindfuss, Cooksey, and Sutterlin (1999).
2. See data in Bachu and O'Connell (2001); Ventura and Bachrach (2000). This upward trend in nonmarital birth rates has also occurred in all other industrialized countries. The United States ranks approximately in the middle. In 1997 Germany, Italy, Greece, and Japan had less than 15% of births occurring out of wedlock, while Norway, Sweden, and Iceland had premarital birth rates hovering between 50% and 65%.
3. See Fremstad and Primus's 2002 report on TANF reauthorization written for the Center on Budget and Policy Priorities.
4. Statistics come from Bachu and O'Connell (2001); Bianchi and Spain (1996).
5. See Hamilton, Martin, and Sutton (2003).
6. See Peterson and DeBarros (2001).
7. See Fields (2003).
8. See Casey and Pitt-Catsouphes (1994).
9. See Casey and Pitt-Catsouphes (1994).
10. Hertz and Ferguson (1998) interviewed women who intentionally planned to be single mothers.
11. Hertz and Ferguson (1998), p. 22.
12. See U.S. Department of Commerce; Bureau of the Census (1997).
13. Of never-married mothers, 69% are in poverty compared to 45% of once-married mothers. See U.S. Department of Commerce; Bureau of the Census (1997); Bianchi (1999); Lichter, Graefe, and Brown (2003).
14. See U.S. Department of Commerce; Bureau of the Census (1997); Bianchi, Subaiya, and Kahn (1999).
15. See Upchurch, Lillard, and Panis (2002); Musick (2002); Sigle-Rushton and McLanahan (2002a).
16. Blumenberg (2002) finds that the barriers have an additive effect on difficulty getting a job.
17. See the analysis by Heymann and Earl (1998).
18. See White and Geddes (2002).
19. See Martin et al. (2002).
20. Wu and MacNeill (2002), p. 199.

21. Statistics come from Bachu and O'Connell (2001); Bianchi and Spain (1996); Bloom and Trussell (1984); Martin (1999).

22. See discussion by Goodman (1991).

23. They are also delaying marriage (see chapter 3).

24. See Forest, Moen, and Dempster-McClain (1995); Martin (1999); Bloom and Trussell (1984). For the Netherlands case, see Corijn, Liefbroer, and Gierveld (1996).

25. See Altucher and Williams (2003).

26. See Barber (2000).

27. See Bachu and O'Connell (2001); Bianchi and Spain (1996).

28. Altucher and Williams (2003) used qualitative data from the "Cornell Couples and Careers Study," a sample of middle-class, dual-earner couples, to examine the impact of employment on childbearing decisions.

29. See Downs (2003), p. 20, for a report from the U.S. Bureau of the Census.

30. CPS June 2002 at www.census.gov/population/socdemo/fertility/tabH2.pdf (accessed March 16, 2004).

31. Data comes from Bachu (1999); Bernhardt (1993); United Nations (2001).

32. See Bernhardt (1993); Bram (1985); Moen (1992).

33. See Bram (1985).

34. See Thomas (1995).

35. See Erbe (1996), p. G 3.

36. See Bloom and Trussell (1984); Heaton (1999); Wu and MacNeill (2002).

37. See Chen and Morgan (1991); Altucher and Williams (2003).

38. See Wilk (1986), p. 44.

39. See Goldin and Katz (2000).

40. See, e.g., Hogan, Berhanu, and Hailemariam (1999).

41. DeOllos and Kapinus (2002) summarize the research on childlessness and life satisfaction and conclude that there are few, if any, differences between the two groups in terms of life satisfaction. When there are differences, they tend to be due to income and age.

42. See DeOllos and Kapinus (2002) for a summary of the research on childlessness and marital satisfaction.

43. See DeOllos and Kapinus (2002).

44. DeOllos and Kapinus (2002) cite a study by Alexander, Rubinstein, Goodman, and Luborsky (1992) in which the researchers interviewed childless women age sixty and over. They found that these women express regrets about not having children. The authors suggest that this regret is due to the fact that the women's lives did not take the traditional trajectory of other women.

45. See King (1999).

46. See Cohen and Bianchi (1999); Desai and Waite (1991); Moen (1985, 1992); Van der Klaauw (1996).

47. See the considerable body of work on this topic: Blossfeld and Hakim (1997); Cerrutti (2000); Drobnic, Blossfeld, and Rohwer (1999); Hakim (1999); Kodera (1994); Ogawa and Ermisch (1996).

48. The Pregnancy Discrimination Act was passed as an amendment to Title VII, the Civil Rights Act, in 1978. This act makes discrimination in the workplace based on pregnancy, childbirth, or other medical conditions unlawful. See www.eeoc.gov/types/pregnancy.html.

49. According to census data, in 1994 23% of children under fifteen had a mother who stayed home with them full time. In 2002, that number had increased to 25%. See Associated Press article in the *Holland Sentinel* (2003, June) for more information. See also Klerman and Leibowitz (1999).

50. Data is from the U.S. Department of Labor, "Employment Characteristics of Families in 2002" (2003b).

51. Human-capital theory was developed by economists to explain differential wages and attainments based on education and experience ("human capital"). Economist Becker (1981) developed this explanation to explain the bread-winner/homemaker gender divide (women have less human capital for paid work and more for family care work).

52. See Lyness, Thompson, Francesco, and Judiesch (1999).

53. See Cerrutti (2000); Desai and Waite (1991); Greenstein (1989); Klepinger, Lundberg, and Plotnick (1999).

54. See Cohen and Bianchi (1999); Desai and Waite (1991); Greenstein (1989); Hofferth (2000).

55. See Greenstein (1989); Lyness, Thompson, Francesco, and Judiesch (1999).

56. Cohen and Bianchi (1999); Schlesinger (2000); Schor (1991, 1998).

57. See the report by Bernstein, Boushey, McNichol, and Zahradnik (2002).

58. See Current Population Survey, June 2000, at www.census.gov/population/socdemo/fertility/tabH6.pdf (accessed October 10, 2003).

59. See Werbel (1998).

60. See Brown (1996) for the value-based model and Hakim (2000) for the preference-based model.

61. See the findings of Lyness, Thompson, Francesco, and Judiesch (1999); Werbel (1998).

62. Studies include those by Kaufman and Uhlenberg (2000); Lundberg and Rose (1999, 2000); Waite, Haggstrom, and Kanouse (1985).

63. See Lundberg and Rose (2000).

64. See Lundberg and Rose (2000).

65. See research from the Cornell Careers Institute; Becker and Moen (1999); Clarkberg and Moen (2001); Han and Moen (1999a, b); Moen (1985); Moen and Yu (1999, 2000). See also Bram (1985); Klerman and Leibowitz (1999); Lee, MacDermid, and Buck (2002); Lundberg and Rose (2000); Waite, Haggstrom, and Kanouse (1985).

66. See Bond, Galinsky, and Swanberg (1998); Lundberg and Rose (2000).

67. See Moen and Sweet (2003).

68. See MacDermid, Lee, and Williams (2001); Lee, MacDermid, and Buck (2002).

69. See Boise and Neal (1996).

70. Among women, childbirth appears to have a short-term adverse impact on income. Based on a nationally representative sample, Lundberg and Rose (2000) found a 5% decline in income after returning to work.

71. Taniguchi (1999) found that the women who have their children between the ages of twenty and twenty-seven have the greatest wage penalty associated with childbirth.

72. Cappelli, Constantine, and Chadwick (2000) followed a nationally representative sample of the graduating class of 1972 and found that having been married was related to higher income among men.

73. See Lundberg and Rose (2002).

74. See Hochschild (1989) for a discussion of the second shift that working women encounter in the home. Bianchi, Milkie, Sayer, and Robinson (2000) explore the reasons for this gender inequity.

75. See Aryee and Luk (1996); Moen (1989); Moore (1995); Roopnarine, Brown, Snell-White, Riegraf, Crossley, Hossain, and Webb (1995).

76. See Crittenden (2001), pp. 82–85, for a fuller discussion of the ways in which other nations provide recognition for unpaid labor.

77. See Brewster (2000).

78. See Deutsch, Servis, and Payne (2001).

79. See Glass (1998); Deutsch and Saxon (1998).

80. See Presser (1994, 1995).

81. According to Presser (1999), among couples with children who have been married less than five years, the likelihood of divorce or separation is six times higher for men who work the night shift and three times higher for women who work the night shift.

82. See Cox and Presser (2000).

83. Cox and Presser (2000) use a nationally representative sample of over nine thousand employed women in their study. They also found that single mothers also opt for nonstandard shifts so that they can attend school.

84. For information on shift work, see Bianchi (1999); Presser (1994, 1995).

85. See Hundley (2001).

86. For more information about gender differences in reasons for self-employment, see Boden (1999), Loscocco (1997); Carr (1996); Hundley (2001).

87. See Edwards and Field-Hendrey (2002).

88. Connelly (1992) examined the reasons for women entering self-employment and being at-home day care providers.

89. See Loscocco (1997).

90. Hundley (2001) references a study by Aronson (1991), which finds that full-time self-employed women earn 36.7% of what full-time self-employed men earn.

91. Hundley (2001) used data from the 1989 and 1990 waves of the "Michigan Panel Study of Income Dynamics" to reach his conclusions about the earning differential between self-employed men and women. See also Hundley (2000) for differentials in time spent on housework and on paid labor between self-employed men and women.

92. See Feldman and Bolino (2000).

93. To identify these work-hour patterns, Moen and Sweet (2003) used data from over 850 dual-earner couples.

94. Becker and Moen (1999) report this finding using interview data from a subset of the subjects used in the Moen and Sweet (2003) study.

95. See Polasky and Holahan's 1998 study of professional married women with young children.

96. See discussion of this issue in Cowan and Cowan (2000); Duxbury, Higgins, Lee, and Mills (1992); Moen (2001a, b); Moen and Yu (2000); Brough and Kelling (2002), p. 32.

97. Frone, Russell, and Barnes (1996) found, using a random sample of employees in upstate New York, that work–family conflict was related to depression,

poor health, and heavy alcohol use. Grzywacz and Marks (2000) found that work–family spillover was related to higher levels of alcohol use. Noor (2002) found a relationship between work–family conflict and distress and job dissatisfaction among a sample of Malaysian employees. See also Becker and Moen (1999); Eagle, Miles, and Icenogel (1997); Gutek, Searle, and Klepa (1991); Higgins, Duxbury, and Irving (1992); Kinnunen and Mauno (1998); Moen, Waismel-Manor, and Sweet (2003); Moen and Yu (2000); Schieman, McBrier, and Van Gundy (2003); Wallace (1999).

98. See, e.g., Brough and Kelling (2002), p. 33; Eagle, Miles, and Icenogle (1997); Kinnunen and Mauno (1998); Williams and Alliger (1994); Roehling, Moen, and Batt (2003).

99. See Gutek, Searle, and Klepa (1991); Higgins, Duxbury, and Lee (1994); Hochschild (1989); Marshall and Barnett (1993); Yu and Moen (2001).

100. See Crouter and Bumpus (2001) for a review of the literature. See also Frone, Russell, and Cooper (1992); Fox and Dwyer (1999); Gutek, Searle, and Klepa (1991); Higgins, Duxbury, and Irving (1992); Moen and Yu (2000); Rydstedt and Johansson (1998); Vinokur, Pierce, and Buck (1998); Wallace (1999).

101. See Kinnunen and Mauno (1998); Moen and Yu (2000).

102. See Beutell and Wittig-Berman (1999); Burley (1991); Frone, Russell, and Cooper (1992); Higgins, Duxbury, and Lee (1994); Kinnunen and Mauno (1998); Marshall and Barnett (1993); Maume and Houston (2001); Moen and Yu (2000).

103. See Higgins, Duxbury, and Lee (1994); Marshall and Barnett (1993).

104. See Frone, Russell, and Cooper (1992); Marshall and Barnett (1993).

105. See Marshall and Barnett (1993).

106. See Barnett and Hyde (2001); Barnett and Rivers (1996); Marshall and Barnett (1993); Repetti, Matthews, and Waldron (1989); Wethington and Kessler (1989).

107. See Barnett and Hyde (2001); Barnett and Rivers (1996); Klumb and Lampert (2004); Marks and MacDermid (1996); Marshall and Barnett (1993); Repetti, Matthews, and Waldron (1989); Wethington and Kessler (1989).

108. See Barnett and Hyde (2001).

109. See Carlson and Perrewe (1999); Kirchmeyer (1992, 1993).

110. See Almeida, Wethington, and Chandler (1999).

111. This point was suggested by Hochschild (1997). For other research evidence, see Barnett and Marshall (1992a, b); Roehling, Moen, and Batt (2003).

112. As part of the "Ecology of Careers Study."

113. See Roehling, Moen and Batt (2003).

114. See Jones and Fletcher (1993); Kirchmeyer (1992).

115. See Roehling, Moen and Batt (2003).

116. See Roehling, Moen, and Batt (2003).

117. See Roehling, Moen, and Batt (2003).

118. See Kirchmeyer (1992).

119. Sandberg and Cornfield (2000) found that women most often terminated their FMLA leaves because of financial or work-related pressures, not because they wanted to return to work.

120. See Heymann (2001).

121. See Hofferth (1996); O'Connell (1990); Waldfogel (1999).

122. See Pleck (1993).
123. See Singley and Hynes (2001).
124. Rapoport, Bailyn, Fletcher, and Pruitt (2002) describe their program for working with employers to construct a workplace that increases gender equity and work–personal life integration while increasing the effectiveness of the organization.

CHAPTER 5: LIVING THE CAREER MYSTIQUE: MAKING IT, GIVING UP, OR SLIPPING BEHIND?

1. Based on a study conducted by consulting firm Watson Wyatt Worldwide as reported in Munk (1999).
2. A study conducted in 1996 by Howard Eglit as reported in Munk (1999).
3. See Bejian and Salomone (1995); Riverin-Simard (1990); Willis and Reid (1999).
4. See Marshall and Barnett (1993).
5. See, e.g., Hochschild (1997); Moen (1992); Orrange (1999).
6. See Evans and Bartolome (1984).
7. See Roehling, Moen, and Batt (2003).
8. As we discussed in chapter 2, many women scale back on their jobs when they have children. See Moen and Sweet (2003); Becker and Moen (1999).
9. See Orrange (1999, 2002, 2003a, b).
10. See Belle, Norell, and Lewis (1997).
11. See Umansky (1999).
12. See Polatnick (1999).
13. See the U.S. Census Bureau report "Who's Minding the Kids? Child Care Arrangements," by Kristin Smith (Smith 2002a, b).
14. See Polatnick (1999).
15. See Belle, Norell, and Lewis (1997).
16. See Moen, Dempster-McClain, Altobelli, Wimonsate, Dahl, Roehling, and Sweet (2004).
17. See Belle, Norell, and Lewis (1997); Feiring and Lewis (1993).
18. See Belle, Norell, and Lewis (1997).
19. See Polatnick (1999), p. 14.
20. See Mattingly and Bianchi (2003).
21. See Almeida, Maggs, and Galambos (1993); Arrighi and Maume (2000); Bianchi and Spain (1996); Coverman (1985); Ferree (1991); Moen (1992); Presser (1994).
22. See Aryee and Luk (1996); Brayfield (1992); Dempsey (1998); Kim and Harrison (1999); Lu, Bellas, and Maume (2000); Moore (1995); Nordenmark and Nyman (2003); Roopnarine, Brown, Snell-White, Riefgraf, Crossley, Hossain, and Webb (1995); Rout, Lewis, and Kagan (1999).
23. See Bianchi, Milkie, Sayer, and Robinson (2000); Coverman and Sheley (1986).
24. Baxter (2002) found a decrease in time spent in housework among Australian women between 1986 and 1997. Kitterod (2002) found a decrease in the amount of housework done by Norwegian women between 1970 and 1990.
25. See Ferree (1991); Presser (1994); Yu and Moen (2001).

26. See Dempsey (1998).

27. See Mederer (1993); Orrange (1999).

28. See South and Spitze (1994); Gupta (1999); Shelton and John (1996).

29. See Gupta (1999).

30. The more time a woman spends at work, the less time she tends to spend on housework. See Almeida, Maggs, and Galambos (1993); Bianchi and Spain (1996); Brayfield (1992); Ferree (1991). This is true of men as well. See Merola (2001); Yu and Moen (2001).

31. See Shelton and John (1996); Ciscel and Sharp (1995).

32. See Bianchi and Spain (1996).

33. See Hays (1996).

34. See Arrighi and Maume (2000); Coverman (1985).

35. See Brayfield (1992).

36. See Brayfield's (1992) study of Canadian couples and Strom's (2002) study of Norwegian couples.

37. See Deutsch (2001) for a summary of this research. Kluwer, Heesink, and van de Vliert (2002) also found an intensification of traditional gender-role behaviors following childbirth among a sample of Dutch couples.

38. See Hays (1996).

39. See Brayfield (1992); Ciscel and Sharp (1995); Coverman, (1985); Ferree (1991); Lu, Bellas, and Maume (2000); Presser (1994).

40. See Ciscel and Sharp (1995); Mederer (1993).

41. See Gupta (1999).

42. See Ferree (1991).

43. See Arrighi and Maume (2000); Dempsey (1998); Ferree (1991); Moore (1995); Shelton and John (1996).

44. See Brayfield (1992); Lu, Bellas, and Maume (2000); Mederer (1993); Presser (1994); Shelton and John (1996).

45. See Brayfield (1992).

46. See Brines (1994); Lu, Bellas, and Maume (2000); Deutsch, Lussier, and Servis (1993).

47. See study by Ferree (1991).

48. See discussion by Hochschild (1999).

49. For example, Brines (1994); Arrighi and Maume (2000).

50. See Arrighi and Maume (2000); Brayfield (1992).

51. See Presser (1994).

52. See Ferree (1990).

53. See Kamo and Cohen (1998).

54. John, Shelton, and Luschen (1995) and Shelton and John (1993), using data from the 1987 National Survey of Families and Households, found evidence that African American men are more likely to participate in household chores than Anglo-American men.

55. See Grote, Naylor, and Clark (2002) for a summary of this literature and also Wilkie, Ferree, and Strother (1998).

56. See Grote, Naylor, and Clark (2002).

57. See Grote, Naylor, and Clark (2002); Wilkie, Ferree, and Strother (1998).

58. See Nordenmark and Nyman (2003) for a study of Swedish couples.

59. See Frisco and Williams (2003); Wilkie, Ferree, and Strother (1998); Mederer (1993), who uses a Korean sample.

60. See Baruch and Barnett (1986); Cohen (1978); Friedman (1990); Gilbert (1990); Hill (1998); Menaghan and Parcel (1995); Sanderson (2000).

61. See Galinsky (1999), p. 49.

62. See Booth, Clarke-Stewart, Vandell, McCartney, and Owen (2002), p. 22, and a review of the literature by Bianchi (2000).

63. Booth, Clarke-Stewart, Vandell, McCartney, and Owen (2002) used a sample of parents who had seven-month-old children (p. 22).

64. See Brewster (2000); Almeida, Maggs, and Galambos (1993); Galinsky (1999); Hoffman (1989); McLoyd (1989); Price, Friedland, Choi, and Caplan (1998); Repetti and Wood (1997).

65. See Galinsky (1999).

66. See Galinsky (1999), p. 189.

67. See Almeida and McDonald (1998); Almeida, Wethington, and Chandler (1999); Galambos and Maggs (1990); Repetti (1994).

68. See Galambos and Maggs (1990); Kim and Moen (2001a).

69. See Galinsky (1999), p. 38.

70. See Galinsky (1999), p. 176.

71. See Galinsky (1999), p. 240.

72. The research summarized in this section was conducted on married, often dual-earner couples. Because the largest number of dual-earner couples falls in the establishment stage (have school-aged children) compared to the other stages addressed in this book, we will report the results of this research in this chapter. However, it is important to remember that the conclusions drawn from these studies apply to couples at all life stages and also to couples without children.

73. See Bolger, DeLongis, Kessler, and Wethington (1989).

74. See Barnett and Brennan (1997).

75. See Jones and Fletcher (1993).

76. See Bolger, DeLongis, Kessler, and Wethington (1989).

77. See Jones and Fletcher (1996).

78. See Kalleberg, Rasell, Cassirer, Reskin, Hudson, Webster, Appelbaum, and Spalter-Roth (1997); Spalter-Roth, Kalleberg, Rasell, Cassirer, Reskin, Hudson, Webster, Appelbaum, and Dooley (1997).

79. See report by the U.S. Census Bureau (May 2004), p. 11.

80. This limits women's entry into fast-track jobs (Adler 1993). A study of male and female attorneys in Ontario showed that female lawyers make less than male lawyers, despite comparable credentials (Kay and Hagan 1995). In Britain, controlling for ability, education level, and work experience, women earn significantly less than men and are apt to hold lower-level managerial jobs than men (Melamed 1995). In a study of five hundred large Turkish organizations, only 2% of top managers are women, with the reason given for this low figure being that women's duties at home prevent them from succeeding at work (Tabak 1997). Albrecht, Bjorklund, and Vroman (2003) found a significant wage differential between Swedish men and women that accelerates as earnings get higher. See also Joshi, Macran, and Dex (1996); Blossfeld and Drobnic (2001).

81. See Adler (1993); Blau and Kahn (2003); Cannings (1991); Cotter, Hermsen, Ovadia, and Vanneman (2001); Groat, Chilson, and Neal (1982); Morgan, Schor, and Martin (1993).

82. The glass ceiling also exists for men of color, particularly Native American, African American, and Hispanic men, as well as for immigrants. A discussion of the barriers facing minorities is beyond the scope of this book.

83. See a summary of the Catalyst study presented by the Business and Professional Women/USA (2003).

84. See Catalyst (1997b).

85. Taniguchi (1999) found the greatest childbearing-related wage penalty among women who had children when they were between the ages of twenty and twenty-seven. Women who had children when in their teens tended to make the least amount of money. See also Landau and Arthur (1992). However, this was directly attributable to their lack of education. See also Van der Klaauw (1996).

86. See Parasuraman and Greenhaus (1993).

87. Altucher and Williams (2003), using qualitative data from the "Ecology of Careers Study," found that childfree women in their forties felt positively about their decision not to have children, particularly with respect to their careers.

88. See Ewen (1994).

89. See Cappelli, Constantine, and Chadwick (2000) and Landau and Arthur (1992), who also found that married women tended to earn more than unmarried women.

90. See Landau and Arthur (1992).

91. According to Lundberg and Rose (2000) men earn 9% more after the birth of their first child.

92. See results in Kay and Hagan (1995); Tharenou, Latimer, and Conroy (1994).

93. See Landau and Arthur (1992).

94. See Moen (2003a, b).

95. For example, evidence of lower pay among women has been documented in Canada (Kay and Hagan, 1995), Britain (Melamed, 1995) and Turkey (Tabek, 1997).

96. See Albrecht, Bjorkland, and Vroman (2003).

97. Schacter (2001), using data from the 2000 "Current Population Survey," finds that 31% of people make a long-distance move for work, second only to moving for housing-related reasons, which 32% of people surveyed cite as their major reason for moving.

98. See Hendershott's 1995 book on relocation for a discussion of corporations' expectations that their top executives will relocate.

99. See Schacter (2001).

100. According to Anne Hendershott (1995), the typical relocated employee is a white male, in his forties, with two children.

101. See Hendershott (1995). Camstra (1996), using a Dutch sample, and Bielby and Bielby (1992), using a sample from 1977, found that women are less likely to relocate than men.

102. Eby, Allen, and Douthitt (1999) examined relocation offers among a sample of employees in the United States and in Canada. They found that women receive lower recommendation ratings for jobs requiring relocation than men and that married women receive fewer offers for relocation than married men.

103. See Bielby and Beilby (1992).

104. See Bielby and Bielby (1992).

105. See Bielby and Bielby (1992).

106. Camstra (1996), using a sample of Dutch employees and their trailing spouses, found that many women quit working following a move for their husband's job.

107. See Eby, Douthitt, Perrin, Noble, Atchley, and Ladd (2002), p. 354.

108. See Hendershott (1995).

109. Topel and Ward (1992) also found that the men in their study held an average of seven jobs in their first ten years of employment.

110. Brett and Stroh (1997), using a sample of executives from twenty Fortune 500 companies, found that female executives who used an external strategy for mobility (changing organizations) had salaries similar to women who used an internal strategy (moving up within a company). For men, the external strategy resulted in higher salaries. Stroh, Brett, and Reilly (1992) found that women who had relocated for their company still had salaries that lagged behind those of men who had relocated.

111. Franklin and Ramage (1999) cite a study by Stroh that reports this statistic regarding commuter marriages and corporate relocation.

112. For a fuller discussion of commuter marriages, see Hendershott (1995).

113. Markham, Bonjean, and Corder (1986) and Presser and Hermsen (1996) found that men travel for work more frequently than women. However, both of these studies used data from the mid-1980s. Roehling and Bultman (2002) found that this relationship continues to exist in a contemporary sample of professional, dual-earner couples.

114. Fisher's (1998) respondents were five hundred frequent business travelers who worked for an international hotel chain.

115. According to Gerald and Hussar (2002) of the National Center for Education Statistics, the trend of increasing numbers of older students entering higher education has leveled off and will decrease slightly over the next ten years. However, it is projected that students over twenty-five will continue to be a significant part of those seeking higher education.

116. See Gerald and Hussar (2002), table 174.

117. See Kim and Creighton (2000). Participants in adult education include those engaged in some form of instruction or educational activity to acquire the knowledge, information, and skills necessary to succeed in the workforce, learn basic skills, earn credentials, or otherwise enrich their lives (this also includes GED courses and English-as-a-second-language courses).

118. For data on the United Kingdom, see Hartley (1998); for data on Australia, see Richardson and King (1998).

119. See AAUW (1999).

120. See AAUW (1999).

121. See U.S. Department of Education (2003).

122. See Kember (1999).

123. See AAUW (1999); Kember (1999).

124. Studies of women returning to school include those by Suitor (1987a, b, c) and Suitor and Keeton (1997).

125. Stettner and Wenger (2003) of the Economic Policy Institute report that the long-term laid-off tend to be college graduates over forty-five who were in executive, professional, or managerial positions (p. 1).
126. See Munk (1999).
127. See Price, Friedland, Choi, and Caplan (1998).
128. Taris (2002) examined the effects of unemployment among a sample of Dutch employees.
129. See Price, Friedland, Choi, and Caplan (1998).
130. See findings by McLoyd (1989).
131. See overview of Blau, Ferber, and Winkler (2001); Goldin (1991). For an international view, see Blossfeld and Hakim (1997).

CHAPTER 6: LIFE MIDCOURSE: ARE RETIREMENT OR SECOND ACTS INEVITABLE, DESIRABLE, OR EVEN POSSIBLE?

1. Family sociologists have traditionally defined midlife as the years when one's children are in (high) school (e.g., Hill and Rogers [1964]). However, along with increases in longevity and the reluctance of the baby boom generation to admit to growing older, there has been both a blurring of the boundaries around and an extension of the middle years. Increasingly, *late midlife* or *midcourse* are terms applied to those in their fifties, sixties, and seventies, whose children have grown and gone, as well as to those without children in this age group. For more on the nature of midlife, see Kim and Moen (2001b); Lachman and James (1997); Moen (2003b); Moen and Wethington (1999); Ryff and Seltzer (1996); Willis and Reid (1999). For more discussion on midcourse, see Moen (2003a, b).
2. Costa (1998); Graebner (1980).
3. Quadagno (1988); Quadagno and Hardy (1996).
4. See Costa (1998); Graebner (1980).
5. Priore and Sabel (1984).
6. See Hardy, Hazelrigg, and Quadagno (1996); Kotter (1995).
7. Quinn and Burkhauser (1994).
8. See Quinn (1997).
9. Employees now develop their expectations about retirement against the backdrop of corporate downsizing. Additionally, the growth in defined-contribution pension programs (as opposed to defined-benefit ones) gives employees greater responsibility for planning their futures. Concurrently, federal policy makers have delayed the age of Social Security eligibility and are evaluating the potentials of placing some portion of Social Security accounts under personal discretion. Contemporary retirement planning, therefore, is taking place in a shifting context of ambiguity and uncertainty.
10. See Moen and Wethington (1992); Riley, Kahn, and Foner (1994).
11. See Quinn (1997); O'Rand and Henretta (1999); Han and Moen (1999a).
12. Clay (2003) summarizes research on the empty-nest syndrome and concludes that relationships are improved after children leave the home.
13. See Evans and Bartolome (1984).

14. See Pixley and Wethington (1998a, b).

15. See Roehling, Moen, and Wilson (2003).

16. Because of its emphasis on timing, process, and context, the life-course perspective directs attention to midcourse variability, including differences by gender, ethnicity, social class, community, and residential location. This midcourse perspective also underscores the importance of specific historical times in shaping options. See Moen (2003b) in *Handbook of the Life Course*, edited by J. Mortimer and M. Shanahan.

17. U.S. Census Bureau, Census 2000, table DP-1, "Profile of General Demographic Characteristics of the United States: 2000."

18. See Day (2001) for the U.S. Census Bureau's national population projections.

19. United Nations Population Division (2001), p. vii.

20. See Hays (1996); Moen (1992); Bianchi and Spain (1996).

21. See various chapters in Moen (2003a).

22. According to the Economic Policy Institute's 2003 *EPI Issue Guide: Retirement Security*, white workers are more likely to have pension coverage (57%) than African American (44%) or Hispanic (28%) workers, and men are more likely to have pension coverage than women (43% and 28%, respectively).

23. Waite and Gallagher (2000).

24. Another life-course issue related to the declining significance of marriage concerns how the individuals who are important to people change over the course of their lives. One researcher, in attempting to get at this issue, asked the people he interviewed two questions: (1) Whom do you spend time with? and (2) Whom do you go to when you're in trouble? People answered this quite differently, depending on their ages. For older people two groups are increasingly important, siblings and friends. For more information on marriage and singleness, see Allen and Demo (1995); Barrett (1999); Cherlin and Furstenberg (1994); Waite and Gallagher (2000).

25. See Riley and Riley (1989).

26. See Emanuel, Fairclough, Slutsman, Alpert, Baldwin, and Emanuel (1999).

27. Kramer and Kipnis (1995) and Starrels, Ingersoll-Dayton, Dowler, and Neal (1997) report that women spend more time in caregiving than men. Kramer and Kipnis (1995) also cite supporting studies by Finley (1989), Horowitz (1985), and Miller and Cafasso (1992). Cicirelli (1995) reviews the literature on siblings and caregiving and finds that daughters are more likely to be primary caregivers for their parents than are sons.

28. See Kramer and Kipnes (1995), Finley (1989), Horwitz (1985), and Miller and Cafasso (1992).

29. See Kramer and Kipnis (1995); Chapman, Ingersoll-Dayton, and Neal (1994); Kossek, Colquitt, and Noe (2001), pp. 35–36.

30. Vitaliano, Zhang, and Scanlan (2003) report these findings based on a meta-analysis of twenty-three studied.

31. The U.S. Census reports that in 1970 3.2% of children lived with their grandparents. In 1998 that number had risen to 5.6%. See www.census.gov/population/www/documentation/twps0026/twps0026.html (accessed June 23, 2004).

32. See Fields (2003), who reports using data from the U.S. Census Bureau.

33. Pavalko and Artis (1997) found a relationship between caregiving and reduced employment using the "National Longitudinal Survey of Mature Women." Contrary to this finding, Couch, Daly, and Wolf (1999), using data from 1988, found no evidence that increased time spent caregiving is related to decreased time spent in the marketplace. Starrels, Ingersoll-Dayton, Neal, and Yamada (1995) cite studies by Mutschler (1994) and Stone and Short (1990) that demonstrate that women accommodate their work schedule to caregiving needs.

34. Starrels, Ingersoll-Dayton, Neal, and Yamada (1995) cite a study by Stone, Cafferata, and Sangl (1987) that demonstrates the relationship between the type of profession and the ability to accommodate work and caregiving.

35. See Hartl (1996).

36. See, e.g., Choi (2002), p. 66; Lowenthal and Robinson (1976); Moen (1998); Reimers and Honig (1989).

37. See Han and Moen (1999a, b); Kohli and Rein (1991); Settersten and Mayer (1997).

38. See Han and Moen (1999b); Moen (1994, 2001a); Kohli (1994); Quinn and Burkhauser (1994).

39. Quinn and Burkhauser (1994) link the declining age of retirement to pension and Social Security work disincentives for older adults. See also Burtless and Quinn (2001).

40. U.S. Census Bureau, 2001 Statistical Abstracts of the United States, No. 568, p. 367.

41. Currently, Social Security is structured such that the age at which a person can receive full benefits will increase from sixty-five to sixty-seven by 2017.

42. See Quinn and Burkhauser (1994).

43. See Dixon and Van Horn (2002), a report from the Heldrich Center for Workforce Development, pp. 5 and 6.

44. Dixon and Van Horn (2002), p. 1.

45. U.S. Census Bureau (2003), p. 79.

46. See Zedlewski and Saha (2003), pp. 111–113.

47. See Elder (1995).

48. See Bronfenbrenner (1995).

49. See, e.g., Han and Moen (1999b); Hoff and Hohner (1986); O'Rand and Henretta (1982); Quick and Moen (1998). Jobs define one's position in the broader opportunity structure, which in turn affects the range of available strategies and options.

50. See Szinovacz (1989) and Szinovacz and Ekerdt (1995).

51. Recall that a key tenet of the life-course perspective is that lives are interdependent. Shifts in occupational and family careers always take place in the context of ongoing social relations; see Elder (1995).

52. See Moen (1996); Quick and Moen (1998); Smith and Moen (1998, 2003); Szinovacz (1989); Szinovacz, Ekerdt, and Vinick (1992); Vinick and Ekerdt (1991a, b, 1992).

53. Couples must increasingly deal with two retirements rather than just the husband's. See Henretta and O'Rand (1983); Henretta, O'Rand, and Chan (1993a, b); O'Rand, Henretta, and Krecker (1992).

54. Until recently, however, retirement has been viewed as an individual's, not a couple's, status change. See Henretta and O'Rand (1983); Henretta, O'Rand, and Chan (1993a, b); O'Rand, Henretta, and Krecker (1992); Smith and Moen (1998, 2003); Szinovacz (1989); Szinovacz and Ekerdt (1995); Szinovacz, Ekerdt, and Vinick (1992).

55. See Dorfman (1992); Vinick and Ekerdt (1992).

56. For discussion of homophily, see Merton (1968). See also studies by Ortega, Whitt, and Williams (1988); Booth, Edwards, and Johnson (1991).

57. See Anderson, Clark, and Johnson (1982); Henretta, O'Rand, and Chan (1993a, b).

58. See Moen, Kim, and Hofmeister (2001); Kim and Moen (2001).

59 See discussion in Moen, Kim, and Hofmeister (2001).

60. Kulik (2002) bases his findings on a sample of Israeli retirees and preretirees.

61. See, e.g., Atchley (1983).

62. See Atchley (1983).

63. See, e.g., Poorkaj (1972).

64. See Cartensen (1992). Baltes and Baltes (1990) further elaborate a theory of selection and optimization.

65. See *Social Integration in the Second Half of Life* by Pillemer, Moen, Wethington, and Glasgow, eds. (2000).

66. See Riley, Foner, and Riley (1999); Marshall et al. (2001); Mayer and Mueller (1986); Moen (1994, 2001a, b).

67. See the writing of Freedman (1999); Pillemer, Moen, Wethington, and Glasgow (2000).

68. For trends in retirement, see American Association of Retired Persons (2000), Han and Moen (1999a); Quinn (1999); Czaja and Moen (2004); Kim and Moen (2001a, b); Wise (1998).

69. Retirees who live alone and whose children are geographically remote, who remain estranged from their children, or who never had children may feel especially cut off as a result of a divorce years earlier.

70. It does not affect women's psychological well-being, however. See the findings reported in Moen, Kim, and Hofmeister (2001).

71. See Freedman (1999); Moen (1998); Moen, Fields, Meador, and Rosenblatt (2000); Moen, Fields, Quick, and Hofmeister (2000); Moen and Fields (2002).

72. See also Han and Moen (1999b).

73. See Wolff (2002).

74. See Caro and Bass (1997); Gillespie and King (1985); Herzog and Morgan (1993).

75. See Chambré (1984, 1987).

76. See Moen and Fields (2002).

77. See Chambré (1984, 1987); Fischer and Schaffer (1993); Moen (1997a); Moen, Dempster-McClain, and Williams (1992); Moen and Fields (2002); Moen, Fields, Meador, and Rosenblatt (2000); Okun, Stock, Haring, and Witter (1984).

78. This is evidenced by high postretirement participation in formal associations and volunteer involvement; see Broderick and Glazer (1983).

79. See Moen and Fields (2002).

80. See Moen and Fields (2002).
81. See Atchley (1993).
82. See Reitzes, Mutran, and Fernandez (1998).
83. See Mutran, Reitzes, Bratton, and Fernandez (1997) for a study of 753 late-midlife retirees.
84. See, e.g., Kim and Moen (2001b); Kolhi (1986); Moen (1998).
85. Japan has already delayed its age of pension eligibility from sixty to sixty-five.
86. See Erikson, Erikson, and Kivnick (1994).

CHAPTER 7: POLICIES AND PRACTICES: MAINTAINING THE STATUS QUO OR CHALLENGING THE CAREER MYSTIQUE?

1. In the form of Aid to Families with Dependent Children.
2. See Burstein, Bricher, and Einwohner (1995); Moen and Forest (1999); Moen and Coltrane (2004); Coltrane (1992).
3. See Gornick and Meyers (2003), p. 294.
4. See Kelly and Dobbin (1999).
5. See U.S. Department of Labor 1995 Family and Medical Leave Commission Report, executive summary.
6. See U.S. Census Bureau report by Smith, Downs, and O'Connell (2001), pp. 3 and 4.
7. See U.S. Department of Labor, Commission on Leave Report, 1996, which includes all public employees and employees in the private sector who have worked for a "covered" employer (those with fifty or more employees) for at least one year and for at least 1,250 hours over the previous twelve months.
8. See Campion and Dill (2000); Gerstel and McGonagle (1999); Kamerman (2000).
9. A report by the Department of Labor authored by Cantor et al. (2001) estimates that between 58% and 61% of employees in the United States are covered by and eligible for the benefits established by the FMLA (chapter 3, p. 2, and forward, p. 2). Only 10% of private employers meet the criteria for the FMLA, but those institutions employ a large number of people (chapter 3, p. 2).
10. See Cantor, Waldfogel, Kerwin, Wright, Levin, Rauch, Hagerty, and Kudela (2001).
11. See Gerstel and McGonagle (1999).
12. See Campion and Dill (2000).
13. See Caputo (2000); Mitchell (1997).
14. See U.S. Department of Labor Commission on Leave Report, 1996.
15. See Border (2002).
16. See Kamerman (2000).
17. See Kamerman (2000).
18. See Kamerman (2000).
19. See Kamerman (2000).
20. According to Gornick and Meyers (2003), 85% of married or cohabiting women in Sweden work, compared to 69% in the United States (p. 60).

21. See Seward, Yeatts, and Zottarelli (2002).

22. See Schwartz (1989).

23. See Galtry (2001) for the benefits of breastfeeding.

24. See Galtry (2001).

25. For an overview of welfare reform and a historical perspective, see Skocpol (1992); Goodwin and Moen (1980).

26. For a description of PRWORA and TANF, see the U.S. Department of Health and Human Services Fact Sheet on the report regarding the Administration for Children and Families (2001).

27. See Boushey (2001).

28. See Monroe, Blalock, and Vlosky (1999) and Hays (1996) for a discussion of challenges facing women who try to exit welfare.

29. Boushey (2002) reports that only 33% of those on welfare encountered a critical financial hardship in 1999 as opposed to 47% of full-time-employed, former welfare recipients.

30. See Chapman and Bernstein (2003).

31. Boushey (2001) found that one third of former welfare recipients worked in retail trade, particularly in eating and drinking establishments, which are especially vulnerable to economic vagaries.

32. See Heymann and Earle (1998) for a fuller discussion of this issue.

33. See Heymann and Earle (1998) for a study using a 1993 nationally representative sample of Americans.

34. Meyers, Heintze, and Wolf (2002) found that only 13% of employed, former welfare recipients in California were using subsidized day care.

35. See Hardina (1999); Monroe, Blalock, and Vlosky (1999); and Meyers, Heintze, and Wolf (2002).

36. See Monroe, Blalock, and Vlosky (1999).

37. Gmiter (2001).

38. See Zedlewski and Saha (2003), pp. 111–113.

39. See Chase-Lansdale, Moffitt, Lohman, Cherlin, Coley, Pittman, Roff, and Botruba-Drzal (2003).

40. See Orthner and Randolph (1999).

41. See McManus and DiPrete (2000) and Esping-Andersen (1990) for more information about European systems of welfare.

42. For a discussion of the use of welfare for single mothers in Europe, see Millar (1998); Millar (2001).

43. Jane Millar (1998) discusses this attempt in the United Kingdom.

44. See Gornick and Meyers (2003), pp. 189–207, for a discussion of child-care legislation in the United States and in Europe.

45. See Gornick and Meyers (2003), pp. 189–190.

46. See report by the National Center for Children in Poverty (2003).

47. See Gornick and Meyers (2003), p. 194.

48. See Knox, London, and Scott (2003).

49. See Gornick and Meyers (2003), p. 189.

50. See Friedman (undated).

51. See Gornick and Meyers (2003), pp. 198–207, for a discussion of child care in Europe.

52. See their website at www.aoa.gov/prof/aoaprog/caregiver/caregiver.asp (accessed June 9, 2004).

53. Kelly and Dobbin (1999) believe that the desire to appear socially responsible is one of the major driving forces behind family-friendly corporate initiatives. The publicity that even a failed government initiative generates may be more motivating to a corporation than the legislation that is eventually passed.

54. See MacDermid, Hertzog, Kensinger, and Zipp (2001); Pitt-Catsouphes and Litchfield (2001).

55. See U.S. Department of Labor, Bureau of Labor Statistics (1999, 2003a).

56. See Catalyst (1997a).

57. See Blair-Loy and Wharton (2002) for a survey of workers in a large financial corporation.

58. See Deitch and Huffman (2001).

59. See Deitch and Huffman (2001).

60. See Gjerdingen and Chaloner (1994).

61. See Klein, Hyde, Essex, and Clark (1998).

62. See Glass and Riley (1998); Hofferth (1996); Thompson, Beauvais, and Lyness (1999).

63. Blair-Loy and Wharton (2002) found that employees working in a company touted for its family-friendly benefits were afraid to take family leaves because of the message that it would send to the company about their commitment.

64. See Judiesch and Lyness (1999); Department of Labor, Commission on Leave (1997); Gerstel and McGonagle (1999); Pleck (1993).

65. See U.S. Department of Labor, Bureau of Labor Statistics (2003a).

66. See U.S. Department of Labor, Bureau of Labor Statistics (1999).

67. See U.S. Department of Labor, Bureau of Labor Statistics (November 2000).

68. See Galinsky and Bond (1998).

69. See Galinsky and Stein (1990); Glass and Riley (1998); Goff, Mount, and Jamison (1990); Kingston (1990); Lyness, Thompson, Francesco, and Judiesch (1999).

70. See Roehling, Roehling, and Moen (2001); Thompson, Beauvais, and Lyness (1999).

71. See Amgen press release at www.ext.amgen.com/news/news00/press Release000612.html.

72. See Wagner and Hunt (1994).

73. According to an article by Martinez (1997), Aetna found a 23% decrease in turnover of professional women following a policy that allowed the women to return to work on a part-time basis. See also Desai and Waite (1991); Glass and Riley (1998); Hofferth (1996); Hofferth (2000).

74. See Catalyst (1997a).

75. See Hyde, Klein, Essex, and Clark (1995).

76. See Gornick and Meyers (2003), p. 153.

77. See Armour (1998).

78. Gornick and Meyers (2003) provide an excellent review of European and U.S. policy regarding work hours.

79. See Gornick and Meyers (2003), pp. 157–164.

80. See Gornick and Meyers (2003), pp. 157–164; see also Appelbaum, Bailey, Berg, and Kalleberg (2002a, b) for more information on protections afforded to parents in selected countries.

81. According to the European Foundation for the Improvement of Living and Working Conditions (2001), ten of the sixteen European countries studied had instituted some form of progressive retirement.

82. According to Martinez (1997) Hewlett-Packard saw productivity double among a group of employees who began working a compressed workweek.

83. See Higgins, Duxbury, Lee, and Mills (1992); U.S. Census Bureau, 2002b, p. 377.

84. See Thompson, Beauvais, and Lyness (1999); Kossek, Barber, and Winters (1999). Blair-Loy and Wharton (2002) found that in the company they surveyed, flexible-time benefits were used equally by both men and women and by those with and without children.

85. See Sharpe, Hermsen, and Billings (2002).

86. McCrate (2002) also found that black workers were less likely than white workers to have flexibility in their daily work schedule.

87. See Roehling, Roehling, and Moen (2001).

88. See Scandura and Lankau (1997).

89. See Christensen and Staines (1990); Glass and Riley (1998); Guelzow, Bird, and Koball (1991); Kingston (1990).

90. See Winett and Neale (1981).

91. See Roehling, Moen, and Wilson (2003).

92. See Blair-Loy and Wharton (2002).

93. See Clacs (2000), Higgins, Duxbury, Lee, and Mills (1994); Roehling, Moen, and Wilson (2003).

94. See Higgins, Duxbury, Lee, and Mills (1994).

95. Bailey and Kurland (2002) in their review of the literature on telework state that the majority of teleworkers work away from the workplace five to six days per month (p. 390).

96. See Bailey and Kurland (2002), p. 391, for a review of the literature; Baruch (2000), p. 43.

97. See Standen, Daniels, and Lamond (1999); Cooper and Kurland (2002), p. 527; Duxbury, Higgins, and Thomas (1996), p. 20; and Roehling, Moen, and Batt (2003).

98. Standen, Daniels, and Lamond (1999) discuss the potential negative effects of telecommuting (p. 373). See also Cooper and Kurland (2002), p. 527; Duxbury, Higgins, and Thomas (1996), p. 20; Roehling, Moen, and Batt (2003).

99. See Hartman, Stoner, and Arora (1991).

100. See Secret (2000); Thompson, Beauvais, and Lyness (1999); Valcour and Batt (2003).

101. See Cropanzano, Howes, Grandey, and Toth (1997); Desai and Waite (1991); Galinsky and Stein (1990); Glass and Riley (1998); Goff, Mount, and Jamison (1990); Haley, Perry-Jenkins, and Armenia (2001); Kossek, Colquitt, and Noe (2001); Lyness, Thompson, Francesco, and Judiesch (1999); Roehling, Roehling, and Moen (2001) for research on the effects of supervisor and coworker support on employee outcomes.

102. See Galinsky and Stein (1990).

103. See York (1991).

104. See Gerstel and Clawson (2001).

105. See Deitch and Huffman (2001) for a discussion of this trend.

106. Osterman (1995), Galinsky (2001), and Deitch and Huffman (2001) found no difference between union members and nonunion members in family-friendly benefits. Glass and Fujimoto (1995) found that union members had fewer child-care benefits, less schedule flexibility, and less availability of reduced hours.

107. See Gerstel and McGonagle (1999); Glass and Fujimoto (1995); Maume and Bellas (2001).

108. See Kelly (1999) for a discussion of how and why companies adopt work–family benefits.

109. See Associated Press (2003).

110. See Kelly (1999).

111. See Bailyn, Drago, and Kochan (2001); Rapoport, Bailyn, Fletcher, and Pruitt (2002).

112. See Martinez (1997).

113. See Galtry (2001) for more information about this recommendation by the American Academy of Pediatrics.

114. Gornick and Meyers (2003) credit British sociologist Rosemary Crompton with the term *dual-earner–dual-career*.

115. See the Third Path Institute website at www.thirdpath.org (accessed June 9, 2004).

116. See Tilly (1992).

117. See Fried (1998).

118. See Rapoport, Bailyn, Fletcher, and Pruitt (2002)

CHAPTER 8: BEYOND THE CAREER MYSTIQUE: RECASTING THE LOCKSTEP LIFE COURSE

1. See Schwartz (1989).

2. Leisure World is a retirement community near Phoenix, Arizona. Its website boasts, "Here you'll discover the perfect permanent haven, a worry-free, hurry-free oasis where new friends beckon and new pursuits abound. Leisure World . . . It's nothing less than residential and recreational magic." See www.leisureworld arizona.com.

3. See, e.g., Frank and Cook (1996).

4. See, e.g., Bailyn (1993); Han and Moen (2001); Kanter (1977); Blair-Loy and Wharton (2002).

5. For a discussion of greedy institutions, see Coser and Coser (1974).

6. See, e.g., Riley (1988); Riley, Kahn, and Foner (1994); Moen (2003a).

7. See Hochschild (1989).

8. See discussions by Williams (2000); Moen (2003a); Bailyn (1993); Rapoport et al. (2002).

9. This is discussed by a number of authors, including Parcel (1999); Perlow (1997); Galinsky and Swanberg (2000).

10. See Fried (1998); Bailyn (1993); Perlow (1997); Osterman (1995, 1996); Pfeffer (1977). See also discussions by Epstein and Kalleberg (2001); Parcel and Cornfield (2000); Tilly (1992); Kanter (1977); Hertz and Marshall (2001).

11. See Merola (2001). See also Clarkberg and Moen (2001).

12. See Jacobs and Gerson (1998a, b); Tilly (1992). For a discussion of part-time work, see Blossfeld and Hakim (1996); Kropf (2001); Wharton and Blair-Loy (2002); Epstein et al. (1999); Fried (1998).

13. See Friedan (1963).

14. See Osterman (1996).

15. Melzer (2002), for example, found that workplace stress was related to domestic violence among men.

16. See Crouter, Bumpus, Head, and McHale (2001).

17. See Repetti and Wood (1997); Repetti (1994).

18. See Barnett and Marshall (1992b); Hyde, Klein, Essex, and Clark (1995); Marshall and Barnett (1993); Pavalko and Smith (1999); Wethington and Kessler (1989) for research relating to the ways in which multiple roles enhance women's well-being. See Repetti, Matthews, and Waldron (1989) for a review of the literature on employment and women's mental health.

19. For information on how work influences experiences at home, see Bowen (1998); Bromet, Dew, and Parkinson (1990); Christensen and Staines (1990); Frone, Russell, and Cooper (1992); Goff, Mount, and Jamison (1990); Greenhaus, Parasuraman, Granrose, Rabinowitz, and Beutell (1989); Higgins, Duxbury, and Irving (1992); Marshall and Barnett (1993); Rydstedt and Johansson (1998); Thomas and Ganster (1995). For information on the ways in which family life influences work life, see Crouter (1984); Duxbury, Higgins, and Lee (1994); Higgins and Duxbury (1992); Kirchmeyer (1993); Marshall and Barnett (1993). See also Judge and Watanabe (1994). According to Simon (1998) work- and family-related stressors are related to alcohol use and abuse among men and depression among women. For evidence relating to a later-life stage, see Moen, Kim, and Hofmeister (2001).

20. See Frone, Russell, and Barnes (1996); Grzywacz (2000); Pisarski, Bohle, and Callan (1998); Rydstedt and Johansson (1998).

21. See Reskin and Padavic (1994); Waldfogel (1998); Budig and England (2001); Crittenden (2001).

22. See Pixley and Moen (2003); Moen and Yu (2000).

23. See Bellas (1992); Han and Moen (1999b); Bianchi (2000); Hertz (1986); Fowlkes (1987). For earlier views on this topic see Rapoport and Rapoport (1977); Bird (1996).

24. See the Conference Board (2002), at www.conference-board.org/utilities/pressPrinterFriendly.crm?press_ID=1707 (accessed June 9, 2004).

25. See Kahn (1994), p. 49.

References

Adler, Nancy J. 1993. "An International Perspective on the Barriers to the Advancement of Women Managers." *Applied Psychology: An International Review* 42, no. 4: 289–300.

Albrecht, James, Anders Bjorklund, and Susan Vroman. 2003. "Is There a Glass Ceiling in Sweden?" *Journal of Labor Economics* 21, no. 1: 145–77.

Alexander, Baine B., Robert L. Rubinstein, Marcene Goodman, and Mark Luborsky. 1992. "A Path Not Taken: A Cultural Analysis of Regrets and Childlessness in the Lives of Older Women." *Gerontologist* 32, no. 5: 618–26.

Allen, Jim, and Karin Sanders. 2002. "Gender Gap in Earnings at the Industry Level." *European Journal of Women's Studies* 9, no. 2: 163–80.

Allen, Katherine R., and David H. Demo. 1995. "The Families of Lesbians and Gay Men: A New Frontier in Family Research." *Journal of Marriage and the Family* 57, no. 1: 111–27.

Allen, Sarah, and Alan Hawkins. 1999. "Maternal Gatekeeping: Mothers' Beliefs and Behaviors That Inhibit Greater Father Involvement in Family Work." *Journal of Marriage and the Family* 61, no. 1: 199–212.

Almeida, David M., and Daniel McDonald. 1998. "Weekly Rhythms of Parents' Work Stress, Home Stress, and Parent-Adolescent Tension." In *Temporal Rhythms in Adolescence: Clocks, Calendars, and Coordination of Daily Life*, edited by A. C. Crouter and R. Larson, 53–67. San Francisco: Jossey-Bass/Pfeiffer.

Almeida, David M., Elaine Wethington, and Amy L. Chandler. 1999. "Daily Transmission of Tensions between Marital Dyads and Parent–Child." *Journal of Marriage and the Family* 61, no. 1: 49–61.

Almeida, David M., Jennifer L. Maggs, and Nancy L. Galambos. 1993. "Wives' Employment Hours and Spousal Participation in Family Work." *Journal of Family Psychology* 7, no. 2: 233–44.

Altucher, Kristine A., and Lindy B. Williams. 2003. "Family Clocks: Timing Parenthood." In *It's About Time: Couples and Careers*, edited by P. Moen, 49–59. Ithaca, N.Y.: Cornell University Press.

American Association of Retired Persons. 2000. *Easing the Transition: A Look at Phased and Partial Retirement Programs in the United States*. Washington, D.C.: American Association of Retired Persons.

American Association of University Women Educational Foundation. 1999. *Gaining a Foothold: Women's Transitions through Work and College*. Washington, D.C.: American Association of University Women.

Anderson, Kathryn, Robert L. Clark, and Thomas Johnson. 1982. "Retirement in Dual-Career Families." In *Retirement Policy in an Aging Society*, edited by R. L. Clark, 109–27. Durham, N.C.: Duke University Press.

Appelbaum, Eileen, Thomas Bailey, Peter Berg, and Arne L. Kalleberg. 2002a. "Shared Work Valued Care." *Economic and Industrial Democracy: An International Journal* 23, no. 1: 125–31.

———. 2002b. *Shared Work, Valued Care: New Norms for Organizing Market Work and Unpaid Care Work*. Washington, D.C.: Economic Policy Institute.

Appelbaum, Eileen, and Rosemary Batt. 1994. *The New American Workplace: Transforming Work Systems in the United States*. Ithaca, N.Y.: ILR Press.

Armas, Genaro C. 2001. *Cohabitation on the Rise*. Washington, D.C.: Associated Press.

Armour, Stephanie. 1998. "More Workers Quick to Pick Perks over Pay." *USA Today*, June 15, 2B.

Aronson, Robert L. 1991. *Self-employment: A Labor Market Perspective*. Ithaca, N.Y.: ILR Press.

Arrighi, Barbara A., and David J. Maume. 2000. "Workplace Subordination and Men's Avoidance of Housework." *Journal of Family Issues* 21, no. 4: 464–87.

Aryee, Samuel, and Vivienne Luk. 1996. "Balancing Two Major Parts of Adult Life Experience: Work and Family Identity among Dual-Earner Couples." *Human Relations* 49, no. 4: 465–87.

Associated Press. 2000. "Child Care Latest Corporate Perk." *The Holland Sentinel* (MI), June 13, at www.hollandsentinel.com/stories (accessed June 25, 2004).

———. 2003. "Number of Stay-at-home Moms Boomed in the '90s." *The Holland Sentinel* (MI), June 17, at www.hollandsentinel.com/stories (accessed June 25, 2004).

———. 2003. "Employees Trim Worker Flexibility Programs." *The Holland Sentinel* (MI), October 23, A1.

Atchley, Robert C. 1983. *Aging: Continuity and Change*. Belmont, Calif.: Wentworth.

———. 1993. "Critical Perspectives on Retirement." In *Voices and Visions of Aging: Toward a Critical Gerontology*, edited by T. R. Cole, W. A. Achenbaum, P. L. Jakobi, and R. Kastenbaum, 3–19. New York: Springer Publishing.

Bachu, Amara. 1999. "Is Childlessness among American Women on the Rise?" *Working Paper Series*, No. 37, Washington, D.C.: U.S. Department of Commerce.

Bachu, Amara,.and Martin O'Connell. 2001. "Fertility of American Women: Population Characteristics June 2000." *Current Population Reports*, P20-543RV. Washington, D.C.: U.S. Department of Commerce.

Bailey, Diane E. and Nancy B. Kurland. 2002. "A Review of Telework Research: Findings, New Directions, and Lessons for the Study of Modern Work." *Journal of Organizational Behavior* 23: 383–400.

Bailyn, Lotte. 1993. *Breaking the Mold: Women, Men, and Time in the New Corporate World.* New York: Free Press.

Bailyn, Lotte, Robert Drago, and Thomas A. Kochan. 2001. *Integrating Work and Family Life: A Holistic Approach.* Boston: MIT School of Management.

Baltes, Paul B., and Margret M. Baltes, eds. 1990. *Successful Aging: Perspectives from the Behavioral Sciences.* Cambridge, Mass.: Cambridge University Press.

Bandura, Albert. 1977. *Social Learning Theory.* Englewood Cliffs, N.J.: Prentice Hall.

Bank, Barbara J., and Dee Ann Spencer. 1998. "Effects of Gender, Race-Ethnicity, High-School Experiences, and Ideology on Commitments after Graduation." *American Sociological Association Paper.*

Barber, Jennifer S. 2000. "Intergenerational Influences on the Entry into Parenthood: Mothers' Preferences for Family and Nonfamily." *Social Forces* 79, no. 1: 319–48.

Barker, Kathleen, and Kathleen Christensen. 1998. *Contingent Work: American Employment Relations in Transition.* Ithaca, N.Y.: ILR Press.

Barnett, Rosalind C., and Robert T. Brennan. 1997. "Change in Job Conditions, Change in Psychological Distress, and Gender: A Longitudinal Study of Dual-Earner Couples." *Journal of Organizational Behavior* 18, no. 3: 253–74.

Barnett, Rosalind C., and Karen C. Gareis. 2002. "Full-Time and Reduced-Hours Work Schedules and Marital Quality." *Work and Occupations* 29, no. 3: 364–79.

Barnett, Rosalind C., and Janet S. Hyde. 2001. "Women, Men, Work, and Family." *American Psychologist* 56, no. 10: 781–96.

Barnett, Rosalind C., and Nancy L. Marshall. 1992a. "Men's Job and Partner Roles: Spillover Effects and Psychological Distress." *Sex Roles* 27, nos. 9–10: 455–72.

———. 1992b. "Worker and Mother Roles, Spillover Effects, and Psychological Distress." *Women and Health* 18, no. 2: 9–40.

———. 1993. "Work-Family Strains and Gains among Two-Earner Couples." *Journal of Community Psychology* 21, no. 1: 64–78.

Barnett, Rosalind C., and Caryl Rivers. 1996. *She Works/He Works: How Two-Income Families Are Happier, Healthier, and Better-Off.* New York: Harper Collins.

Barrett, Anne E. 1999. "Marital Trajectories and Mental Health: A Typological Approach to the Social Causation Hypothesis. (Marital Status, Medical Sociology)," *Dissertation Abstracts International Section A: Humanities and Social Sciences* 60, no. 5-A: 1781.

Baruch, Grace K., and Rosalind C. Barnett. 1986. "Fathers' Participation in Family Work and Children's Sex-Role Attitudes." *Child Development* 57, no. 5: 1210–23.

Baruch, Yehuda. 2000. "Teleworking: Benefits and Pitfalls as Perceived by Professionals and Managers." *New Technology, Work, and Employment* 15, no. 1: 34–49.

Baumol, William J., Alan S. Blinder, and Edward N. Wolft. 2003. *Downsizing in America: Reality, Causes, and Consequences.* New York: Russel Sage Foundation.

Baxter, Janeen. 1981. *A Treatise on the Family.* Cambridge, Mass.: Harvard University Press.

———. 2002. "Patterns of Change and Stability in the Gender Division of Household Labour in Australia, 1986–1997." *Journal of Sociology* 34, no. 4: 399–424.

Becker, Gary S. 1981. "Division of Labor in Households and Families." In *A Treatise on the Family*, edited by G. S. Becker, 30–53. Cambridge, Mass.: Harvard University Press.

Becker, Penny, and Phyllis Moen. 1999. "Scaling Back: Dual Career Couples' Work–Family Strategies." *Journal of Marriage and the Family* 61, no. 4: 995–1007.

Bejian, Donna V., and Paul R. Salomone. 1995. "Understanding Midlife Career Renewal: Implications for Counseling." *Career Development Quarterly Special Issue: Career Transitions* 44, no. 1: 52–63.

Bellas, Marcia L. 1992. "The Effects of Marital Status and Wives' Employment on the Salaries of Faculty Men: The (House) Wife Bonus." *Gender and Society* 6, no. 4: 609–22.

Belle, Deborah, Sara Norell, and Anthony Lewis. 1997. "Becoming Unsupervised: Children's Transitions from Adult-Care to Self-Care in the after School Hours." In *Stress and Adversity over the Life Course: Trajectories and Turning Points*, edited by I. H. Gotlib and B. Wheaton, 159–78. Cambridge: Cambridge University Press.

Benson, John, and Ying Zhu. 1999. "Markets, Firms, and Workers in Chinese State-Owned Enterprises." *Human Resource Management Journal* 9, no. 4: 58–74.

Bergmann, Barbara. 1986. *The Economic Emergence of Women*. New York: Basic Books.

Bernhardt, Eva M. 1993. "Fertility and Employment." *European Sociological Review* 9, no. 1: 25–41.

Bernstein, Jared, Heather Boushey, Elizabeth McNichol, and Robert Zahradnik. 2002. *Pulling Apart: A State-by-State Analysis of Income Trends*. Washington, D.C.: Economic Policy Institute.

Beutell, Nicholas J., and Ursula Wittig-Berman. 1999. "Predictors of Work–Family Conflict and Satisfaction with Family, Job, Career, and Life." *Psychological Reports* 85, no. 3, pt. 1: 893–903.

Bianchi, Suzanne M. 1999. "Feminization and Juvenilization of Poverty: Trends, Relative Risks, Causes, and Consequences." *Annual Review of Sociology* 25: 307–33.

———. 2000. "Maternal Employment and the Time with Children: Dramatic Change or Surprising Continuity?" *Demography* 37, no. 4: 401–14.

Bianchi, Suzanne M., Melissa A. Milkie, Liana C. Sayer, and John P. Robinson. 2000. "Is Anyone Doing the Housework? Trends in the Gender Division of Household Labor." *Social Forces* 79, no. 1: 191–228.

Bianchi, Suzanne M., and Daphne Spain. 1996. "Women, Work, and Family in America." *Population Bulletin* 51, no. 3: 2–46.

Bianchi, Suzanne M., Lekha Subaiya, and Joan R. Kahn. 1999. "The Gender Gap in the Economic Well-Being of Nonresident Fathers and Custodial Mothers." *Demography* 36, no. 2: 195–203.

Bielby, William T., and Denise D. Bielby. 1992. "I Will Follow Him: Family Ties, Gender-Role Beliefs, and Reluctance to Relocate for a Better Job." *American Journal of Sociology* 97, no. 5: 1241–67.

Bird, Chloe E. 1996. "An Analysis of Gender Differences in Income among Dentists, Physicians and Veterinarians in 1987." *Research in the Sociology of Health Care* 13, A: 31–61.

Blair-Loy, Mary, and Amy S. Wharton. 2002. "Employees' Use of Work–Family Policies and the Workplace Social Context." *Social Forces* 80, no. 3: 813–45.

Blau, Francine D. 1977. *Equal Pay in the Office*. Lexington, Mass.: Lexington Books.

Blau, Francine, and Marianne A. Ferber. 1986. *The Economics of Women, Men, and Work*. Englewood Cliffs, N.J.: Prentice Hall.

Blau, Francine D., Marianne A. Ferber, and Anne E. Winkler. 2001. *The Economics of Men and Women at Work*, 4th ed. Upper Saddle River, N.J.: Prentice Hall.

Blau, Francine D., and Lawrence M. Kahn. 2003. "Understanding International Difference in the Gender Pay Gap." *Journal of Labor Economics* 21, no. 1: 106–44.

Blau, Francine D., Lawrence M. Kahn, and Jane Waldfogel. 2000. "Understanding Young Women's Marriage Decisions: The Role of Labor and Marriage Market Conditions." *Industrial and Labor Relations Review* 53, no. 4: 624–47.

Bloom, David E., and James Trussell. 1984. "What Are the Determinants of Delayed Childbearing and Permanent Childlessness in the United States?" *Demography* 21, no. 4: 591–611.

Blossfeld, Hans-Peter, and Sonja Drobnic, eds. 2001. *Careers of Couples in Contemporary Societies: A Cross-National Comparison of the Transition from Male Breadwinner to Dual-Earner Families*. Oxford: Oxford University Press.

Blossfeld, Hans-Peter, and Catherine Hakim, eds. 1996. "Part-time Work in the United States of America." In *Between Equalization and Marginalisation: Women Working Part Time in Europe and the United States of America*, edited by H.-P. Blossfeld and C. Hakim, 289–314. Oxford: Oxford University Press.

———. 1997. *Between Equalization and Marginalization: Women Working Part Time in Europe and the United States of America*. Oxford: Oxford University Press.

Blumenberg, Evelyn. 2002. "On the Way to Work: Welfare Participants and Barriers to Employment." *Economic Development Quarterly* 16, no. 4: 314–25.

Boden, Richard. 1999. "Flexible Working Hours, Family Responsibilities, and Female Self-Employment: Gender Differences in Self-Employment Selection." *American Journal of Economics and Sociology* 58, no. 1: 71–83.

Boise, Linda, and Margaret B. Neal. 1996. "Family Responsibilities and Absenteeism: Employees Caring for Parents Versus Employees Caring for Children." *Journal of Managerial Issues* 8, no. 2: 218–38.

Bolger, Niall, Anita Delongis, Ronald C. Kessler, and Elaine Wethington. 1989. "The Contagion of Stress across Multiple Roles." *Journal of Marriage and the Family* 51, no. 1: 175–83.

Bond, James T., Ellen Galinsky, and Jennifer E. Swanberg. 1998. *The 1997 National Study of the Changing Workforce*. New York: Families and Work Institute.

Bookman, Ann. 2004. *Starting in Our Own Backyards, How Working Families Can Build Community and Survive the New Economy*. New York: Routledge.

Booth, Alan, Ann C. Crouter, and Michael J. Shanahan, eds. 1999. *Transitions to Adulthood in a Changing Economy: No Work, No Family, No Future?* Westport, Conn.: Praeger.

Booth, Alan, John N. Edwards, and David R. Johnson. 1991. "Social Integration and Divorce." *Social Forces* 70, no. 1: 207–24.

Booth, Cathryn L., Alison K. Clarke-Stewart, Deborah L. Vandell, Kathleen McCartney, and Margaret T. Owen. 2002. "Child-Care Usage and Mother-Infant 'Quality Time.'" *Journal of Marriage and the Family* 64, no. 1: 16–26.

Border, John M. 2002. "Family Leave in California Now Includes Pay Benefit." *New York Times*, September 24, A 20.

Boserup, Ester. 1995. *Women's Role in Economic Development*. London: Earthscan Publications.

Boushey, Heather. 2001. "Last Hired, First Fired Job Losses Plague Former TANF Recipients." *EPI Issue Brief*, #171. Washington, D.C.: Economic Policy Institute.

———. 2002. "Former Welfare Families Need More Help: Hardships Await Those Making Transition to Workforce." *EPI Briefing Paper*. Washington, D.C.: Economic Policy Institute, April.

Bowen, Gary. 1998. "Effects of Leader Support in the Work Unit on the Relationship between Work Spillover and Family Adaptation." *Journal of Family and Economic Issues* 19: 25–52.

Bradburn, Ellen. 2002. "Short-Term Enrollment in Postsecondary Education: Student Background and Institutional Differences in Reasons for Early Departure, 1996–1998." NCES 2003–2153. Washington, D.C.: U.S. Department of Education, National Center for Education Statistics, at http://nces.ed.gov/das/epubs/2003153/factors2.asp (accessed October 1, 2003).

Bram, Susan. 1985. "Childlessness Revisited: A Longitudinal Study of Voluntary Childlessness Couples, Delayed Parents, and Parents." *Lifestyles: A Journal of Changing Patterns*: 46–65.

Brayfield, April. 1992. "Employment Resources and Household Work in Canada." *Journal of Marriage and the Family* 54, no. 1: 19–30.

Brett, Jeanne M., and Linda K. Stroh. 1997. "Jumping Ship: Who Benefits from an External Labor Market Career Strategy?" *Journal of Applied Psychology* 82, no. 3: 331–41.

Brett, Jeanne M., Linda K. Stroh, and Anne H. Reilly. 1993. "Pulling Up Roots in the 1990s: Who's Willing to Relocate?" *Journal of Organizational Behavior* 14, no. 1: 49–60.

Brewster, Karin L. 2000. "Contextualizing Change in Fathers' Participation in Child Care, 1977–1994." Paper presented at Work and Family Conference, San Francisco, Calif., March.

Brines, Julie. 1994. "Economic Dependency, Gender, and the Division of Labor at Home." *American Journal of Sociology* 100, no. 3: 652–88.

Broderick, Tara, and Belinda Glazer. 1983. "Leisure Participation and the Retirement Process." *American Journal of Occupational Therapy* 37, no. 1: 15–22.

Bromet, Evelyn J., Mary A. Dew, and David K. Parkinson. 1990. "Spillover between Work and Family: A Study of Blue-Collar Working Wives." In *Stress between Work and Family: The Plenum Series on Stress and Coping*, edited by J. Eckenrode and S. Gore, 133–51. New York: Plenum Press.

Bronfenbrenner, Urie. 1995. "Developmental Ecology through Space and Time." In *Examining Lives in Context: Perspectives on the Ecology of Human Development*, edited by P. Moen, G. H. Elder Jr., and K. Lüscher, 619–47. Washington, D.C.: American Psychological Association.

Brough, Paula, and Anouk Kelling. 2002. "Women, Work and Well-Being: The Influence of Work-Family and Family-Work Conflict." *New Zealand Journal of Psychology* 31, no. 1: 29–38.

Brown, Duane. 1996. "Brown's Value-Based Holistic Model of Career and Life-Role Choices and Satisfaction." In *Career Choice and Development*, edited by D. Brown and L. Brooks, 3rd ed. San Francisco: Jossey-Bass.

Bryant, Alyssa N. 2003. "Changes in Attitudes towards Women's Roles: Predicting Gender-Role Traditionalism among College Students." *Sex Roles* 48, nos. 3–4: 131–42.

Buchmann, Marlis. 1989. *The Script of Life in Modern Society: Entry into Adulthood in a Changing World*. Chicago: University of Chicago Press.

Budig, J. Michelle, and Paula England. 2001. "The Wage Penalty for Motherhood." *American Sociological Review* 66, no. 2: 204–25.

Bumpass, Larry, and Hsien-Hen Lu. 2000. "Trends in Cohabitation and Implications for Children's Family Contexts in the United States." *Population Studies* 54, no. 1: 29–41.

Burley, Kim A. 1991. "Family to Spillover in Dual-Career Couples: A Comparison of Two Time Perspectives." *Psychological Reports* 68, no. 2: 471–80.

Burstein, Paul, Marie R. Bricher, and Rachel L. Einwohner. 1995. "Policy Alternatives and Political Change: Work, Family, and Gender on the Congressional Agenda, 1945–1990." *American Sociological Review* 60, no. 1: 67–83.

Burtless, Gary, and Joseph F. Quinn. 2001. "Retirement Trends and Policies to Encourage Work among Older Americans." In *Ensuring Health and Income Security for an Aging Workforce*, edited by P. Budetti, R. Burkhauser, J. Gregory, and A. Hunt, 375–415. Kalamazoo, Mich.: W. E. Upjohn Institute for Employment Research.

Business and Professional Women. 2003. "101 Facts on the Status of Working Women (Women in the Fortune 500, Facts 32–47)," January, at www.bpwusa.org/content/PressRoom/101Facts/101_Fortune500.htm (accessed June 25, 2004).

Campion, William J., and Janice C. Dill. 2000. "An Investigation of the Impact on Higher Education of the Family and Medical Leave Act of 1993." *Public Personnel Management* 29, no. 1: 147–56.

Camstra, Ronald. 1996. "Commuting and Gender in a Lifestyle Perspective." *Urban Studies* 33, no. 2: 283–300.

Cannings, Kathleen. 1991. "An Interdisciplinary Approach to Analyzing the Managerial Gender Gap." *Human Relations* 44, no. 7: 679–95.

Cantor, David, Jane Waldfogel, Jeffrey Kerwin, Mareena M. Wright, Kerry Levin, John Rauch, Tracey Hagerty, and Martha S. Kudela. 2001. "Balancing the Needs of Families and Employers: The Family and Medical Leave Surveys 2000 Update." Washington, D.C.: U.S. Department of Labor.

Cappelli, Peter, Jill Constantine, and Clint Chadwick. 2000. "It Pays to Value Family: Work and Family Trade-Offs Reconsidered." *Industrial Relations* 39, no. 2: 175–98.

Caputo, Richard K. 2000. "The Availability of the Traditional and Family-Friendly Employee Benefits among a Cohort of Young Women, 1968–1995." *Families in Society: The Journal of Contemporary Human Services* 81, no. 4: 422–36.

Carlson, Dawn, and Pamela A. Perrewe. 1999. "The Role of Social Support in the Stressor-Strain Relationship: An Examination of Work–Family Conflict." *Journal of Management* 25, no. 4: 513–40.

Caro, Francis G., and Scott A. Bass. 1997. "Receptivity to Volunteering in the Immediate Postretirement Period." *Journal of Applied Gerontology* 16, no. 4: 427–44.

Carr, Deborah. 1996. "Two Paths to Self-Employment? Women's and Men's Self-Employment in the United States, 1980." *Work and Occupations* 23, no. 1: 26–53.

Carstensen, Laura L. 1992. "Social and Emotion Patterns in Adulthood: Support for Socioemotional Selectivity Theory." *Psychology and Aging* 7: 331–38.

Casey, Judith C., and Marcie Pitt-Catsouphes. 1994. "Employed Single Mothers: Balancing Job and Homelife." *Employee Assistance Quarterly* 9, nos. 3/4: 37–53.

Casper, Lynne M., and Suzanne M. Bianchi. 2002. *Continuity and Change in the American Family*. Thousand Oaks, Calif.: Sage Publications.

Catalyst. 1997a. *Factsheet. A New Approach to Flexibility: Managing the Work/Time Equation*. New York: Catalyst.

———. 1997b. *Women of Color in Corporate Management: A Statistical Picture*. New York: Catalyst.

———. 2000. *2000 Catalyst Census of Women Corporate Officers and Top Earners*. New York: Catalyst.

———. 2001. *2001 Catalyst Census of Women Board Directors of the Fortune 1000*. New York: Catalyst.

Cerrutti, Marcela. 2000. "Intermittent Employment among Married Women: A Comparative Study of Buenos Aires and Mexico City." *Journal of Comparative Family Studies* 31, no. 1: 19–44.

Chafe, William H. 1972. *The American Woman: Her Changing Social, Economic, and Political Roles, 1920–1970*. New York: Oxford University Press.

Chambré, Susan M. 1984. "Is Volunteering a Substitute for Role Loss in Old Age: An Empirical Test of Activity Theory." *Gerontologist* 24, no. 3: 292–98.

———. 1987. *Good Deeds in Old Age: Volunteering by the New Leisure Class*. Lexington, Mass.: Lexington Books.

Chapman, Jeff, and Jared Bernstein. 2003. "Falling through the Safety Net: Low-Income Single Mothers in the Jobless Recovery." *EPI Issue Brief*, #191. Washington, D.C.: Economic Policy Institute.

Chapman, Nancy J., Berit Ingersoll-Dayton, and Margaret B. Neal. 1994. "Balancing the Multiple Roles of Work and Caregiving for Children, Adults, and Elders." In *Job Stress in a Changing Workforce: Investigating Gender Diversity and Family Issues*, edited by G. P. Keita and J. J. Hurrell Jr., 283–300. Washington, D.C.: American Psychological Association.

Chase-Lansdale, Lindsay P., Robert A. Moffitt, Brenda J. Lohman, Andrew J. Cherlin, Rebekah L. Coley, Laura D. Pittman, Jennifer Roff, Elizabeth Botruba-Drzal. 2003. "Mothers' Transitions from Welfare to Work and the Well-Being of Preschoolers and Adolescents." *Science* 299: 1548–52.

Chen, Renbao, and S. Philip Morgan. 1991. "Recent Trends in the Timing of First Births in the United States." *Demography* 28, no. 4: 513–33.

Cherlin, Andrew. 1992. *Marriage, Divorce, Remarriage*. Cambridge, Mass.: Harvard University Press.

Cherlin, Andrew J., and Frank F. Furstenberg. 1994. "Stepfamilies in the United States: A Reconsideration." *Annual Review of Sociology* 20: 359–81.

Choi, Namkee G. 2002. "Self-Defined Retirement Status and Engagement in Paid Work among Older Working-Age Women: Comparison between Childless Women and Mothers." *Sociological Inquiry* 72, no. 1: 43–71.

Christensen, Kathleen E., and Graham Staines. 1990. "Flextime: A Viable Solution to Work/Family Conflict?" *Journal of Family Issues* 11, no. 4: 455–76.

Cicirelli, Victor G. 1995. *Sibling Relationships across the Life Span.* New York: Plenum Press.

Ciscel, David H., and David C. Sharp. 1995. "Household Labor in Hours by Family Type." *Journal of Forensic Economics* 8, no. 2: 115–23.

Clacs, Rita. 2000. "Meaning of Atypical Working: The Case of Potential Telehomeworkers." *European Review of Applied Psychology* 50, no. 1: 27–36.

Clarkberg, Marin. 1999. "The Price of Partnering: The Role of Economic Well-Being in Young Adults' First Union Experiences." *Social Forces* 77, no. 3: 945–68.

———. 2000. "The Time Squeeze in American Families: From Causes to Solutions." In *Balancing Acts: Easing the Burdens and Improving the Options for Working Families,* edited by E. Appelbaum, 25–36. Washington, D.C.: Economic Policy Institute.

Clarkberg, Marin, and Phyllis Moen. 2001. "Understanding the Time-Squeeze: Married Couples' Preferred and Actual Work-Hour Strategies." *American Behavioral Scientist* 44, no. 7: 1115–36.

Clay, Rebecca. 2003. "An Empty Nest Can Promote Freedom, Improved Relationships." *Monitor on Psychology* 34, no. 4: 40.

Clayton, Kermeta K., Gonzalo Garcia Jr., Rachel Underwood, Phil McEndree, and Richard Sheppard. 1993. "Family Influence over the Occupational and Educational Choices of Mexican American Students." Paper presented at the meeting of the American Vocational Association, Nashville, Tenn., December.

Cohen, Philip N. 2002. "Cohabitation and the Declining Marriage Premium for Men." *Work and Occupations* 29, no. 3: 346–63.

Cohen, Philip N., and Suzanne M. Bianchi. 1999. "Marriage, Children and Women's Employment: What Do We Know?" *Monthly Labor Review* 122, no. 12: 22–31.

Cohen, Sarale E. 1978. "Maternal Employment and Mother—Child Interaction." *Merrill-Palmer Quarterly* 24: 189–97.

Cohn, Samuel. 1985. *The Process of Occupational Sex-Typing: The Feminization of Clerical Labor in Great Britain.* Philadelphia: Temple University Press.

Collins, Glenn. 1997. "Tug of Home is Stronger Than the Pull of the Office." *New York Times,* September 25, D4.

Coltrane, Scott. 1996. *Family Man: Fatherhood, Housework, and Gender Equity.* New York: Oxford University Press.

Conference Board, The. 2002. "Job Satisfaction on the Decline." *Special Consumer Survey Report,* July, at www.conference-board.org/utilities/pressDetail.cfm?press_ID=1707 (accessed June 25, 2004).

Connelly, Rachel. 1992. "Self-Employment and Providing Child Care." *Demography* 29, no. 1: 17–29.

Cooper, Cecily D., and Nancy B. Kurland. 2002. "Telecommuting, Professional Isolation, and Employee Development in Public and Private Organizations." *Journal of Organizational Behavior* 23: 511–32.

Corijn, Martine, Art C. Liefbroer, and Jenny de John Gierveld. 1996. "It Takes Two to Tango, Doesn't It? The Influence of Couple Characteristics on the Timing of the Birth of the First Child." *Journal of Marriage and the Family* 58, no. 1: 117–26.

Cornfield, Daniel B., Karen E. Campbell, and Holly J. McCammon. 2001. *Working in Restructured Workplaces: Challenges and New Directions for the Sociology of Work.* Thousand Oaks, Calif.: Sage Publications.

Correll, Shelley J., and Chris Bourg. 1999. "Trends in Gender Role Attitudes, 1976–1997: The Continued Myth of Separate Worlds." Paper presented at the annual meeting of the American Sociological Association, Chicago, Ill., August.

Coser, Lewis A. 1974. *Greedy Institutions: Patterns of Undivided Commitment.* New York: Free Press.

Coser, Lewis A., and Rose Laub Coser. 1974. "The Housewife and Her Greedy Family." In *Greedy Institutions*, edited by L. A. Coser. New York: Free Press.

Costa, Dora L. 1998. *The Evolution of Retirement: An American Economic History, 1880–1990.* Chicago: University of Chicago Press.

Cott, Nancy, and Elizabeth H. Pleck. 1979. *A Heritage of Her Own: Toward a New Social History of American Women.* New York: Simon and Schuster.

Cotter, David A., Joan M. Hermsen, Seth Ovadia, and Reeve Vanneman. 2001. "The Glass Ceiling Effect." *Social Forces* 80, no. 2: 655–82.

Couch, Kenneth A., Mary C. Daly, and Douglas A. Wolf. 1999. "Time? Money? Both? The Allocation of Resources to Older Parents." *Demography* 36, no. 2: 219–32.

Coverdill, James E. 1988. "The Dual Economy and Sex Differences in Earnings." *Social Forces* 66, no. 4: 970–93.

Coverman, Shelley. 1985. "Explaining Husbands' Participation in Domestic Labor." *Sociological Quarterly* 26, no. 1: 81–98.

Coverman, Shelley, and Joseph F. Sheley. 1986. "Change in Men's Housework and Child-Care Time, 1965–1975." *Journal of Marriage and the Family* 48, no. 2: 413–22.

Covin, Teresa J., and Christina C. Brush. 1991. "An Examination of Male and Female Attitudes toward Career and Family." *Sex Roles* 25, nos. 7–8: 393–415.

Cowan, Carolyn P., and Philip A. Cowan. 2000. *When Partners Become Parents.* Mahwah, N.J.: Lawrence Erlbaum.

Cox, Amy G., and Harriet Presser. 2000. "Nonstandard Employment Schedules among American Mothers." In *Work and Family*, edited by T. L. Parcel and D. B. Cornfield, 97–130. Thousand Oaks, Calif.: Sage Publications.

Crittenden, Ann. 2001. *The Price of Motherhood: Why the Most Important Job in the World Is Still the Least Valued.* New York: Metropolitan Books.

Crittenden, Danielle. 1999. "Being with the Kids Beats Life in the Rat Race." *Sunday Times* (London), July 25.

Crompton, Rosemary, and Fiona Harris. 1997. "Women's Employment and Gender Attitudes: A Comparative Analysis of Britain, Norway, and the Czech Republic." *Acta Sociologica* 40, no. 2: 183–202.

Cropanzano, Russell, John C. Howes, Alicia A. Grandey, and Paul Toth. 1997. "The Relationship of Organizational Politics and Support to Work Behaviors, Attitudes, and Stress." *Journal of Organizational Behavior* 18, no. 2: 159–80.

Crouter, Ann C. 1984. "Spillover from Family to Work: The Neglected Side of the Work–Family Interface." *Human Relations* 37, no. 6: 425–42.

Crouter, Ann C., and Matthew F. Bumpus. 2001. "Linking Parents' Work Stress to Children's and Adolescents' Psychological Adjustment." *Current Directions in Psychological Science* 10, no. 5: 156–59.

Crouter, Ann C., Matthew F. Bumpus, Melissa R. Head, and Susan M. McHale. 2001. "Implications of Overwork and Overload for the Quality of Men's Family Relationships." *Journal of Marriage and the Family* 63, no. 2: 404–16.

Czaja, Sara J., and Phyllis Moen. 2004. "Technology and Employment." In *Technology for Adaptive Aging*, edited by Richard Pew and Susan Van Hemel. National Research Council, Steering Committee for the Workshop on Adaptive Aging. Washington, D.C.: National Academies Press.

Daly, Kerry J. 1996. *Families and Time: Keeping Pace in a Hurried Culture*. Thousand Oaks, Calif.: Sage Publications.

Day, Jennifer C. 2001. "National Population Projections." U.S. Census Bureau, Population Division and Housing and Household Economic Statistics Division, January 18, at www.census.gov/population/www/pop-profile/natproj.html (accessed November 15, 2002). Government Publication.

Deitch, Cynthia H., and Matt L. Huffman. 2001. "Family Responsive Benefits and the Two-Tiered Labor Market." In *Working Families: The Transformation of the American Home*, edited by R. Hertz and N. L. Marshall, 103–30. Berkeley: University of California Press.

Dempsey, Kenneth, C. 1998. "Increasing the Workload of the Overloaded Housewife." *Journal of Family Studies* 4, no. 1: 3–20.

DeOllos, Ione Y., and Carolyn A. Kapinus. 2002. "Aging Childless Individuals and Couples: Suggestions for New Directions in Research." *Sociological Inquiry* 72, no. 1: 72–80.

Desai, Sonalde, and Linda J. Waite. 1991. "Women's Employment during Pregnancy and after the First Birth: Occupational Characteristics and Work Commitment." *American Sociological Review* 56, no. 4: 551–66.

Desmarais, Serge, and James Curtis. 1999. "Gender Differences in Employment and Income Experiences among Young People." In *Young Workers: Varieties of Experience*, edited by J. Barling and E. K. Kelloway, 59–88. Washington, D.C.: American Psychological Association.

Deutsch, Francine M. 2001. "Equally Shared Parenting." *Current Directions in Psychological Science* 10, no. 1: 25–28.

Deutsch, Francine M., Julianne B. Lussier, and Laura J. Servis. 1993. "Husbands at Home: Predictors of Paternal Participation in Childcare and Housework." *Journal of Personality and Social Psychology* 65, no. 6: 1154–66.

Deutsch, Francine M., and Susan E. Saxon. 1998. "Traditional Ideologies, Nontraditional Lives." *Sex Roles* 38, nos. 5–6: 331–62.

Deutsch, Francine M., Laura L. Servis, and Jessica D. Payne. 2001. "Paternal Participation in Child Care and Its Effects on Children's Self-Esteem and Attitudes toward Gendered Roles." *Journal of Family Issues* 22, no. 8: 1000–24.

Dillard, John M., and N. Jo Campbell. 1981. "Influences of Puerto Rican, Black, and Anglo Parents' Career Behavior on Their Adolescent Children's Career-Development." *Vocational Guidance Quarterly* 30, no. 2: 139–48.

Dixon, K. A., and Carl E. Van Horn. 2002. "Taking Stock of Retirement: How Workers and Employers Assess Pensions, Trust, and the Economy." Heldrich Work Trends Survey 3.5 in *Work Trends: Americans' Attitudes about Work, Employers and Government*, May, at http://heldrich.rutgers.edu/Resources/Publication/22/PDF_Work_Trends_XI_Taking_Stock_of_Retirement_Final_Report.pdf (accessed May 21, 2003).

Dorfman, Lorraine T. 1992. "Couples in Retirement: Division of Household Work." In *Families and Retirement*, edited by M. Szinovacz, D. J. Ekerdt, and B. H. Vinick, 159–73. Thousand Oaks, Calif.: Sage Publications.

Downs, Barbara. 2003. "Fertility of American Women: June 2002." *Current Population Reports*, P20-548. Washington, D.C.: U.S. Census Bureau, at www.census.gov/prod/2003pubs/p20–548.pdf (accessed October 6, 2003).

Drobnic, Sonja, Hans-Peter Blossfeld, and Gotz Rohwer. 1999. "Dynamics of Women's Employment Patterns over the Family Life Course: A Comparison of the United States and Germany." *Journal of Marriage and the Family* 61, no. 1: 133–46.

Duxbury, Linda E., Christopher A. Higgins, and Catherine Lee. 1994. "Work–Family Conflict: A Comparison by Gender, Family Type, and Perceived Control." *Journal of Family Issues* 15, no. 3: 449–66. ·

Duxbury, Linda E., Christopher A. Higgins, Catherine Lee, and Shirley Mills. 1992. "An Examination of Organizational and Individual Outcomes." *Journal of Public Sector Management* 23, no. 2: 46–59.

Duxbury, Linda E., Christopher A. Higgins, and D. Roland Thomas. 1996. "Work and Family Environments and the Adoption of Computer-Supported Supplemental Work-at-Home." *Journal of Vocational Behavior* 49, no. 1: 1–23.

Eagle, Bruce W., Edward W. Miles, and Marjorie L. Icenogle. 1997. "Interrole Conflicts and the Permeability of Work and Family Domains: Are There Gender Differences?" *Journal of Vocational Behavior* 50, no. 2: 168–84.

Eby, Lillian T., Tammy D. Allen, and Shane S. Douthitt. 1999. "The Role of Nonperformance Factors on Job-Related Relocation Opportunities: A Field Study and Laboratory Experiment." *Organized Behavior and Human Decision Processes* 79, no. 1: 29–55.

Eby, Lillian T., Shane S. Douthitt, Towers Perrin, Carrie L. Noble, Kate P. Atchley, and Robert Ladd. 2002. "Managerial Support for Dual-Career Relocation Dilemmas." *Journal of Vocational Behavior* 60, no. 3: 354–73.

Economic Policy Institute. 2003. *EPI Issue Guide: Retirement Security.* Washington, D.C.: Economic Policiy Institute, at www.epinet.org/Issueguides/retire/retirement_security_issue_guide-epi.pdf (accessed November 14, 2003).

Edwards, Linda N., and Elizabeth Field-Hendrey. 2002. "Home-Based Work and Women's Labor Force Decisions." *Journal of Labor Economics* 20, no. 1: 170–200.

Elder, Glen H., Jr. 1995. "The Life Course Paradigm: Social Change and Individual Development." In *Examining Lives in Context: Perspectives on the Ecology of Human Development*, edited by P. Moen, G. H. Elder Jr., and K. Lüscher, 101–39. Washington, D.C.: American Psychological Association.

Emanuel, Ezekiel J., Diane L. Fairclough, Julia Slutsman, Hillel Alpert, DeWitt Baldwin, and Linda L. Emanuel. 1999. "Assistance from Family Members, Friends, Paid Care Givers, and Volunteers in the Care of Terminally Ill Patients." *New England Journal of Medicine* 341, no. 13: 956–63.

England, Paula, and George Farkas. 1986. *Households, Employment, and Gender: A Social, Economic, and Demographic View.* New York: Aldine.

Epstein, Cynthia F., and Arne L. Kalleberg. 2001. "Time and the Sociology of Work: Issues and Implications." *Work and Occupations* 28, no. 1: 5–16.

Epstein, Cynthia Fuchs, Robert Saute, Martha Gever, and Bonnie Oglensky. 1999. *The Part-time Paradox: Time Norms, Professional Lives, Family and Gender.* New York and London: Routledge.

Erbe, Bonnie. 1996. "There's No Room for a Child in Her Life." *San Diego Union-Tribune*, May 12, G3.

Erikson, Erik H., Joan M. Erikson, and Helen Q. Kivnick. 1994. *Vital Involvement in Old Age*. New York: W. W. Norton and Co.

Esping-Andersen, Gosta. 1990. *The Three Worlds of Welfare Capitalism*. Princeton, N.J.: Princeton University Press.

European Foundation for the Improvement of Living and Working Conditions. 2001. "Progressive Retirement in Europe," at www.eiro.eurofound.ie/2001/09/study/tn0109184s.html (accessed December 2, 2003).

Evans, Paul, and Fernando Bartolome. 1984. "The Changing Pictures of the Relationship between Career and Family." *Journal of Occupational Behaviour* 5, no. 1: 9–21.

Ewen, Ida M. 1994. "Women in Midlife/Midcareer: An Exploratory Study of Their Changes and Transitions." *Dissertation Abstracts International Section A: Humanities and Social Sciences* 54, no. 9-A: 3327.

Farmer, Helen S. 1997. "Why Women Don't Persist in Their High School Career Aspirations." In *Diversity in Women's Career Development: From Adolescence to Adulthood*, edited by H. S. Farmer, 62–80. Thousand Oaks, Calif.: Sage Publications.

Federal Interagency Forum on Child and Family Statistics. 2001. "America's Children: Key National Indicators of Well-Being 2001." *Federal Interagency Forum on Child and Family Statistics*. Washington, D.C.: U.S. Government Printing Office.

———. 2003. "America's Children: Key National Indicators of Well-Being, 2003." *Federal Interagency Forum on Child and Family Statistics*. Washington, D.C.: U.S. Government Printing Office, at www.childstats.gov/ac2003/pdf/front.pdf (accessed October 6, 2003).

Feiring, Candice, and Michael Lewis. 1993. "Do Mothers Know Their Teenagers' Friends—Implications for Individuation in Early Adolescence." *Journal of Youth and Adolescence* 22, no. 4: 337–54.

Feldman, Daniel C., and Mark C. Bolino. 2000. "Career Patterns of the Self-Employed: Career Motivations and Career Outcomes." *Journal of Small Business Management* (July), 53–67.

Felmlee, Diane H. 1982. "Women's Job Mobility Processes." *American Sociological Review* 47, no. 1:142–50.

———. 1984. "The Dynamics of Women's Job Mobility." *Work and Occupations* 11, no. 3: 259–81.

Ferguson, Susan J. 2000. "Challenging Traditional Marriage: Never Married Chinese American and Japanese American Women." *Gender and Society* 14, no. 1: 136–59.

Ferree, Myra M. 1990. "Beyond Separate Spheres: Feminism and Family Research." *Journal of Marriage and the Family* 52, no. 4: 866–84.

———. 1991. "The Gender Division of Labor in Two-Earner Marriages: Dimensions of Variability and Change." *Journal of Family Issues* 12, no. 2: 158–80.

Fields, Jason. 2003. "Children's Living Arrangements and Characteristics: March 2002." *Current Population Reports*, P20-547. Washington, D.C.: U.S. Census Bureau.

Fields, Jason, and Lynne M. Casper. 2001. "America's Families and Living Arrangements: March 2000." *Current Populations Reports*, P20-537. Washington, D.C.: U.S. Census Bureau.

Finch, Jonet. 1983. *Married to the Job: Wives' Incorporation in Men's Work.* London: Allen and Unwin.

Finley, Nancy J. 1989. "Theories of Family Labor as Applied to Gender Differences in Care Giving for Elderly Parents." *Journal of Marriage and the Family* 51, no. 1: 79–86.

Fischer, Lucy R., and Kay B. Schaffer. 1993. *Older Volunteers: A Guide to Research.* Thousand Oaks, Calif.: Sage Publications.

Fisher, Christy. 1998. "Business on the Road." *American Demographics* 20, no. 6: 44–47.

Fisher, Teresa A., and Inna Padmawidjaja. 1999. "Parental Influences on Career Development Perceived by African American and Mexican American College Students." *Journal of Multicultural Counseling and Development* 27, no. 3: 136–52.

Flammer, August, Francoise D. Alsaker, and Peter Noack. 1999. "Time Use by Adolescents in an International Perspective: The Case of Leisure Activities." In *The Adolescent Experience: European and American Adolescents in the 1990s,* edited by F. D. Alsaker and A. Flammer, 33–60. Mahwah, N.J.: Lawrence Erlbaum.

Forest, Kay B., Phyllis Moen, and Donna Dempster-McClain. 1995. "Cohort Differences in the Transition to Motherhood: The Variable Effects of Education and Employment before Marriage." *Sociological Quarterly* 36, no. 2: 315–36.

Forman, Gayle. 1999. "We Are Invisible: Slave Wage Teens." *Seventeen Magazine* 58, no. 11: 174–77.

Fowlkes, Martha. 1980. *Behind Every Successful Man: Wives of Medicine and Academe.* New York: Columbia University Press.

———. 1987. "The Myth of Merit and Male Professional Career: The Role of Wives." In *Families and Work,* edited by N. Gerstel and H. E. Gross, 347–60. Philadelphia: Temple University Press.

Fox, Marilyn L., and Deborah J. Dwyer. 1999. "An Investigation of the Effects of Time and Involvement in the Relationship between Stressors and Work–Family Conflict." *Journal of Occupational Health Psychology* 4, no. 2: 164–74.

Frank, Robert H., and Philip J. Cook. 1996. *The Winner Take All Society. Why the Few at the Top Get So Much More Than the Rest of Us.* New York: Penguin.

Franklin, Mary B., and James Ramage. 1999. "Till a Long-Distance Job Do Us Part." *Kiplinger's Personal Finance Magazine* 53, no. 1: 56–59.

Freedman, Marc. 1999. *Prime Time: How Baby Boomers Will Revolutionize Retirement and Transform America.* New York: Public Affairs.

Freeman, Richard B., ed. 1994. *Working under Different Rules.* New York: Russell Sage Foundation.

Fremstad, Shawn, and Wendell Primus. 2002. *Strengthening Families: Ideas for TANF Reauthorization.* Washington, D.C.: Center on Budget and Policy.

Fried, M. 1998. *Taking Time: Parental Leave Policy and Corporate Culture.* Philadelphia: Temple University Press.

Friedan, Betty. 1963. *The Feminine Mystique.* New York: Bantam Doubleday Dell.

Friedman, Dana E. 1990. "Corporate Responses to Family Needs." *Marriage and Family Review* 15, nos. 1–2: 77–98.

Friedman, Michele. Undated. "Child Care." *Almanac of Policy Issues,* at www.policyalmanac.org/social_welfare/childcare.shtml (accessed October 27, 2003).

Friedman, Stewart D., and Jeffrey H. Greenhaus. 2000. *Work and Family: Allies or Enemies?* New York: Oxford University Press.

Frisco, Michelle L., and Kristi Williams. 2003. "Perceived Housework Equity, Marital Happiness, and Divorce in Dual-Earner Households." *Journal of Family Issues* 24, no. 1: 51–73.

Frone, Michael R. 1999. "Developmental Consequences of Youth Employment in Young Workers: Varieties of Experience." In *Young Workers: Varieties of Experience*, edited by J. Barling and E. D. Kelloway, 89–128. Washington, D.C.: American Psychological Association.

Frone, Michael R., Marcia Russell, and Grace M. Barnes. 1996. "Work–Family Conflict, Gender, and Health-Related Outcomes: A Study of Employed Parents in Two Community Samples." *Journal of Occupational Health Psychology* 1, no. 1: 57–69.

Frone, Michael R., Marcia Russell, and M. Lynne Cooper. 1992. "Antecedents and Outcomes of Work–Family Conflict: Testing a Model of the Work–Family Interface." *Journal of Applied Psychology* 77, no. 1: 65–78.

Fuchs, Victor R. 1988. *Women's Quest for Economic Equality.* Cambridge, Mass.: Harvard University Press.

Gager, Constance T., Teresa M. Cooney, and Kathleen T. Call. 1999. "The Effects of Family Characteristics and Time Use on Teenagers' Household Labor." *Journal of Marriage and the Family* 61, no. 4: 982–94.

Galambos, Nancy L., and Jennifer L. Maggs. 1990. "Putting Mothers' Work-Related Stress in Perspective: Mothers and Adolescents in Dual-Earner Families." *Journal of Early Adolescence* 10: 313–28.

———. 1993. "Wives' Employment Hours and Spousal Participation in Family Work." *Journal of Family Psychology* 7: 233–44.

Galinsky, Ellen. 1999. *Ask the Children: What America's Children Really Think about Working Parents.* New York: William Morrow and Co.

———. 2001. "Toward a New View of Work and Family Life." In *Working Families: The Transformation of the American Home*, edited by R. Hertz and N. L. Marshall, 168–86. Berkeley: University of California Press.

Galinsky, Ellen, and James T. Bond. 1998. "The 1998 Business Work–Life Study." New York: Families and Work Institute.

Galinsky, Ellen, Stacy S. Kim, James T. Bond, and Kimberlee Salmond. 2001. "Youth and Employment: Today's Students Tomorrow's Workforce." Ask the Children Series. Families and Work Institute, at www.familiesandwork .org/summary/yande.pdf (accessed June 2, 2003).

Galinsky, Ellen, and Peter J. Stein. 1990. "The Impact of Human Resource Policies on Employees." *Journal of Family Issues* 11, no. 4: 368–83.

Galinsky, Ellen, and Jennifer E. Swanberg. 2000. "Employed Mothers and Fathers in the United States." In *Organizational Change and Gender Equity*, edited by L. L. Haas, P. Hwang, and G. Russell, 15–28. Thousand Oaks, Calif.: Sage Publications.

Galtry, Judith. 2001. "Maternal Employment and Breastfeeding: Policies and Practices in the United States and Sweden." Working Paper 01-12, Bronfenbrenner Life Course Center, Cornell University, Ithaca, N.Y.

Garey, Anita I. 1999. *Weaving Work and Motherhood.* Philadelphia: Temple University Press.

Gendell, Murray. 1998. "Trends in Retirement Age in Four Countries, 1965–95." *Monthly Labor Review* (August): 20–30.

Gerald, Debra E., and William J. Hussar. 2002. "Projections of Education Statistics to 2012" (NCES 2002-030). Washington, D.C.: U.S. Department of Education, National Center for Education Statistics.

Gerson, Kathleen. 1985. *Hard Choices: How Women Decide about Work, Career, and Motherhood.* Berkeley: University of California Press.

Gerstel, Naomi, and Dan Clawson. 2001. "Unions' Responses to Family Concerns." *Social Problems* 48, no. 2: 277–98.

Gerstel, Naomi, and Katherine McGonagle. 1999. "Job Leave and the Limits of the Family and Medical Leave Act." *Work and Occupations* 26, no. 4: 510–34.

Giele, Janet. Z., and Glen. H. Elder Jr., eds. 1998. *Methods of Life Course Research: Qualitative and Quantitative Approaches.* Thousand Oaks, Calif.: Sage Publications.

Gilbert, Evelyn. 1990. "Employers Who Help Working Moms." *National Underwriter (Property/Casualty/Employee Benefits)* 94: 48–49.

Gill, Leroy H., and Donald R. Haurin. 1998. "Wherever He May Go: How Wives Affect Their Husband's Career Decisions." *Social Science Research* 27, no. 3: 264–79.

Gillespie, David F., and Anthony E. King. 1985. "Demographic Understanding of Volunteerism." *Journal of Sociology and Social Welfare* 12, no. 4: 798–816.

Giranda, Melanie, James Luk, and Kathryn A. Atchison. 1999. "Social Networks of Elders without Children." *Journal of Gerontological Social Work* 31, nos. 1–2: 63–84.

Gjerdingen, Dwenda K., and Kathryn M. Chaloner. 1994. "The Relationship of Women's Postpartum Mental Health to Employment, Childbirth, and Social Support." *Journal of Family Practice* 38, no. 5: 465–72.

Glass, Jennifer. 1998. "Gender Liberation, Economic Squeeze, or Fear of Strangers: Why Fathers Provide Infant Care in Dual-Earner Families." *Journal of Marriage and the Family* 60, no. 4: 821–34.

Glass, Jennifer, and Tetsushi Fujimoto. 1995. "Employer Characteristics and the Provision of Family Responsive Policies." *Work and Occupations* 22, no. 4: 380–411.

Glass, Jennifer, and Lisa Riley. 1998. "Family Responsive Policies and Employee Retention Following Childbirth." *Social Forces* 76, no. 4: 1401–35.

Gmiter, Tanda. 2001. "Case Highlights Demand for Reliable Child Care for Needy." *Grand Rapids Press* (Mich.), March 2, A1.

Goff, Stephen J., Michael K. Mount, and Rosemary L. Jamison. 1990. "Employer Supported Child Care, Work/Family Conflict, and Absenteeism: A Field Study." *Personnel Psychology* 43, no. 4: 793–809.

Goldin, Claudia. 1991. *Understanding the Gender Gap: An Economic History of American Women.* New York: Oxford University Press.

Goldin, Claudia, and Lawrence F. Katz. 2000. "The Power of the Pill: Oral Contraceptives and Women's Marriage Career and Marriage Decisions." Working Paper No. 7527, Washington, D.C.: National Bureau of Economic Research.

Goldscheider, Frances K., and Linda J. Waite. 1986. "Sex Differences in the Entry into Marriage." *American Journal of Sociology* 92, no. 1: 91–109.

Goode, William I. 1960. "A Theory of Role Strain." *American Sociological Review* 25, no. 4: 483–96.

Goodman, Norman. 1991. *Marriage and the Family in the United States: Dying Institution?* New Brunswick, N.J.: Transaction.

Goodwin, Leonard, and Phyllis Moen. 1980. "The Evolution and Implementation of Family Welfare Policy." In *Effective Policy Implementation*, edited by D. A. Mazmanian and P. A. Sebatier, 147–68. Lexington, Mass.: Lexington Books. First Published in *Policy Studies Journal* 8, no. 4: 633–51.

Gore, Susan, Robert Aseltine Jr., Mary E. Colten, and Bin Lin. 1997. "Life after High School: Development, Stress, and Well-Being." In *Stress and Adversity over the Life Course: Trajectories and Turning Points*, edited by I. H. Gotlib and B. Wheaton, 197–214. Cambridge: Cambridge University Press.

Gornick, Janet C., and Marcia K. Meyers. 2003. *Families That Work*. New York: Russell Sage.

Gottfredson, Linda S. 1981. "Circumscription and Compromise: A Developmental Theory of Occupational Aspirations." *Journal of Counseling Psychology* 28, no. 6: 545–79.

Gowan, Mary, and Melanie Trevino. 1998. "An Examination of Gender Differences in Mexican American Attitudes toward Family and Career Roles." *Sex Roles* 38, nos. 11–12: 1079–93.

Graebner, William. 1980. *A History of Retirement: The Meaning and Function of an American Institution, 1885–1978*. New Haven, Conn.: Yale University Press.

Graefe, Deborah R., and Daniel T. Lichter. 1999. "Life Course Transitions of American Children: Parental Cohabitation, Marriage, and Single Motherhood." *Demography* 36, no. 2: 205–17.

Greenhaus, Jeffrey H., and Nicholas J. Beutell. 1985. "Sources and Conflict between Work and Family Roles." *Academy of Management Review* 10, no. 1: 76–88.

Greenhaus, Jeffrey, Saroj Parasuraman, Cherlyn Granrose, Samuel Rabinowitz, and Nicholas J. Beutell. 1989. "Sources of Work–Family Conflict among Two-Career Families." *Journal of Vocational Behavior* 34, no. 2: 133–53.

Greenstein, Theodore. 1989. "Human Capital, Marital, and Birth Timing and the Postnatal Labor Force Participation of Married Women." *Journal of Family Issues* 10, no. 3: 359–82.

Groat, Theodore H., David W. Chilson, and Arthur G. Neal. 1982. "Sex Stratification among Three Cohorts of Recent University Graduates." *Sociology and Social Research* 66, no. 3: 269–88.

Grote, Nancy K., Kristen E. Naylor, and Margaret S. Clark. 2002. "Perceiving the Division of Family Work to Be Unfair: Do Social Comparisons, Enjoyment, and Competence Matter?" *Journal of Family Psychology* 17, no. 4: 510–22.

Grzywacz, Joseph G. 2000. "Work–Family Spillover and Health during Midlife: Is Managing Conflict Everything?" *American Journal of Health Promotion* 14, no. 4: 236–43.

Grzywacz, Joseph G., and Nadine Marks. 2000. "Family, Work, Work–Family Spillover, and Problem Drinking during Midlife." *Journal of Marriage and the Family* 62, no. 2: 336–48.

Guelzow, Maureen G., Gloria W. Bird, and Elizabeth H. Koball. 1991. "An Exploratory Path Analysis of the Stress Process for Dual-Career Men and Women." *Journal of Marriage and the Family* 53, no. 1: 151–64.

Gupta, Sanjiv. 1999. "The Effects of Transitions in Marital Status on Men's Performance of Housework." *Journal of Marriage and the Family* 61, no. 3: 700–11.

Gutek, Barbara A., Sabrina Searle, and Lilian Klepa. 1991. "Rational versus Gender Role Explanations for Work–Family Conflict." *Journal of Applied Psychology* 76, no. 4: 560–68.

Hakim, Catherine. 1999. "Diversity and Choice in the Sexual Contracts: Models for the 21st Century." In *Rewriting the Sexual Contract*, edited by G. Dench, 165–79. New Brunswick, N.J.: Transaction.

———. 2000. *Work-Lifestyle Choices in the 21st Century: Preference Theory*. London: Oxford University Press.

Haley, Heather-Lyn, Maureen Perry-Jenkins, and Amy Armenia. 2001. "Workplace Policies and the Psychological Well-Being of First-Time Parents: The Case of Working-Class Families." In *Working Families: The Transformation of the American Home*, edited by R. Hertz and N. L. Marshall, 207–26. Berkeley: University of California Press.

Hallett, Mary B., and Lucia A. Gilbert. 1997. "Variables Differentiating University Women Considering Role-Sharing and Conventional Dual-Career Marriages." *Journal of Vocational Behavior* 50, no. 2: 308–22.

Hamilton, Brady E., Joyce A. Martin, and Paul D. Sutton. 2003. "Births: Preliminary Data for 2002." *National Vital Statistics Reports* 51, no. 11, at www.cdc.gov/nchs/data/nvsr/nvsr51/nvsr51_11.pdf (accessed October 7, 2003).

Han, Shin-Kap, and Phyllis Moen. 1999a. "Clocking Out: Temporal Patterning of Retirement." *American Journal of Sociology* 105, no. 1: 191–236.

———. 1999b. "Work and Family over Time: A Life Course Approach." *Annals of the American Academy of Political and Social Science* 562 (March): 98–110.

———. 2001. "Coupled Careers: Pathways through Work and Marriage in the United States." In *Careers of Couples in Contemporary Societies: From Male Breadwinner to Dual Earner Families*, edited by H.-P. Blossfeld and S. Drobnic, 201–31. Oxford: Oxford University Press.

Hardina, Donna. 1999. "Employment and the Use of Welfare among Male and Female Heads of AFDC Households." *Affilia* 14, no. 2: 217–34.

Hardy, Melissa A., Lawrence E. Hazelrigg, and Jill Quadagno. 1996. *Ending a Career in the Auto Industry: Thirty and Out*. New York: Plenum Publishing.

Harrington, Mona. 1999. *Care and Equality: Inventing a New Family Politics*. New York: Knopf.

Hartl, Gregory. 1996. "Reconciling Work and Elder Care." *World of Work* 18: 29.

Hartley, James. 1998. *Learning and Studying: A Research Perspective*. London: Rutledge.

Hartman, Richard I., Charles R. Stoner, and Raj Arora. 1991. "An Investigation of Selected Variables Affecting Telecommuting Productivity and Satisfaction." *Journal of Business and Psychology* 6, no. 2: 207–25.

Hays, Sharon. 1996. *The Cultural Contradictions of Motherhood*. New Haven, Conn.: Yale University Press.

Heaton, Tim B. 1999. "The Next Generation: Implications of Fertility for the Growth, Composition, and Well-Being of New York in the Coming Years." In *New York State in the 21st Century*, edited by T. A. Hirschl and T. B. Heaton, 241–54. Westport, Conn.: Praeger.

Heinz, Walter R., ed. 1999. *From Education to Work: Cross-National Perspectives.* New York: Cambridge University Press.

———. 2001. "Work and the Life Course: A Cosmopolitan-Local Perspective." In *Restructuring Work and the Life Course*, edited by V. W. Marshall, W. R. Heinz, H. Krüger, and A. Verma, 3–22. Toronto: University of Toronto Press.

Hendershott, Anne B. 1995. *Moving for Work: The Sociology of Relocating in the 1990s.* New York: University Press of America.

Henretta, John C., and Angela M. O'Rand. 1983. "Joint Retirement in the Dual Worker Family." *Social Forces* 62, no. 2: 504–20.

Henretta, John C., Angela M. O'Rand, and Christopher G. Chan. 1993a. "Gender Differences in Employment after Spouses' Retirement." *Research on Aging* 15, no. 2: 148–69.

———. 1993b. "Joint Role Investments and Synchronization of Retirement: A Sequential Approach to Couples Retirement Timing." *Social Forces* 71, no. 4: 981–1000.

Henretta, John C., Angela M. O'Rand, and Margaret Krecker. 1992. "Family Pathways to Retirement." In *Families and Retirement*, edited by M. Szinovacz, D. J. Ekerdt, and B. H. Vinick, 81–98. Thousand Oaks, Calif.: Sage Publications.

Hernandez, Donald J., and David E. Myers. 1993. *America's Children: Resources from Family, Government, and the Economy.* New York: Russell Sage Foundation.

Hersch, Joni, and Leslie S. Stratton. 2000. "Household Specialization and the Male Marriage Wage Premium." *Industrial and Labor Relations Review* 54, no. 1: 78–94.

Hertz, Rosanna. 1986. *More Equal Than Others: Women and Men in Dual-Career Marriages.* Berkeley: University of California Press.

———. 1991. "Dual-Career Couples and the American Dream: Self-Sufficiency and Achievement." *Journal of Comparative Family Studies* 22, no. 2: 247–63.

Hertz, Rosanna, and Faith I. Ferguson. 1998. "Only One Pair of Hands: Ways That Single Mothers Stretch Work and Family Resources." *Community, Work, and Family* 1, no. 1: 13–37.

Hertz, Rosanna, and Nancy L. Marshall. 2001. *Working Families: The Transformation of the American Home.* Berkeley: University of California Press.

Herzog, Anna R., and James N. Morgan. 1993. "Formal Volunteer Work among Older Americans." In *Achieving a Productive Aging Society*, edited by S. A. Bass, F. G. Caro, and Y. P. Chen, 119–42. Westport, Conn.: Auburn House.

Hewlett, Sylvia A. 2002. *Creating a Life: Professional Women and the Quest for Children.* New York: Talk Miramax Books.

Heymann, S. Jody. 2001. *The Widening Gap: Why America's Working Families Are in Jeopardy and What Can Be Done about It.* New York: Basic Books.

Heymann, S. Jody, and Alison Earle. 1998. "The Work–Family Balance: What Hurdles Are Parents Leaving Welfare Likely to Confront?" *Journal of Policy Analysis and Management* 17, no. 2: 313–21.

Higgins, Christopher A., and Linda E. Duxbury. 1992. "Work–Family Conflict: A Comparison of Dual-Career and Traditional-Career Men." *Journal of Organizational Behavior* 13, no. 4: 389–411.

Higgins, Christopher A., Linda E. Duxbury, and Richard H. Irving. 1992. "Work–Family Conflict in the Dual-Career Family." *Organizational Behavior and Human Decision Processes* 51, no. 1: 51–75.

Higgins, Christopher A., Linda E. Duxbury, and Catherine Lee. 1994. "Impact of Life-Cycle Stage and Gender on the Ability to Balance Work and Family Responsibilities." *Family Relations* 43, no. 2: 144–50.

Higgins, Christopher A., Linda E. Duxbury, Catherine Lee, and Shirley Mills. 1994. "An Examination of Work-Time and Work-Location Flexibility." *Journal of Public Sector Management* 23, no. 2: 29–37.

Hill, Patricia K. 1998. "Maternal and Infant Factors Related to the Security of the Infant–Mother Attachment Relationship When Considering Employed and Stay-at-Home Mothers." *Dissertation Abstracts International: Section B: The Sciences and Engineering* 58, no. 11-B: 6258.

Hill, Reuben. 1970. *Family Development in Three Generations.* Cambridge, Mass.: Schenkman Publishing.

Hill, Reuben, and Roy H. Rogers. 1964. "The Developmental Approach." In *Handbook of Marriage and the Family*, edited by H. T. Christensen, 171–211. Chicago: Rand McNally.

Hochschild, Arlie. 1989. *The Second Shift.* New York: Avon Books.

———. 1997. *The Time Bind: When Work Becomes Home and Home Becomes Work.* New York: Metropolitan Books.

———. 1999. "The Nanny Chain." *American Prospect* 11, no. 4: 32–36.

Hoff, Ernst H., and Hans-Uwe Hohner. 1986. "Occupational Careers, Work, and Control." In *The Psychology of Control and Aging*, edited by M. M. Baltes and P. B. Baltes, 345–71. Hillsdale, N.J.: Lawrence Erlbaum.

Hofferth, Sandra L. 1996. "Effects of Public and Private Policies on Working after Childbirth." *Work and Occupations* 23, no. 4: 378–404.

———. 2000. "Effects of Public and Private Policies on Working after Childbirth." In *Work and Family*, edited by T.L. Parcel and D.B. Cornfield, 131–159. Thousand Oaks, CA: Sage Publications.

Hofferth, Sandra L., and John F. Sandberg. 2001a. "Changes in Children's Time with Parents: United States, 1981–1997." *Demography* 38, no. 2: 423–36.

———. 2001b. "How American Children Spend Their Time." *Journal of Marriage and the Family* 63, no. 2: 295–308.

Hoffman, Lois W. 1989. "Effects of Maternal Employment in the Two-Parent Family." *American Psychologist* 44, no. 2: 283–92.

Hogan, Dennis P., Betemariam Berhanu, and Assefa Hailemariam. 1999. "Household Organization, Women's Autonomy, and Contraceptive Behavior in Southern Ethiopia." *Studies in Family Planning* 30, no. 4: 302–14.

Horowitz, Amy. 1985. "Sons and Daughters as Caregivers to Older Parents: Differences in Role Performance and Consequences." *Gerontologist* 25, no. 6: 612–17.

Huffman, Matt L., and Lisa Torres. 2002. "It's Not Only 'Who You Know' That Matters: Gender, Personal Contacts, and Job Lead Quality." *Gender and Society* 16, no. 6: 793–813.

Hundley, Greg. 2000. "Male/Female Earnings Differences in Self-Employment: The Effects of Marriage, Children, and the Household Division of Labor." *Industrial and Labor Relations Review* 54, no. 1.

———. 2001. "Why Women Earn Less Than Men in Self-employment." *Journal of Labor Research* 22, no. 4: 817–29.

Hyde, Janet S., Marjorie H. Klein, Marilyn J. Essex, and Roseanne Clark. 1995. "Maternity Leave and Women's Mental Health." *Psychology of Women Quarterly* 19, no. 2: 257–85.

Ingels, Steven J., Thomas R. Curtin, Phillip Kaufman, Martha N. Alt, and Xianglei Chen. 2002. "Coming of Age in the 1990s: The Eighth-Grade Class of 1998 12 Years Later" (NCES 2002-321). Washington, D.C.: U.S. Department of Education, National Center for Education Statistics.

Institute for Women's Policy Research. 1999. "Equal Pay for Working Families." *IWPR Publication*, #C344. Washington, D.C.: IWPR, June.

———. 2001. "The Gender Wage Ratio: Women's and Men's Earnings." *IWPR Publication*, #C350. Washington, D.C.: IWPR, October.

Jackson, Dorothy, and Jenn-Yun Tein. 1998. "Adolescents' Conceptualization of Adult Roles: Relationships with Age, Gender, Work Goal, and Maternal Employment." *Sex Roles* 38, nos. 11–12: 987–1008.

Jacobs, Jerry A., and Kathleen Gerson. 1998a. "Toward a Family-Friendly, Gender-Equitable Work Week." *University of Pennsylvania Journal of Labor and Employment Law* 1, no. 2: 457–72.

———. 1998b. "Who Are the Overworked Americans?" *Review of Social Economy* 56, no. 4: 442–59.

———. 2000. "Do Americans Feel Overworked? Comparing Ideal and Actual Working Time." In *Work and Family*, edited by T. L. Parcel and D. B. Cornfield, 71–96. Thousand Oaks, Calif.: Sage Publications.

———. 2001. "Overworked Individuals or Overworked Families? Explaining Trends in Work, Leisure, and Family Time." *Work and Occupations* 28, no. 1: 40–64.

John, Daphne, Beth Anne Shelton, and Kristen Luschen. 1995. "Race, Ethnicity, Gender, and Perceptions of Fairness." *Journal of Family Issues* 16, no. 3: 357–79.

John J. Heldrich Center for Workforce Development and Center for Survey Research and Analysis. 1998. "Work Trends: Americans' Attitudes about Work, Employers, and the Government." *Work Trends Survey* Vol. I:1. New Brunswick, N.J.: Rutgers University, September 1, at www.heldrich .rutgers.edu/Resources/Publication/23/Fall%201998%20Report.doc (accessed June 25, 2004).

Johnson, Monica K., and Jeylan T. Mortimer. 2000. "Work-Family Orientations and Attainments in the Early Life Course." In *Work and Family*, edited by T. L. Parcel and D. B. Cornfield, 215–48. Thousand Oaks, Calif.: Sage Publications.

Jones, Fiona, and Ben C. Fletcher. 1993. "An Empirical Study of Occupational Stress Transmission in Working Couples." *Human Relations* 46, no. 7: 881–903.

———. 1996. "Taking Work Home: A Study of Daily Fluctuations in Work Stressors, Effects on Moods, and Impacts on Marital Partners." *Journal of Occupational and Organizational Psychology* 69, no. 1: 89–106.

Joshi, Heather, Susan Macran, and Shirley Dex. 1996. "Employment after Childbearing and Women's Subsequent Labour Force Participation: Evidence from the British 1958 Birth Cohort." *Journal of Population Economics* 9, no. 3: 325–48.

Judge, Timothy A., and Shinichiro Watanabe. 1994. "Individual Differences in the Nature of the Relationship between Job and Life Satisfaction." *Journal of Occupational and Organizational Psychology* 67, no. 2: 101–7.

Judiesch, Michael K., and Karen S. Lyness. 1999. "Left Behind? The Impact of Leaves of Absence on Managers' Career Success." *Academy of Management Journal* 42, no. 6: 641–51.

Kahn, Robert L. 1994. "Opportunities, Aspirations, and Goodness of Fit." In *Age and Structural Lag: Society's Failure to Provide Meaningful Opportunities in Work, Family, and Leisure,* edited by M. W. Riley, R. L. Kahn, and A. Foner, 37–56. New York: John Wiley & Sons.

Kalleberg, Arne L., Edith Rasell, Naomi Cassirer, Barbara F. Reskin, Ken Hudson, David Webster, Eileen Appelbaum, and Roberta M. Spalter-Roth. 1997. *Nonstandard Work, Substandard Jobs.* Washington, D.C.: Economic Policy Institute.

Kamerman, Sheila B. 2000. "Parental Leave Policies: An Essential Ingredient in Early Childhood Education and Care Policies." *Social Policy Report* 14, no. 2: 3–15.

Kamo, Yoshinori, and Ellen Cohen. 1998. "Division of Household Work between Partners: A Comparison of Black and White Couples." *Journal of Comparative Family Studies* 29, no. 1: 131–45.

Kanter, Rosabeth M. 1977. *Work and Family in the United States: A Critical Review and Agenda for Research and Policy.* New York: Russell Sage Foundation.

———. 1993. *Men and Women of the Corporation.* New York: Basic Books.

Kaufman, Gayle, and Peter Uhlenberg. 2000. "The Influence of Parenthood on the Work Effort of Married Men and Women." *Social Forces* 78, no. 3: 931–49.

Kay, Fiona M., and John Hagan. 1995. "The Persistent Glass Ceiling—Gendered Inequalities in the Earnings of Lawyers." *British Journal of Sociology* 46, no. 2: 279–310.

Kelly, Erin. 1999. "Theorizing Corporate Family Policies: How Advocates Built 'the Business Case' for 'Family-Friendly' Programs." *Research in the Sociology of Work* 7: 169–202.

Kelly, Erin, and Frank Dobbin. 1999. "Civil Rights Law at Work: Sex Discrimination and the Rise of Maternity Leave Policies." *American Journal of Sociology* 105, no. 2: 455–92.

Kember, David. 1999. "Integrating Part-Time Study with Family, Work, and Social Obligations." *Studies in Higher Education* 24, no. 1: 109–24.

Kerpelman, Jennifer L., and Paul S. Schvaneveldt. 1999. "Young Adults' Anticipated Identity Importance of Career, Marital, and Parental Roles: Comparisons of Men and Women with Different Role Balance Orientations." *Sex Roles* 41, nos. 3–4: 189–217.

Kessler-Harris, Alice. 2001. *In Pursuit of Equity: Women, Men and the Quest for Economic Citizenship in 20th-Century America.* New York: Oxford University Press.

Kim, Jungmeen E., and Phyllis Moen. 2001a. "Is Retirement Good or Bad for Subjective Well-Being?" *Current Directions in Psychological Science* 10, no. 3: 83–86.

———. 2001b. "Moving into Retirement: Preparation and Transitions in Late Midlife." In *Handbook of Midlife Development,* edited by M. E. Lachman, 487–527, New York: John Wiley & Sons.

Kim, Kwang, and Sean Creighton. 2000. "Participation in Adult Education in the United States: 1998–1999." *Education Statistics Quarterly: Lifelong Learning.* Washington, D.C.: National Center for Education Statistics.

Kim, Yu-Soon, and Dianne F. Harrison. 1999. "Housework, Gender Role Attitudes, Perceived Fairness, and Marital Quality of Korean Working Wives." *Arete* 23, no. 2: 21–32.

King, Rosalind B. 1999. "Time Spent in Parenthood Status among Adults in the United States." *Demography* 36, no. 3: 377–85.

Kingston, Paul W. 1990. "Illusions and Ignorance about the Family-Responsive Workplace." *Journal of Family Issues* 11, no. 4: 438–54.

Kinney, David A., Janet S. Dunn, and Sandra L. Hofferth. 2000. "Family Strategies for Managing the Time Crunch." Working Paper 011-00, Center for the Ethnography of Everyday Life, Ann Arbor, Mich.

Kinnunen, Ulla, and Saija Mauno. 1998. "Antecedents and Outcomes of Work–Family Conflict among Employed Women and Men in Finland." *Human Relations* 51, no. 2: 157–77.

Kirchmeyer, Catherine. 1992. "Perceptions of Nonwork-to-Work Spillover: Challenging the Common View of Conflict-Ridden Domain." *Basic and Applied Social Psychology* 13, no. 2: 231–49.

———. 1993. "Nonwork-to-Work Spillover: A More Balanced View of the Experiences and Coping of Professional Women and Men." *Sex Roles* 28, nos. 9–10: 531–52.

Kitterod, Ragni H. 2002. "Mothers' Housework and Childcare: Growing Similarities or Stable Inequalities?" *Acta Sociologica* 45, no. 2: 127–49.

Klein, Marjorie H., Janet S. Hyde, Marilyn J. Essex, and Roseanne Clark. 1998. "Maternity Leave, Role Quality, Work Involvement, and Mental Health One Year after Delivery." *Psychology of Women Quarterly* 22, no. 2: 239–66.

Klepinger, Daniel, Shelly Lundberg, and Robert Plotnick. 1999. "Teen Childbearing and Human Capital: Does Timing Matter?" Working Paper 98-02, Center for Public Health Research and Evaluation, Battelle Memorial Institute.

Klerman, Jacob A., and Arleen Leibowitz. 1999. "Job Continuity among New Mothers." *Demography* 36, no. 2: 145–55.

Klumb, Petra, and Thomas Lampert. 2004. "Women, Work, and Well-Being, 1950–2000: A Review and Methodological Critique." *Social Science and Medicine* 58, no. 6: 1007–24.

———. 1997. "Labor Supply Effects of State Maternity Leave Legislation." In *Gender and Family Issues in the Workplace*, edited by F. D. Blau and R. G. Ehrenberg, 65–85. New York: Russell Sage Foundation.

Kluwer, Esther S., Jose A. M. Heesink, and Evert van de Vliert. 2002. "The Division of Labor across the Transition to Parenthood: A Justice Perspective." *Journal of Marriage and the Family* 64 (November): 930–43.

Knox, Virginia, Andrew S. London, and Ellen K. Scott. 2003. "Welfare Reform, Work and Child Care: The Role of Informal Care in the Lives of Low-Income Women and Children." (2003) Washington, D.C.: MDRC, at www.mdrc.org/publications/353/policybrief.html (accessed December 2, 2003).

Kodera, Kyoko. 1994. "The Reality of Equality for Japanese Female Workers: Women's Careers within the Japanese Style of Management." *Social Justice* 21, no. 2(56): 136–54.

Kohli, Martin. 1986. "Social Organization and Subjective Construction of the Life Course." In *Human Development and the Life Course: Multidisciplinary Perspectives*, edited by A. B. Sorenson, F. E. Weinert, and L. R. Sherrod, 271–92. Hillside, N.J.: Lawrence Erlbaum.

———. 1994. "Work and Retirement: A Comparative Perspective." In *Age and Structural Lag: Society's Failure to Provide Meaningful Opportunities in Work, Family, and Leisure,* edited by M. W. Riley, R. L. Kahn, A. Foner, and K. A. Mack, 80–106. Oxford: John Wiley & Sons.

Kohli, Martin, and Martin Rein. 1991. "The Changing Balance of Work and Retirement." In *Time for Retirement: Comparative Studies of Early Exit from the Labor Force,* edited by M. Kohli, M. Rein, A. Guillmard, and H. van Gunsteren, 1–35. Cambridge: Cambridge University Press.

Kohli, Martin, Martin Rein, Anne-Marie Guillemard, and Herman van Gunsteren. 1991. *Time for Retirement: Comparative Studies of Early Exit from the Labor Force.* Cambridge: Cambridge University Press.

Komarovsky, Mirra. 1962. *Blue-Collar Marriage.* New Haven, Conn.: Yale University Press.

Kossek, Ellen E., Alison E. Barber, and Deborah Winters. 1999. "Using Flexible Schedules in the Managerial World: The Power of Peers." *Human Resource Management* 38, no. 1: 33–46.

Kossek, Ellen E., Jason A. Colquitt, and Raymond A. Noe. 2001. "Caregiving Decisions, Well-Being, and Performance: The Effects of Place and Provider as a Function of Dependent Type and Work–Family Climates." *Academy of Management Journal* 44, no. 1: 29–44.

Kotter, John P. 1995. *The New Rules: How to Succeed in Today's Post-Corporate World.* New York: Free Press.

Kramer, Betty J., and Stuart Kipnis. 1995. "Eldercare and Work-Role Conflict: Toward an Understanding of Gender Differences in Caregiver Burden." *Gerontologist* 35, no. 3: 340–48.

Kropf, Marcia Brumit. 2001. "Part-Time Work Arrangements and the Corporation: A Dynamic Interaction." In *Working Families: The Transformation of the American Home,* edited by R. Hertz and N. L. Marshall, 152–67. Berkeley: University of California Press.

Krüger, Helga. 1996. "Normative Interpretations of Biographical Processes." In *Society and Biography: Interrelationships between Social Structure, Institutions, and the Life Course,* edited by A. Weymann and W. R. Heinz, 129–46. Weinheim, Germany: Deutscher Studienverlag.

Kruse, Douglas L., and Douglas Mahony. 2000. "Illegal Child Labor in the United States: Prevalence and Characteristics." *Industrial Labor Relations Review* 54, no. 1: 17–40.

Kulik, Liat. 2002. "Equality in Marriage, Marital Satisfaction, and Life Satisfaction: A Comparative Analysis of Pre-retired and Retired Men and Women in Israel." *Families in Society* 83, no. 2: 197–208.

Lachman, Margie E., and Jacquelyn B. James. 1997. *Multiple Paths of Midlife Development.* Chicago: University of Chicago Press.

Landau, Jacqueline, and Michael B. Arthur. 1992. "The Relationship of Marital Status, Spouse's Career Status, and Gender to Salary Level." *Sex Roles* 27, nos. 11–12: 665–81.

Larson, Reed W., and Suman Verma. 1999. "How Children and Adolescents Spend Time across the World: Work, Play, and Developmental Opportunities." *Psychological Bulletin* 125, no. 6: 701–36.

Lee, Courtland C. 1984. "Predicting the Career Choice Attitudes of Rural Black, White, and Native American High School Students." *Vocational Guidance Quarterly* 32, no. 3: 177–84.

Lee, Mary D., Shelley M. MacDermid, and Michelle L. Buck. 2002. "Reduced-Load Work Arrangements: Response to Stress or Quest for Integrity of Functioning?" In *Gender, Work, Stress, and Health*, edited by D. L. Nelson and R. J. Burke, 169–90. Washington, D.C.: American Psychological Association.

Lichter, Daniel T., Deborah R. Graefe, and Brian J. Brown. 2003. "Is Marriage a Panacea? Union Formation among Economically Disadvantaged Unwed Mothers." *Social Problems* 50, no. 1: 60–86.

Loscocco, Karyn A. 1997. "Work–Family Linkages among Self-Employed Women and Men." *Journal of Vocational Behavior* 50, no. 2: 204–26.

Loughlin, Catherine A., and Julian Barling. 1999. "The Nature of Youth Employment." In *Young Workers: Varieties of Experience*, edited by J. Barling and E. K. Kelloway, 17–36. Washington, D.C.: American Psychological Association.

Lowenthal, Marjorie F., and B. Robinson. 1976. "Social Networks and Isolation." In *Handbook of Aging and the Social Sciences*, edited by R. H. Binstock and E. Shanas, 1st ed., 432–56. New York: Van Nostrand Reinhold.

Lu, Zai Zai, Marcia L. Bellas, and David J. Maume. 2000. "Chinese Husbands' Participation in Household Labor." *Journal of Comparative Family Studies* 31, no. 1: 191–215.

Lundberg, Shelly, and Elaina Rose. 1999. "The Determinants of Specialization within Marriage." Working paper.

———. "Parenthood and the Earnings of Married Men and Women." *Labour Economics* 7, no. 6: 689–710.

———. 2002. "The Effects of Sons and Daughters on Men's Labor Supply and Wages." *Review of Economics and Statistics* 84, no. 2: 251–68.

Lyness, Karen S., Cynthia A. Thompson, Anne M. Francesco, and Michael K. Judiesch. 1999. "Work and Pregnancy: Individual and Organizational Factors Influencing Organizational Commitment, Timing of Maternity Leave, and Return to Work." *Sex Roles* 41, nos. 7–8: 485–508.

MacDermid, Shelley M., Jodie L. Hertzog, Katherine B. Kensinger, and John F. Zipp. 2001. "The Role of Organizational Size and Industry in Job Quality and Work–Family Relationships." *Journal of Family and Economic Issues* 22, no. 2: 191–216.

MacDermid, Shelley M., Mary D. Lee, and Margaret L. Williams. 2001. "Alternative Work Arrangements among Professionals and Managers: Rethinking Career Development and Success." *The Journal of Management Development* 20, no. 4: 305–18.

Machung, Anne. 1989. "Talking Career, Thinking Job: Gender Differences in Career and Family Expectations of Berkeley Seniors." *Feminist Studies* 15, no. 1: 35–58.

Macmillan, Ross, and Scott R. Eliason. 2003. "Characterizing the Life Course as Role Configurations and Pathways: A Latent Structure Approach." In *Handbook of the Life Course,* edited by J. T. Mortimer and M. J. Shanahan, 529–54. New York: Kluwer Academic/Plenum Publishers.

Mahaffy, Kimberly A., and Sally K. Ward. 2002. "The Gendering of Adolescents' Childbearing and Educational Plans: Reciprocal Effects and the Influence of Social Context." *Sex Roles* 46, nos. 11–12: 403–17.

Maines, David R., and Monica J. Hardesty. 1987. "Temporality and Gender: Young Adults' Career and Family Plans." *Social Forces* 66, no. 1: 102–20.

Markham, William T., Charles M. Bonjean, and Judy Corder. 1986. "Gender, Out-of-Town Travel, and Occupational Advancement." *Sociology and Social Research* 70, no. 2: 156–60.

Marks, Stephen, and Shelley MacDermid. 1985. "Initiation of the Process of Adult Role Entry." *Population and Environment* 8, nos. 3–4: 240–74.

———. 1996. "Multiple Roles and the Self: A Theory of Role Balance." *Journal of Marriage and the Family* 58, no. 2: 417–32.

Marshall, Nancy L., and Rosalind C. Barnett. 1993. "Work–Family Strains and Gains among Two-Earner Couples." *Journal of Community Psychology* 21, no. 1: 64–78.

Marshall, Victor W., Walter R. Heinz, Helga Krüger, and Anil Verma. 2001. *Restructuring Work and the Life Course.* Toronto: University of Toronto Press.

Martin, Joyce A., Brady E. Hamilton, Stephanie J. Ventura, Fay Menacker, Melissa M. Park, and Paul D. Sutton. 2002. "Births: Final Data for 2001." *National Vital Statistics Reports* 51, no. 2: 1–20.

Martin, Paige D., Don M. Martin, and Maggie Martin. 2001. "Adolescent Premarital Sexual Activity, Cohabitation, and Attitudes toward Marriage." *Adolescence* 36, no. 143: 601–9.

Martin, Robin. 1999. "Adjusting to Job Relocation: Relocation Preparation Can Reduce Relocation Stress." *Journal of Occupational and Organizational Psychology* 72, no. 2: 231–35.

Martin, Steven P. 1999. "U.S. Women Who Delay Childbearing: Interpreting Recent Marriage and Fertility Patterns." Paper presented at the American Sociological Association Annual Meeting, August, Chicago, Ill.

Martinez, Michelle N. 1997. "Work-Life Programs Reap Business Benefits." *HR Magazine* 42, no. 6: 110–14.

Martinez, Yolanda G., and Ann Cranston-Gingras. 1996. "Migrant Farmworker Students and the Educational Process: Barriers to High School Completion." *High School Journal* 80, no. 1: 28–38.

Mattingly, Marybeth J., and Suzanne M. Bianchi. 2003. "Gender Differences in the Quantity and Quality of Free Time: The U.S. Experience." *Social Forces* 81, no. 3: 999–1030.

Maume, David J., Jr., and Marcia L. Bellas. 1999. "Do Workers Prefer the Workplace to Home? An Empirical Assessment of 'The Time Bind.'" In *Workplace/Women's Place,* edited by P. J. Dubeck and D. Dunn, 197–205. Los Angeles: Roxbury.

———. 2001. "The Overworked American or the Time Bind? Assessing Competing Explanations for the Time Spent in Paid Labor." *American Behavioral Scientist* 44, no. 7: 1137–56.

Maume, David J., Jr., and Paula Houston. 2001. "Job Segregation and Gender Differences in Work–Family Spillover among White-Collar Workers." *Journal of Family and Economic Issues* 22, no. 2: 171–89.

Mayer, Karl U., and Walter Mueller. 1986. "The State and the Structure of the Life Course." In *Human Development and the Life Course: Multidisciplinary Perspectives F.E.W.*, edited by A. B. Sorensen and L. R. Sherrod, 217–45. Hillsdale, N.J.: Lawrence Erlbaum.

McCabe, Kristen, and Douglas Barnett. 2000. "First Comes Work, Then Comes Marriage: Future Orientation among African American Young Adolescents." *Family Relations* 49, no. 1: 63–70.

McCrate, Elaine. 2002. "Working Mothers in a Double Bind." *Briefing Paper*, #124. Washington, D.C.: Economic Policy Institute.

McLanahan, Sara, and Lynne Casper. 1995. "Growing Diversity and Inequality in the American Family." In *State of the Union: America in the 1990s*, edited by R. Farley, 1–46. New York: Russell Sage Foundation.

McLoyd, Vonnie C. 1989. "Socialization and Development in a Changing Economy: The Effects of Parental Job and Income Loss on Children." *American Psychologist* 44, no. 2: 293–302.

McManus, Patricia A., and Thomas A. DiPrete. 2000. "Market, Family, and State Sources of Income Instability in Germany and the United States." *Social Science Research* 29, no. 3: 405–40.

McMullin, Julie A., and Victor W. Marshall. 1996. "Family, Friends, Stress, and Well-Being: Does Childlessness Make a Difference?" *Canadian Journal of Aging* 15, no. 3: 355–73.

Mederer, Helen J. 1993. "Division of Labor in Two-Earner Homes: Task Accomplishment versus Household Management as Critical Variables in Perceptions about Family Work." *Journal of Marriage and the Family* 55, no. 1: 133–45.

Melamed, Tuvia. 1995. "Barriers to Women's Career Success: Human Capital, Career Choices, Structural Determinants, or Simply Sex Discrimination." *Applied Psychology: An International Review* 44, no. 4: 295–314.

Melzer, Scott A. 2002. "Gender, Work and Intimate Violence: Men's Occupational Violence Spillover and Compensatory Violence." *Journal of Marriage and the Family* 64, no. 4: 820–32.

Menaghan, Elizabeth G., and Toby L. Parcel. 1995. "Social Sources of Change in Children's Home Environments: The Effects of Parental Occupational Experiences and Family Conditions." *Journal of Marriage and the Family* 57, no. 1: 69–84.

Merola, Stacey S. 2001. "Leisure and the Life Course: American Workers' Free Time 1977 and 1997." Unpublished Ph.D. dissertation, Cornell University.

Merton, Robert K. 1968. "The Matthew Effect in Science." *Science* 159, no. 3810: 56–63.

Meyers, Marcia K., Theresa Heintze, and Douglas A. Wolf. 2002. "Child Care Subsidies and the Employment of Welfare Recipients." *Demography* 39, no. 1: 165–79.

Millar, Jane. 1998. "Family Obligations and Social Policy: Attitudes, Behaviour and Policy Change." Paper presented at the Fourteenth World Congress of Sociology, Montreal, Quebec, July.

———. 2001. "Work Requirements and Labour Market Programmes for Lone Parents." In *Lone Parents and Employment in Cross-National Perspective*, edited by J. Millar and K. Rowlingson, 189–201. Bristol: Policy Press.

Miller, Baila, and Lynda Cafasso. 1992. "Gender Differences in Caregiving: Fact or Artifact?" *Gerontologist* 32, no. 4: 498–507.

Mills, C. Wright 1956. *White Collar: The American Middle Class*. New York: Oxford University Press.

Mitchell, Olivia S. 1997. "Work and Family Benefits in the Corporate Setting." In *Gender and Family Issues in the Workplace*, edited by F. D. Blau and R. G. Ehrenberg, 269–76. New York: Russell Sage Foundation.

Modell, John. 1989. *Into One's Own: From Youth to Adulthood in the United States, 1920–1975*. Berkeley: University of California Press.

Moen, Phyllis. 1985. "Women Who Work: A National Survey—A 1984 Newsweek Report." *Contemporary Sociology* 14, no. 4: 480–81.

———. 1989. *Working Parents: Transformations in Gender Roles and Public Policies in Sweden*. Madison: University of Wisconsin Press.

———. 1998. "Recasting Careers: Changing Reference Groups, Risks, and Realities." *Generations* 22, no. 1: 40–45.

———. 1992. *Women's Two Roles: A Contemporary Dilemma*. Westport, Conn.: Auburn House.

———. 1994. "Women, Work, and Family: A Sociological Perspective on Changing Roles." In *Age and Structural Lag: The Mismatch between People's Lives and Opportunities in Work, Family, and Leisure*, edited by M. W. Riley, R. L. Kahn, and A. Foner, 151–70. New York: John Wiley & Sons.

———. 1996. "A Life Course Perspective on Retirement, Gender, and Well-Being." *Journal of Occupational Health Psychology* 1, no. 2: 131–44.

———. 1997a. "Women's Roles and Health: A Life Course Approach." In *Women, Stress, and Heart Disease*, edited by K. Orth-Gomer, 111–32. Los Angeles: Lawrence Erlbaum.

———. 1997b. "Women's Roles and Resilience: Trajectories of Advantage or Turning Points?" In *Stress and Adversity over the Life Course: Trajectories and Turning Points*, edited by I. H. Gotlib and B. Wheaton, 133–56. New York: Cambridge University Press.

———. 2001a. "The Career Quandary." *Population Reference Bureau Reports on America* 2, no. 1 (February), at www.prb.org/Content/NavigationMenu/PRB/AboutPRB/Reports_on_America/The_Career_Quandary.htm (accessed June 25, 2004).

———. 2001b. "The Gendered Life Course." In *Handbook of Aging and the Social Sciences*, edited by L. George and R. H. Binstock, 5th ed., 179–96. San Diego: Academic Press.

———. 2003a. *It's About Time: Couples and Careers*. Ithaca, N.Y.: Cornell University Press.

———. 2003b. "Midcourse: Navigating Retirement and a New Life Stage." In *Handbook of the Life Course*, edited by J. Mortimer and M. J. Shanahan. New York: Kluwer Academic/Plenum.

Moen, Phyllis, and Steve Coltrane. 2004. "Families, Theories, and Social Policy." In *Sourcebook of Family Theory and Methods*, edited by Bengtson, Klein, Acock, Allen, and Wilworth-Anderson. Thousand Oaks, Calif.: Sage Publications (in press).

Moen, Phyllis, Donna Dempster-McClain, Joyce Altobelli, Wipas Wimonsate, Lisa Dahl, Patricia Roehling, and Stephen Sweet. 2004. *The New "Middle" Work Force*. Ithaca, N.Y.: Bronfenbrenner Life Course Center.

Moen, Phyllis, Donna Dempster-McClain, and Robin Williams Jr. 1992. "Successful Aging: A Life Course Perspective on Women's Roles and Health." *American Journal of Sociology* 97, no. 6: 1612–38.

Moen, Phyllis, and Mary A. Erickson. 1995. "Linked Lives: A Transgenerational Approach to Resiliency." In *Examining Lives in Context: Perspectives on the Ecology of Human Development*, edited by P. Moen, G. H. Elder Jr., and K. Luscher, 169–210. Washington, D.C.: American Psychological Association.

Moen, Phyllis, Mary A. Erickson, and Donna Dempster-McClain. 1997. "Their Mother's Daughters? The Intergenerational Transmission of Gender Role Orientations." *Journal of Marriage and the Family* 59, no. 2: 281–93.

Moen, Phyllis, and Vivian Fields. 1998. "Retirement, Social Capital, and Well-Being: Does Community Participation Replace Paid Work." Working Paper 98-10, Bronfenbrenner Life Course Center, Cornell University, Ithaca, N.Y.

———. 2002. "Midcourse in the United States: Does Unpaid Community Participation Replace Paid Work?" *Aging International* 27: 21–48.

Moen, Phyllis, Vivian Fields, Rhoda Meador, and Helene Rosenblatt. 2000. "Fostering Integration: A Case Study of the Cornell Retirees Volunteering in Service (CRVIS)." In *Social Integration in the Second Half of Life*, edited by K. Pillemer, P. Moen, E. Wethington, and N. Glasgow, 247–64. Baltimore: Johns Hopkins University Press.

Moen, Phyllis, Vivian Fields, Heather Quick, and Heather Hofmeister. 2000. "A Life Course Approach to Retirement and Social Integration." In *Social Integration in the Second Half of Life*, edited by K. Pillemer, P. Moen, E. Wethington, and N. Glasgow, 75–107. Baltimore: Johns Hopkins University Press.

Moen, Phyllis, and Kay B. Forest. 1995. "Family Policies for an Aging Society: Moving to the Twenty-First Century." *Gerontologist* 35, no. 6: 825–30.

———. 1999. "Strengthening Families: Policy Issues for the Twenty-first Century." In *Handbook of Marriage and the Family*, edited by M. B. Sussman, S. K. Steinmetz, and G. W. Peterson, 633–63. New York: Plenum Press.

Moen, Phyllis, and Shin-Kap Han. 2001a. "Gendered Careers: A Life Course Perspective." In *Families and Work: Today's Realities and Tomorrow's Possibilities*, edited by R. Hertz and N. Marshall, 42–57. Berkeley: University of California Press.

———. 2001b. "Reframing Careers: Work, Family, and Gender." In *Restructuring Work and the Life Course*, edited by V. Marshall, W. Heinz, H. Krueger, and A. Verma, 424–45. Toronto: University of Toronto Press.

Moen, Phyllis, Jungmeen E. Kim, and Heather Hofmeister. 2001. "Couples' Work/Retirement Transitions, Gender, and Marital Quality." *Social Psychology Quarterly* 64, no. 1: 55–71.

Moen, Phyllis, and Robert Orrange. 2002. "Careers and Lives: Socializiation, Structural Lag, and Gendered Ambivalence." In *Advances in Life Course Research: New Frontiers in Socialization*, Vol. 7, edited by R. Settersten and T. Owens, 231–60. London: Elsevier Science.

Moen, Phyllis, and Stephen Sweet. 2003. "Time Clocks: Couples' Work Hour Strategies." In *It's about Time: Couples and Careers*, edited by P. Moen, 17–34. Ithaca, N.Y.: Cornell University Press.

Moen, Phyllis, Ronit Waismel-Manor, and Stephen Sweet. 2003. "Successful Living in Dual-Earner Households: Perceptions of Success at Work, at Home and in Balancing the Two." In *It's about Time: Couples and Careers*, edited by P. Moen, 133–52. Ithaca, N.Y.: Cornell University Press.

Moen, Phyllis, and Elaine Wethington. 1992. "The Concept of Family Adaptive Strategies." *Annual Review of Sociology* 18: 233–51.

———. 1999. "Midlife Development in a Life Course Context." In *Life in the Middle*, edited by S. L. Willis and J. D. Reid, 3–23. San Diego: Academic Press.

Moen, Phyllis, and Yan Yu. 1999. "Having It All: Overall Work/Life Success in Two-Earner Families." In *Research in the Sociology of Work*, edited by T. Parcel, Vol. 7, 107–37. Greenwich, Conn.: JAI Press.

———. 2000. "Effective Work/Life Strategies: Working Couples, Work Conditions, Gender, and Life Quality." *Social Problems* 47, no. 3: 291–326.

Monroe, Pamela A., Lydia B. Blalock, and Richard P. Vlosky. 1999. "Work Opportunities in a Non-traditional Setting for Women Exiting Welfare: A Case Study." *Journal of Family and Economic Issues* 20, no. 1: 35–60.

Moore, Dahlia. 1995. "Role Conflict: Not Only for Women? A Comparative Analysis of 5 Nations." *International Journal of Comparative Sociology* 36, nos. 1–2: 17–35.

Morgan, Sandra, Susan M. Schor, and Linda R. Martin. 1993. "Gender Differences in Career Paths in Banking." *Career Development Quarterly* 41, no. 4: 375–82.

Morris, Kathleen. 1998. "The Rise of Jill Barad." *Business Week*, May 25, 112–19.

Mortimer, Jeylan T. 2003. *Working and Growing Up in America*. Boston: Harvard University Press.

Mortimer, Jeylan T., and Michael D. Finch. 1996. "Work, Family, and Adolescent Development." In *Adolescent, Work, and Family: An Intergenerational Developmental Analysis*, edited by J. T. Mortimer and M. D. Finch, 1–24. Thousand Oaks, Calif.: Sage Publications.

Mortimer, Jeylan T., Carolyn Harley, and Pamela J. Aronson. 1999. "How Do Prior Experiences in the Workplace Set the Stage for Transitions to Adulthood?" In *Transitions to Adulthood in a Changing Economy: No Work, No Family, No Future?* edited by A. Booth, A. C. Crouter, and M. J. Shanahan, 131–59. Westport, Conn.: Praeger.

Mortimer, Jeylan T., Ellen Efron Pimentel, Seongryeol Ryu, Katherine Nash, and Chaimun Lee. 1996. "Part-Time Work and Occupational Value Formation in Adolescence." *Social Forces* 74, no. 4: 1405–18.

Munk, Nina. 1999. "Finished at Forty." *Fortune* 139, no. 2: 50–66.

Musick, Kelly. 2002. "Planned and Unplanned Childbearing among Unmarried Women." *Journal of Marriage and the Family* 64, no. 4: 915–29.

Mutran, Elizabeth J., Donald C. Reitzes, Kathleen A. Bratton, and Maria E. Fernandez. 1996. "Preretirement Influences of Postretirement Self-Esteem." *Journals of Gerontology* 51, no. 5: 242–49.

———. 1997. "Self-Esteem and Subjective Responses to Work among Mature Workers: Similarities and Differences by Gender." Psychological Sciences and Social Sciences Series. *Journal of Gerontology* 52B, no. 2: 89–96.

Mutschler, Phyllis H. 1994. "From Executive Suite to Production Line: How Employees in Different Occupations Manage Elder Care Responsibilities." *Research on Aging Special Issue: Work and Elder Care* 16, no. 1: 7–26.

Myrdal, Alva, and Viola Klein. 1956. *Women's Two Roles, Home and Work*. London: Routledge & Kegan Paul.

National Center for Education Statistics. 2003. "The Condition of Education: 2003," table 18.1, at nces.ed.gov/programs/coe/2003/section3/tables/t18.1.asp (accessed March 23, 2004).

Nelson, Debra L., James C. Quick, Michael A. Hitt, and Doug Moesel. 1990. "Politics, Lack of Career Progress and Work/Home Conflict: Stress and Strain for Working Women." *Sex Roles* 23, nos. 3–4: 169–85.

Newburger, Eric C., and Andrea E. Curry. 2000. "Educational Attainment in the United States (Update): March 2000." *Current Populations Reports*, P20-536. Washington, D.C.: U.S. Census Bureau.

Nippert-Eng, Christena. 1996. *Home and Work: Negotiating Boundaries through Everyday Life.* Chicago: University of Chicago Press.

Noor, Noraini M. 2002. "Work-Family Conflict, Locus of Control, and Women's Well-Being: Tests of Alternative Pathways." *Journal of Social Psychology* 142, no. 5: 645–62.

Nordenmark, Mikael, and Charlott Nyman. 2003. "Fair or Unfair? Perceived Fairness of Household Division of Labour and Gender Equality among Women and Men: The Swedish Case." *European Journal of Women's Studies* 10, no. 2: 181–209.

Nurmi, Jari-Erik, Aurora Liiceanu, and Hanna Liberska. 1999. "Future Oriented Interests." In *The Adolescent Experience: European and American Adolescents in the 1990s*, edited by F. D. Alsaker and A. Flammer, 85–98. Mahwah, N.J.: Lawrence Erlbaum.

O'Connell, Lenahan, Michael Betz, and Suzanne Kurth. 1989. "Plans for Balancing Work and Family Life: Do Women Pursuing Nontraditional and Traditional Occupations Differ?" *Sex Roles* 20, nos. 1–2: 35–45.

O'Connell, Martin. 1990. "Maternity Leave Arrangements: 1961–1985." In *Work and Family Patterns of American Women, Current Population Reports*, P23-165. Washington, D.C.: U.S. Census Bureau.

Ogawa, Naohiro, and John Ermisch. 1996. "Family Structure, Home Time Demands and the Employment Patterns of Japanese Married Women." *Journal of Labor Economics* 14, no. 4: 677–702.

Okun, Morris, William A. Stock, Marilyn J. Haring, and Robert A. Witter. 1984. "The Social Activity/Subjective Well-Being Relation: A Quantitative Synthesis." *Research on Aging* 6, no. 1: 45–65.

O'Rand, Angela M., and John C. Henretta. 1982. "Delayed Career Entry, Industrial Pension Structure, and Early Retirement in a Cohort of Unmarried Women." *American Sociological Review* 47, no. 3: 365–73.

———. 1999. *Age and Inequality: Diverse Pathways through Later Life.* Boulder, Colo.: Westview Press.

O'Rand, Angela M., John C. Henretta, and Margaret L. Krecker. 1992. "Family Pathways to Retirement." In *Families and Retirement*, edited by M. Szinovacz, D. Ekerdt, and B. Vinick, 81–98. Thousand Oaks, Calif.: Sage Publications.

Orrange, Robert. 1999. "Women as Household Managers." Working Paper No. 99-05, Cornell Employment and Family Careeers Institute, Cornell University, Ithaca.

———. 2002. "Aspiring Law and Business Professionals' Orientations to Work and Family Life." *Journal of Family Issues* 23, no. 2: 287–317.

———. 2003a. "Individualism, Family Values, and the Professional Middle Class: In-Depth Interviews with Advanced Law and MBA Students." *Sociological Quarterly* 44, no. 3: 451–80.

———. 2003b. "The Emerging Mutable Self: Gender Dynamics and Creative Adaptations in Defining Work, Family, and the Future." *Social Forces* 82, no. 1: 1–34.

Ortega, Suzanne T., Hugh P. Whitt, and Allen J. Williams Jr. 1988. "Religious Homogamy and Marital Happiness." *Journal of Family Issues* 9, no. 2: 224–39.

Orthner, Dennis K., and Karen A. Randolph. 1999. "Welfare Reform and High School Dropout Patterns for Children." *Children and Youth Services Review* 21, nos. 9–10: 881–900.

Osterman, Paul. 1995. "Work/Family Programs and the Employment Relationship." *Administrative Science Quarterly* 40, no. 4: 681–700.

———. 1996. "Introduction." In *Broken Ladders: Managerial Careers in the New Economy,* edited by P. Osterman, 1–22. New York: Oxford University Press.

Parasuraman, Saroj, and Jeffrey H. Greenhaus. 1993. "Personal Portrait: The Life-Style of the Woman Manager." In *Women in Management,* edited by E. A. Fagenson, 186–211. Thousand Oaks, Calif.: Sage Publications.

Parcel, Toby. 1999. "Work and Family in the 21st Century: Its about Time." *Work and Occupations* 26, no. 2: 264–74.

Parcel, Toby, and Daniel B. Cornfield. 2000. *Work and Family Research in Framing Policy.* Thousand Oaks, Calif.: Sage Publications.

Parsons, Talcott, and Robert Bales. 1955. *The Family: Socialization and Interaction Process.* New York: Free Press.

Pavalko, Eliza K., and Julie E. Artis. 1997. "Women's Caregiving and Paid Work: Causal Relationships in Late Midlife." Psychological Sciences and Social Sciences Series. *Journals of Gerontology* 52B, no. 4: S170–S179.

Pavalko, Eliza K., and Brad Smith. 1999. "The Rhythm of Work: Health Effects of Women's Work Dynamics." *Social Forces* 77, no. 3: 1141–62.

Peake, Amy, and Karen L. Harris. 2001. "Young Adults' Attitudes toward Multiple Role Planning: The Influence of Gender, Career Traditionality and Marriage Plans." *Journal of Vocational Behavior* 60, no. 3: 405–21.

Perlow, Leslie A. 1997. *Finding Time: How Corporations, Individuals, and Families Can Benefit from New York Practices.* Ithaca, N.Y.: Cornell University Press.

Peterson, Karen S., and Anthony DeBarros. 2001. "Single-Father Households in USA Increased 62%." *USA Today,* More News: Census 2000, May 17, A01.

Pfeffer, Jeffrey. 1977. "Effects of an MBA and Socioeconomic Origins on Business School Graduates' Salaries." *Journal of Applied Psychology* 62: 698–705.

Pillemer, Karl, Phyllis Moen, Elaine Wethington, and Nina Glasgow, eds. 2000. *Social Integration in the Second Half of Life.* Baltimore: Johns Hopkins University Press.

Piotrkowski, Chaya S., and Joanne Carrubba. 1999. "Child Labor and Exploitation." In *Young Workers: Varieties of Experience,* edited by J. Barling and E. K. Kelloway, 129–57. Washington, D.C.: American Psychological Association.

Pisarski, Anne, Philip Bohle, and Victor Callan. 1998. "Effects of Coping Strategies, Social Support and Work–Nonwork Conflict on Shift Worker's Health." *Scandinavian Journal of Work, Environment and Health* 24, no. 3: 141–45.

Pitt-Catsouphes, Marcie, and Leon Litchfield. 2001. "How Are Small Businesses Responding to Work and Family Issues?" *Working Families: The Transformation of the American Home,* edited by R. Hertz and N. L. Marshall, 131–51. Berkeley: University of California Press.

Pixley, Joy E., and Elaine Wethington. 1998a. "Life Events, Turning Points, and Generativity." *Multiple Dimensions of Social Responsibility,* edited by A. Rossi. Chicago: University of Chicago Press.

———. 1998b. "Turning Points in Work Careers: Gender and Life Course Factors." Working Paper No. 98-13, Bronfenbrenner Life Course Center, Cornell University, Ithaca, N.Y.

Pixley, Joy E., and Phyllis Moen. 2003. "Prioritizing Careers." In *It's about Time: Couples and Careers*, edited by P. Moen, 183–200. Ithaca, N.Y.: Cornell University Press.

Pleck, Joseph H. 1977. "The Work–Family Role System." *Social Problems* 24, no. 4: 417–27.

———. 1985. *Working Wives/Working Husbands*. Thousand Oaks, Calif.: Sage Publications.

———. 1993. "Are 'Family-Supportive' Employer Policies Relevant to Men?" In *Men, Work, and Family*, edited by J. C. Hood, 217–37. Thousand Oaks, Calif.: Sage Publications.

Polasky, Lynn J., and Carole K. Holahan. 1998. "Maternal Self-Discrepancies, Interrole Conflict, and Negative Affect among Married Professional Women with Children." *Journal of Family Psychology* 12, no. 3: 388–401.

Polatnick, M. Rivka. 1999. "Too Old for Child Care? Too Young for Self-Care? Negotiations between Preteens and Their Employed Parents." Working Paper No. 10, Center for Working Parents, University of California, Berkeley, November.

Poorkaj, Houshang. 1972. "Social-Psychological Factors and Successful Aging." *Sociology and Social Research* 56, no. 3: 289–300.

Powell, Walter, and Paul DiMaggio. 1991. *The New Institutionalism in Organizational Analysis*. Chicago: University of Chicago Press.

Presser, Harriet B. 1994. "Employment Schedules among Dual-Earner Spouses and the Division of Household Labor by Gender." *American Sociological Review* 59, no. 3: 348–64.

———. 1995. "Are the Interests of Women Inherently at Odds with the Interests of Children or the Family? A Viewpoint." In *Gender and Family Change in Industrialized Countries*, edited by K. O. Mason and A. Jensen, 297–319. Oxford: Clarendon Press.

———. 1999. "Toward a 24-Hour Economy." *Science* 284, no. 5421: 1778–79.

Presser, Harriet, and Joan Hermsen. 1996. "Gender Differences in the Determinants of Work-Related Overnight Travel among Employed Americans." *Work and Occupations* 23, no. 1: 87–115.

Price, Richard H., Daniel S. Friedland, Nam J. Choi, and Robert D. Caplan. 1998. "Job-Loss and Work Transitions in a Time of Global Economic Change." In *Addressing Community Problems: Psychological Research and Interventions*, edited by X. B. Arriaga and S. Oskamp, 195–222. Thousand Oaks, Calif.: Sage Publications.

Priore, Michael J., and Charles F. Sabel. 1984. *The Second Industrial Divide: Possibilities for Prosperity*. New York: Basic Books.

Quadagno, J. 1988. *The Transformation of Old Age Security*. Chicago: University of Chicago Press.

Quadagno, Jill, and Melissa A. Hardy. 1996. "Private Pensions, State Regulation and Income Security for Older Workers: The Case of the Auto Industry." In *The Privatization of Social Policy? Occupational Welfare and the Welfare State in American, Scandanavia, and Japan*, edited by M. Shalev. London: Macmillan.

Quick, Heather, and Phyllis Moen. 1998. "Gender, Employment, and Retirement Quality: A Life Course Approach to the Differential Experiences of Men and Women." *Journal of Occupational Health Psychology* 3, no. 1: 44–64.

Quinn, Joseph F. 1997. "Retirement Trends and Patterns in the 1990s: The End of an Era?" *Public Policy and Aging Report* 8: 10–14.

———. 1999. "Retirement Patterns and Bridge Jobs in the 1990s." *EBRI Issue Brief*, #206. Washington, D.C.: Employee Benefit Research Institute.

Quinn, Joseph F., and Richard V. Burkhauser. 1994. "Retirement and Labor Force Behavior of the Elderly." In *Demography of Aging*, edited by L. Martin and S. Preston, 50–101. Washington, D.C.: National Academy of Science.

Raley, Kelly R. 2001. "Increasing Fertility in Cohabiting Unions: Evidence for the Second Demographic Transition in the United States?" *Demography* 38, no. 1: 59–66.

Rapoport, Rhona, Lotte Bailyn, Joyce Fletcher, and Bettye H. Pruitt. 2002. *Beyond Work–Family Balance: Advancing Gender Equity and Workplace Performance.* San Francisco: Jossey-Bass.

Rapoport, Rhona, and Robert Rapoport. 1977. *Dual-Career Families Reexamined: New Integrations of Work and Family.* New York: Harper Colophon.

Reimers, Cordelia W., and Marjorie Honig. 1989. "The Retirement Process in the United States: Mobility among Full-Time Work, Partial Retirement, and Full Retirement." In *Redefining the Process of Retirement: An International Perspective*, edited by W. Schmall, 115–31. New York: Springer-Verlag.

Reitzes, Donald C., Elizabeth J. Mutran, and Maria E. Fernandez. 1998. "The Decision to Retire: A Career Perspective." *Social Science Quarterly* 79, no. 3: 607–19.

Repetti, Rena L. 1989. "Effects of Daily Workload on Subsequent Behavior during Marital Interaction: The Roles of Social Withdrawal and Spouse Support." *Journal of Personality and Social Psychology* 57, no. 4: 651–59.

———. 1994. "Short-Term and Long-Term Processes Linking Job Stressors to Father–Child Interaction." *Social Development* 3, no. 1: 1–15.

Repetti, Rena L., Karen A. Matthews, and Ingrid Waldron. 1989. "Employment and Women's Health: Effects of Paid Employment on Women's Mental and Physical Health." *American Psychologist* 44, no. 11: 1394–1401.

Repetti, Rena L., and Jennifer Wood. 1997. "Effects of Daily Stress at Work on Mothers' Interactions with Preschoolers." *Journal of Family Psychology* 11, no. 1: 90–108.

Reskin, Barbara F., and Irene Padavic. 1994. *Women and Men at Work.* Thousand Oaks, Calif.: Pine Forge Press.

Reskin, Barbara F., and Patricia A. Roos. 1990. *Job Queues, Gender Queues: Explaining Women's Inroads into Male Occupations.* Philadelphia: Temple University Press.

Richard, Judy W., and Carol D'Amico. 1999. *Workforce 2020: Work and Workers in the 21st Century.* Indianapolis: Hudson Institute.

Richardson, John T. E., and Estelle King. 1998. "Adult Students in Higher Education: Burden or Boom?" *Journal of Higher Education* 69, no. 1: 65–88.

Riley, M. W., ed. 1988. *Social Structures and Human Lives.* Vol. 1, Social Change and the Life Course. Thousand Oaks, Calif.: Sage Publications.

Riley, Matilda W., Anne Foner, and John W. Riley. 1999. "The Aging and Society Paradigm." *Handbook of Theories of Aging: In Honor of Jim Birren*, edited by V. L. Bengtson and K. W. Schaie, 327–43. New York: Springer Publishing.

Riley, Matilda W., Robert L. Kahn, and Anne Foner. 1994. *Age and Structural Lag: The Mismatch between People's Lives and Opportunities in Work, Family, and Leisure.* New York: John Wiley & Sons.

Riley, Matilda W., and John W. Riley. 1989. "The Lives of Older People and Changing Social Roles." *Annals of the American Academy of Political and Social Science* 503 (May): 14–28.

———. 1994. "Structural Lag: Past and Future." In *Age and Structural Lag: Society's Failure to Provide Meaningful Opportunities in Work, Family, and Leisure,* edited by J. W. Riley, M. W. Riley, and A. Foner, 12–36. New York: John Wiley and Sons.

Rindfuss, Ronald R., Elizabeth C. Cooksey, and Rebecca L. Sutterlin. 1999. "Young Adult Occupational Achievement: Early Expectations versus Behavioral Reality." *Work and Occupations* 26, no. 2: 220–63.

Riverin-Simard, Danielle. 1990. "Adult Vocational Trajectory." *Career Development Quarterly* 39, no. 2: 129–43.

Robinson, John P., and Geoffrey Godbey. 1997. *Time for Life: The Surprising Ways Americans Use Their Time.* University Park: Pennsylvania State University Press.

Roehling, Patricia V., and Marta Bultman. 2002. "Does Absence Make the Heart Grow Fonder? Work-Related Travel and Marital Satisfaction." *Sex Roles: A Journal of Research* 46, nos. 9–10: 279–93.

Roehling, Patricia V., Phyllis Moen, and Rosemary Batt. 2003. "When Work Spills over into the Home and Home Spills over into Work." In *It's about Time: Couples and Careers,* edited by P. Moen, 101–21. Ithaca, N.Y.: Cornell University Press.

Roehling, Patricia V., Phyllis Moen, and Elizabeth Wilson. 2003. "The Cornell Careers Institute: Studying the Working Environments of Dual Earner Couples." Paper presented at the Society for Research on Child Development, Tampa, Fla., April.

Roehling, Patricia V., Mark V. Roehling, and Phyllis Moen. 2001. "The Relationship between Work-Life Policies and Practices and Employee Loyalty: A Life Course Perspective." *Journal of Family and Economic Issues* 22, no. 2: 141–70.

Rollins, Judy, and Priscilla N. White. 1982. "The Relationship between Mothers' and Daughters' Sex-Role Attitudes and Self-concepts in Three Types of Family Environment." *Sex Roles* 8, no. 11: 1141–55.

Roopnarine, Jaipaul L., Janet Brown, Priscilla Snell-White, Nancy Riegraf, B. Devon Crossley, Ziarat Hossain, and Wayne Webb. 1995. "Father Involvement in Child Care and Household Work in Common-Law Dual-Earner and Single-Earner Jamaican Families." *Journal of Applied Developmental Psychology* 16, no. 1: 35–52.

Rose, Peter I. 2001. "Immigration and Opportunity: Race, Ethnicity, and Employment in the United States." *Contemporary Sociology* 30, no. 1: 19–20.

Rout, Usha R., Sue Lewis, and Carolyn Kagan. 1999. "Work and Family Roles: Indian Career Women in India and the West." *Indian Journal of Gender Studies* 6, no. 1: 91–108.

Rubin, Beth A. 1996. *Shifts in the Social Contract: Understanding Change in American Society.* Thousand Oaks, Calif.: Pine Forge Press.

Ruhm, Christopher J., and Jackqueline L. Teague. 1997. "Parental Leave Policies in Europe and North America." In *Gender and Family Issues in the Workplace,* edited by F. D. Blau and R. G. Ehrenberg, 133–56. New York: Russell Sage Foundation.

Rydstedt, Leif W., and Gunn Johansson. 1998. "A Longitudinal Study of Workload, Health, and Well-Being among Male and Female Urban Bus Drivers." *Journal of Occupational and Organizational Psychology* 71, no. 1: 35–45.

Ryff, Carol D., and Marsha M. Seltzer. 1996. *The Parental Experience.* Chicago: University of Chicago Press.

Sandberg, Joanne C., and Daniel B. Cornfield. 2000. "Returning to Work: The Impact of Gender, Family, and Work on Terminating a Family or Medical Leave." In *Work and Family,* edited by T. L. Parcel and D. B. Cornfield, 161–84. Thousand Oaks, Calif.: Sage Publications.

Sanderson, Susan L. 2000. "Factors Influencing Paternal Involvement in Childrearing." *Dissertation Abstracts International: Section B: The Sciences and Engineering* 60, no. 11-B: 5790.

Sassler, Sharon, and Robert Schoen. 1999. "The Effect of Attitudes and Economic Activity on Marriage." *Journal of Marriage and the Family* 61, no. 1: 147–59.

Scandura, Terri A., and Melenie J. Lankau. 1997. "Relationships of Gender, Family Responsibility and Flexible Work Hours to Organizational Commitment and Job Satisfaction." *Journal of Organizational Behavior* 18: 377–91.

Schacter, Jason. 2001. "Why People Move: Exploring the March 2000 Current Population Survey." *Current Population Reports Special Studies,* P23-204. Washington, D.C.: U.S. Census Bureau.

Schieman, Scott, Debra B. McBrier, and Karen Van Gundy. 2003. "Home-to-Work Conflict, Work Qualities, and Emotional Distress." *Sociological Forum* 18, no. 1: 137–64.

Schlesinger, Jacob M. 2000. "Working Full Time Is No Longer Enough." *Wall Street Journal,* June 29, 2.

Schofield, John. 1999. "Back to School Online." *Maclean's* 112, no. 36: 22–26.

Schor, Juliet. 1991. "Global Equity and Environmental Crisis: An Argument for Reducing Working Hours in the North." *World Development* 19, no. 1: 73–84.

———. 1992. *The Overworked American: The Unexpected Decline of Leisure.* New York: Basic Books.

———. 1998. "Time, Labour, and Consumption: Guest Editor's Introduction." *Time and Society* 7, no. 1: 119–27.

Schwartz, Felice. 1989. "Management Women and the New Facts of Life." *Harvard Business Review* 67, no. 1: 65–77.

Secret, Mary. 2000. "Identifying the Family, Job, and Workplace Characteristics of Employees Who Use Work–Family Benefits." *Family Relations* 49, no. 2: 217–25.

Settersten, Richard A., Jr. 1999. *Lives in Time and Place: The Problems and Promises of Developmental Science.* Amityville, N.Y.: Baywood Publishing Company.

Settersten, Richard A., Jr., and Karl U. Mayer. 1997. "The Measurement of Age, Age Structuring, and the Life Course." *Annual Review of Sociology* 23: 233–61.

Seward, Rudy R., Dale E. Yeatts, and Lisa K. Zottarelli. 2002. "Parental Leave and Father Involvement in Child Care: Sweden and the United States." *Journal of Comparative Family Studies* 33, no. 3: 387–99.

Shanahan, Michael J., Richard A. Miech, and Glen H. Elder Jr. 1998. "Changing Pathways to Attainment in Men's Lives: Historical Patterns of School, Work, and Social Class." *Social Forces* 77, no. 1: 231–56.

Sharpe, Deanna L., Joan M. Hermsen, and Jodi Billings. 2002. "Gender Differences in Use of Alternative Full-Time Work Arrangements by Married Mothers." *Family and Consumer Sciences Research Journal* 31, no. 1: 78–111.

Shelton, Beth Anne, and Daphne John. 1993. "Ethnicity, Race, and Difference: A Comparison of White, Black, and Hispanic Men's Household Labor Time." In *Men, Work, and Family*, edited by J. C. Hood, 131–50. Thousand Oaks, Calif.: Sage Publications.

———. 1996. "The Division of Household Labor." *Annual Review of Sociology* 22: 299–322.

Sigle-Rushton, Wendy, and Sara McLanahan. 2002a. "For Richer or Poorer? Marriage as an Anti-poverty Strategy in the United States." *Population-E* 57, no. 3: 509–26.

———. 2002b. "The Living Arrangements of New Unmarried Mothers." *Demography* 39, no. 3: 415–33.

Simon, Robin W. 1998. "Assessing Sex Differences in Vulnerability among Employed Parents: The Importance of Marital Status." *Journal of Health and Social Behavior* 39, no. 1: 38–54.

Singley, Susan G., and Kathryn Hynes. 2001. "Examining Couples' Work/Family Strategies through the Transition to Parenthood: Gender, Workplace Policies, and the Couple Context." Paper presented at the Alfred P. Sloan Foundation Working Family Centers Conference, University of Michigan, Ann Arbor, Mich., May.

Skocpol, Theda. 1992. *Protecting Soldiers and Mothers: The Political Origins of Social Policy in the United States*. Cambridge, Mass.: Harvard University Press.

———. 2000. *The Missing Middle: Working Families and the Future of American Social Policy*. New York: W. W. Norton.

Smelser, Neil. 1959. *Social Change in the Industrial Revolution*. Chicago: University of Chicago Press.

Smith, Deborah B., and Phyllis Moen. 1998. "Spousal Influence on Retirement: His, Her, and Their Perceptions." *Journal of Marriage and the Family* 60, no. 3: 734–44.

———. 2003. "Retirement Satisfaction for Retirees and Their Spouses: Do Gender and the Retirement Decision-Making Process Matter?" *Journal of Family Issues* 24, no. 10: 1–24.

Smith, Kristin. 2002a. "Who's Minding the Kids? Child Care Arrangements: Spring 1997." *Current Population Reports*, P70-86. Washington, D.C.: U.S. Census Bureau, at www.census.gov/prod/2002pubs/p70–86.pdf (accessed April 24, 2003).

———. 2002b. "Who's Minding the Kids? Child Care Arrangements: Spring 2002." *Current Population Reports*, P70-86. Washington, D.C.: U.S. Census Bureau.

Smith, Kristin, Barbara Downs, and Martin O'Connell. 2001. "Maternity Leave Employment Patterns: 1961–1995." *Current Population Reports*, P70-79. Washington, D.C.: U.S. Census Bureau.

South, Scott. 1993. "Racial and Ethnic Differences in the Desire to Marry." *Journal of Marriage and the Family* 55, no. 2: 357–70.

South, Scott, and Glenna D. Spitze. 1994. "Housework in Marital and Non-Marital Households." *American Sociological Review* 59, no. 3: 327–47.

Spain, Daphne, and Suzanne Bianchi. 1996. *Balancing Act: Motherhood, Marriage, and Employment among American Women.* New York: Russell Sage Foundation.

Spalter-Roth, Roberta M., Arne L. Kalleberg, Edith Rasell, Naomi Cassirer, Barbara F. Reskin, Ken Hudson, David Webster, Eileen Appelbaum, and Betty Dooley. 1997. *Managing Work and Families: Nonstandard Work Arrangements among Managers and Professionals.* Washington, D.C.: Economic Policy Institute.

Standen, Peter, Kevin Daniels, and David Lamond. 1999. "The Home as a Workplace: Work–Family Interaction and Psychological Well-Being in Telework." *Journal of Occupational Health Psychology Special Issue: Relationship between Work and Family Life* 4, no. 4: 368–81.

Stark, David. 1995. "Not by Design: The Myth of Designer Capitalism in Eastern Europe." In *Strategic Choice and Path Dependency in Post-Socialism: Institutional Dynamics in the Transformation Process,* edited by J. Hausner, B. Jessop, and K. Nielsen, 67–83. Brookfield, Vt.: Edward Elgar.

Starrels, Marjorie E., Berit Ingersoll-Dayton, David W. Dowler, and Margaret B. Neal. 1997. "The Stress of Caring for a Parent: Effects of the Elder's Impairment on an Employed, Adult Child." *Journal of Marriage and the Family* 59, no. 4: 860–72.

Starrels, Marjorie E., Berit Ingersoll-Dayton, Margaret B. Neal, and Hiroko Yamada. 1995. "Intergenerational Solidarity and the Workplace: Employees' Caregiving for Their Parents." *Journal of Marriage and the Family* 57, no. 3: 751–62.

Stettner, Andrew, and Jeffrey Wenger. 2003. "The Broad Reach of Long-Term Unemployment." *EPI Issue Brief,* #194. Washington, D.C.: Economic Policy Institute.

Stevens, Constance J., Laura A. Puchtell, Seongryeol Ryu, and Jeylan T. Mortimer. 1992. "Adolescent Work and Boys' and Girls' Orientations to the Future." *Sociological Quarterly* 33, no. 2: 153–69.

Stone, James R., and Jeylan T. Mortimer. 1998. "The Effect of Adolescent Employment on Vocational Development: Public and Education Policy Implications." *Journal of Vocational Behavior* 53: 184–214.

Stone, Robyn I., Gail L. Cafferata, and Judith Sangl. 1987. "Caregivers of the Frail Elderly: A National Profile." *Gerontologist* 27, no. 5: 616–26.

Stone, Robyn I., and Pamela F. Short. 1990. "The Competing Demands of Employment and Informal Caregiving to Disabled Elders." *Medical Care* 28, no. 6: 513–26.

Straussner, Shulamith L. A., and Norma Kolko Phillips. 1999. "The Impact of Job Loss on Professional and Managerial Employees and Their Families." *Families in Society* 80, no. 6: 642–48.

Stroh, Linda K., Jeanne M. Brett, Anne H. Reilly. 1992. "All the Right Stuff: A Comparison of Female and Male Managers' Career Progression." *Journal of Applied Psychology* 77, no. 3: 251–60.

Strom, Sara. 2002. "Unemployment and Gendered Divisions in Domestic Labor." *Acta Sociologica* 45, no. 2: 89–106.

Suitor, J. Jill. 1987a. "Friendship Networks in Transition: Married Mothers Return to School." *Journal of Social and Personal Relationships* 4: 445–61.

———. 1987b. "Marital Happiness of Returning Women Students and Their Husbands: Effects of Part and Full Time Enrollment." *Research in Higher Education* 24, no. 4: 311–31.

———. 1987c. "Mother–Daughter Relations When Married Daughters Return to School: Effects of Status Similarity." *Journal of Marriage and the Family* 49, no. 2: 435–44.

Suitor, J. Jill, and Shirley Keeton. 1997. "Once a Friend, Always a Friend? Effects of Homophily on Women's Support Networks across a Decade." *Social Networks* 19, no. 1: 51–62.

Swisher, Raymond, Stephen Sweet, and Phyllis Moen. 2004. "The Family-Friendly Community and Its Life Course Fit for Dual-Earner Couples." 66, no. 12: 281–292.

Szinovacz, Maximiliane. 1989. "Decision-Making on Retirement Timing." In *Dyadic Decision-Making*, edited by D. Brinberg and J. Jaccard, 286–310. New York: Springer-Verlag.

Szinovacz, Maximiliane, and David J. Ekerdt. 1995. "Families and Retirement." In *Handbook of Aging and the Family*, edited by R. Blieszner and V. H. Bedford, 375–400. Westport, Conn.: Greenwood Press.

Szinovacz, Maximiliane, David J. Ekerdt, and Barbara H. Vinick, eds. 1992. *Families and Retirement*. Thousand Oaks, Calif.: Sage Publications.

Tabak, Filiz. 1997. "Women's Upward Mobility in Manufacturing Organizations in Istanbul: A Glass Ceiling Initiative?" *Sex Roles* 36, nos. 1–2: 93–102.

Taniguchi, Hiromi. 1999. "The Timing of Childbearing and Women's Wages." *Journal of Marriage and the Family* 61, no. 4: 1008–19.

Taris, Toon W. 2002. "Unemployment and Mental Health: A Longitudinal Perspective." *International Journal of Stress Management* 9, no. 1: 43–57.

Tharenou, Phyllis, Shane Latimer, and Denise Conroy. 1994. "How Do You Make It to the Top? An Examination of Influences on Women's and Men's Managerial Advancement." *Academy of Management Journal* 37, no. 4: 899–931.

Thomas, Irene M. 1995. "Childless by Choice: Why Some Latinas Are Saying No to Motherhood." *Hispanic Magazine.com*, May, at www.hispanicmagazine.com/PDF/may 1995 Childless by Choice.pdf (accessed July 15, 2002).

Thomas, Linda T., and Daniel C. Ganster. 1995. "Impact of Family-Supportive Work Variables on Work–Family Conflict and Strain: A Control Perspective." *Journal of Applied Psychology* 80, no. 1: 6–15.

Thompson, Cynthia A., Laura L. Beauvais, and Karen S. Lyness. 1999. "When Work–Family Benefits Are Not Enough: The Influence of Work–Family Culture on Benefits Utilization, Organizational Attachment, and Work–Family Conflict." *Journal of Vocational Behavior* 54, no. 3: 392–415.

Thorn, Brian L., and Lucia A. Gilbert. 1998. "Antecedents of Work and Family Role Expectations of College Men." *Journal of Family Psychology* 12, no. 2: 259–67.

Tilly, Chris. 1992. "Dualism in Part-Time Employment." *Industrial Relations* 31, no. 2: 330–47.

Tilly, Louise A., and Joan W. Scott. 1978. *Women, Work, and Family*. New York: Holt, Rinehart, and Winston.

Topel, Robert H., and Michael P. Ward. 1992. "Job Mobility and the Careers of Young Men." *Quarterly Journal of Economics* 107, no. 2: 439–79.

Townsend, Nicholas W. 2002. *The Package Deal: Marriage, Work and Fatherhood in Men's Lives*. Philadelphia: Temple University Press.

Umansky, Diane. 1999. "The Middle-School Squeeze." *Working Mother* 22, no. 2: 26–30.

United Nations. 2001. "World Population Prospectus: The 2000 Revision." Population Division, Department of Economic and Social Affairs. New York: United Nations.

Upchurch, Dawn M., Lee A. Lillard, and Constantijn W. A. Panis. 2002. "Nonmarital Childbearing: Influences of Education, Marriage, and Fertility." *Demography* 39, no. 20: 311–29.

U.S. Bureau of the Census. 1998. *World Population Profile: 1998.* Washington, D.C.: U.S. Government Printing Office, at www.census.gov/ipc/prod/wp98/wp98.pdf (accessed April 6, 2004).

———. 2000. *Statistical Abstract of the United States 2000,* no. 644, p. 403. Washington, D.C.: U.S. Census Bureau.

———. 2001. *Statistical Abstract of the United States 2001.* Washington, D.C.: U.S. Census Bureau.

———. 2002a. *Fertility of American Women.* Washington, D.C.: U.S. Census Bureau, at www.census.gov/population/socdemo/fertility/tabH1.pdf.

———. 2002b. *Statistical Abstract of the United States 2002.* Washington, D.C.: U.S. Census Bureau.

———. 2003a. *National Compensation Survey: Employee Benefits in Private Industry in the United States.* Washington, D.C.: U.S. Census Bureau, at www.bls.gov/ncs/ebs/sp/ebbl0019.pdf (accessed November 13, 2003).

———. 2003b. *Statistical Abstract of the United States 2003.* Washington, D.C.: U.S. Census Bureau.

———. 2004. *Evidence from Census 2000 about Earnings by Detailed Occupation for Men and Women.* Washington, D.C.: U.S. Census Bureau, at www.census.gov/prod/2004pubs/censr-15.pdf (accessed June 23, 2004).

U.S. Department of Commerce. 1997. "Children with Single Parents—How They Fare." *Census Brief,* 97-1. Washington, D.C.: U.S. Department of Commerce, Economics and Statistics Administration, September, at www.census.gov/prod/3/97pubs/cb-9701.pdf (accessed July 10, 2002).

U.S. Department of Education, National Center for Education Statistics. 2000. "Digest of Education Statistics Tables and Figures," table 175, at www.nces.ed.gov/programs/digest/d00/dt175.asp.

———. 2003. "Distance Education at Degree-Granting Postsecondary Institutions: 2000–2001." National Center for Education Statistics, Tiffany Waits and Laurie Lewis. Washington, D.C.: U.S. Department of Education, at http://nces.ed.gov/pubs2003/2003017.pdf (accessed August 27, 2004).

U.S. Department of Health and Human Services. 2001. "Administration for Children and Families." Washington, D.C.: U.S. Department of Health and Human Services, January 25, at www.acf.dhhs.gov/programs/opa/facts/tanf.htm (accessed May 31, 2001).

U.S. Department of Labor. 1995. "1995 Family and Medical Leave Commission Report." Washington D.C.: U.S. Department of Labor, at www.dol.gov/esa/regs/compliance/whd/fmla/family.htm (accessed October 28, 2003).

———. 1996. "A Workable Balance: Report to Congress on Family and Medical Leave Policies, Executive Summary." Washington, D.C.: Department of Labor, Women's Bureau, Commission on Leave, April 30, at www.ilr.cornell.edu/library/downloads/keyWorkplaceDocuments/FamilyMedical.pdf (accessed May 29, 2001).

———. 1999. "Employee Benefits in Medium and Large Private Establishments, 1997." Washington, D.C.: Department of Labor, Bureau of Labor Statistics, January 7, at www.bls.gov/news.release/ebs3.toc.htm (accessed June 6, 2003).

———. 2000. "Pilot Survey on the Incidence of Child Care Resource and Referral Services in June 2000." Report 946. Washington, D.C.: U.S. Department of Labor Bureau of Labor Statistics, November, at www.bls.gov/ncs/ocs/sp/ncrp0002.pdf (accessed June 6, 2003).

———. 2001. "Contingent and Alternative Employment Arrangements." Washington, D.C.: Department of Labor, Bureau of Labor Statistics, at www.bls.gov/news.release/conemp.toc.htm.

———. 2003a. "National Compensation Survey: Employee Benefits in Private Industry in the United States, 2000." Bulletin 2555. Washington, D.C.: U.S. Department of Labor, Bureau of Labor Statistics, January, at http://stats.bls.gov/ncs/ebs/sp/ebbl0019.pdf (accessed June 6, 2003).

———. 2003b. "Employment Characteristics of Families in 2002." Washington, D.C.: Department of Labor, Bureau of Labor Statistics, July 9, at www.bls.gov/news.release/famee.pdf (accessed March 17, 2004), government site.

———. 2004. "Comparative Civilian Labor Force Statistics, Ten Countries, 1959–2002." Washington D.C.: Department of Labor, Bureau of Labor Statistics, February 11, at www.bls.gov/fls/flslforc.pdf (accessed April 6, 2004).

Valcour, Monique P., and Rosemary Batt. 2003. "Work-Life Integration: Challenges and Organizational Responses." In *It's about Time: Couples and Careers*, edited by P. Moen, 310–32. Ithaca, N.Y.: Cornell University Press.

Valenti, Catherine. 2003. "Vacation Deprivation: Americans Get Short-Changed When It Comes to Holiday Time." ABC News.com, June 26, at www.abc news.go.com/sections/business/US/vacation_030625.html (accessed October 7, 2003).

Van der Klaauw, Wilbert. 1996. "Female Labour Supply and Marital Status Decisions: A Life-Cycle Model." *Review of Economic Studies* 63, no. 2: 199–235.

Ventura, Stephanie J., and Christine Bachrach. 2000. "Non-Marital Childbearing in the United States, 1940–1999." Centers for Disease Control and Prevention, U.S. Department of Health and Human Services. *National Vital Statistics Reports* 48, no. 16: 1–40.

Vinick, Barbara H., and David J. Ekerdt. 1991a. "Retirement: What Happens to Husband–Wife Relationships?" *Journal of Geriatric Psychology* 24, no. 1: 23–40.

———. 1991b. "The Transition to Retirement: Responses of Husbands and Wives." In *Growing Old in America*, edited by B. B. Hess and E. W. Markson, 4th ed., 305–17. New Brunswick, N.J.: Transaction.

———. 1992. "Couples View Retirement Activities: Expectation versus Experience." In *Families and Retirement*, edited by M. Szinovacz, D. J. Ekerdt, and B. H. Vinick, 129–44. Thousand Oaks, Calif.: Sage Publications.

Vinokur, Amiram D., Penny F. Pierce, and Catherine L. Buck. 1998. "Work–Family Conflicts of Women in the Air Force: Their Influence on Mental Health and Functioning." *Journal of Organizational Behavior* 20: 865–78.

Vitaliano, Peter P., Jianping Zhang, and James Scanlan. 2003. "Is Caregiving Hazardous to One's Physical Health? A Meta-Analysis." *Psychological Bulletin* 129, no. 6: 946–72.

Vondracek, Fred W., and Erik J. Profeli. 2003. "The World of Work and Careers." In *Blackwell Handbook of Adolescence*, edited by G. R. Adams and M. D. Berzonsky, 109–28. Malden, Mass.: Blackwell Publishing.

Wagner, Donna L., and Gail G. Hunt. 1994. "The Use of Workplace Eldercare Programs by Employed Caregivers." *Research on Aging Special Issue: Work and Eldercare* 16, no. 1: 69–84.

Waite, Linda J., and Maggie Gallagher. 2000. *The Case for Marriage: Why Married People Are Happier, Healthier, and Better Off Financially*. New York: Doubleday.

Waite, Linda J., Gus W. Haggstrom, and David E. Kanouse. 1985. "Changes in the Employment Activities of New Parents." *American Sociological Review* 50, no. 2: 263–72.

Waldfogel, Jane. 1998. "The Effect of Children on Women's Wages." *American Sociological Review* 62, no. 2: 209–17.

———. 1999. "Family Leave Coverage in the 1990s." *Monthly Labor Review* 122, no. 10: 13–21.

Wallace, Jean E. 1999. "Work-to-Nonwork Conflict among Married Male and Female Lawyers." *Journal of Organizational Behavior* 20, no. 6: 797–816.

Weinger, Susan. 2000. "Opportunities for Career Success: Views of Poor and Middle Class Children." *Children and Youth Services Review* 22, no. 1: 13–35.

Werbel, James. 1998. "Intent and Choice Regarding Maternal Employment Following Childbirth." *Journal of Vocational Behavior* 53, no. 3: 372–85.

Wethington, Elaine, and Ronald C. Kessler. 1989. "Employment, Parental Responsibility, and Psychological Distress." *Journal of Family Issues* 10, no. 4: 527–46.

Wharton, Amy S., and Mary Blair-Loy. 2002. "The 'Overtime Culture' in a Global Corporation: A Cross-National Study of Finance Professionals' Interest in Working Part-Time." *Work and Occupations* 29, no. 1: 32–63.

White, Sammis B., and Lori A. Geddes. 2002. "The Impact of Employer Characteristics and Workforce Commitment on Earnings of Former Welfare Recipients." *Economic Development Quarterly* 16, no. 4: 326–41.

Whitehead, Barbara D., and David Popenoe. 1999. "Changes in Teen Attitudes toward Marriage, Cohabitation, and Children 1975–1995." Piscataway, N.J.: National Marriage Project, Rutgers, University of New Jersey.

———. 2001. "Who Wants to Marry a Soul Mate? New Survey Findings on Young Adults' Attitudes about Love and Marriage." In *The State of Our Unions: The Social Health of Marriage in America 2001*, 6–16. Piscataway, N.J.: National Marriage Project, Rutgers, University of New Jersey.

———. 2002. "Why Men Won't Commit: Exploring Young Men's Attitudes about Sex, Dating, and Marriage." In *The State of Our Unions: The Social Health of Marriage in America 2002*, 6–16. Piscataway, N.J.: National Marriage Project, Rutgers, University of New Jersey.

Whyte, William H. 1956. *The Organization Man*. New York: Simon and Schuster.

Wilk, Carole A. 1986. *Career Women and Childbearing: A Psychological Analysis of the Decision Process*. New York: Van Nostrand Reinhold Company.

Wilkie, Jane R., Myra M. Ferree, and Kathryn S. R. Strother. 1998. "Gender and Fairness: Marital Satisfaction in Two-Earner Couples." *Journal of Marriage and the Family* 60, no. 3: 577–94.

Williams, Joan. 2000. *Unbending Gender: Why Family and Work Conflict and What to Do about It*. New York: Oxford University Press.

Williams, Kevin J., and George M. Alliger. 1994. "Role Stressors, Mood Spillover, and Perceptions of Work–Family Conflict in Employed Parents." *Academy of Management Journal* 37, no. 4: 837–68.

Williger, Beth. 1993. "Resistance and Change: College Men's Attitudes toward Family and Work in the 1980s." In *Men, Work, and Family*, edited by J. C. Hood, 108–30. Thousand Oaks, Calif.: Sage Publications.

Willis, Sherry L., and James D. Reid, eds. 1999. *Life in the Middle*. San Diego: Academic Press.

Wilson, Sloan. 1955. *The Man in the Grey Flannel Suit*. Mattituck, N.Y.: Amereon House.

Wilson, William J. 1996. *When Work Disappears: The World of the New Urban Poor*. New York: Knopf.

Winett, Richard A., and Michael S. Neale. 1981. "Flexible Work Schedules and Family Time Allocation: Assessment of a System Change on Individual Behavior Using Self-Report Logs." *Journal of Applied Behavior Analysis* 14: 39–46.

Wise, David, ed. 1998. *Frontiers in the Economics of Aging*. Chicago: University of Chicago Press.

Wolff, Edward. 2002. *Retirement Insecurity: The Income Shortfalls Awaiting the Soon-to-Retire*. Washington, D.C.: Economic Policy Institute.

Wu, Zheng, and Lindy MacNeill. 2002. "Education, Work, and Childbearing after Age 30." *Journal of Comparative Family Studies* 33, no. 2: 191–213.

Yu, Yan, and Phyllis Moen. 2001. "Chores and Childcare: Domestic Work Time among Men and Women in Dual-Earner Households." *Journal of Marriage and the Family*.

York, Carolyn. 1991. "The Labor Movement's Role in Parental Leave and Child Care." In *Parental Leave and Child Care*, edited by J. S. Hyde and M. J. Essex, 176–86. Philadelphia: Temple University Press.

Zandvakili, Sourushe. 2000. "Dynamics of Earnings Inequality among Female-Headed Households in the United States." *Journal of Socio-Economics* 29, no. 1: 73–89.

Zedlewski, Sheila R., and Rumki Saha. 2003. "Social Security and Single Mothers: Options for 'Making Work Pay' into Retirement." In *Social Security and the Family*, edited by M. M. Favreault, F. J. Sammartino, and C. E. Steurerle, 89–122. Washington, D.C.: Urban Institute Press.

Zerubavel, Eviatar. 1981. *Hidden Rhythms: Schedules and Calendars in Social Life*. Chicago: University of Chicago Press.

Zhou, Xueguang, and Phyllis Moen. 2001a. "Explaining Life Chances in China's Economic Transformation: A Life Course Approach." *Social Science Research* 30, no. 4: 552–77.

———. 2001b. "Job-Shift Patterns of Husbands and Wives in Urban China." In *Careers of Couples in Contemporary Societies: From Male Breadwinner to Dual Earner Families*, edited by H.-P. Blossfeld and S. Drobnic, 332–67. New York: Oxford University Press.

Zuo, Jiping, and Shengming Tang. 2000. "Breadwinner Status and Gender Ideologies of Men and Women Regarding Family Roles." *Sociological Perspectives* 43, no. 1: 29–43.

Subject Index

271

Name Index

About the Authors

Phyllis Moen holds the McKnight Presidential Chair in Sociology at the University of Minnesota. She is the author, co-author, and editor of numerous articles and books, including *It's About Time: Couples and Careers* (2003). While at Cornell University she headed the Cornell Careers Institute, an Alfred P. Sloan Foundation Working Family Center. Moen is a member of the Conference Board's *Work Life Leadership Council*, as well as vice chair of the Board of Directors for *Civic Ventures*. She lives with her husband, Dick Shore.

Patricia Roehling is a professor of psychology and chairperson of the Psychology Department at Hope College in Holland, Michigan. She formerly served as director of research at the Cornell Careers Institute. She has a Ph.D. in clinical psychology and has authored articles and chapters on topics ranging from family members of alcoholics to the work–family interface. She lives with her husband and two teenage children.